PLANETARY
ASTRONOMY

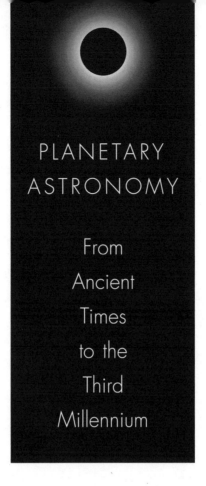

PLANETARY ASTRONOMY

From
Ancient
Times
to the
Third
Millennium

RONALD A. SCHORN

Texas A&M University Press
College Station

LIBRARY OF CONGRESS
CATALOGING-IN-PUBLICATION DATA

Schorn, Ronald A. (Ronald Anthony), 1935–
    Planetary astronomy : from ancient times to the third millennium /
Ronald A. Schorn.
        p.   cm.
    Includes bibliographical references and index.
    ISBN 0-89096-807-1
    1. Astronomy—History.   2. Planetology.   I. Title.
QB15.S39   1998
523.4'09—dc21
                                                          97-51563
                                                              CIP

CONTENTS

ILLUSTRATIONS

COLOR SECTION
FOLLOWING PAGE 166

Lunar and solar eclipses
Mars as it looks from far away
Mars as it looks from orbit
Martian afternoon
Jupiter as seen from a Voyager spacecraft
Rings of Saturn
Atmospheric structure on Neptune
Upper atmosphere of Neptune
Triton
Titan
Comet Shoemaker-Levy 9
Mars rock
Jupiter with dark spots

PROLOGUE

Humans of the distant past must have had a strong sense of place and time, due to their awareness of the heavens. In early times the apparent motions of the Sun and the Moon in the sky drew attention, for they were important guides to the times of day and night, the progress of the month, and the passing of the year. For these reasons, people began to keep track of these movements and depended on their regular recurrence. By contrast, the rare lunar and solar eclipses inspired awe and wonder.

To a casual observer on a clear night, all the "lights" in the sky—except the Moon—look alike except for their different brightnesses and, for some of the brightest, their reddish color. However, a few of the most outstanding luminaries move slowly with respect to all the others. Once the peculiar apparent motions of the five objects that we call Mercury, Venus, Mars, Jupiter, and Saturn were recognized, these bodies drew special attention. Because of their unusual behavior, they have long been called *planets,* a name that derives from the Greek word for "wanderer."

Early sky observers at first recorded only special events such as the first appearances of Venus in the evening or morning sky, close approaches of planets to each other, what stars had just risen or were about to set, and the like. Later, regular observations were made and recorded, and much later came attempts to predict such events.

There are myriad other points of light in the night sky; ones that, by contrast with the planets, never change positions with respect to one another. That is, they keep an unchanging pattern, even as that design moves across the night sky. The Big Dipper, for example, always looks like a dipper. These "fixed" stars serve useful purposes in telling time and direction at night, for following the progress of the year and its seasons, and as visual and memory aids in the retelling of legends and myths. But to almost all who studied the heavens seriously once records began to be kept, these stars merely formed a backdrop against which to measure the positions and motions of the planets (which amounted to seven in all if the Sun and Moon were included, a number that still survives in the days of our week).

For millennia, the main interests of astronomers were the observation and prediction of certain events that were considered important, such as interesting groupings of planets or the first or last visibility of a planet or star in the dusk or dawn. This emphasis lasted until shortly before the invention of the telescope. During this long period astronomy was essentially mathematics of one kind or another (observations were few by modern standards), and the greatest professional and public triumphs of mathematics were scored in astronomy. Thus it is no surprise that advances in one field depended in many respects on advances in the other.

For us, it is easy to look back at the past and wonder why ancient astronomers made so little progress in understanding the real nature of the universe, why they traveled so far down so many wrong roads for so long. But we have the advantages of hindsight and know, for example, that the Sun and other stars shine with the energy of nuclear reactions, while the planets merely reflect the light of their nearest star, and that the Earth is a sphere that orbits our Sun. To appreciate the hard-won advances of earlier times, we must try to put ourselves in the place of early astronomers and try to forget what we may know now. To understand the beginnings of planetary astronomy, we must imagine ourselves ignorant of the fact that apparent motions in the heavens are not always what they seem, and we must look at the sky with only our eyes and the aid of a few simple instruments.

WHAT CAN YOU SEE?

Because artificial light was rare many thousands of years ago and the skies were not as full of civilization's dust and smoke, it might seem obvious that knowledge of the heavens was fairly extensive back then. But how much did our distant ancestors really know? One can find out simply by going outside and looking.

NIGHT AND DAY

The constant changing from dark to light and back to dark again as the Sun rises and sets is one phenomenon of the heavens that everybody knows. Another is the strange behavior of the Moon, which appears to have different shapes on different nights. Even today, those are the only two observational facts about the sky that many people know, for the most casual, irregular glances reveal them.

It takes only one night of watching to notice that the stars, and the Moon too if present, appear to move in parallel paths. Most of them rise from the eastern half of the horizon, moving upward and westward across the sky in curved paths until they reach their greatest height. Then they begin to descend, still keeping their relentless westward motion, until they disappear at the western horizon. Observers living near the equator see that the paths near the horizon are almost straight up and down, but the farther north or south the observer, the shallower the angle at which the stars rise from and approach the horizon.

One notices something else, too, away from the equator. Some stars do *not* rise or set. Instead, they move in circles around a point in the sky above that direction on the horizon midway between east and west (call that direction north if you live in the northern hemisphere). Again, things look different depending on where you are. For a viewer near the equator, only a few objects in a small circular portion of the sky near the horizon never rise or set, but the farther north or south you live, the bigger that circle is, and the more stars are in it.

One other thing would strike you about these tiny sparks of light. Almost all of them are strewn across the heavens in patterns that do not change through the night, as if representing the view from inside a huge spangled bowl or hemisphere of crystal that spins on an invisible axle. As the night passes, you can see more and more of this "celestial sphere."

By day, if it is clear, you can see that the Sun moves like some stars do at night, rising in the east and generally moving westward to set at the western horizon. You can also follow the great luminary's daily motion by putting a straight stick (a *gnomon*) vertically into the ground. This is one of simplest and probably earliest of astronomical instruments. All you need is a stick, something to pound it into the ground, and a string with a weight at the end to check that the stick is standing straight up, though even that is not strictly necessary. A properly placed hole in a wall serves many of the same purposes, except that now a moving spot of light in the shadow of the wall traces out the Sun's motions.

The path of the tip of the stick's shadow always lies on the ground exactly opposite the Sun. In fact, the shadow tip lies at one end of a straight line, with the Sun at the other and the tip of the stick in between. The shadow is shortest at midday, when the Sun is highest. If you mark the shadow's direction at noon and wait till dark, it will be plain that this is the same direction in which lies the point in the sky about which the stars appear to wheel—north if you live north of the equator.

To learn even more, watch the sky for several nights in a row, starting when the Moon is a thin crescent low in the west just after sunset. Each night the Moon waxes a bit "fatter" and is also higher above the horizon and sets later. In fact, while never stopping its grand westward sweep every night, it is at the same time moving much more slowly in an *eastward* direction with respect to the stars. The Moon moves eastward through the stars by its own diameter every hour, so if it is near a bright luminary, you can easily detect that second motion in a few hours.

After ten or twelve days the Moon looks perfectly round and is at its brightest. Now it rises as the Sun sets, coming up exactly opposite the Sun on the horizon. On following nights the Moon rises later and later after sunset as it simultaneously wanes. About twenty-nine or thirty days after you began your observations, you once again spy a thin crescent in the west just after sunset. A *lunar month* has passed.

By now you may have noticed something else. The Moon's slow eastward motion is seldom exactly opposite to the nightly westward movement of nearby stars. Instead, it moves in a path that takes it north and south with respect to the stars, so that in the course of a month it sometimes ranges higher or lower in the sky than at other times, and it rises and sets at different points on the horizon. But no matter where it is with respect to the stars, the Moon's nightly westward wheel is in general similar to those of the stars immediately around it.

At the end of that first month, the sky does not look exactly the same as it did earlier, for the stars around the young crescent Moon are different ones than those of thirty or so days ago. Turning around to the east, you already see stars above the horizon that a month ago did not rise until two hours after dark had set in. It appears that the entire bowl of stars has slid westward toward the Sun—or the Sun eastward with respect to the stars. Motions in the sky, you have learned, are not simple.

In the daytime, now, the gnomon's noon shadow is a different length than a mark shows it was a month ago. Not only that, but the Sun now rises and sets at different places on the horizon than it did last month. It appears that the Sun, like the Moon, has a slower, eastward motion in addition to its daily western motion across the sky. As in the case of the Moon, this second motion is not exactly the opposite of the daily one, because it has shifted the Sun's midday altitude above the horizon. So there is a "north-south" variation here as well. It will take time to learn more.

Suppose you persist with your day- and nighttime observations. After about 365 days, you find that in the interval the Sun's midday shadow has reached a least and a greatest length and has returned to the value it had when you started. If you are not near the equator, that finding agrees with something else you already knew—that the changing seasons return in the same length of time, so you call 365 days a *solar year*. Knowledge of such a year made it possible for our ancestors to keep hunting trips or crop plantings in step with the seasons.

Another advantage of the solar year is that the same stars will again be setting in the sky just after the Sun or rising just before the Sun (*helical* settings and risings) after one year passes. This provides a rough but easy way to tell when a year has elapsed. Moreover, by noting which stars or star groupings are rising or setting at dusk and dawn, you can gauge where you are in the course of a year.

But there is a problem in that the Moon does not have the same phase as it had one year ago—it is fatter and also higher in the sky than it was just after sunset back then. As a result, your year does not have a whole number of months but twelve and part of a thirteenth.

Your neighbor may prefer to calling twelve lunar months a year, which has the advantages of not needing any tedious observations and of providing an even number of months in the year. But that year is several days shorter that 365 days; even within a single lifetime, it gets badly out of step with the seasons unless one adds extra days or months from time to time.

Your year of daytime observations has shown that the Sun's slow eastward motion takes it along an "inclined" path (the *ecliptic*) that, as far as you can tell, is nearly the same as the Moon's, but needing a year instead of a month to complete the circuit.

Nighttime observations over the same interval reveal something else. Five of the brightest stars—precisely those that seldom twinkle like the others—also move slowly with respect to all the rest! The unusual quintet are "wandering stars" or planets; all the other stars are "fixed" compared to each other even though they move constantly every night.

It takes several years to sort out the planetary motions. Curiously, none of the five (nor the Moon, for that matter) ever strays far from the yearly path of the Sun through the stars (the ecliptic), and they always remain within the *zodiac*, a band that extends equally on either side of the ecliptic. Three of the planets move similarly amid the fixed stars. They spend much of their time migrating eastward, but when they are nearly opposite the Sun in the sky ("in opposition"), they slow, stop, and reverse their course, moving westward for a time ("retrograde motion"). Then they again slow, stop, and finally resume their eastward motion through the stars.

The slowest mover, Saturn, which glows with a yellowish light, takes about thirty years to complete its path through the stars, retrograding almost every year. Jupiter, brighter and whiter, moves faster, taking about twelve years for its circuit, retrograding about every thirteen months. Ruddy Mars moves much faster than the other two and retrogrades only every two years or so. Besides its baleful color, reminding many cultures of bloody war, it is easier to see that this planet is much brighter near opposition than at any other time.

The remaining two planets move very differently. Neither strays far from the Sun in the sky, although they sometimes rise before the Sun and sometimes set after it. Brilliant Venus is often a striking sight for several hours in the morning or evening sky, but fainter Mercury stays so close to the Sun that it is seldom glimpsed, and even then never in a totally dark sky.

Some groups of lights in the sky, however, are more constant. To help in finding directions and the hour at night, to follow planetary motions, or to point to a place in the dark sky, our predecessors found it convenient to name groups of stars, or *constellations,* as aids to memory. Connecting stories with those arrays helped even more. An outstanding example is the myth of the champion Perseus, who astride his winged horse Pegasus rescued Andromeda, the daughter of King Cepheus and Queen Cassiopeia, from the sea monster Cetus. The characters in the tale are all names of constellations today. Early in the evening, in late autumn, they are visible in the northern and western skies from Greece, whence the story reached us.

There are other things to see in the heavens. Nearly everyone has seen an eclipse of the Moon. Sometimes the full Moon is devoured by darkness, then for a while it shines feebly with a dull red glow like an ember before gradually regaining its former brightness. A lucky few will experience a solar eclipse, when the Sun is suddenly blotted out and day turns to night for a few moments. But the vast majority of people never see this latter phenomenon, so records that can be passed around or handed down are needed if others are even to know that it exists.

Easily visible on any clear night are the mysterious swift streaks of differently colored light that cross the dark sky and can even illuminate the landscape like day. These "shooting stars" were long believed to be phenomena of the upper atmosphere (indeed, *meteor* means any changeable aspect of the sky, which is why the study of weather is called meteorology). They do occur in the upper atmosphere, but an ancient observer could not know that they came from outer space.

From time to time—many years may pass between examples—a fuzzy glow with a faint tail appears in the sky for a period of a few days to a few months before fading away. These *comets* move with the stars during the night, but from night to night move with an additional motion with respect to the fixed stars. The mysterious visitors can appear anywhere in the sky, not just near the Sun's annual path, like the Moon and the planets, and can move in any direction relative to the stars. Are they omens for empires or persons of high rank? For a long time, many thought so.

Rarely, a new star appears temporarily, one visible to anyone who looks at the night sky. But this happens so infrequently that permanent records are needed if future generations are to hear of it. Such occurrences were also considered to portend important events for rulers.

Though this list is not complete, it indicates about how far civilization progressed in knowledge of the heavens until around 500 B.C. While this lore was slight and hard-won, it was significant. In those early days planetary science was the one field of human knowledge in which definite predictions of natural phenomena could be made, and it could be clearly shown to anyone who cared to look that indeed they did come true.

INTRODUCTION

The history of planetary astronomy is fascinating. The field experienced a dramatic rebirth in the last half of the twentieth century, and today the study of the amazing array of bodies in our solar system fascinates scientists and the general public alike. Planetary astronomy is often in the news—on television, in national magazines, and on the front pages of newspapers. Men and women who work in the field are widely respected and some, such as the late Carl Sagan, became celebrities. The field is now a prestigious and popular one, and in addition astronomy has generally escaped the distrust or even fear that many people feel toward the sciences. With a history more ancient than that of any other of the physical sciences, the field of planetary astronomy is vigorous, confident, and healthy.

It has not always been that way, for things were very different not so long ago. It is hard to believe the lowly state of planetary astronomy during most of the first half of the twentieth century. The field had become dormant. The ancient triumphs of Galileo and the glories of Copernicus were faint memories. What was once the "queen of sciences," perceived as one of the noblest examples of the immense power of human intelligence, languished. Even worse, planetary astronomy became a field to be avoided by astronomers and scientists interested in earning a livelihood. But, in its darkest hours at midcentury, planetary astronomy took an unexpected and almost miraculous turn, entering an era of solid achievement, mushrooming growth, and spectacular triumphs. How and why did this Horatio Alger story happen?

The clear and simple answer, it seems, is the rise of the U.S. space program, and in particular the programs beginning in 1958 administered by the National Aeronautics and Space Administration (NASA). NASA programs enabled relatively large numbers of scientists to earn their living doing planetary science. NASA funds provided both ground-based facilities and spacecraft that made it possible for those scientists, most of whom worked in the United States, to make a series of stunning discoveries, the consequences of which continue to unfold.

The story of this rebirth of planetary astronomy is the crux of this book, but it is only part of the story. As interesting, and certainly more puzzling, is why the field "fell from grace" earlier in the century. There are few other examples of areas of human knowledge that were preeminent for so long and yet fell into such disfavor.

The effective death of planetary astronomy is much more obscure than its rebirth. The paper trail of documents relating to its demise is thin and scattered. In addition, personal recollections are contradictory. For example, some (nonplanetary) astronomers who remember the past fifty years or so deny that there was any prejudice against planetary work or workers. On the other hand, every single planetary astronomer I have interviewed, and whose experience goes back that far, believes in no uncertain terms that there was indeed a bias against the field.

This double reversal of fortune in only about fifty years is a dramatic story, but it is only a recent development in a long, long history. Just how far back the story goes poses an interesting question. Some make a good case that planetary astronomy did not begin until 1609, when Galileo first trained his self-made telescope on the heavens. On the other hand, most planetary astronomers to whom I have talked take it for granted that their field goes back at least to the classical Greeks and late Babylonians. Many would go back more than a thousand years earlier, to ancient Sumerian records, even though these did not include any systematic scheme of the heavens. There is indeed strong evidence that the ancients, and certainly the classical Greeks, really did do planetary astronomy. In any case, modern scientists in the field take great pride in their ancient heritage.

Another reason for going as far back as possible is to illustrate how times, ways of thinking, and planetary astronomy itself have changed over the millennia. One misses most of that panorama of change if the time frame is too compressed. Galileo's Europe, for example, considered itself quite modern, while from our distance in time we can see that it was still steeped in much older traditions. However, it was already showing features familiar to the modern world: printing with movable type was established, universities were centuries old, the Earth had been circumnavigated, the New World was being explored, big business had become a force in society, and many of the rivalries that bedevil Europe to this day were well developed.

More to the point, there were enough scientists, and they could communicate quickly enough, that they could argue or agree with one another about current developments as a matter of course. They were aided by the fact that interest in the sciences was great among both the educated public and those with power.

The latter part of our story covers the time from the beginnings of NASA to the present. This was a period of ups and downs for planetary astronomy: times have never been as good as in the early 1960s, yet were almost as bad in the 1980s as a generation earlier. In this era more of the important facts are in the record than in past ages, and personal memories are clearer and still available. Also, by this time the field was an established one, with its own organizations, journals, awards, and even with political clout in locales as different as Washington, D.C., and university campuses.

Such are the limits of our story in time. But where do we set the bounds as regards content? One simply cannot cover all of planetary astronomy in detail. Books about Copernicus and his system alone would make a hefty pile.

I have omitted topics that did not contribute directly to the development of modern planetary astronomy, such as Mayan and Chinese astronomy, fascinating though they are. Sumerian and Egyptian work, as far as it is known, receive modest mentions and late Babylonian efforts only a little more.

As in so many fields of human knowledge, planetary astronomy begins with the classical Greeks, who might be called the first "modern" people because much of their thinking is still with us today. Be the idea democracy or tyranny, the Greeks had a word for it. Arabic astronomy, in turn, transferred classical ideas to later times and other cultures. Medieval European studies are relevant but offered little infusion of new knowledge and here receive only a sparse treatment.

With the birth of the "New Astronomy"—Copernicus, Tycho, Galileo, Kepler, and their contemporaries—planetary astronomy entered a new age. For example, systems of the "world" (the observable universe, in its older meaning) play lesser parts in the story. Our range of topics narrows through time, to compensate for the ever growing number of scientists and their rapidly increasing outputs in ever more restricted fields.

As examples of this trend, modern work on the Sun and kindred topics like the solar wind and the aurora borealis, although interesting, is secondary to the central story of planetary astronomy. Karl Hufbauer's *Exploring the Sun: Solar Science since Galileo* (1991) provides strong coverage on the subject. Similarly, at the time of this writing, there are in progress two other NASA-sponsored studies that relate to the study of planetary astronomy: Joseph N. Tatarewicz's discussion of planetary geophysics and Andrew J. Butrica's examination of planetary radar astronomy. These works provide in-depth treatment of areas only touched upon here. In addition, Stephen G. Brush's three-volume *A History of Modern Planetary Physics* (1996) gives a detailed account of such matters as how the analysis of lunar samples provided by the Apollo missions led to a better understanding of our satellite's origin and development. Works of this kind fill in the broader and longer-range account I am attempting.

This history also narrowly defines celestial mechanics, the science of how heavenly bodies move, as relating only to the solar system. Even that narrow portion of the subject is further pared back as we near the present, which eliminates areas such as the vital (but not in the scope of this history) navigation of interplanetary probes.

Likewise, coverage of the geology and meteorology of the planets and their satellites is limited ever further as our story goes on. The nature of our Moon is a good example. The Moon ceases to be solely of astronomical interest when scientists start studying lunar rocks in their laboratories. And, of course, studies of our own planet, Earth, fill libraries. However, the impact of astronomical observations on our understanding of our own planet is properly within the scope of this work. A third set of limits to this work is geographic. In the twentieth century, the focus of attention narrows to planetary astronomy in the United States of America, and with good reason. In the rest of the world, Europe in particular, planetary astronomy never fell into the utter disrepute that it suffered in the United States, but America had a monopoly on large telescopes until only a few decades ago, and American astronomers made most of the observational and theoretical advances. Here is where the action was, though little of it was in planetary astronomy.

In our contemporary Space Age, except for a few early Soviet successes with Moon probes and a long series of Venus lander probes, virtually every other discovery, whether by way of space vehicles or terrestrial observations, belongs to the United States. This situation lasted until fairly recently, when other nations began to send probes to bodies such as Halley's comet, and large telescopes were no longer an American monopoly. But the rejuvenation of the field of planetary astronomy is largely an American phenomenon.

The renewal can be partly attributed to the new technology provided by radio astronomy. That science essentially began after World War II and is important to our history because, in contrast to those in optical astronomy, radio astronomers never had a condescending attitude toward planetary studies. Why? Opinions vary; the fact that both fields were outside the mainstream of astronomy is a popular view. This is an interesting and unusual circumstance, which requires closer examination.

Having indicated the limits of the current study, I must explain the processes and procedures for researching and it. Written documentation is of course the standard basis for history, and for the more distant past that is often all that is available. Yet, it is common experience that many important things are never written down, sometimes unintentionally, and sometimes very intentionally indeed. Thus many reasons, opinions, excuses, hopes, fears, and ideas are lost, making it much harder—and often impossible—to find out why people did certain things at particular times. The historian employs historical imagination and intuitive reasoning in attempting to fill out the picture.

Fortunately, many of the actors who played roles in the rebirth of planetary astronomy are still on the stage, and there are even some who experienced the dark times that came before. While memories may be imperfect, it is true that what people *think* happened is sometimes as significant as what did happen. This inquiry into the modern age of planetary astronomy owes much to interviews with participants and observers, especially as regards the climate in which they worked and the often unspoken problems they faced.

One may yet ask what is here rendered differently—why read this book? The first answer is simple: at this writing there are no other modern histories of planetary astronomy from earliest times to the present, although many writers have worked on specific areas of the story.[1] Studies on classical astronomy are numerous. Otto Neugebauer's monumental *A History of Ancient Mathematical Astronomy* (1975) provides a full presentation of the subject. Likewise, Arab, medieval, and Renaissance astronomy have held their own in the book trade. Moving ahead in time, studies of the field's progress in the last few centuries are not rare. Agnes M. Clerke's *A Popular History of Astronomy during the 19th Century* (first published in 1885) went through four editions by 1902 and may never be equaled. And, it goes without saying, the explosion of knowledge about our solar system in the past forty years has produced an enormous number of books. Good examples of recent scholarship are Joseph N. Tatarewicz's *Space Technology and Planetary Astronomy* (1990) and Oran W. Nicks's story of planetary probes—*Far Travelers: The Exploring Machines* (1985).

So what can be added? First, one can put the whole picture together, as those working in the field before us have tried to do for millennia. Second, one can try to provide answers about why things were done when and how they were, and not merely give a simple list of events—which brings up a further question: Should those who took part in the rebirth of planetary astronomy write about it?

Why not? My own work, for example, was at NASA Headquarters in the 1960s as chief of planetary astronomy, then as researcher in planetary and radio astronomy, before becoming a professor of physics and astronomy and then technical editor of *Sky & Telescope* magazine. One of the consultants on this project, Oran W. Nicks, was NASA's director of lunar and planetary programs when growth in the field was most explosive, and he held direct responsibility for most of the successful lunar and planetary probes that have ever been launched. Another consultant, Henry C. Dethloff, an economic historian, is author of *Suddenly Tomorrow Came: A History of the Johnson Space Center.* We certainly were and are in the picture, yet we all feel that we should help paint it.

Is there a bias in this work? Probably yes. Do we lack the perspective that only the passage of time can give? Certainly. Would not the comparatively narrow ranges of our personal experiences hinder us from arriving at the big picture? Possibly. On the other hand, there is one positive and vitally important viewpoint that participants can contribute, one that future historians can never provide. *We were there* when things happened, from the 1960s to the present, which enables us to render events with a sense of immediacy and reality, a sense of being there, an idea of what things were like when nobody knew the answers. Our aim is to give every reader the feeling that you, too, have been there, been there through all the triumphs and failures.

This is a good time to write a book like this, as many of the characters in the story are still around, but the day is getting long. The deaths, in the past few years, of major players such Art Adel, Jim Pollock (who unfortunately could not be interviewed in time), Carl Sagan, Harlan Smith, and Gerard de Vaucouleurs, underline how important it is to write at least some history soon after the events.

Finally, the world of planetary astronomy, though it may seem remote, nonetheless affects us all. An oceanic navigator must know not only his own ship but also the seas on which she sails; the coasts and islands she may encounter; the winds and storms she may meet; the invisible reefs and shoals that may imperil her, and the currents that may speed or hinder her voyage. In the same way, we who are the crew of planet Earth would do well to learn all we can about the sea of space through which we sail.

This book was made possible by the generous financial support of the National Aeronautics and Space Administration under contract NASW-4780. During the three years that the contract ran, work was supervised by Roger D. Launias, NASA's chief historian, who also enthusiastically provided sound advice, valuable suggestions, and much needed encouragement, while at the same time guiding us through the archives at NASA Headquarters.

Henry C. Dethloff put in a lot of hard work, his expertise as a historian and writer invaluable and his efforts in keeping track of the details of the contract indispensable. Oran W. Nicks, my old chief at NASA Headquarters, provided the solid background and clear points of view that his unique, hard-won experience in planetary exploration provides. Both of these men read every word of this book many times and made no bones about catching errors, asking for changes, and so forth, yet they kept proper perspective and an excellent sense of humor through the whole process.

In addition, three reviewers selected by the NASA History Office carefully read over an earlier draft. Their comments and suggestions were well taken. None of these people, nor anyone else who helped me, is responsible for mistakes of fact or interpretation; those are my responsibility.

While writing this book, I talked to hundreds of planetary astronomers and scientists in related fields and encountered almost universal cooperation. All in all that was a pleasant surprise, although in retrospect it might not have been. A list of everyone involved would run to several pages—I thank them one and all. In particular, I appreciate the time many people gave me in interviews; they are named in the bibliographical essay.

Planetary scientists may ask such questions as why was this not included or why give so much emphasis to that? Some may firmly state that I got it all wrong. Historians may pose queries like where is the documentation for this or why is there not more about background, details, or repercussions? To both, my answer is that I did the best I could in the time I had, and that this work is not intended to be a history of the "What General Lee ate for breakfast on the Third Day at Gettysburg" school but rather an attempt at broader perspective—more a case of "Why in heaven's name did Lee order Pickett's Charge?"

Libraries and archives were universally helpful: the National Science Foundation, the National Academy of Sciences, the Huntington Memorial Library, the University of Arizona, and the U.S. Naval Observatory. It was eye-opening to find out just how little of what I knew had happened is actually documented.

Special thanks go to the Astronomy Department of the University of Texas at Austin, and in particular to its McDonald Observatory and Peridier Library, for generous assistance. My thanks are also due to Texas A&M University's Cushing Library, and in particular to the TAMU Archives. To TAMU Press, a hearty "well done."

To one and all, sincere thanks for your aid, for it has helped make this book a lot of fun to write. And to my wife, Marcia-Ellen, sincere thanks for support and understanding during the past four years (and much longer than that). She, too, remembers the good old days and knows all too well how difficult many of them were for those of us who were there.

PLANETARY ASTRONOMY

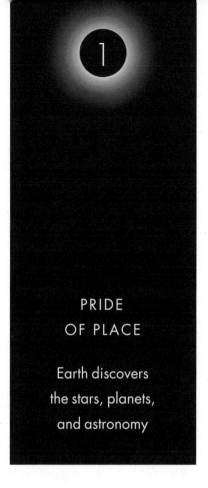

1

PRIDE
OF PLACE

Earth discovers
the stars, planets,
and astronomy

Watchers of the night sky probably began to associate groups of stars in early times as an aid to finding direction and telling the time at night. Some arrays may be very ancient indeed, probably older than any known records. For example, many native North American peoples traditionally considered the stars of the Big Dipper to form a bear, while today we designate these stars as the hind part of a bear. This similarity may be the result of a common tradition that goes back more than ten thousand years, but we will probably never know for certain.

There are good reasons for believing that the three constellations of Leo, Scorpius, and Taurus (including the distinctive Pleiades star cluster), which lie along the ecliptic, were known in their present form at least as early as 3500 B.C., and possibly may trace their origins to the region of lower Mesopotamia then peopled by the Sumerians. Other star groups recognized by Babylonians around 1000 B.C. have names that betray a

Sumerian origin. As the constellations form the background against which planetary positions are charted, there is a legitimate reason to begin the story of planetary astronomy with the Sumerians in the fourth millennium before Christ.

By sometime in the first millennium B.C., the entire zodiac seems to have been marked off into the twelve equal divisions that survive in our renderings of it to the present day. However, the oldest known record of our modern zodiacal constellations is a late Babylonian cuneiform tablet from 400 B.C. or so. At about that time the zodiac appeared in Greece without a trace of any long development there, which strongly suggests that the classical Greeks simply borrowed it from the East. The oldest known Greek description of modern constellations, by Eudoxus of Cnidus, also dates from this era.

In general, the constellations apparently developed from the mingling of a number of traditions, "giving us," in Owen Gingerich's words, "a sweeping pattern of something old, something new, something borrowed, and something going back to the ice ages."[1]

THE FIRST ACCOUNTS

How far back do astronomical records go? The oldest known are the famous "Venus Tablets," dating from the end of the First Dynasty of Babylon. Their date is uncertain, in part because the precise chronology of the ancient Middle East is still very much in dispute, but 1700 to 1600 B.C. is probably not far off. The cuneiform writing describes omens that depend on the appearance of Venus and makes certain predictions. There are also some actual observational data on Venus; not precise positions with respect to the stars, but statements of how long the planet was invisible (due to its closeness in the sky to the Sun), when it reappeared, and so on.[2] In fact, "the wisdom of the ancients" was pretty meager in that case, and in fact, the Babylonian astronomy of that era was, as Otto Neugebauer put it, "rather primitive and crude."[3]

There are later scattered Middle Eastern texts relating to astronomy. For example, the Assyrians were attentive to the skies, mainly because they were interested in what the omens they saw there portended here on Earth, particularly for emperors and empires. The observations and predictions involved were still "general"—the sort of thing that in our terms might read, "When Venus first appears in the western dusk, there will be rain." Whatever the reasons, neither observations nor predictions had improved much in a millennium.[4]

When one thinks about ancient astronomy, one might suspect that the astronomical lore of Egypt was the most ancient and advanced. Egyptian astronomy does go back a long way, but it was not very advanced, for the inhabitants preferred to depend upon traditions rather than upon experimentation and new information.

To take one case, the calendar in use in ancient Egypt was extremely simple. It was so simple and crude that its origin must go back far beyond historic times, probably further back than any but the most basic astronomical observations. Every Egyptian year had exactly 365 days, and since the true year is roughly a quarter of a day longer than that, after only a century a calendar that started out synchronized with the seasons would be almost a month "off," in the sense that the time to plant would be one month later. As a result the Egyptians kept two calendars—one practical and one theoretical—a system that worked well for millennia.

Whatever the origins of their calendar, which may be agricultural and related to the annual rising of the Nile, there does not seem to be any reason to assume that the Egyptians relied on a sophisticated knowledge of astronomy.[5] While their impressive practical knowledge of surveying and leveling enabled them to turn the entire swampy Nile delta into fertile farmland, they were less accomplished in mathematics and astronomy.

Early Egyptians did observe the daily and yearly motions of the celestial sphere, for some of their results are painted on coffin lids from as early as the twenty-first century B.C. However, their star groupings were so different from ours that so far we have been able to connect only a few of their descriptions of stars and star groups with our own: the star Sirius, the constellation Orion, and the Big Dipper, for example.[6]

The astronomy of the ancient Egyptians was not very advanced in part because their mathematics never advanced to the point where it could describe astronomical events. Their astronomical work, such as it was, contributed little to the development of the science in future ages.[7] Egyptian astronomy was a dead end.

CHINA

There is little evidence that Chinese astronomical study predated that of the Middle East or Egypt. Astronomy became a serious field of study in China only after the Babylonians and even the Greeks began their advances. Moreover, China was effectively isolated from the civilizations to the west, so that despite off-and-on trade contacts over the millennia, it never affected developments elsewhere to any noticeable extent.[8]

Confusion between astrology and astronomy is all too common. Contrary to widespread folklore, astrology is *not* the more ancient science, and it did not precede or "father" astronomy. It is true that "signs in the heavens," such as eclipses, comets, and close approaches of planets to each other, were often seen as omens in ancient times and still are by many today. After all, some events in the heavens do affect Earth. If one lives away from the equator, it is hotter when the Sun arcs higher in the sky and stays up longer, and it is colder when the Sun does not rise very high or stay up as long. The fixed stars tell the same story, for they indicate how the seasons are passing, and what to expect next, by the appearances and positions of familiar star groups at dawn and dusk. Thus it seemed only reasonable to believe that other celestial phenomena would be the causes of good or bad to kings, empires, or the people at large.

But the "personal" astrology that we know today, based on the casting of horoscopes that depend on the exact time of a person's birth and the celestial positions of the planets then, is actually fairly "modern." It could not exist before the zodiac was clearly defined, for example, or before it was possible to predict for the future, or reconstruct for the past, planetary positions with respect to the fixed stars. Thus astronomy needed to be fairly advanced both observationally and theoretically before there could be any personal astrology at all. Such evidence as we have is that astrology arose along with the clearly defined zodiac in Chaldea—another name for lower Mesopotamia—in early times but not before about 700 B.C. Eventually, although not rapidly, astrology made its way westward. Astrology did not give rise to astronomy, planetary astronomy in particular, because by the time personal horoscopes appeared, detailed descriptions and predictions of how the planets moved were already known.[9]

THE EMERGING SCIENCE OF PLANETARY ASTRONOMY

Writing probably began in the fourth millennium B.C. in Mesopotamia, and there must have been some form of record keeping even earlier. Thus the means for recording at least some astronomical events were available in very ancient times, yet there were no substantial advances in the ability to predict planetary astronomy for thousands of years. Why? There are no convincing answers.

When substantial progress did occur, it came in a most curious manner. In one of the most remarkable coincidences in the history of science, two separate and entirely different ways of predicting planetary phenomena advanced to a previously unparalleled degree of sophistication in roughly the same era in separate, but neighboring, cultures. Planetary observations and methods of prediction by the late Babylonians and then the Chaldeans, as well as the Hellenistic Greeks, advanced to remarkable levels of sophistication.

About 750 B.C., when Greece was still emerging from the Mediterranean Dark Ages embodied by the fall of Mycenae, astronomer-priests at Babylon began a series of planetary observations that continued to roughly 50 B.C.[10] From their records we also have lists of the relative positions of the constellations, and from these early astronomers' work we derive our circle of 360 degrees and its division of one degree into sixty minutes of arc and one minute into sixty seconds.[11] This advanced method of dealing with numbers is called the sexidecimal system and was used in all their calculations, including business and astronomical, and may be one reason the advances took place.

The "Babylonian" observations were not long lists of angular positions of an object at different times, as in the modern sense. Because measuring instruments in antiquity were so inaccurate, observations were more qualitative than quantitative—and rather sparse as well. The lack of precision was compensated for to some degree by the observations covering an extended time, so that the periods of different phenomena, and the relations between them, became clear. A relatively few observations at selected times were then analyzed by very complex mathematics to produce predictions. (The use of only a few well-chosen observations also characterized classical Greek astronomy—with the notable exception of Hipparchus—and remained the rule right up to the time of Tycho Brahe many centuries later.)[12]

By 400 or 300 B.C. the Babylonians in some way—there is no hard evidence of how or when they did it—had developed arithmetic methods capable of producing accurate predictions of planetary motions and the even more complex movement of the Moon, methods that eventually allowed them to predict lunar and later solar eclipses. The Mesopotamian procedures made no use whatever of geometric models or combinations of circular motions, in stark contrast with Greek (or our own) astronomical techniques. What the Mesopotamians did do was look for recurrences of phenomena and time differences between those repetitions. They looked for patterns in the observations, and through complex arithmetic predicted future events and calculated past ones.[13]

While Greek science advanced, the city of Babylon lost its position as a center of trade and culture, becoming mostly a ruin by the end of the first century A.D. Babylonian planetary theory died and was forgotten, not to be rediscovered until almost two thousand years had passed. Only a century ago was the city's astronomy rediscovered. Interestingly, we have learned the names of some of its astronomers and scribes, and we know how they made a living. They were practical workers attached to temples, engaged in the religious duty of describing how luminous deities made their way across the heavens.[14]

Meanwhile, Greeks made significant strides in every facet of knowledge, including astronomy. Just how much they borrowed from or were inspired by Babylonian astronomy, science, or knowledge in general is uncertain. In any case, the Greeks developed a new and entirely different form of mathematical planetary astronomy, one based on geometric models and not just on looking for arithmetical relations between the recurrences of events. Their way of apprehending their world apparently was original and there is no evidence that it owed anything to any previous civilization. Essentially, their view was to dominate astronomy for two thousand years. As with so many fields of human knowledge, modern astronomy really begins with the Greeks. Their interest in the heavens no doubt had practical aspects—determining the time of day or night, the date, and direction, for example—but they also loved to theorize for theory's sake.

There are mentions of the heavens in Homer and Hesiod, but these are merely references to the simple facts that a sailor, a farmer, or a shepherd of the "Dark Ages" might know. Interestingly, the new ideas first came from Greek colonists on the coast of Asia Minor and its adjoining islands, as well as those in southern Italy, rather than from natives who stayed on in the old homeland.[15] These early "philosophers" were not astronomers or scientists in the modern sense. They used no scientific method, nor did they observe a lot. They wished to explain all the world and had to do so with only very primitive mathematics. Still, they were the people who opened the way to modern astronomy and science in general.

The Greek historian Herodotus relates that Thales of Miletus predicted at least the year in which a total solar eclipse took place (probably in 585 B.C.) and thus stopped a battle between the Lydians and the Medes in full career. It's a great story, but the fact is that even the Babylonians, who were substantially ahead of the Greeks in astronomical prediction at that time, did not then have the ability to predict eclipses of the Sun accurately.[16]

Pythagoras of Samos is another shadowy figure who flourished in southern Italy later in the sixth century B.C. Later writers attribute to him many kinds of knowledge, including the "Pythagorean Theorem" for right triangles (which, however, was known long before in many civilizations) and the spherical shape of the Earth. In the following century his followers, the Pythagoreans, devised a bizarre world picture in which the Earth, which they held to be just another spherical planet, and all other celestial bodies revolve about a "central fire" at the true center of the universe. In this construction, Earth rotates in such a way that its uninhabited (western) hemisphere always faces the fire, so we cannot see it. Even if we could travel halfway around the Earth, we still could not see the central fire because a "counter Earth" always hides it from view.[17]

There are other similar figures in the history of Greek thought before Socrates, philosophers who illustrate how widely and wildly classical Greeks could theorize. For example, we apparently owe the concept of concentric celestial spheres, which bulked so large in later centuries, to Parmenides of Elea, who lived during the first half of the fifth century B.C.[18] However, none of these early speculators really contributed to the advancement of theoretical or observational planetary astronomy. In particular, they did not provide any specific theories of, or practical methods for calculating, planetary motions.

Still, whether or not these classical Greek philosophers proposed or even held the opinions credited to them, it seems clear that the idea of the Earth being the center of the universe, though wrong, was beginning to be generally accepted in Greece by this time. So too was the spherical shape of Earth, for Greek merchants and soldiers of fortune had had been north to the Crimea and beyond, and south to Egypt, and they had seen the night and day skies change as they went their ways. Then too, seafarers well knew that mountaintops appeared long before the lowlands that bore them. This belief in a spherical Earth *was* accurate, and significantly it never afterward disappeared from Western thought, even when a preponderance of scholarly opinion placed our planet motionless in the center of the universe.[19]

But alongside the efforts of technically minded navigators, engineers, surveyors, traders, warriors, adventurers, and the like were the powerful influences of the truly classical philosophers, above all the mighty trio of Socrates, Plato, and Aristotle. They were not astronomers, but their thoughts influenced the development of astronomy, and planetary astronomy in particular, for two millennia.

Socrates has only small bearing on our story, for nature held little interest for him. But he did teach Plato, and that philosopher held that only ideas were real and that the world revealed by our senses was merely an appearance. Plato's influence was enormous in antiquity and continues to this day. In fact, his opinions may have been responsible to some extent for the dearth of scientific inquiry in classical times.[20]

Aristotle, who flourished in the fourth century B.C., was Plato's most distinguished pupil. This Macedonian was a philosopher foremost, striving to explain the entire world by means of a unified system derived by strict logic from general principles. When those principles were wrong, they led to conclusions ludicrous by our standards. On the other hand, he was the world's first real natural scientist (especially in biology), who insisted on observation and experimentation as the basis of knowledge.[21]

The universe according to Aristotle was finite, spherical, and centered on a spherical, unmoving Earth, which was surrounded by nested concentric spheres.[22] The concept of such spheres or shells had originated with Eudoxus of Cnidus in the first half of the fourth century B.C. They both used a number of them, all rotating uniformly about the Earth, but at different rates and with their axes in different directions, and thus made the first known attempt to explain planetary motions physically.[23] These concepts later were refined by Callippus of Cyzicus, a friend of Aristotle.[24]

For Eudoxus and Callippus, the celestial spheres were merely mathematical constructs, but for Aristotle they were real; solid crystalline shells that carried the stars and planets along. The outermost sphere carried the fixed stars around once a day. The "prime mover" propelled this outermost shell, which transferred its impetus to the one below it, and so on down to the lowest sphere. It took fifty-five shells to account for the motions of the stars, Sun, Moon, and five other "planets." Inside the sphere of the fixed stars were shells carrying Saturn, Jupiter, Mars, Venus, Mercury, the Sun, and the Moon, in that order "downward" toward the spherical Earth.[25]

According to Aristotle the heavens were the unchanging realm of uniform, circular motions, the only type appropriate there, and contained the "fifth element," ether (the other four were earth, water, air, and fire). Below the sphere of the Moon, however, things were completely different, with change and straight-line motion—objects fall toward the center of the Earth, for example—being the rule. In the sublunar region the four elements were, in general, arranged with earth at the center and water, air, and fire at higher and higher levels. In his view, shooting stars and comets were produced in the upper part of the atmosphere, which rotated from east to west like the stars. According to this picture these phenomena must lie beneath the Moon because they were changeable, and thus could not belong to the higher, unchanging heavens. (Aristotle was correct as regards meteors, which are indeed produced in the upper atmosphere, but he was dead wrong about comets.) His system of spheres was superseded in a relatively short time by better models. Still, many of his mistaken ideas about the physical world, such as the stark difference between the heavens and the Earth, would remain in vogue for two millennia.[26]

The fourth century B.C. also saw the pioneering ideas of Heraclides Ponticus, Aristotle's contemporary and perhaps also a student of Plato's. According to Heraclides, the Earth turned on its axis once a day, causing the heavens to appear to move in the opposite direction. Apparently he also suggested that Mercury and Venus revolve about the Sun, and not the Earth, which was the first step toward a Sun-centered or heliocentric theory.[27]

In addition to his efforts in many fields of knowledge, Aristotle tutored Alexander the Great, who had conquered the Persian Empire by the time of his death in 323 B.C. The subsequent fusion of Greek and Oriental ideas gave rise to a culture known as Hellenistic. This civilization extended from Bactria and India in the east to far into the Mediterranean in the west, and in the next few centuries it gave rise to a surprisingly large number of advances in science and technology.

Aristarchus of Samos, who lived from about 310 to 230 B.C., was the first to propose a completely heliocentric theory. His model, with the Earth rotating once a day, the Moon revolving around Earth once a month, and all the planets, including our own, revolving around the central Sun, turned out to be correct.

Unfortunately, while Aristarchus' theory was never completely forgotten, it had little impact in antiquity. There was then no proof that Earth moved but plenty of everyday, "commonsense" indications that it did not. Moreover, instruments and thus observations were getting better, mathematics was advancing, and the heliocentric theory offered no advantages to those interested in ever more elaborate calculations that could reproduce the ever more complex planetary motions. Mathematical formalisms would dominate astronomy for centuries, and Aristarchus' promising theory failed to stir new inquiry about what the world was *really* like.

But Aristarchus was not just another spinner of theories. He made the first known attempt to determine the relative distances of the Sun and the Moon from Earth, and thus their relative sizes. He did so by observing the Moon when it appeared exactly half-lit (at "first quarter," for example) and determining its angular distance from the Sun at that time. He found that the Moon was then *less* than one quarter of the way around the sky, in fact 87 degrees instead of the 90 degrees expected if the Sun were infinitely far away. This 3-degree difference indicated that the Sun was about nineteen times as far from the Earth as the Moon was, a value that would be quoted for millennia.

The number he got was much too small (400 is closer to the truth), because it is quite difficult to determine with the unaided eye exactly when the Moon is half lit, so he put the Sun much too close and calculated it to be much too small. In addition, from lunar eclipses he determined the relative sizes of the Earth and Moon (his result, roughly 3 to 1, is not far from the true ratio of 4 to 1). With some estimate of the true size of the Earth, he could then get estimates of the true sizes of the Moon and Sun. While his value for Sun was much smaller than it was eventually found to be, it was still enormous compared to Earth, and it may have been for this reason that he put the Sun at the center of his system.[28]

The best ancient measurement of the size of the Earth was made by Eratosthenes of Alexandria, a geographer who headed the great Alexandrian Library. Late in the third century B.C. he used the fact that vertical objects cast no shadows at noon in Syene, Egypt, while they did farther north at Alexandria. His result was probably close to correct (how close depends on the uncertain length of the unit of distance called a "stadia" he used in his calculations.).[29]

EPICYCLES TRIUMPHANT

The so-called epicycle theory is a mathematical formalism that dominated theoretical astronomy for nearly two thousand years. Its basic principles are simple. A planet moves on a small circle (the epicycle), the center of which center moves along a larger circle (the deferent) that has Earth at the center. Both motions are circular and at constant speed—properties assumed as "natural" for celestial bodies—but the resultant motion as seen from Earth can be irregular in speed and direction.

One can see how an epicycle works by sticking a piece of chewing gum on a rotating phonograph turntable while riding on a merry-go-round and noting the complex motions the gum performs with respect to the fixed ground below. The same idea is used in carnival rides to produce fast, slow, forward, and backward motions in bewildering succession; one can even be momentarily stationary with respect to the ground or other riders.

In particular, an epicycle can reproduce a planet's retrograde behavior and also, for example, can explain why Mars appears brightest when in opposition to the Sun. More complex apparent departures from uniform motion can be produced by adding epicycles upon epicycles, letting an epicycle's center not stay on the deferent, reversing the direction of motion on the epicycle, and various other clever devices. In fact, if they are complex enough—and they soon became so—epicycle theories can reproduce *any* celestial motion, for they are in effect geometric versions of the algebraic equations we use today. Epicycle theories were excellent candidates to "save the phenomena," which means that they could reproduce the observed planetary motions. Whether the epicycles and deferents really existed was immaterial to mathematical scientists of the time, as long as the theory worked.[30]

Besides the intellectual challenge involved in making sense of planetary motions, there was no doubt a practical motive as well. Personal astrology became ever more popular during Hellenistic times, in particular among royalty; people who could predict planetary positions accurately could use that knowledge to better their personal positions. In those days planetary astronomy was a very practical science.[31] The earliest great exponent of epicycles was the mathematician Apollonius of Perga, who worked in Alexandria about 230 B.C. His theory may have originated earlier in some form, but we do not know.[32]

Hipparchus of Nicaea made significant advances in epicycle theory, and in many other areas, for he was the greatest astronomer of antiquity. Hipparchus worked mostly on the island of Rhodes about the middle of the second century B.C. and was superb in both theory and observation. Besides his own abilities, he was able to exploit a number of advances: technology had reached the point of providing angle-measuring instruments with graduated circles (the protractor is a humble example), mathematics was much improved, and Hipparchus had access to extensive Alexandrian and Babylonian observational records. He took full advantage of them all.

By comparing older records with his observations, Hipparchus discovered the phenomenon known as the precession of the equinoxes, which is due to the motion of the orientation of Earth's axis in space and results in the north pole of the sky sweeping out a small circle in the sky every 25,800 years, thus giving us a variety of "pole stars" in that interval. He determined the lengths (of several varieties) of the month and the year to unprecedented accuracy (his value for the length of the solar year was only about six minutes too long), and he was able to represent the motions of the Sun and Moon very well by epicycle theory. This ability enabled him to predict eclipses with much more precision than anyone before him—to within an hour or so for lunar eclipses, although not quite so closely for solar eclipses. Hipparchus never produced a theory of the five planets— perhaps because there were not enough observations, or perhaps because he did not have the time—though he did determine their mean times of revolution about the Sun more precisely.

For good measure, Hipparchus determined the distance and size of the Moon (he got essentially the true values), made significant advances in both plane and spherical geometry, and, supposedly stimulated by the appearance of a "new star," probably compiled a catalogue of almost a thousand fixed stars.[33]

Hipparchus left astronomy a natural science in the modern sense of the word—the only one in antiquity. Surprisingly, two and a half centuries passed before anyone picked up the torch that he had carried. There is no certain explanation for this gap, but it does indicate how rare serious professional astronomers, mathematicians, or scientists in general were in classical times; indeed, they are not common even today. We should also remember that astronomy at that time was the most difficult and technical subject known. Few had the intelligence and mathematical training to tackle it, and fewer still the financial support to devote their lives to doing so.

Claudius Ptolemaeus of Alexandria was Hipparchus's only worthy follower in antiquity. He worked in the second century A.D., during the best and greatest times of the Roman Empire. As a geographer, mathematician, and astrologer as well as an astronomer, he wrote on a wide variety of subjects but is most famous for his *Syntaxis*, known to us familiarly as the *Almagest* (mutilated Arabic for "The Greatest").[34] This is the foremost surviving astronomical work from classical times, and its influence was wide and profound in many cultures for almost fifteen hundred years.[35]

Ptolemy built upon and extended Hipparchus's efforts. He refined the epicycle theory in general and was able to predict the positions of the planets to about 10 arc minutes (about one-third of the Moon's apparent diameter), which was about the precision of most astronomical observations at the time. In addition, he discovered and accounted for additional irregularities in the Moon's motion. Ptolemy made relatively few observations. For example, he essentially reissued an updated version of Hipparchus' star catalogue, but in so doing preserved his predecessor's work for posterity. For each star in the catalogue Ptolemy gave its brightness in "magnitudes," with first the brightest and sixth the faintest visible to the naked eye. This system has been modified over the centuries but is still used by astronomers today.

As good as the epicycle theory was in Ptolemy's polished version, there were certain glaring problems of which he—and his mentor Hipparchus—must have been aware. Their theory demanded, for instance, that the Moon's distance from Earth, and thus its apparent angular diameter, should vary so much during a month that the effect would be easily visible to the unaided eye. Of course no such thing happened, but the silence of Hipparchus and Ptolemy on the subject is probably as good a proof as any that these two excellent astronomers considered the epicycle theory a mere mathematical scheme to calculate the positions of the Sun, Moon, and planets on the sky, and not a real physical description of the universe.[36]

Ptolemy's work established him as the foremost authority on astronomy until well after the time of Copernicus. In this connection, there is a widely held belief that a unified "Aristotelian-Ptolemaic" worldview dominated Europe and the Middle East during much of that interval. That is a plausible idea, but Liba Chaia Taub has made a convincing case that Ptolemy "was no Aristotelian, but rather, a mathematician greatly influenced by Platonism."[37] After all, Aristotle was not responsible for everything that his students took down as class notes (Nothing definitely from his hand is generally acknowledged to have survived).

The *Almagest* was so influential that it erased most earlier works on astronomy—why spend a scribe's valuable time copying outmoded books, now that the latest and best was available?—which as a result are now lost. On the other hand, it does provide a superb example of the high level reached by the science of astronomy in late classical times. It was never lost, and today it is possible to read it in the original Greek or in numerous modern translations, many of which provide helpful commentaries and explanations.

After Ptolemy, there was for a long time little that was new in observational or theoretical astronomy. There were compendia, popular works, and elementary texts, but no real advances. Why? True, in the three centuries following Ptolemy the Roman Empire underwent hard times, but the Greeks of earlier days had advanced all forms of knowledge while fighting for their lives against the Persians, engaging in bitter warfare among themselves, and conquering much of the known world. Probably we shall never know the reason.

In any case, the Roman Empire abandoned its relatively uncivilized, underpopulated, and certainly less rich western provinces in the fifth century. "Rome" did not "fall" then but instead concentrated on the richer and more productive provinces of the East. The resulting Byzantine Empire lasted for a thousand years more and poses yet another puzzle. Preserve and improve as it did, why did this splendid civilization produce no substantial advances in astronomy, science, or other fields of endeavor? There is no definite answer.

In abandoned western Europe, the level of intellectual activity sank as matters of sheer survival came to the fore. For centuries, astronomical and other technical knowledge generally would be on a primitive level, though classical lore was never entirely forgotten.

Meanwhile, there were striking developments that originated in the Middle East. During the seventh century the followers of Mohammed spread their rule eastward and westward from Arabia. The resultant culture is often called "Arabian" for its place of origin, though few of its members were Arabs. These people picked up knowledge from those they overran: Greeks, Syrians, Persians, Indians, and others. "Arabic" numerals are a case in point, for they originated in India and were merely transmitted to western Europe by the Arabs. There were translations into Arabic of many works originally produced in other languages. The *Almagest* was translated sometime around 800.[38]

But the Arabs did not just translate (and thus in many cases preserve) manuscripts, because astronomy was important to them for many reasons. Accurate times were needed to determine when to pray, directions and orientations were required for people to face Mecca while praying, and lunar theory was of importance because the calendar was a lunar one. Moreover, astrology was an important part of life, and rulers would pay well for knowledge of the future. Thus Islamic scholars both observed the heavens and attempted to improve Ptolemaic-style planetary theory. However, they never attempted to go beyond Ptolemy's conception of the universe, and so their astronomy remained essentially that of classical times.

Meanwhile, Europe was reviving, and by the end of the eleventh century was strong and confident enough to launch the First Crusade. Intellectual life was advancing apace, and the twelfth century saw the founding of universities such as at Bologna, Paris, and Oxford, with astronomy as an integral part of the curriculum. In the same period there began to appear a spate of translations of Greek and Latin authors from Arabic into Latin, primarily via Spain. This work continued in the next century, supplemented by translations directly from the Greek.[39]

By now European astronomy was roughly back up to the level of classical antiquity. Thus, for example, it was possible for Alfonso X, The Wise, King of Castile and Leon, to gather a group of scholars in Toledo who produced an improved set of tables for calculating planetary motions. The so-called *Alfonsine Tables* appeared in 1252 and remained the standard throughout Europe for some three hundred years.[40] Nevertheless, as long as astronomy remained wedded to the Ptolemaic system there could be no substantial progress in theory. So while the number of astronomers and their published works rose, and interest in astrology, navigation, and commerce cried out for better ways to predict planetary motions, there were few real advances of the kind that held up in the light of later work. We now know that the state of mathematics and instrumentation were prime causes of this situation, but it must have been frustrating at the time.

The unlikely revolutionary was a Pole, Nicolaus Copernicus. This modest shaker of worlds was born in Torun in 1473 and studied at universities in Krakow and then in Italy, where he pursued medicine among other subjects and received a doctorate in law. He then returned to Poland, where he held the ecclesiastical position of canon. Copernicus eventually settled in the town of Frombork and, in the time between his official duties, worked out a new system of the universe.[41]

Copernicus's construction has the Sun at the center, with Mercury, Venus, Earth, Mars, Jupiter, and Saturn revolving about it in that order outward. The Moon revolves around Earth, which is just another planet and which rotates once a day.[42] His universe was vastly larger than Ptolemy's, so as to be consistent with the lack of measurable change of position of any fixed stars on the celestial sphere due to the effect of Earth's motion around its orbit ("annual parallax"). If he was right, the stars had to be extremely far away, much more distant than just outside the sphere of Saturn, as had previously been believed.[43]

His system was basically the solar system as we know it today. Still, Copernicus could not escape the Ptolemaic tradition completely, and he kept the notion of uniform circular motion. He also retained the deferents and the epicycles—thirty-four "circles" in all—needed to reproduce the observed planetary motions even with the Sun at the center of the system.[44] Nor was he a great observer like Hipparchus, for he made relatively few measurements. However these were important—just those that he needed.[45]

Copernicus delayed publishing his full work for many years, although word of it spread around Europe and there were a few short summaries. It appears that he was not the kind of person who relished the controversy that publication seemed sure to bring on, and so his magnum opus, *De revolutionibus (On the Revolutions),* appeared only in 1543, the year of its author's death.[46]

Before and for some years after publication, there is little evidence that the novel system proposed in On the Revolutions caused much of a stir in general, though there were a few pointed criticisms.[47] For one thing, the work was extremely technical and mathematical, and few persons had the knowledge and the time to work through it.[48] For another, although Copernicus's new world system is clearly laid out early in the book, by far the greater part of the work *looks* Ptolemaic to the core as far as all its formalism goes.[49]

Among the small fraternity of European professional astronomers, however, *On the Revolutions* was an instant success. They promptly elevated Copernicus to a place alongside the great astronomers of antiquity and placed great store in his new numerical data and new mechanism for reproducing the finer points of planetary orbits, using both extensively. In particular, Erasmus Reinhold published the *Prussian Tables* in 1551, which relied on Copernicus's work and became the new standard.[50] This new information was all the more welcome because the *Alfonsine Tables* were getting more and more out of date, calendar reform was in the air, and the needs of navigators were ever more pressing.

On the other hand, there were almost no Copernicans among astronomers, even though they applauded his skill at predicting celestial motions—there was no proof for his new system, and it was no simpler than Ptolemy's. Professionals praised the author because he was better able to explain the phenomena, but they did not believe in the physical reality of his view of the solar system and the universe.[51] Though Copernican ideas gradually found increased favor, this curious situation lasted for half a century until another innovator entered the stage.

The agent of change was Tycho Brahe, the greatest observational astronomer who ever lived. This proud Danish nobleman was born in 1546 and had an early interest in astronomy. However, it was the sighting of a bright "new star" in 1572 that really began his career. He found that the heavenly intruder, a supernova later dubbed "Tycho's Star," showed no change of position through the night with respect to the stars ("diurnal parallax") and so must be "above" the Moon in Ptolemaic terms. Here was proof that the heavens were not unchangeable after all.[52]

Tycho believed in astrology but felt that it was an uncertain science because its basis—astronomy—needed a thorough overhaul. He got his chance when the King of Denmark, Frederick II, gave him the island of Hven and financial support in 1576. Here Tycho built an observatory complex named Uraniborg (Castle of the Heavens), and produced astronomical measuring instruments of far greater accuracy and precision than any before made.[53] Even without the aid of a telescope, he was able to measure positions in the sky to within 1 minute of arc or so—a previously unheard of feat.[54]

A brilliant comet appeared in the sky in 1577, before Tycho's improved instruments were ready, but he observed the unexpected visitor as best he could. In particular, he looked for and failed to find any diurnal parallax. If the comet were as close as the Moon, the displacement would have been about 1 degree, an amount that would have been obvious to him. This negative result showed that Aristotle's teaching that comets were phenomena in Earth's atmosphere was wrong, and definitely placed them among celestial bodies.[55]

For two decades Tycho carried on a systematic series of precise observations of the positions of the Sun, Moon, planets, and fixed stars, something that had never been done before. In addition to these labors, he produced theories of the motions of the Sun and the Moon, a new star catalogue, and a new theory of the world.[56] Tycho's new system of the universe was a hybrid, with the Earth at the center, circled by the Moon and also by the Sun, around which all the other planets revolved. He believed that Earth was fixed because, among other reasons, he had been unable to detect any annual stellar parallaxes. His was just one example of a "geoheliocentric" theory, several varieties of which were quite popular in seventeenth century. Real crystalline spheres had no place in these models, because here the orbits of various bodies actually intersected.[57]

After the old king died Tycho lost his financial backing. He left Hven in 1597 and accepted the post of Imperial Mathematician under the Holy Roman Emperor Rudolph II in Bohemia. Tycho died shortly thereafter and never did produce a detailed new planetary theory. Instead, that task would be accomplished in a completely unexpected manner by a young assistant of Tycho's last few years.[58]

That man was Johannes Kepler, a mystic and a Copernican. Born in 1571, he was invited to Bohemia by Tycho, where the young astronomer first arrived around the beginning of 1600 and worked on and off with Tycho for that year and the next.[59] Kepler started by attempting to reproduce the motion of Mars as determined by Brahe's observations. This was a stroke of good fortune, because Mars is the only planet that has an orbit departing enough from a circle, and that comes close enough to Earth, for the elliptical nature of its path to show up in Tycho's observations.[60]

Shortly after Tycho's death, Kepler was appointed the new Imperial Mathematician and later gained control of most of the data accumulated at Hven. He continued his attack on Mars's motion by methods that were laborious, painstaking, wandering, and often fruitless. The mathematics of his age was barely sufficient for the job (for example, logarithms were invented during his career), but at last he discovered two of the three "laws" that bear his name. What has come to be known as Kepler's First Law of Planetary Motion states that a planet moves in an elliptical orbit with the Sun at one focus of the ellipse. The second law, often called the "area rule" or the "law of areas," declares that a line joining the Sun and a planet sweeps out equal areas in equal times. This means that a planet moves fastest when it is closest to the Sun (at perihelion) and slowest when it is farthest away (at aphelion).[61]

Kepler finished his work on Mars in 1605, but legal wrangles with Tycho's heirs delayed publication of *Astronomia nova (The New Astronomy)* until 1609.[62] Although old ideas hung on for a while, his concepts eventually swept onto the scrap heap of history the hoary dogma of circular motion at constant speed as the only possible type of heavenly motion.

In 1618 Kepler happened upon his third, or "harmonic" law, which states that the ratio of the squares of the orbital periods of any two planets is the same as the ratio of the cubes of their mean distances—the more distant a planet is from the Sun, the more slowly it moves. This rule also holds for any two bodies in orbit around a third, and in particular he later showed that it held for the satellites of Jupiter.[63] The third law provides a scale model of planetary orbits—that is, it gives their relative sizes in terms of that of Earth's orbit—but cannot give absolute distances in miles. To do that requires measuring in some way the true distance between two planets, say Earth and Mars, or that from Earth to the Sun.

In 1627 Kepler published the *Rudolphine Tables,* which were based on his laws of planetary motion. The new tables were widely used because they reduced the typical differences between predicted and observed planetary positions from a few degrees to a few minutes of arc.[64] But as Kepler was laboring in the vineyard of theory, a brash and self-assured Italian to the south was also changing astronomy forever, though in an entirely different way.

No one knows for certain just who invented the telescope, or where, or when, but there is no doubt at all that Galileo Galilei made the most of it. Born in Pisa in 1564, he was not a mathematical astronomer in the time-honored sense but rather a mathematician and natural philosopher.

Telescopes appeared in Europe early in the 1600s—probably first in the Netherlands. At this time Galileo was already famous in Italy, in part because of his studies of moving bodies, work that demolished a good part of Aristotle's physics. He first heard of the invention in 1609, soon made one for himself, and later constructed others.[65] Galileo's primitive instruments were all similar; a simple tube of lead, cardboard, or some other material, with a convex lens at the front and a concave one at the rear—a type now known as the Galilean telescope. It gave upright images, a useful property for viewing objects on Earth, but the field of view was small, and because of the poor quality of the lenses, the images it gave were also poor. Magnifications ranged up to some thirty times, but the views through these and other early telescopes were so bad that considerable skill and practice were needed to see anything at all.[66]

While Galileo was not the first to look at the heavens through a telescope, he was the first to do so systematically, and beginning late in 1609 he made a series of stunning discoveries. He found that the Moon was rough, not smooth as Aristotle taught, with mountains and many curious circular craters, but still a body much like Earth. He also confirmed that the sky contained many fixed stars too faint to be seen with the unaided eye, and he established that the Milky Way was composed of a multitude of "small" stars.

Galileo noted that his telescopes showed planets as disks with definite angular diameters, whereas stars remained twinkling points of light, even though they appeared brighter through his tubes. This finding destroyed the ancient notion that the apparent angular sizes of stars as seen with the naked eye are real (brighter stars do "look" bigger than fainter ones, as one can see easily, but that effect is in the eye, not in the sky). Here was the answer to a serious objection against the Copernican theory. If the apparent naked-eye sizes were real, the stars would have to be truly enormous to *look* that large and still be so far away that they showed no annual parallax. Now that objection vanished.

Most startling of all, Galileo found that Jupiter had four moons revolving about it, which proved that Earth was not the only possible center of celestial motions. These discoveries were announced in *Sidereus nuncius* (*The Starry Messenger*), a small book that was published in March, 1610, and caused a sensation.[67] None of these telescopic observations proved either Copernicus right or Ptolemy wrong, but several were hard blows against Aristotle's teachings.

In July, 1610, Galileo was puzzled by Saturn's appearance, for that planet seemed to have three disks, with a smaller one on either side of a larger central one. These features were not like the satellites of Jupiter, for they did not move with respect to the planet. These appendages were the rings of Saturn seen imperfectly, something that Galileo could not know. Their disappearance in 1612, followed by their reappearance in 1613, left him and other observers baffled for decades.[68]

Galileo had been observing Venus as well, and by the autumn of 1610 had found that the planet went through all the phases of the Moon, from crescent to full. This behavior was conclusive evidence against the Ptolemaic theory, which held that Venus was always roughly between us and the Sun and so could never be seen as full. However, the Copernican theory still was not proven, because various Tychonic systems could also explain the phases.[69]

Large sunspots had long been spied with the unaided eye, but Thomas Harriot in London was the first to observe them telescopically. Galileo also studied them and, typically, claimed priority for himself in the matter, as he had for the invention of the telescope. In any event, continued observations showed that these spots were indeed on the Sun and demonstrated solar rotation, another blow against Aristotle.[70]

Galileo's celestial discoveries were not far from the limit of what could be discerned by the naked eye; they required little telescopic aid. He neatly skimmed the cream off the top of what could be done with the instruments of the day. A true Renaissance man, and not one to remain in an ivory tower, he skillfully used the prominence he gained to advance his personal situation. The telescopic observations and discoveries that brought him fame, position, and money probably would have been made by others within a few years.

On the other hand, Galileo's advances in physics, and particularly in the motions of bodies, were far ahead of his time. For example, he was the first to grasp the principle of inertia, according to which an object naturally keeps on moving *unless* something changes its motion. This is dead against the "commonsense" Aristotelian notion that bodies are naturally at rest and move only as long as they are acted upon by some impetus. That mistaken idea results from ignoring effects such as friction, which we cannot escape on Earth.[71]

Galileo's later life was tragic. His overt Copernicanism got him into trouble with the Catholic Church, and his 1632 book *Dialogue Concerning the Two Chief World Systems, the Ptolemaic and the Copernican* brought matters to a head. In a blunder of epic proportions, the Church allowed the Holy Office to pronounce on a matter of natural science. Galileo's sentence was a pro forma penance and benign house arrest, first in the custody of his friend the Archbishop of Sienna and then in a villa at Arcetri, near Florence.[72]

The effects of the "Galileo Affair" were widespread but not permanent. The Holy Office (a Church Tribunal dealing with faith and morals) had decreed in 1616 that Copernicus's *De revolutionibus* be suspended until corrected (in fact, only a few corrections were ordered in 1620). Galileo's treatment had a serious effect in Catholic countries, but it seems that only in Italy was research on the new system of the world seriously affected. Curiously, when Copernicus's work first became known, it was the Protestants who attacked it, but in the century that followed there was a complete reversal. By the seventeenth century most Protestant astronomers were Copernicans and it was the Catholic Church that condemned the heliocentric theory—though probably far from all the astronomers who were Catholics subscribed to that condemnation. This cosmological "split," which once loomed so important, lasted for a century before it began fading away.[73]

DISCOVERING THE NATURE OF THE UNIVERSE

From Galileo
to Newton
and Herschel

By the mid-1600s European science, and especially astronomy, had advanced far beyond the level of classical times. In addition, there were more astronomers alive and working at one time than ever before, due in good part to the numerous universities scattered across the continent and the many courts of powerful figures, both kinds of institutions providing financial support for scholars. Accurate information could also spread faster and more easily. Printing from movable type was well and widely established, and the extensive public postal service of the house of Thurn and Taxis had been delivering the mails reliably for a century.[1]

But compared to the dizzying pace of general advance in the recent past, progress in astronomy was slow. On the theoretical side, studies of motions in the solar system ("celestial mechanics") were hobbled because the useful mathematics of the day was still limited to difficult geometry and laborious arithmetic. In observations, progress was slow because telescopic performance was poor and improved only slowly. Still, in the seventeenth and eighteenth centuries, there was slow but certain progress toward a better understanding of the solar system and the nature of the universe.

TOWARD A NEW UNDERSTANDING OF THE SOLAR SYSTEM

During the seventeenth century opinion among astronomers gradually but generally swung over to a belief in the daily rotation of the Earth about its axis, for it seemed much more reasonable than having the huge celestial sphere with its now much larger number of much more distant of stars rotate at a furious rate. The entirely separate question of whether the Earth revolved around the Sun (or, more generally, just what revolved about what in the solar system) was more complicated. There were three basic choices for the system of the world: Ptolemaic, Copernican, and a number of Tychonic (geoheliocentric) choices.

The Ptolemaic system fell by the wayside before midcentury, in large part because its competitors were so much more useful and precise. Choosing between the remaining contestants was more difficult, for the Copernican and Tychonic systems were equivalent for practical purposes. Copernicus's scheme was simple and regular and was buttressed by Kepler's newly found laws. On the other hand, Tycho had a tremendous reputation as an observer, and his failure to find any annual stellar parallax argued against an Earth revolving around the Sun once a year. The debate went on, with the Copernican view gradually gaining ground, until it had clearly won out by about 1700.[2]

Two theories of the physical nature of the universe—as contrasted to how it moves—made quite a stir in this era, even though both were dead ends, both seem bizarre today, and neither was quantitative. Their popularity is surprising, for neither contained any schemes for calculating much of anything, and hence both were useless for practical purposes such as reproducing observed planetary motions in detail, computing almanacs, or casting horoscopes.

The earlier failure was the creation of William Gilbert, born in 1544 and later chief physician to Queen Elizabeth I of England. Today he is remembered as the first serious student of magnetism and for his discovery that Earth can be considered a gigantic magnet. His great work, *De magnete* (*On the Lodestone*), was published in 1600. Gilbert's findings drew wide attention because of their obvious importance to oceanic navigation, but they also had cosmological implications. He believed that magnetism could account for Earth's rotation, though he did not apply it to the possible motion of our own planet around the Sun or to the motions of other planets. Astronomers quickly did so.[3]

Among other enthusiasts, Kepler embraced magnetism as the physical basis of his laws of planetary motion, while Galileo flirted with it briefly. The concept got a lot of attention because both Copernicans and anti-Copernicans used various magnetic theories to buttress their arguments. However, magnetism as the moving or controlling force for planetary motions was essentially a dead letter by the mid-1600s.[4]

The second and more influential dead end was the vortex theory of René Descartes, a French philosopher and mathematician who was born in 1596. Among other accomplishments, he devised new laws of motion to take the place of Aristotle's as well as a new concept of the universe (both were mostly wrong). In 1644 he first presented his views in print in a book titled *Principia philosophia.*

Descartes believed that the universe was filled with a curious fluid ether that was rotating in whirls, or vortices, of various sizes. These eddies somehow moved the planets and their satellites. There was no proof whatever for Descartes' theory, which provided only vague ideas about how vortices produced the observed planetary motions. Moreover, there was nothing in his concepts that could be used to calculate planetary motions. But despite the fact that they were no more than creative speculations, Descartes' ideas spread widely through Europe and took deep root. They remained and were taught for a century or so, until Isaac Newton's concepts finally ousted them.[5]

For a century after Kepler, the adoption and development of his new insights were the main reasons for improvements in the prediction of planetary motions.[6] In addition, two observational developments greatly boosted theory.

First, the estimated distance from the Earth to the Sun kept increasing toward its modern value, correcting the mistakes of Ptolemy, and even Tycho, in placing Earth much too close to the Sun.[7] Because of the way in which this distance was estimated, the problem is often stated in terms of the "solar parallax," which is the angular size of Earth's radius as seen from the Sun. (Later on the term *astronomical unit,* the mean distance between Earth and the Sun, would come into use.)

During the seventeenth century, values of the solar parallax decreased from minutes to seconds of arc, getting smaller by roughly sixty times, which implied a corresponding increase in the distance between the Earth and the Sun. Eliminating the wrong parallax "correction" that had previously been applied to various observations of where the planets are clearly helped predictions of where they would be later. An improved solar parallax helped in another way as well, as better values for it enabled astronomers to turn Kepler's scale model of the solar system into one with real, absolute distances.[8]

The second improvement was a better knowledge of refraction, an effect of our atmosphere that makes celestial objects look higher in the sky than they really are. It is a complex matter, because the amount of this "raising" varies from nothing at the zenith to about 30 arc minutes at the horizon (thus the setting Sun appearing to touch the sea horizon has already just set), but during the seventeenth century astronomers greatly improved their understanding of the phenomenon.[9] Obviously, it is useful to know exactly where a planet is in the sky right now if one wants to predict where it will be in the future.

There were other nagging problems. For example, the "fixed" stars did not seem to stay in place but rather seemed to vary their positions by as much as a good part of a minute of arc. Thus no matter what the advances in observing instruments, it was impossible to improve upon knowledge of planets' positions when these were measured with respect to the stars. The problem would be resolved later in a most unexpected manner, but in the meanwhile this enigma would be the cause of several erroneous claims of the discovery of annual parallaxes for stars.

Other puzzles were the substantial "irregularities" (differences between prediction and observation) in the motions of Jupiter and Saturn. These discrepancies were far larger than any conceivable errors in the observations and could not be explained theoretically. Lunar theory was in even worse shape. Because our satellite is so close and moves so fast over the celestial sphere, even the relatively primitive observations then available revealed a wide variety of non-uniform motions that defied explanation. It would take until the next century to see these problems resolved.[10]

While the theory of celestial mechanics slowly improved as regards planetary and satellite motions, comets were another matter. The shapes of their orbits were an open question: straight-line, curved, or even sinuous? Nobody knew, and seventeenth-century astronomers could not decide among the alternatives. Observers of the sixteenth century had confirmed that comet tails generally pointed away from the Sun, which gave support to the idea that comets were true celestial bodies, but opinions about their physical nature varied wildly. The majority opinion held that comets were ephemeral bodies that somehow appeared and then died away, though some held that they were permanent objects but visible only when they came close to us. In this, as in many other areas, advances had to wait for new ideas.

On the observational side, telescopes were a big problem. Galileo had, right at the start, almost exhausted the capabilities of his type of instrument. It was Kepler, of all people, who thought of a way to improve telescopic performance. His 1611 work, *Dioptrice* (*Dioptrical Researches*), contained a correct explanation of how light rays passed through a telescope and formed images. Moreover, he suggested that a *convex* eyepiece would give a brighter and wider field of view as well as increased magnification—fifty times, for example.[11] His innovation gave an upside down view that was useless for terrestrial activity such as war or commerce but made little difference in the heavens. Kepler was neither a good observer nor a mechanic, and he never made an instrument of this kind. Others did, however, and improved telescopes first pointed at the skies in the 1630s and eventually spread widely.[12]

"Keplerian" telescopes made possible a much more precise method of measuring small angles, because one could put a micrometer at their focus.[13] In its developed form, this device was simply a pattern of wires or threads, with perhaps one movable, that appeared in the same field of view as the stars. There were other improvements at the end of the telescope as well, for compound eyepieces (composed of more than one lens) came into use. The Dutch astronomer Christiaan Huygens made an early example and reaped the benefits of the advantage it gave him over other observers, in particular in the study of Saturn.[14]

But even the new and improved refracting telescopes had a serious flaw that severely limited their performance. The single convex objective lens at the front brought different colors of light to different focuses, so that the focus was never sharp and stars and planets appeared surrounded by disconcerting and garishly colored halos. One way to reduce this "chromatic aberration" is to make the curve of the objective lens very gradual, which also means that the telescope has a very long focal length. That is, the eyepiece is a long way from the objective.[15]

The struggle against chromatic aberration went to extremes, and by the end of the seventeenth century refractors had focal lengths more than one hundred times as great as the diameters ("apertures") of their objective lenses. Even if the objective were only a few inches in diameter, such a telescope had to be enormously long. Because of this, tubes were dispensed with and the optics were attached to a long spar hung from a tall mast, a whole crew of assistants moving the weird and spectacular apparatus around. The ultimate variation of these "aerial" telescopes just had an objective on a swivel mounting, attached to the distant eyepiece by a string—and nothing else! These clumsy contraptions were difficult to use and their improvement was impossible. As a result, observational discoveries petered out. Only new ideas and new technologies would again open the door to advances.[16]

In a different but related area, clocks improved greatly when pendulums were introduced to regulate keeping of time. Galileo first realized that a pendulum's length determined the period of its swing, and his successors put that fact to practical use. In 1656 Huygens developed the first practical regulated clock. As a result, the relative east-and-west positions of planets and stars could be determined precisely by reference to a timepiece, rather than by the old method of directly measuring angles in the sky.[17] The time difference between crossings of two celestial objects across the meridian (the imaginary arc from the north point of the horizon through the zenith to the south point of the horizon), gave the difference in "right ascension" directly in hours, minutes, and seconds. This method of expressing angles in terms of time originated in the way east-west differences were measured by the clock, and has been used until the present day.

As a result of these improvements and barriers, observational astronomy lurched forward slowly during the seventeenth century. Early on, even though Kepler predicted passages, or transits, of Mercury and Venus across the face of the Sun in 1631, results were sparse. Only three observers, Pierre Gassendi in Paris being the most notable, watched Mercury pass across the face of the Sun, while in the case of Venus the event happened after the Sun set in Europe. There was another transit of Venus in 1639, but only Jeremiah Horrocks and William Crabtree in England observed it.[18]

The transit of 1631 showed that the apparent angular diameter of Mercury, even when that planet was closest to Earth, was much smaller than previous estimates. Gassendi estimated that Mercury was about 20 arc seconds (one third of an arc minute) across rather than the expected 3 arc minutes.[19]

Of course Jupiter's satellites drew attention because they might solve the problem of finding the longitude (one's east-west position) at sea. The important point is that their positions in orbit around Jupiter are essentially the same as seen from anywhere on Earth. Thus the local time at which, for instance, a satellite is eclipsed by Jupiter's shadow, compared with the local time the same event occurred at another location, gives the difference in longitude between the two places. Galileo tried to peddle this concept to the Spanish court, and later the Dutch, for a substantial price, but neither observation nor theory was good enough to make the method practical, and the deals fell through.[20] Several astronomers observed Jupiter's four largest moons extensively, and Simon Mayr ("Marius") may have seen them shortly before Galileo did; the Bavarian gave them the names we use today: Io, Europa, Ganymede, and Callisto.[21]

In the late 1630s Francesco Fontana observed the Moon and planets and detected the phases of Mercury, noted belts on Jupiter, and identified possible surface features on Mars. His results were published in 1646 as *Novae coelestium terrestriumque rerum observationes* (*New Observations of Celestial and Terrestrial Things*).[22]

LUNAR OBSERVATIONS AND MAPS

The Moon was a prime candidate for examination with the telescope, but progress was by fits and starts. After the first revelations of its mountains, plains, and craters, nothing much happened, for Galileo had seen about all that could be seen with a "Galilean" telescope.

What got lunar observations going again was the possibility of finding a practical method of determining longitude at sea by observing eclipses of the Moon—and perhaps thereby making a fortune. The main idea is that particular features on our satellite will be covered by Earth's shadow at the same time as viewed by all observers on one side of Earth. Then, by comparing the local times at which this happens (predicted for one place, observed at another), the difference in time will give difference in longitude directly. The method never worked, because Earth's shadow on the Moon is so ill-defined, but it did produce some improved Moon maps.[23]

The founder of lunar map making was Michael Florent Van Langren ("Langrenus"), who tried to win the "longitude prize" by observing the times when lunar peaks would first or last be lit up by the Sun. That scheme never worked out, but he did publish the first "modern" Moon map in 1645. He decided to name lunar features after illustrious men, a scheme is that has been followed to this day for naming places on the Moon, other planets, and planetary satellites.[24]

Langrenus's work stimulated a flurry of activity in the subject, but the real landmark was the 1647 publication of Johannes Hevelius's *Selenographia,* which became the standard work on the Moon. The Polish brewer observed our satellite at many phases and produced engravings of and a running commentary on what he saw. He avoided personal names and instead used classical Greek and Roman place names, a few of which—the Apennines and Alps, for example—are still used.[25]

The next improvement was a lunar map drawn by Francesco Maria Grimaldi and published in 1651 as a feature of Giambattista Riccioli's *Almagestum novum.* Riccioli returned to Van Langren's scheme of dubbing lunar formations after noted scholars, and in many cases the names he assigned are the ones we use today.[26]

A revealing indication of how uncertain was knowledge of the Moon in the seventeenth century is the fact that these and other early lunar maps all gave "watery" names to the smoother, darker areas of our satellite, even though these "maria" are actually smooth lava plains. In his 1665 work *Micrographia,* the English scientist Robert Hooke considered but rejected an impact theory for lunar craters and suggested some sort of vulcanism as the cause, an explanation that would prevail for centuries, though remnants of his suggested process might just be active today—we are not sure.[27]

OBSERVING THE PLANETS

Looking farther out in the solar system, Huygens discovered Saturn's largest and brightest satellite, Titan, in 1655. He followed up on this feat with the 1659 book *Systema Saturnium,* in which he finally explained that planet's bizarre, changing appearance. The Dutch scholar used better telescopes and, perhaps more important, a new idea to deduce that Saturn is surrounded by a wide flat ring, which appears in different aspects as Earth and Saturn revolve around the Sun and which is so thin that it disappears from view when seen edge on. This behavior and the poor telescopes of the time explain the wide variety of early drawings of Saturn.[28]

Indefatigable, Huygens also used a micrometer to measure the apparent diameters of planets, the positions of satellites relative to them, and Saturn's rings. However, his results were too large because of "irradiation," a defect of the eye that causes bright objects seen against a dark background to seem bigger than they really are.[29]

But it was Jean Domenique Cassini, the first of four generations of Cassinis who were astronomers and directors of the Paris Observatory, who coaxed the most out of the clumsy very-long-focus refracting telescopes of the time.[30] In the 1660s, while still working in Italy, he took advantage of lenses made from high quality Venetian glass to detect features on the disks of Mars and Jupiter and to estimate the rotation periods of those planets. He also monitored the motions of the Galilean satellites and timed the passages (transits) of their shadows across the disk of Jupiter, again with the terrestrial longitude problem in mind.[31]

Cassini moved to Paris in 1669, and in 1671–72 discovered two more Saturnian moons, Rhea and Iapetus, followed by Tethys and Dione in 1684. Iapetus showed bizarre behavior, for it was visible only when west of Saturn and disappeared when it moved to the east of the planet. Cassini hit on what turned out to be the correct explanation; the satellite has two east-west hemispheres, one of which reflects sunlight much better than the other. If Iapetus circles Saturn with the same side always facing the planet, as the Moon does with respect to Earth, we will see first the light and then the dark half of the satellite. Ironically, he rejected his own idea![32]

In 1675 Cassini discerned the division in Saturn's rings that is named for him, and the next year observed a dark belt on the planet that ran parallel to the ring plane. Among other things, he was the first to notice that Jupiter is oblate; that is, its disk is not circular but rather "squashed" at the poles. Cassini I, as he is sometimes called, was a superb observer and, for good measure, also produced one of the best Moon maps of the century.[33]

Observers such as Huygens and Cassini were just able to make out the most prominent features on Mars and Jupiter. Beginning in 1659 Huygens used markings on Mars to determine that the planet turned once on its axis in 25 hours and 40 minutes; the Martian day is just a little longer than Earth's. Cassini used observations of Jovian features to determine that, though the planet is the largest in the solar system, it has a rapid rotation period (near the equator) of only 9 hours, 56 minutes.[34] Both Huygens and Cassini made out the bright white polar caps of Mars, which showed from their positions on the planet that Mars's axis of rotation is tilted with respect to its orbit about as much as Earth's is.[35] The red planet seemed to be much like our own.

As for the remaining planets, Mercury has such a small apparent size, and always remains so close to the Sun in the sky, that no real surface features were detected. On the other hand, a number of observers claimed to have seen faint markings on Venus—the consensus was that they were atmospheric—and Cassini I even derived a rotation period of a little less than 24 hours. Down to the middle of the twentieth century, astronomers continued to announce various rotation periods (about one Earth day was a popular value), all of which were wrong.[36] Venus does show atmospheric features in visible light, but they have low contrast and are difficult to see even with modern instruments. Most if not all of these early sightings were probably spurious, and the determination of Venus's rotation period would have to wait until the advent of planetary radar astronomy.

Since Earth was now obviously just another planet, it was only natural to speculate on whether it was the only abode of life. Kepler had speculated on the subject, and Huygens believed that there was no reason why there could not be extraterrestrial beings. He noted that Jupiter's belts changed their appearance, indicating that they were clouds similar to those in Earth's atmosphere and that better telescopes might also find clouds on Mars. If clouds, why not water—and why not life? In 1686 the French writer Bernard Le Bovier de Fontenelle published *Entretiens sur la Pluralité des Mondes* (*Conversations of the Plurality of Worlds*), a popular book on a popular level, in which even Jupiter's moons are considered fit for inhabitants.[37] Such optimistic outlooks, based mostly on hopes, wishes, or analogies, would remain in vogue for two centuries.

A decade before Fontenelle's book, Ole Römer, a Danish astronomer working in Paris, came up with an explanation for the curious behavior of Jupiter's innermost and fastest moving known satellite, Io. New observations and improved theory had produced better predictions of eclipses of the satellite by Jupiter's shadow, but the events came later than expected when Jupiter was at its greatest distance from Earth (on the opposite side of the Sun from us and near conjunction) and early when the giant planet was closest to Earth (on the same side of the Sun as Earth and near opposition). By 1676 or possibly 1675, Römer—or perhaps Cassini as early as 1674; the details of what happened are not clear—realized that the maximum deviation of about 11 minutes (the modern value is a little more than 8 minutes) from the mean was just the time that it took for light to travel between Earth and the Sun.[38]

It was a revelation that light had a finite speed and did not travel instantly from place to place; this finding dealt another blow at Aristotle, and Descartes too. However, there were no immediate attempts to pin down the speed of light more accurately, though improved estimates of the solar parallax made that possible. Astronomers probably did not bother because all they needed for predictions of phenomena were the time for light to pass from Earth to the Sun, along with planetary distances in terms of Earth's orbital radius, which Kepler's third law provided.[39]

THE SOCIAL STRUCTURES OF ASTRONOMY

By now astronomy was getting organized. In the seventeenth century Paris became the center of the astronomical world because the Sun King, Louis XIV, supported science in general and astronomy in particular in a royal manner. Not for the last time, financial support attracted astronomers from far and wide—Cassini and Römer are two examples. In 1666 the Academie des Sciences received official status. Its members got a salary from the government, which in return held control over actions such as the admission of new members and the delivery of formal addresses. There was even a new publication, the *Journal des Savants,* to print research results.[40]

In England diverse "natural philosophers" started meeting informally in 1645 and in 1662 got a charter as the Royal Society from Charles II. In contrast to the situation in France, not only did members not get an official salary, but also they had to pay dues. On the other hand, they were freed of much in the way of governmental interference. To report on advances in knowledge, the *Philosophical Transactions* began publishing in 1666, and is still going to press regularly to this day.[41]

The two monarchies were also close together in establishing permanent official observatories. France led, for in 1667 Louis XIV ordered construction of the Paris Observatory, which was to become the headquarters of the Academie des Sciences, and appointed Cassini as first director. England was not far behind, and in 1675 Charles II decreed the establishment of the Royal Greenwich Observatory and appointed John Flamsteed Astronomer Royal, with the job of finding longitudes and improving navigation, items of vital practical importance to commerce and empire. But the king of England was less generous than the French monarch, for while Flamsteed got a building, he had to pay for his instruments himself.[42]

The establishment of these two royal observatories solidified a trend to which Tycho had given a powerful boost. Until the twentieth century the main task of observers would be to measure ever more accurately and precisely the positions of planets and stars, viewing the latter primarily as aids to improving planetary theory.[43] Similarly, theorists would produce ever more complex and precise descriptions of lunar and planetary motions. Astronomy confirmed its status as by far the most rarefied, advanced, and difficult of all the physical sciences. But despite all this effort, there was little new knowledge gained about what the planets or stars really were. That would have to wait for centuries.

By the latter half of the 1600s, theoretical and observational astronomy sorely needed new ideas, and they came, unexpectedly, from an island at the edge of Europe.

NEWTON

The year 1687 saw the publication of *Principia mathematica philosophiae naturalis*, (*The Mathematical Principles of Natural Philosophy*),[44] a work that revolutionized astronomy and, indeed, all of physical science. The English scientist Isaac Newton provided the concepts that thrust these fields ahead sharply after decades of slow progress.

The *Principia* is as difficult to read as anything ever written, but it changed physics and astronomy dramatically and forever. In it Newton presented his three Laws of Motion, which applied to celestial and terrestrial behavior alike. Here was another revolution, for it sealed the doom of the long-held belief that those two realms were different.

The first law says that a body continues to move in a straight line at constant speed *unless a force acts upon it* (or it stays at rest, which Newton believed could be shown by reference to the fixed stars, for he believed in "absolute" space, and time as well). This destroyed the old ideas that circular motion was natural and that some sort of impetus had to work continuously to keep a body moving. According to the new law, the fact that the planets move in nearly circular orbits implies that something must be acting on them continuously so that they do not fly off into space along straight-line paths.

The first law also answers the problem of what keeps the planets moving, by stating that nothing is needed. On the contrary, some force would be needed to stop them. On Earth, moving objects are slowed and eventually brought to a halt by friction, air resistance, and the like, a circumstance that leads to the commonsense—but wrong—notion that something is always needed to keep a body moving. However, motions in the vacuum of space reveal the true situation.

The second law states that a change in a body's momentum is equal to the force applied to it. (Momentum is mass multiplied by velocity, which explains why a light, swift baseball can knock one over as easily as a slow, massive bowling ball.) There was another advance as well, for Newton realized that velocity involves not just speed but also *direction*. Thus a force is needed to change the direction of a body's path from a straight line just as much as it is needed to slow down or speed up the object. (Since the mass of a body is usually constant, this law is often stated in some form such as "the acceleration is proportional to the force applied." Acceleration here is a change in either speed or direction.)

The third law says that forces occur only in equal and opposite pairs (each member of the pair acts on a different body). This idea is subtle, hard to believe in many cases, and often runs against common sense. But one has only to hold a rock to realize that it is pressing against one's hand, and the muscles concerned will soon send one a message that it really does take a force to hold the rock up.[45]

Newton also presented his Law of Universal Gravitation, which states that every two material particles in the universe, including those that make up Earth, attract each other. The force of attraction is proportional to the product of the masses. This means that, for example, if one mass is doubled, so is the force of attraction between them, while if both masses are doubled, the force becomes four times as great. The attraction decreases if the bodies are farther apart, but as the *square* of the separation, an "inverse square" relationship. Thus if the distance is doubled, the force is only one-fourth of what it was; if the separation becomes ten times larger, the attraction is reduced to one hundredth of its original value, and so on.[46]

Gravity keeps the Moon orbiting Earth and the planets orbiting the Sun, and in Newton's view it is the only force needed to explain *all* heavenly motions. It also controls the motion of falling bodies on Earth, thus connecting terrestrial and celestial events. Indeed gravity does it all!

Newton used his law of gravity to derive all three of Kepler's laws of planetary motion. For example, he showed that a planet moving under the influence of a force (such as gravity) that always acts toward a fixed point (such as the Sun) obeys the area rule. He also showed this "the other way around"—that a planet following the area rule must be acted on by such a "central" force. In addition, if that force decreases as the inverse square of the distance, as gravity does, then Kepler's first and third laws must follow.

In an extension of Kepler's first law, Newton showed to his satisfaction that bodies under the influence of an inverse square force of attraction can move in any "conic section" (circle, ellipse, parabola, or hyperbola), with the Sun at one focus.[47]

Unfortunately, the Universal Law of Gravitation presents tremendous complications just because it *is* universal. For one thing, this means that while the Sun attracts a planet, a planet also attracts the Sun, and in fact both actually revolve around their common center of gravity.[48] Newton was able to modify Kepler's harmonic law to take this effect into account, thus solving the so-called two-body problem.[49]

But the real universe is more complicated, for the planets attract each other as well, introducing complex deviations from simple "Keplerian" motion. The possible effects of these mutual interactions or "perturbations" worried Newton, but the fact that Jupiter's satellites did not appear to be influenced by the Sun to any observable degree reassured him.[50] In reality, the relatively poor state of observational astronomy at the time concealed all but a few of the myriad perturbations that exist in the solar system. Fortunately, the masses of the planets are small compared to that of the Sun, which allowed the development of approximate techniques for calculating the effects of mutual attractions. However, one major effect *was* beginning to surface at the time, namely long-term irregularities in the motions of Jupiter and Saturn; the explanation of that behavior would not come for another century.[51]

For the first time, Newton was able to estimate the masses, relative to Earth, of planets with known satellites—Jupiter and Saturn—and his results were not far different from modern ones. These masses were enormous compared to Earth's, but even though true distances in the solar system were still only roughly known, it was clear that the densities of these "giant" planets was surprisingly low, much less than those of ordinary rocks. As for the other planets—Mercury, Venus, and Mars—he knew only that their masses must be so small that they caused no observed perturbations in the motions of other bodies.[52]

The motions of the Moon defied Newton. Though he explained much, neither in the *Principia* nor later was he able to make substantial improvements in the prediction of our satellite's complex and uneven motion. In particular, the errors remained so big that our satellite still could not be used to determine longitude at sea to within the much desired single degree.[53]

On the other hand, Newton provided the first and basically the correct explanation for the precession of the equinoxes. He assumed that Earth's rotation produces an equatorial "bulge" in our planet and showed to his satisfaction that the gravitational effects of the Sun and Moon on that bulge cause the orientation in space of Earth's axis of rotation to move slowly, tracing out a small circle on the celestial sphere. Newton also discussed the effects of the Sun and the Moon in producing ocean tides, but neither observation nor theory was then good enough to produce useful results. However, he was able to make the first realistic estimate of the Moon's mass, which was about twice the modern value.[54]

Results were better in the case of comets, which "came in from the cold" in the *Principia*. From then on they were regular, if eccentric, members of the solar system, moving in response to the Universal Law of Gravitation. Newton showed that a comet's orbit must have the shape of one of the so-called conic sections. If the path is a parabola or hyperbola, the body makes but a single sweep around the Sun, but if the orbit is an ellipse (a circle is most unlikely), the comet will keep returning. However, if the ellipse is very elongated, the comet will spend a long time far from the Sun, where it is invisible. Only at long but periodic intervals will the comet reappear, when it approaches the Sun.[55]

Newton could do what he did in part because of the mathematics he had developed as early as 1666. Advanced for the time, his methods were geometric in nature and required superb physical and mathematical insight at every step in solving a problem. In the hands of a Newton, these techniques produced results the world had never seen before, but there are few such geniuses. As a result, England, where Newton's methods were taught for many years, lagged far behind continental Europe in theoretical astronomy for a century. During that period, advances in celestial mechanics would come almost entirely from across the English Channel, where different mathematics were developed. These methods were easier to use, for in them the intermediate steps involve only the manipulation of algebraic symbols by formal rules.[56]

But England scored a triumph due to Edmond Halley. The epitome of a hale fellow well met, he was the exact opposite of Newton in personality, yet the two were good friends and Halley personally shepherded Newton's *Principia* through the press and even paid some of the related expenses out of his own pocket. Later, Halley looked into past observations of various comets and found that the orbits of those of 1531 and 1607 were so alike, and so similar to that of a 1682 comet he observed, that he believed they must be reappearances of the same object. On this basis he announced that the comet would reappear in 1758. His unprecedented prediction was very near the mark and led to the body's being named Halley's comet.

This was the first known example of a "periodic" (or "short period") comet, one that returns in less than two hundred years. Owen Gingerich has noted that Halley was extremely lucky in this case, for "the comet that would later bear his name is the *only* really bright one among the 100 or so periodic comets now known. It represented Halley's only chance for finding multiple returns of a comet from the old naked-eye observations."[57]

Among his other scientific work, Newton investigated the well-known ability of a glass prism to "disperse" or spread out a beam of sunlight into a rainbow of colors. Violet light is bent, or refracted, the most and appears at one end of this spectrum, while red is bent the least and forms the other end. He found that white light is made up from myriad colors (we now know that these are different wavelengths, with violet being the shortest and red the longest visible ones). An unfortunate result of these studies was Newton's mistaken idea that different transparent materials all had the same dispersive power, and that there was thus no solution to the problem of chromatic aberration produced by lenses.[58]

Newton's 1668 solution to this impasse was to design and build a reflecting telescope that used a curved, concave mirror—instead of a lens—to collect and focus light. (The Scot James Gregory had the same idea in 1663 but never got an instrument made.) Mirrors have no chromatic aberration and for this and other reasons, all large modern telescopes are reflectors. However, there were serious practical problems in making a mirror of the correct shape out of material that would reflect light efficiently and would not tarnish rapidly.[59] There was also a difficulty in supporting such a mirror so that it did not change its shape as the telescope was pointed in different directions. For these reasons, refractors—with a few conspicuous exceptions—remained the telescopes of choice among professional astronomers until the twentieth century. And to this day, *telescope* means a refractor to most people.

Another unfortunate result of Newton's optical studies was that his solar spectra appeared "continuous," with one color merging smoothly with another and no distinguishing bright or dark features in the rainbow to act as benchmarks. Actually, the Sun's visible spectrum has thousands of dark "lines" in it, each due to absorption of a particular wavelength by a particular atom or molecule, but he could not see them. The simple reason for this failure was that Newton used a circular hole or a wide rectangular one to form the beam that hit the prism. As a result, he got myriad overlapping images—one for each wavelength—that smeared out real spectral details. Had he used a narrow slit, Newton would have seen the dark lines. But he did not, and so "spectroscopy," which would become a vital part of astronomy, languished for a more than a century.[60]

AFTER NEWTON

During the first half of the eighteenth century theoretical astronomy, which was still limited to describing and predicting motions in the solar system, made few advances. The development that eventually got the field moving again occurred on the continent of Europe in 1675, when the wide-ranging German scholar and diplomat Gottfried Wilhelm von Leibniz invented differential and integral calculus in a form close to that used today. As Newton had done basically the same thing—though in a different way—by 1666, there was a hot controversy for some time between supporters of the two men as to who did what first.[61] Probably the discoveries were independent, but Leibniz's methods were easier to use and eventually won the day. Meanwhile, development of the new techniques took time, during which observers also strove to improve their work.

Things were entirely different when it came to observational astronomy, for England led the world in that field during the eighteenth century. As early as 1676, Flamsteed, the first Astronomer Royal, began systematic observations of the Moon, Sun, planets, and above all the stars.[62] In 1720 Halley became the second Astronomer Royal but first had to order new instruments for the Greenwich Observatory, because Flamsteed's equipment was his personal property.[63] Significantly, English artisans were able to make the needed devices, and as the century progressed they got better and better at the job. While astronomers' needs for ever more precise measurements stimulated this development, the driving force was the booming market in navigation instruments for England's expanding merchant and naval fleets; science, commerce, and imperial expansion all gained as a result.

British expertise extended to clocks as well, and it enabled Flamsteed to be the first to use them routinely in determining stars' right ascensions. John Harrison epitomized this development by making, starting in 1735, clocks so accurate ("chronometers") that they could be used along with astronomical observations to determine longitude at sea. Solving this long-standing problem eventually brought Harrison a substantial fortune from the British government and reinforced the position of astronomy as the most useful and financially rewarding of sciences. The practical collaboration of astronomers, navigators, inventors, and artisans had far-ranging effects, for it was one reason that the Industrial Revolution began in England, a revolution that would make the British Empire the greatest that the world had ever seen.[64]

Halley's 1718 discovery that the bright stars Aldebaran, Sirius, and Arcturus had moved with respect to other stars since the time of Hipparchus astonished astronomers. For the first time the "fixed" stars were not so, a situation that had never been considered seriously before. Now that astronomers had to deal with "proper motion," they would have to observe stars repeatedly. One position determination, no matter how precise, no longer was enough.[65]

Two more motions of the "fixed" stars were discovered by James Bradley, the third Astronomer Royal. These were the unexpected results of a fruitless search for annual stellar parallax, detection of which might finally give direct proof of the Copernican theory—there still was none—and measure the distances to the stars as well.

Bradley's first discovery came in 1725–26 from observations of the star Gamma Draconis. In the course of a year it changed its position on the sphere of the stars by a total of about 40 seconds of arc, ending up where it started. But this was not the effect of parallax, for the motions were in the wrong directions. By 1728 Bradley concluded that he was observing the "aberration of starlight," an effect due to a combination of the finite speed of light and the Earth's orbital motion. This phenomenon is the same as that seen while driving in the rain on a windless day; no matter what direction you go, the raindrops appear to be coming at you, changing their direction as your car does. From this unexpected quarter came the first real proof that Earth does indeed orbit the Sun.[66]

Bradley pressed on, because the stars still did not seem to want to "stand still." He observed Gamma Draconis for two decades before publicly announcing another effect in 1748. This was the "nutation" of Earth's axis of rotation, covering a range of some 18 seconds of arc. That axis, it seemed, did not precess uniformly in a circle with respect to the stars but instead had a small "nodding" motion as well. When projected onto the sphere of the stars, our planet's pole in effect describes a "wavy" circle. This phenomenon has a period of a little less than nineteen years and is due to the gravitational attraction of the Moon on Earth's equatorial bulge.[67]

Bradley's discoveries explained many of the discrepancies in stellar positions that long had plagued astronomers, revealed the causes of a number of false "measurements" of stellar parallax, and resulted in more precise locations of stars and planets. Now that the effects proper motion, aberration, and nutation could be allowed for, improved instruments at last could provide improved positions.

In stark contrast, observational discoveries concerning the Moon and planets were few during most of the eighteenth century. Little was done on the Moon, and Mercury showed no surface detail at all. Neither did Venus, but in 1761 the Russian scientist Mikhail Vasilievitch Lomonosov observed a solar transit of that planet and concluded that its blurred appearance at the edge of the Sun meant that Venus had an atmosphere at least equal to Earth's. He was right, but his conclusion was largely ignored.[68] In the case of the other known planets, the situation was also grim because for most of a century, there were no important observational discoveries. Planetary astronomy was at a standstill in this area.

This lack of progress was no doubt due in large part to limitations of the instruments then in use, but during the eighteenth century telescopes, refractors in particular, improved greatly. In 1729, despite Newton's disbelief, the British barrister Chester Moore Hall devised a compound objective lens (containing more than one optical element) that greatly reduced the effects of chromatic aberration. He combined two lenses, one convex and one concave, made of different kinds of glass that refracted light of the same color by different amounts. Hall's "achromatic" objective made little impression at the time, and it took a professional optician to alter the situation.[69]

John Dolland of London heard of Hall's invention in 1750 and after numerous experiments produced his first achromatic lenses in 1757.[70] Not only did they produce much better telescopic images; they also made it possible for refractors of manageable length to have larger apertures that collected more light and revealed fainter objects. But there was the practical problem that it was impossible to make large pieces of optical quality glass with the technology of the time. "Big" lenses (more than 4 inches in diameter) were rare.[71] This barrier would not fall until the next century.

While little was learned about the nature of the planets, estimates of their distances improved greatly. Astronomers backed by their governments fanned out across the globe to observe the Venus transits of 1761 and 1769. Unfortunately, because of the effects of Venus's atmosphere, it proved difficult to tell just when that planet was first fully on or off the Sun's disk, but still the resulting solar parallaxes were closer to the true value than earlier ones had been.[72]

In the theoretical field, eighteenth-century astronomers in Europe made tremendous strides. They could do so because, once they discarded Cartesian doctrines for Newtonian ideas, they could apply the methods of the calculus invented by Leibniz and developed by others. But advances in celestial mechanics did not come easily. Newton solved exactly the problem of the motions of two attracting bodies, but in the case of three (the "Three Body Problem") or more, it could not be done.[73]

During the middle part of the eighteenth century, developments in celestial mechanics were attributable to only a few men. The Swiss-born Leonhard Euler and the Frenchmen Alexis Claude Clairaut and Jean-le-Rond D'Alembert were active.[74] In particular, Clairaut calculated the gravitational effects of Jupiter and Saturn on the path of Halley's comet, which was expected to appear again about 1758. It duly showed up late in that year and passed closest to the Sun ("perihelion") in 1759, just one month and one day earlier than he had predicted. Clairaut's work, and the fact that at least one comet was now proven periodic beyond doubt, caused a great stir and was hailed as a triumph for Newton's and Halley's views.[75]

By this time it was clear that there were no exact solutions to the complex equations that governed lunar and planetary motions, so theoretical astronomers tried *approximate* methods, in which each successive approximation gets closer to the truth. Interestingly, these approaches have a similarity to epicycle theories, in which more and more, and smaller and smaller, complications are added to approximate the observed motions better and better. But by the eighteenth century the mathematics described real motions in space due to real forces, a far cry from models to save the phenomena and merely make observation agree with theory.

Celestial mechanics in the latter part of the eighteenth century and the first part of the nineteenth was dominated by two names: Lagrange and Laplace. These two men made enormous advances in the study of motions in the solar system and reinforced the position of theoretical astronomy as by far the most advanced and precise of all the natural sciences. Joseph Louis Lagrange, who was born in Italy and worked there, then in Berlin, and eventually in Paris, may have been the greatest mathematician of the eighteenth century. He developed general methods of attacking problems involving motions of any kind and his great work *Méchanique Analytique* appeared in 1787.[76]

The Frenchman Pierre Simon de Laplace devoted a larger part of his efforts to astronomy. The several volumes of his monumental *Traité de Méchanique Céleste* were published starting in 1799. In them he attempted to give a general derivation and explanation for all motions in the solar system, assuming only Newton's Laws of Motion and the Law of Universal Gravitation. He almost did it, too, and his efforts spawned the widely held nineteenth-century view of the universe (and in particular of the solar system) as a perfect and eternal "mechanism" that, once set in motion, would go on forever, and for which the future and past could, in theory, be calculated with absolute accuracy and precision.[77]

By 1784, Laplace had solved the puzzle of the long-term deviations of Jupiter and Saturn from their expected paths in the sky. He showed that these irregularities are due to the fact that five revolutions of Jupiter around the Sun take nearly the same time as two of Saturn, so that every fifty-nine years the two planets meet at about the same place on the ecliptic. Because of this "resonance," small gravitational influences add up, much as small pushes on a swing do when done repeatedly at just the right times.[78] After Laplace's work, what had seemed to be a serious challenge to Newton's ideas became a powerful confirmation.

Laplace also explained Halley's 1693 discovery of the fact that records of ancient eclipses, when compared to those of modern ones, seemed to show that the period of the Moon's revolution around Earth, and thus its distance from us, was steadily decreasing. What caused this mysterious change? Would our satellite eventually crash into Earth with disastrous effect? The truth is that the attraction of other planets on Earth causes our mean distance from the Sun to vary over a long period, which in turn increases and decreases the size of the Moon's orbit over a period of tens of thousands of years. Once again, what had seemed to be a grave difficulty for Newtonian science became instead a triumphant vindication.[79]

One of Laplace's great aims was to determine whether the solar system, as a system, was stable. That is, would the planets continue essentially in their present orbits more or less forever? His work, along with that of Lagrange, indicated that probably they would.[80]

But Laplace did something else besides publish technical writings, for in 1796 he produced *Exposition du Système du Monde,* a popular account of his researches. In this amazing book he demonstrates that he really knows his subject by explaining difficult, complicated, and subtle things clearly and simply without using a single algebraic equation or geometric diagram.[81] In addition, the book presents Laplace's idea of how the solar system—and the fixed stars, for that matter—came to be. He speculated that the origin was in a vast, diffuse, rotating body of matter—perhaps similar to one of the softly glowing "nebulae" that then were being discovered in increasing numbers—out of which the Sun and planets condensed. The details of how all this happened were left hazy; Laplace suggested that rings of material were left behind as the rest of the matter contracted toward what was to become the Sun, and that these rings later formed planets. Although the particulars were wrong, his is essentially the accepted explanation today.[82]

Amazingly, this "nebular hypothesis" was first proposed in 1755 by the German philosopher Immanuel Kant, who was definitely *not* an astronomer or even a natural scientist either in our own terms or those accepted at the time. Still, somehow he got the right idea. Unfortunately, Kant labored in what was then Koenigsberg, East Prussia, which must have seemed a provincial backwater to astronomers in centers of learning like Paris, and there is no evidence that Laplace ever heard or read of the German's theory about the origin of the solar system. If indeed he did not, this is a classic example of the improbable, but not all that uncommon, independent conception of the same idea by two different minds at about the same time—when the time was ripe.[83]

Toward the end of the eighteenth century it appeared to many that the main questions relating to the nature of the universe had effectively been solved. Of course theory and observations always could be refined, but the motions of bodies in the solar system were well under control, as it were. Of physical conditions on the planets, little was known and there was little hope of ever knowing much. Basically, the universe was still our solar system: the Sun, six planets, ten satellites, and some comets. Except that distances were greater, it was almost as if the cozy, familiar, predictable Ptolemaic universe was back again. The stars were out there at some far and unknown remove, and there were a few faint patches of light, the nebulae, scattered across the celestial sphere, but next to nothing was known about them. However, even as Lagrange and Laplace labored, one man began a revolution that would burst the boundaries of the solar system and dramatically transform our view of the universe.

On March 13, 1781, William Herschel, a German-born professional musician and amateur astronomer working in England, did something that no one had ever done before; he discovered a new planet. This find was not an accident, for he was in the midst of a systematic survey of the entire sky visible to him (his aim was to find close pairs of stars that might provide evidence of annual stellar parallax), but it certainly *was* unexpected. In his telescope a small, pale, bluish-greenish disk stood out among the stars and moved with respect to them from night to night. At first Herschel believed this was an unusual comet, but after further observations by himself and others, the orbit turned out to be roughly circular and twice as big as Saturn's. Here was a sensation, for at a single stroke the size of the solar system was doubled![84]

Herschel dubbed his find Georgium Sidus (the Georgian Star) after his king, George III, but for obvious nationalistic and dynastic reasons the name was not popular outside Great Britain. Herschel and Neptune were among the many other suggestions, but the planet eventually came to be called Uranus, a name first proposed by a German, Johann Elert Bode.[85] In the meantime, King George rewarded Herschel with an annual pension (effectively a salary) of £200, compared to the Astronomer Royal's £300. This financial support enabled the amateur skywatcher finally to quit the music business and become a full-time astronomer.[86]

Not only was Herschel an indefatigable observer, but he also made his own telescopes. These were reflectors with metal primary mirrors which he cast, ground into shape, and polished himself. Herschel made the best instruments available, and eventually produced giants with apertures far greater than any seen before.[87] Because of the excellence and light-gathering ability of these instruments, along with his industrious observing habits, Herschel dominated observational astronomy for decades.

In 1787 he used a reflector with an aperture of almost 19 inches to discover two satellites of Uranus, later called Titania and Oberon. From their motions he estimated the planet's mass as much larger than Earth's, and its density as much less than our planet's.[88] In these traits Uranus resembles its neighbors, Saturn and Jupiter. Uranus's satellites are unusual in that they move in orbits that are almost at right angles to the planet's path around the Sun. In fact the orbits are inclined *past* the perpendicular (almost 98 degrees), so that the satellites actually move "backward" in their orbits, providing the first examples of true retrograde motion among the planets and their satellites. Because of these tilts, as Uranus circles the Sun, we see the apparent orbital paths change from almost circles, when seen "face on," to straight lines when viewed "on edge."[89]

Uranus's polar flattening was first suspected by Herschel in 1783, and he also suspected at one time that the planet might have rings, though the latter were illusory.[90] By a strange coincidence, Uranus does have a number of equatorial rings, but they are so thin and faint that their discovery would have to wait more than two centuries. He announced the "discovery" of four more Uranian moons, which also turned out to be illusory.[91]

Herschel discovered two more faint, but real, satellites of Saturn in

1789, Enceladus and Mimas. He designated the moons by numbers, and it was his son, John Herschel, who later gave them the names we now use. In addition, the elder Herschel found that the brightness of Iapetus varied with perfect regularity and with the orbital period around the planet. This behavior confirmed Cassini's abandoned hypotheses that the satellite has two very different hemispheres and always keeps the same face toward Saturn.

Herschel also observed the disk of Saturn and its rings. When the latter were nearly edge on—they became very thin and eventually disappeared—he noticed some bright spots on them that seemed not to be additional satellites but structures of some sort on the rings themselves. On the body of the planet, he found a number of variable dark belts and bright zones as well as spots. From such features he derived a rotation period of a little more than 10 hours, which is close to the modern value. He also detected and measured Saturn's polar flattening.[92]

On Venus, Herschel saw some faint, changeable features that he believed were atmospheric. His telescopes were good enough for him probably to have seen actual cloud formations, but he wisely did not try to derive a rotation period from them. He did, however, correctly conclude that Venus had a cloudy atmosphere.[93]

On the subject of life on other worlds, Herschel was optimistic. He speculated about inhabitants of the Moon, planets, and even the Sun.[94] Because physical science was so undeveloped, he could hold that the Sun, and other stars, were actually dark bodies surrounded by luminous atmospheres, sunspots being "holes" that gave us a glimpse of a cooler world below. That is not true, but it was ingenious and remained a popular idea until the middle of the nineteenth century.

Despite his notable planetary work, Herschel's main interests lay outside the solar system. And, as we shall see, his larger efforts were a giant step in dethroning planetary astronomy from the dominance in both theory and observation that it had held for thousands of years.

3

AUTUMN GLORY

Planetary astronomy
is eclipsed by its own
offspring, a "New
Astronomy" that explores
a larger universe

Discoveries and studies of asteroids, meteors, comets, a new major planet, and additional planetary satellites, along with advances on wide fronts along observational and theoretical lines appeared to maintain the high standing of planetary astronomy among the sciences during the first half of the nineteenth Century. In addition, improved telescopes, along with the development of techniques such as spectroscopy and photography, provided new and better tools for studying the universe. But in reality planetary science reached a plateau in this period. The introduction of new technologies resulted in a de-emphasis of solar system studies as a result of the emergence of a "New Astronomy." Astronomers began to probe a vastly larger universe than they had ever imagined before.

WILLIAM HERSCHEL AND A LARGER UNIVERSE

Herschel's discovery of Uranus in 1781 brought him fame and led him to probe beyond the solar system. His most important work dealt with bodies far beyond that planet. Not trained in the dull routine of observatories such as those at Paris and Greenwich, he brought to bear on the heavens new ideas, new approaches, and new points of view.[1] He became the founder of the new field of stellar astronomy. Before him, the stars were just points of light, observed merely so that planetary positions or locations on Earth could be determined more accurately, though a few stars were known to have proper motions and a handful more showed brightness variations. As for the nebulae, more than a hundred had been catalogued to aid observers, who often confused them with comets. That was about all anyone knew about things outside the solar system, but Herschel changed the situation dramatically.[2]

Among other things, Herschel discovered hundreds of double stars (close pairs as seen through the telescope) and by observing them over the decades demonstrated that some form real physical systems. Eventually, observations showed that these "binary" stars revolve around their common centers of gravity under the influence of gravity. This showed that Newton's laws of motion and gravity applied far beyond the solar system and, in time, provided a means of measuring stellar masses.[3]

Herschel used the accumulating stellar proper motions he and others derived to establish that the Sun itself moves through the stars. This "solar motion" causes stars directly ahead of the Sun to appear to move away from the point on the celestial sphere toward which the solar system is headed, while those behind appear to "close up." Though much, much slower to unfold, the appearance is the same as that seen when driving down a straight highway.[4]

But it was in the realm of the mysterious nebulae that Herschel made his greatest advances: finding, describing, and cataloguing thousands of new star clusters and nebulae over the entire sky visible from England. He was able to resolve into stars many objects that lesser telescopes had seen only as hazy patches of light, but he eventually came to believe that at least some nebulae might be partially or wholly made of a diffuse, "shining fluid" of some sort.[5]

By counting stars seen in the field of his telescope when it was pointed at different places on the celestial sphere, Herschel seemed to have demonstrated that the Milky Way has the highly flattened shape of a grindstone. This was a concept that Thomas Wright of Durham and Immanuel Kant had speculated about earlier, but Herschel was the first to try to demonstrate it through observations. His methods, however, proved incorrect, because he used a number of assumptions that were wrong, such as that all stars have about the same true luminosity and that stars are distributed about evenly in space where they do occur. In addition, Herschel did not know that obscuring dust between the stars in the Milky Way hid most of it from his view; he had shown only that the part he could study was flattened.[6] The same dust also blocked his view at roughly the same distance all around the Milky Way, so that the Sun seemed to be near the center of the system. Interestingly, Herschel had the right shape anyway, for we now know that our Milky Way galaxy would look something like a fried egg when seen from outside, though the Sun is far from the center of the system.

In 1799, Herschel made a discovery that at first seemed to have little to do with astronomy in general or planetary studies in particular. He noticed that a thermometer placed *beyond* the red end of the solar spectrum showed a greater rise of temperature than when placed in any visible color. He concluded that a substantial part of the Sun's radiant heat was composed of "invisible light," or infrared radiation, as we now call it.[7] Eventually, infrared studies were to play a large part in expanding our knowledge of the solar system, but that would have to wait until twentieth-century advances in technology and physics.[8]

Shortly after Herschel's discovery, the German scientist R. W. Ritter found that there was also solar "light" beyond the violet end of the spectrum.[9] "Ultraviolet" astronomy would also play a big role in twentieth-century astronomy, but because Earth's atmosphere strongly absorbs these short wavelengths, it took the advent of the Space Age before this part of the spectrum could be studied well.

Not content with observation and experiment, Herschel labored with theory and speculation as well. His wide-ranging discussions covered subjects such as the origins and development of and the relations among nebulae, star clusters, and the Milky Way. His conclusions were mostly wrong because his data were insufficient, and because the physics of the day was woefully inadequate for dealing with celestial phenomena—with the conspicuous exception of motions under the influence of gravity. Still, though his idea of nebulous matter somehow condensing into stars had no true physical basis at the time, this is what astronomers believe today. More important, it was a novel and significant idea, for it was the first suggestion that the universe had not been "finished" long ago but, on the contrary, stars and stellar systems were still forming. Perhaps for this reason, his speculations were not well received in the Europe of his day.[10]

Herschel's work was a watershed in that now stars and nebulae were an integral part of a vast universe, which no longer consisted merely of our solar system. From this point on, planetary studies are only a part of astronomy, instead of constituting essentially all of it.

However, Herschel's efforts had little immediate effect on the work of other astronomers. Some bought the reflectors he made, but few did anything with them, and then or later there were few who could or would build large reflectors (his son John was one exception).[11] Meanwhile, observatories were producing ever more, and ever more precise, planetary and stellar positions, using ever better achromatic refracting telescopes.[12] Unfortunately, due to the difficulty of producing optical glass in large pieces, refractors continued to have small apertures compared to Herschel's giant reflectors. As a result, for decades many of his results could not even be duplicated, let alone improved upon.

Besides the effect of telescopic limitations, progress beyond Herschel's achievements was held back by the rudimentary state of physical science and the lack of any observing techniques beyond looking through a telescope. As a result, stellar and galactic studies would advance slowly for some time, giving planetary astronomy a reprieve for its dominant role.

INTO THE NEW CENTURY

One astronomer to buy Herschel's telescopes and use them to advantage was his German contemporary, Johann Hieronymous Schröter. For three decades, Schröter spent a good part of his spare time observing the Moon and planets with instruments he had bought or made. While no Herschel as an observer (for example, he saw tall but imaginary mountains on Venus),[13] he was a persistent one. His *Selenotopographische Fragmente,* the two volumes of which appeared in 1791 and 1802, became classic books on the Moon's appearance, while his use of almost all of Riccioli's names for lunar features helped force more cumbersome designations out of use.[14]

Schröter also played a role in the first sensational planetary discovery of the nineteenth century. The story begins in 1766, by which time Johann Daniel Titius, a German mathematics professor, had realized that there seemed to be a "missing" planet in the solar system.[15] The omission was suggested by a curious numerical relation among the distances of the planets from the Sun. To see this, write down a series of 4's in a vertical column. Then to the second 4 add 3 (3 × 1), to the third add 6 (3 × 2), to the fourth add 12 (3 × 4), and so on, each time doubling the number added to 4. Dividing all the sums by 10 gives a series of numbers, the first members of which are: 0.4, 0.7, 1.0, 1.6, 2.8, 5.2, and 10.0. Surprisingly, these numbers are close to the mean distances from the Sun (in units of Earth's distance from the Sun) of the planets from Mercury right out to Saturn! But there is one glaring exception, for there is no major planet, one that could be easily observed, corresponding to 2.8, in the gap between the orbits of Mars and Jupiter.[16]

Johann Elert Bode, a German astronomer, popularized this curious "Titius-Bode law" in a book published in 1772. When Uranus was discovered a few years later, Bode showed that it too fitted the relation; its mean distance from the Sun was just that "predicted" for the next planet beyond Saturn. Now the absence of a planet between Mars and Jupiter was *really* puzzling.[17]

In 1800 Schröter was elected president of an informal society dedicated to finding the "missing" planet, and Franz Xavier von Zach used his journal *Monatliche Correspondenz* to drum up support for the effort.[18] The body could not be large and bright, or someone (probably Herschel) would have found it already, so quick positive results were not expected. But to the contrary, on the first day of the nineteenth century, January 1, 1801, Giuseppe Piazzi at Palermo, Sicily, found a tiny "star" that was not on his charts. Moreover, it changed position from night to night with respect to the stars. While the object appeared to move like a planet, it passed into the evening twilight before anyone else could add to Piazzi's few observations.[19]

Was the object lost? The young German mathematician Carl Friedrich Gauss came to the rescue in spectacular style. He applied a new method of determining an orbit, one that assumed no special shape for the path and that worked even if only a small part of the orbit were observed. With surprising speed and accuracy he predicted where the new planet should be found—and there it was. This was a development of great importance for practical celestial mechanics. His method was far more general and yet less cumbersome and time-consuming than all previous ones, and it was widely used during the nineteenth century.[20]

Piazzi dubbed the new planet Ceres Ferdinandea to honor his king, Ferdinand IV of the Two Sicilies, but like other such efforts, that one also failed, and the name Ceres became established.[21] Its orbit was indeed between those of Mars and Jupiter, but satisfaction turned to surprise when a similar object, Pallas, was discovered in 1802, a third, Juno, in 1804, and a fourth, Vesta, in 1807. They were all so small that no one could observe any disks, and Herschel proposed that these objects be called *asteroids* to distinguish them from the major planets.[22] The name caught on, though they were and are still called minor planets by some.

Thus, unexpectedly, instead of one modest planet, there were four small ones. No more were found for nearly forty years, but by 1807 Wilhelm Olbers, the German physician who had discovered Pallas, was looking for many more asteroids because he suspected that they were the fragments of a disintegrated major planet. This plausible theory, though now no longer generally accepted, would stay alive and well for more than a century.[23] Asteroid discoveries resumed with Astrea in 1845, and there were a dozen of these small bodies known by 1850. Many, many more were to come.

THEY CAME FROM OUTER SPACE

For millennia, people had seen "shooting stars" streaking across the sky, and on rare occasions "stones" had been observed to fall to earth with a roar. Opinions about these striking phenomena varied from ancient notions that these were messages from the gods to the prevalent eighteenth-century idea that they were atmospheric phenomena. Even though Halley had actually calculated the orbit of a bright meteor in 1719, as late as 1790, when meteorites fell on the province of Gascogne, the French Academy dismissed the reports as idle superstition.[24]

But the tide was soon to change, for about 1794 the German scientist Ernst F. F. Chladni proposed that space was full of small particles, some of which enter our atmosphere at great speeds and, heated by friction with the surrounding air, produce meteors. A small fraction of these objects survive their fiery entry and reach the ground as what we call meteorites. Starting in 1798, two German students, H. W. Brandes and J. F. Benzenberg, began to test Chladni's theory by the simple method of making simultaneous observations from two separate locations. By triangulation they soon showed that meteors move at speeds similar to those of the planets and blaze at altitudes of about 60 miles.[25]

Skepticism about the cosmic origin of meteorites was finally buried by the report that the French scientist Jean B. Biot made on the falling of stones that descended on L'Aigle, France, in 1803. From then on, the cosmic nature of meteorites was established. Once chemists realized that meteorites were samples of extraterrestrial matter, they began to analyze these. However, the origins of the objects remained unclear, and many scientists, including Laplace in 1802, proposed that they were shot out of lunar volcanos. While there are lunar meteorites, they were blasted off our satellite by impacts rather than by volcanic action.[26]

The field of meteor astronomy got a tremendous boost on the night of November 12–13, 1833, when a spectacular shower of falling stars lit up the skies over North America. Suggestively, as seen by all observers, the meteors seemed to radiate from the constellation Leo (the "radiant" point). This proved that they came from space and exhibited a perspective effect. The cosmic projectiles were, in fact, moving on parallel paths, as Denison Olmstead of Yale University showed in 1834.[27] Interestingly, there was no evidence that a single meteor from this shower survived to reach Earth's surface. Evidently they were not made of strong stuff. Indications slowly turned up that the "Leonids" might be periodic phenomena, as they had provided a great shower in 1799, and indeed they did return in all their glory on the night of November 13–14, 1866, this time favoring Europe.[28]

It was well known that August nights have an unusually high rate of shooting stars. In medieval times they were called the "tears of Saint Lawrence," whose feast day is the tenth of that month. In 1834 John Locke in the United States showed that these meteors have a radiant in the constellation Perseus, and in 1836 Lambert A. J. Quetelet of Belgium showed from old records that the Perseids appeared every year at about the same date. Meanwhile, various scientists developed methods for determining the orbits of meteor swarms, work that would have important consequences later on.[29]

COMETS

During the first half of the nineteenth century, comet research was confined to measuring their positions, calculating their orbits, drawing their heads and tails, and eventually trying to explain the shapes, behaviors, and constitutions of the wispy features emanating from their nuclei.

There were several "great" comets in this period, especially those of 1811 and 1843 (the latter passing less than 100,000 miles from the Sun's surface), and Halley's comet duly reappeared in 1835. On June 19, 1819, Earth probably passed through a comet's tail, but there were absolutely no observed effects resulting from this passage.[30]

In 1818 astronomers discovered a comet with a bizarre orbit. Johann Franz Encke of Germany computed its orbit and found that the period was a mere three and a half years. Such short-period comets differ from long-period specimens in several ways: none gets very bright (except for Halley's, the first known of the breed); they tend to revolve around the Sun in the same direction as the planets; they tend to keep relatively close to the ecliptic; and their paths are much less elongated. A short-period comet owes its orbital characteristics to the alteration of its original long-period orbit during a close encounter with a giant planet (most often Jupiter).[31]

Encke also found that "his" comet orbited the sun under the influence of some unknown force *in addition to* gravity. Even when planetary influences were accounted for, each time that Encke's comet returned to perihelion it was a few hours earlier than expected (later observations showed that this effect was subject to change). A rarefied interplanetary "resisting" medium could account for the effect but would also affect other bodies in the solar system, an influence of which there is no trace. Scientists of the era were baffled.[32]

The next recognized short-period comet, discovered by Austria's Wilhelm von Biela, would prove even more fascinating than Encke's. Recognized in 1826, Biela's comet proved to have an orbital period of between six and seven years. Its return in 1845–47 provided a sensation, for by the end of 1845 the once single body had divided into two separate comets, which moved in parallel paths! As neither body disturbed the motion of the other in a measurable way, it was clear that their masses were very small.[33]

Biela's comet returned in 1852, with its two parts now separated by more than a million miles. Neither has been seen since. A close pass to mighty Jupiter in 1841 probably triggered the breakup and, if so, indicated that this comet at least had little internal strength. The disappearance, behavior duplicated by other comets in later years, was even in the mid-nineteenth century taken as evidence that comets have only a finite amount of material forming their tails, and therefore have finite lifetimes.[34] In particular, this holds for the short-period comets. In that they approach the Sun frequently, their supply of volatile material is depleted rather rapidly, so none of the present ones—again except for Halley's—appears very bright.

Besides sketching the delicate and variable structures of comets' tails, the better telescopes of the eighteenth century showed a wide variety of structures in the heads of comets: fans, jets, halos, and the like. All these features—not to mention the tails—are tenuous in the extreme, letting faint stars shine right through without perceptible dimming.

In an 1836 work on Halley's comet, stimulated by his observations of that object, the German astronomer Friedrich Wilhelm Bessel put the theory of cometary forms on a firm basis. He noted that material comes off the tiny nucleus, often on the sunlight side, but then is pushed away from our star by some sort of repulsive force or forces.[35] Nobody knew what they might be, though the word *electrical* was sometimes used in a vague sense.

Although there were some significant advances, science in general and physics in particular in the first half of the nineteenth century were not yet able to determine much about the physical nature of comets. That knowledge would only come later.

At the beginning of the nineteenth century, belief in a volcanic origin for the craters of the Moon was almost universal, although a competing impact theory probably had been around since Galileo's day. This situation is understandable, for no impact craters were then known on Earth (none would be accepted as such until well into the twentieth century), and some people still considered meteorites to be phenomena of Earth's atmosphere. On the other hand, terrestrial volcanos of various types were well known.[36]

More surprising is that the volcanic theory kept its dominant position even after asteroids were discovered and meteorites were shown to be celestial bodies. A German astronomer, F. von P. Gruithuisen, championed the impact theory, but his odd views on other matters made his speculations suspect. Meanwhile, geologists kept comparing volcanic features on Earth with lunar craters, and the volcanic theory held sway until well into the twentieth century.[37]

As for the physical nature of the Moon, little was known or learned, except that a variety of evidence indicated that it had little or no atmosphere. On another front, mapping of lunar features proceeded at a slow pace, employing small refractors but improved map-making techniques. A few such maps provided real advances. The work was concentrated in Germany. In the 1830s, W. G. Lohmann, using a 5-inch refractor, published a small but good Moon map and a few sections of a larger one. In 1837, Wilhelm Beer, a banker and part-time astronomer, and Johann Heinrich Mädler, a school teacher turned professional astronomer, published their landmark book, *Der Mond,* along with a large new map that showed almost all the features visible in their 3 3/4-inch refractor. They too followed Riccioli's nomenclature, which thus became firmly established. Their work was so thorough, and lunar studies were so dormant, that it took years for anyone to do better work in the field.[38]

New information about the planets came slowly. In 1848, observers on both sides of the Atlantic Ocean simultaneously found Hyperion, the seventh satellite of Saturn. One discoverer was William Cranch Bond, who used the 15-inch refractor at Harvard College Observatory. The other was William Lassell, an English brewer who employed a 24-inch-aperture reflector he had made himself.[39]

Incredibly, there was another "double discovery" concerning the system of Saturn just two years later. This was the so-called crepe ring—a tenuous, dusky feature inside the previously known bright rings—which Bond found in September, 1850. Later in the month but before news of

Bond's find had crossed the ocean (this was a decade before the first Atlantic cable), W. R. Dawes in England found the new ring as well. Once the ring was known to be there, it turned out to be fairly easy to see, and searches in old records turned up several probable sightings by earlier observers.[40]

In addition, Saturn's bright rings were becoming more interesting. Sightings of divisions other than Cassini's had been reported off and on, and in 1837, Encke saw and measured a thin, dark division in the outer ("A") ring. George Bond, William's son, wrote in 1851 that he had frequently detected additional fine, dark divisions in the rings (he was proven right more than a century later). But the true nature of Saturn's rings was revealed in 1859, by the Scottish scientist James Clerk Maxwell. His theoretical investigations showed that the rings could only be composed of myriad small particles—their exact sizes are uncertain to this day—each of which orbits Saturn as an individual satellite. The idea had been around for about two centuries, but Maxwell proved it to be true.[41]

In 1830, Beer and Mädler began to observe and draw Mars. The improved telescopes they used revealed a definite pattern of bright and dark markings on the tiny disk of the ruddy planet. These features reappeared periodically, so they were not mere clouds, and from them Beer and Mädler estimated the planet's rotation period to be a little less than 24 hours and 38 minutes.[42]

PROBLEMS AND PROGRESS AT THE OUTER LIMITS

Meanwhile, interesting things were happening in the outer solar system. Since no features were visible on the tiny disk of Uranus, the tilt of the planet's axis of rotation was unknown. In 1829 Laplace was probably the first to suggest in print that if Uranus's satellites orbit in its equatorial plane, then the planet's axis lies nearly in the ecliptic. In other words, Uranus rotates "on its side." Because of this orientation the planet's orbital motion causes its north pole to point sometimes almost directly toward the Sun and sometimes almost directly away. As a result, during a Uranian "year" we sometimes see only the northern, sometimes only the southern hemisphere, and in between, we see various portions of both. Here was another blow to the vaunted "regularity" of motions in the solar system.[43]

Several observers searched for additional satellites of Uranus, but definite success did not come until October, 1851, when Lassell used a reflector with an aperture of 24 inches to discover Ariel and Umbriel (names given by John Herschel), which orbit the planet more closely than the pair of moons discovered by William Herschel.[44]

Well before these finds, Uranus was posing another troubling problem, because it would not move "properly." As the planet is fairly bright (just visible to the naked eye in a clear dark sky if one knows where to look), it is not surprising that astronomers over the years after Herschel's discovery uncovered earlier accidental telescopic observations of Uranus. These observations went back a century but would not "fit" with recent ones, even when the disturbing effects of other planets were taken into account. Did Newton's Laws of Motion break down at the edge of the solar system, or was the Law of Gravity subtly different at great distances from the Sun? Such possibilities worried many scientists.[45]

As the years passed, even the "recent" positions of Uranus did not fit with each other, and the problem kept growing worse. True, the discrepancies between Uranus's predicted and observed positions were small, amounting to only a few minutes of arc by the early 1840s, so that the unaided eye could hardly tell the difference. But the precision of positional observations and the power of theory were now sufficient for even such a small discrepancy to pose a serious problem.[46]

Many explanations of Uranus's behavior were proposed, but during the 1830s the idea gradually took hold that the culprit was an unknown planet orbiting beyond Uranus. Still, how could the position of a body be predicted merely from its effects on another? That problem had never been tackled, for perturbations until then had always been calculated based on the known positions of objects. Amazingly, the problem was independently solved in theory more or less at the same time by two young mathematicians, John Couch Adams in England and Urbain J. J. Leverrier in France.[47]

Great Britain might have gained the laurels of yet another planetary discovery, were it not for the murky role played by the hidebound Astronomer Royal, George Biddell Airy. Neptune was actually seen, but not recognized, on August 4 and 12, 1846, by James Challis at the observatory at Cambridge University. In fact, both French and British astronomers, busy with their routine positional tasks, were loath to look for the presumed new planet, but Leverrier had the foresight to send his predictions to Johann Gottfried Galle at the Berlin Observatory. On the night of September 23, 1846, Galle, along with Heinrich Louis d'Arrest, turned a 9-inch refractor on the predicted spot and, after a short time, found a point of light that was not on their star chart. They were the first to see the planet Neptune and recognize it for what it was.[48]

News of the discovery made a worldwide sensation. For the first time the existence and position of a previously unknown planet had been predicted theoretically, and the planet *had been found* where expected. Perhaps even more important, what had seemed to be a serious problem for Newton's theories turned out to be their most triumphant vindication. Planetary astronomy, both theoretical and observational, was triumphant.

Leverrier's reward was to see his initial proposed name for the planet, Neptune, eventually prevail. Things were different in Britain, where Airy and Challis both came under severe attack for their skepticism and oversight in the matter. Airy had shown no encouragement of Adams's work, while Challis's search for the planet had been slow and unenthusiastic. As for poor Adams, who was at first slighted in the euphoria over the discovery, his feelings can only be imagined. As recorded in the press, for a while relations between France and Britain were strained over the matter of who discovered what first. But when the smoke cleared, Adams and Leverrier were given joint credit for the prediction, a verdict that still stands.[49]

Soon after Neptune was spotted, several scientists identified published positions of the planet made before its discovery as a planet, by observers who mistakenly took it for a star. Theoretical astronomers used these earlier observations along with recent ones to calculate Neptune's orbit— and found a startling result. As Adams's and Leverrier's predicted positions for the planet as well as their "elements of the orbit" (numerical quantities that describe its size and orientation in space) agreed closely, astronomers were taken aback when the actual orbit turned out to be very different from the predictions. For one thing, Neptune's path was almost circular instead of noticeably eccentric. In addition, the Titius-Bode law, which had proven correct in the cases of Uranus and the asteroids, failed miserably for Neptune, for which the mean distance from the Sun was only some 30 astronomical units (the mean Earth-Sun distance), instead of the "expected" 39 or so. The only element on which theory and observations came close to agreeing was the "mean longitude" on January 1, 1847. This is the position along the ecliptic where Neptune was on that date, and near which one should look for it for some time before and after.

The difference between the observed and predicted orbits was so striking that it seemed to some a wonder that the planet was found at all. Doubts about the predictions were voiced strongly in the United States, where scientists were in the process of "catching up" with their European counterparts. Noted Harvard mathematician Benjamin Peirce called the discovery a "happy accident," his negative view setting off a hot controversy that added yet another dimension to the debate over who first predicted the position where Neptune would be found.

Still, despite all, the planet *had* been found. Probably the differences between the assumed and true distances of Neptune from the Sun did not affect either Adams's or Leverrier's predictions to any great extent. However, that situation held true only for the first half of the nineteenth century. In hindsight, it seems that perhaps some luck did indeed ride with those who prepared well and worked hard.[50]

As word of the new planet's discovery spread, astronomers everywhere observed it, and one struck gold. On October 10, 1846, less than three weeks after Galle first recognized the planet, Lassell caught the first glimpse of a satellite orbiting about it. He confirmed the existence of the moon, dubbed Triton, the next year. As Neptune was so far from the Sun, its companion was evidently large in size and shared with the satellites of Uranus a retrograde motion around its primary. Even though estimates of Neptune's size were not precise, it appeared that the planet's density was low compared to that of Earth, and similar to those of the other outer planets.[51]

Planetary astronomy now seemed more secure than ever in its position as premier science, but even as the field basked in glory, developments in vastly different areas were paving the way for its fall from grace. The search for shifts in the positions of the fixed stars due to Earth's yearly revolution around the Sun had frustrated observers since Tycho Brahe. Over the years the astronomical landscape had been littered with mistaken claims of such detections, so it was a stunning surprise when there were no less than three successful measurements of such stellar displacements in short order. The substantial improvement in telescopes was the reason for this coincidence, but all the same it seemed amazing at the time—and does even today. In 1839 Bessel announced a parallax for a faint star dubbed 61 Cygni; in 1839 Thomas Henderson announced a parallax for Alpha Centauri from observations made at the Cape of Good Hope; and in 1840 Wilhelm Struve in Russia announced a parallax for Vega (Alpha Lyrae).[52]

There was now simple and direct evidence that Earth did indeed revolve around the Sun, and new and exciting opportunities opened for stellar astronomy. Among other things, estimates of stars' true distributions in space and their intrinsic luminosities were now possible. For many astronomers, work on the solar system now became rather mundane. Then too, ever larger telescopes and the new technologies that would soon emerge from other, widely different fields (as we shall soon see), would have a vast impact on all of astronomy. But that influence would be mainly on studies of objects far beyond the planets for a long time to come.

Reflecting telescopes have several advantages over refractors: per inch of aperture they are easier and cheaper to make, they are truly achromatic, and they can be supported at the back as well as along their edges—though it was not until the twentieth century that engineers learned how to do the last properly. But in the nineteenth century, telescope mirrors were made of "speculum" metal, which was composed of copper, tin, and sometimes a bit of arsenic and had a host of drawbacks. The material is dense, which makes mirrors heavy; it is hard, which makes it difficult to grind and polish; it is brittle, and so tends to crack to pieces when being worked on or even in a cold snap; and it changes shape greatly when temperature varies, thus often producing poor images. Worst of all, speculum metal tarnishes rapidly, and the only remedy is to repolish a mirror, which is a tedious and delicate affair.[53]

The limit to these metallic monsters was reached, and probably surpassed, by the 6-foot-diameter giant that the Earl of Rosse placed in operation in Ireland in 1845. However, the "Leviathan of Parsonstown," as the 72-inch telescope was called, made only one significant discovery—the spiral forms of some nebulae. This poor record was due in large part to the miserable Irish observing climate, for astronomers had not yet learned that big telescopes need superior sites to perform well.[54] Lassell demonstrated the importance of clear and steady skies when he took a 48-inch reflector to Malta in 1852, but large instruments would still be installed in bad locations for decades to come.[55]

Speculum metal began to fade from the scene in the 1850s when it became possible to deposit chemically a thin layer of silver on glass to produce a bright mirror. Glass is lighter than speculum metal and easier to grind and polish into shape, but its biggest advantage is that even though the silver coat tarnishes, one merely needs to dissolve the old metal film and deposit a new one, without affecting the shape of the glass. While the refractor remained by far the most common form of telescope for a long time to come, eventually all large telescopes would be metal-on-glass reflectors.[56]

STAR LIGHT, HOW BRIGHT?

Until well into the nineteenth century, estimates of the brightnesses of celestial objects were rough and ready, for there did not seem to be any way to measure that quantity precisely. Astronomers knew that the Moon, Mars, Saturn, Iapetus, and a few stars vary in brightness but were not sure just how much. Were smaller changes in other objects merely unnoticed? And how much brighter than a 6th-magnitude star *is* a 1st-magnitude star? Nobody knew for certain. The whole subject of light intensity was in a primitive state.

In 1760 the German scholar Johann Heinrich Lambert published a theory of the diffuse (that is, not mirrorlike) reflection of light from matt (even, but again not mirrorlike) surfaces. In this work he used the term *albedo* for the fraction of light reflected. If all the light is reflected, as from a perfect white surface, the albedo is 1; if no light is reflected, as from a perfect black surface, the albedo is 0. Accurate values of a body's albedo can reveal hints of its nature. Venus, for example, has a high albedo because it is completely covered by clouds.[57]

In the 1830s John Herschel compared the brightnesses of stars to that of the Moon. His measures seemed contradictory, and it took decades to clear up the matter. The solution came from the German scientist Johann K. F. Zöllner, who had invented an instrument that used polarizing prisms to make a celestial object and an artificial star appear equal in brightness.[58] The principle he used is easy to see by rotating two superimposed pieces of Polaroid polarizing film with respect to each other; the view through them will vary from clear to black.

Using his instrument, Zöllner found that the Moon is much brighter when full than when only a few days from that phase. The reason is that our satellite's surface is irregular, and hence when it is very near full, the shadows of small features on its surface shorten until they all but disappear. Herschel's measurements, it turned out, were fine. Unfortunately he had used Lambert's theory to calculate the Moon's brightness from day to day, and that theory did not apply because it assumed a relatively smooth surface. Thus, from an unexpected source, the variation of the Moon's brightness with phase, Zöllner derived an important fact about our satellite's surface—it was rough at small scales.[59] A glance at any close-up photograph of the Moon taken by Apollo astronauts shows that Zöllner was right.

Zöllner estimated the albedo of the Moon at 0.17. This is high compared to the modern value of about 0.07, but he did establish that our satellite, which looks so silvery in the night sky, actually resembles a dark rock. In the 1860s he estimated the Martian albedo at 0.27, not too far from the modern value, and those for the giant planets—Jupiter, Saturn, Uranus, and Neptune—were about 0.5 or higher, which means that they reflect light quite efficiently (they should, for all are completely surrounded by clouds).[60]

Until long after 1800, all astronomy was conducted by looking through a telescope and drawing or measuring what could be seen. But during the first half of the nineteenth century, a variety of new techniques revolutionized astronomy and much, much more. It is a fascinating insight into human nature to note that, while some astronomers played important roles in these advances, the new technologies generally came from outside their ranks, and many astronomers resisted the new methods.

The first important new development was the beginning of "spectroscopy," the study of light drawn out into a rainbow. The story begins with an 1802 publication by the English scientist William H. Wollaston, who used sunlight admitted to a dark room through a narrow slit, compared to Newton's apertures. That was the key! He found a number of dark "lines"—this was the first use of this term.[61] Wollaston's discovery eventually led, though often slowly and sometimes in spurts, to great and unexpected advances.

The next big advance was due to the German scientist and technician Joseph Fraunhofer. He was interested in improving the performance of all kinds of optical instruments, and this quest led him to investigate the optical properties of glasses. While he at first used prisms, he later began using an actual grating of fine parallel wires wound on a frame, which led to the modern use of term. As reported beginning in 1814, he used a small telescope to view the solar spectrum—another advance—and found hundreds of dark lines that are now called "Fraunhofer lines" in his honor. He dubbed ten of the strongest features with letters from A (in the far red) to H (in the violet), designations that are still used today.[62] Fraunhofer was able to determine the wavelengths of the various colors (blue was shortest and red longest) because, in addition to prisms, he also used a "ruled" surface to disperse the light.[63] When light falls on any surface, transparent or reflecting, that has a large number of parallel striations, or "rulings" close together, some wavelengths of light will interfere and cancel out, others will reinforce each other, and the result will be to produce several spectra. These light-dispersing elements have become known as "diffraction gratings," and a glance at a compact disc shows the effect clearly.

Fraunhofer was two generations ahead of his time and, not satisfied with the Sun, he also observed the spectra of the Moon, Mars, Venus, and several bright stars. He found various dark lines in all but could go no further because he did not know what to make of his spectra.[64]

Efforts to make sense of spectra made little progress in the first half of the nineteenth century. The dark lines in the Sun and the bright lines seen in flames and electric sparks defied explanation. In particular, a single false lead held up progress for decades. The culprit was a bright yellow line (actually a close double) that seemed to appear in the spectra of all flames, no matter what substance was sprinkled into the fire or spark, and as a dark line of the same color in the Sun. Was this some "fundamental" line common to all matter? Not at all, as we now know. It is due to sodium, which is widely distributed on Earth, especially in common table salt, and the "D" line of which, to use Fraunhofer's designation, is so easily produced that even minute amounts of the element give strong lines.[65] The baffled experimenters of the early 1800s did not know this, and so it was a long wait until a pair of German scientists finally pieced the puzzle together.

The two were Robert Bunsen and Gustav Kirchhoff, who first published the results of their studies in 1860. They stated that the dark lines in the solar (and other stellar) spectra are produced by cooler gases in our star's atmosphere absorbing certain particular wavelength from the continuous spectrum emitted by lower, hotter, denser layers. The upper solar atmosphere by itself would produce a spectrum with the same lines in the same locations, but with all the lines appearing *bright* on a dark background.[66]

Kirchhoff and Bunsen set out three laws of spectral formation. They state that what kind of spectrum a luminous body gives off depends on its state. A hot, incandescent solid, a liquid, or a dense gas produces a purely continuous spectrum with no lines (in other words, a rainbow); a hot rarefied gas emits isolated bright lines; and a cooler rarefied gas in front of a hotter source of a continuous spectrum absorbs specific wavelengths, forming dark lines in the rainbow of color.[67]

As each element has its own unique pattern of lines, whether bright or dark (molecules composed of two or more atoms display "bands" made up of many lines each), scientists now had a way to tell the chemical makeup of luminous bodies from afar. Kirchoff followed up by showing that the Sun's outer layers contained elements common on Earth, such as iron, calcium, and sodium. Evidently the stars and our planet were made of similar materials![68]

This discovery was a revelation and appeared almost magical at the time, for it long had been a widely and deeply held belief that we could never, ever, determine the physical compositions of celestial bodies or the physical conditions on them. The teachings of Auguste Comte provide a relatively late and certainly the most famous example of such mistaken thinking. In the nineteenth lecture of his *Cours de Philosophie Positive,* first given in 1829 and published six years later, the French philosopher stated:

> We can see the possibility of determining their [heavenly bodies'] forms, their distances, their magnitudes and their movements, but it is inconceivable that we should ever be able to study by any means whatsoever their chemical compositions or mineralogical structure, still less the nature of organic bodies living on their surface. . . . The positive knowledge we can have of the stars is limited to their geometrical and mechanical phenomena, and can never be extended by physical, chemical, physiological and social research.[69]

Comte was referring not only to the distant stars but also to the much closer objects in the solar system. For example, he mentions the "celebrated problem of the atmospheres of the celestial bodies" and goes on to assert that:

> in no way can we determine their chemical composition or even their density; we should err gravely, for instance, if we supposed, as some have done, that the atmosphere of Venus is as dense as that of the earth because the horizontal refraction of about half a degree [known for Venus from the extensions of the cusps, or ends of the crescent of the planet, near inferior conjunction] that they have in common, for the chemical nature of the gases influences their refractive power, quite as much as their density.[70]

These are not offhand remarks, taken out of context, but an essential part of Comte's philosophy.

He also declared that "the aim of astronomical research is to predict with certainty what will be the actual state of the sky in a more or less distant future." Astronomy, he continued, had "attained the highest philosophical perfection possible to any science" by reducing essentially all the observed phenomena to the workings out of a single physical law, that of gravitation.[71] Such beliefs were common at the time, not least among professional astronomers. Comte provides a striking illustration of how limited was the scope of astronomy in the early nineteenth century, and how dramatic and revolutionary was the change ushered in by the advent of spectroscopy. Comte, who died in 1857, missed by only a few years seeing his views on astronomy proven disastrously wrong.

The spectroscopic method proved powerful. As the case of the sodium D line illustrates all too well, minute quantities of a substance can be detected from its spectrum. In addition, analytical chemists in terrestrial laboratories now had a strong new tool at their service. For astronomers, there was the bonus that spectroscopy did not depend upon distance, as long as the source appeared bright enough to make out its spectrum. As a result, celestial discoveries made with the new technique were soon to come in torrents—but relatively few would be in the realm of planetary studies.

PHOTOGRAPHY TAKES THE STAGE

A second critical development was photography, even though in its early stages it promised to be of little use to astronomy. To begin with, it had long been known that certain substances were affected by light. For example, silver chloride, which occurs as an important silver ore, rapidly turns from gray or colorless to violet-brown when exposed to the Sun.[72] A flat surface coated with such a substance forms an image (a "negative" in modern terms), in which the areas struck by bright light would turn dark, and those "in the shade," so to speak, would remain light. But there was a serious problem, for to see the image one had to *use* light, which would soon turn the entire surface dark. How to "fix" the image was the vital question.

Unexpectedly, two entirely different practical solutions to this problem became public in 1839. As with the prediction of Neptune, the subject of who did what and when in early photography has been argued long and loud.[73] The better known process is the Daguerreotype, introduced by the French painter Louis Jaques Mande Daguerre. He used silver plates exposed to iodine vapor to form a layer of silver iodide. When an image was projected on the plate by a pinhole camera (a small box with a pinhole or lens in one side) and the plate then exposed to mercury fumes, the mercury condensed on the plate, forming a positive image. Dipping the plate in a bath of table salt dissolved the unexposed silver iodide and left a permanent, positive image. That is, bright areas are rendered as bright and dark as dark. (One peculiarity of the Daguerreotype is that it gives a mirror image, in which left and right are reversed. In a historical curiosity, this gave rise to the myth of Billy the Kid as "the Left-Handed Gun"; he was really right-handed.) The later use of silver bromide instead of the chloride reduced exposures made in sunlight to a few seconds, but there was only one image possible from a single plate.[74]

Lesser known by far is the work of the Englishman William Henry Fox Talbot, who concentrated on using sensitized paper to make photographs. He bathed his paper in a series of silver compounds and exposed them while still wet. At the suggestion of John Herschel, he used sodium thiosulfate ("hypo," as it used to be called hyposulfate) to fix the image, which was a negative, and from which any number of positives could be made.[75]

John Herschel, who as noted was an important astronomer in his own right, most of his work involving nebulae and star clusters, also had an important role in the early development of photography. Besides suggesting to Fox Talbot the use of hypo (first used by the English Reverend Joseph B. Reade), Herschel seems to have been the first to use the terms *positive* and *negative* for those types of photographic images and to have coined the word *photography* itself. Even that is not the end of the story. Late in 1839 he decided to tear down his father's 48-inch reflector, which was becoming a danger due to neglect. Using the results of his own researches in photography, he managed to secure an image of the famous instrument, which became, fittingly, the subject of one of the first "pictures" ever made.[76]

It was clear that photography might help astronomy, for it can "store up" light during long exposures and reveal things too faint for the eye to see, and it can provide permanent and objective records of many objects at once. Unfortunately, several severe practical problems barred the way. First was the fact that early photographic emulsions (whatever was spread out on the surface to receive the light) were relatively insensitive to light; that is, they were very "slow." Another factor was that all the early processes responded only to blue (and ultraviolet) light and not to the other colors. Finally, primitive photography was a messy, complicated business that demanded a great deal of skill—much of it exercised of necessity in the dark. The introduction of glass plates and the "wet collodion" process improved the situation somewhat, but it was only the appearance in the 1870s of "dry" plates with reasonable speed made photography at the telescope possible with less than heroic efforts.[77]

The slow speeds of early emulsions meant that exposures had to be relatively long in most cases. To take these exposures, telescopes had to be mounted and moved so as to follow celestial objects smoothly and continuously as Earth rotated, but this kind of sophisticated performance was just being attempted in the first half of the nineteenth century. Then too, even for the Moon and bright planets, for which exposures were relatively short, they were long enough to blur fine details because of the effects of our ever changing atmosphere. Photography could not match the eye's ability to record delicate lunar and planetary features.

Further, the so-called "achromatic" refractors of the time really were not. They were built to focus "visible light," and in particular the yellow-green where the eye is most sensitive; as a result they gave fuzzy photographs. The situation started to change only in 1864, when Lewis M. Rutherford of New York City began to use a photographic refractor expressly built for such work. In the meantime what astronomical photography there was came mainly from reflectors.[78]

Under such conditions, it is not surprising that early celestial photographs were few. J. W. Draper of New York City took the first Daguerreotypes of the Moon in 1840, and one of the solar spectrum the next year.[79] In 1850, William Bond of Harvard College Observatory, with the aid of professional photographer J. A. Whipple, succeeded in making the first Daguerreotypes of stars; Alpha Lyrae (Vega) and Alpha Geminorum (Castor).[80] The Sun posed a unique difficulty, for in its case the problem was to get the very short exposures needed. Nonetheless, Armand H. L. Fizeau and Jean B. L. Foucault made the first Daguerreotype of our star in 1845, capturing an image that showed two sunspots.[81]

Still, for years after these early triumphs progress was slow and there were few workers in astronomical photography. Among these was Rutherford, who made some improved photographs in the 1860s, and especially the Englishman Warren De la Rue, who made his own telescopes. In 1852 he began to experiment with wet plates and soon photographed the Moon's main features. Later he added a clock drive to his 13-inch reflector and by 1865 published a set of lunar photographs that were far better than any made before. He also took many images of the lunar crater Linné to see if its appearance changed (it did not) and designed a refractor to pursue a regular photographic patrol of the Sun.[82] Celestial imaging was just getting started on a grand career that has not yet ended, but one that until recently had little to offer planetary studies.

As the nineteenth century entered its second half, the refracting telescope was *the* instrument in observatories of all types.[83] This was especially the case for professionals working at government, university, and privately funded facilities. Their refractors had relatively small apertures, but these were adequate for most of the routine and enormously extended series of precise positional measurements that were the bread and butter of the profession. The few amateurs, such as De la Rue, Lassell, and Rosse, who built their own giant reflectors and reaped a surprising harvest of discoveries, were exceptions. Ironically, many of these amateurs would blaze trails for the astronomy of the future. But the next version of "the New Astronomy" would take some time to establish itself as the process began in the last half of the nineteenth century.

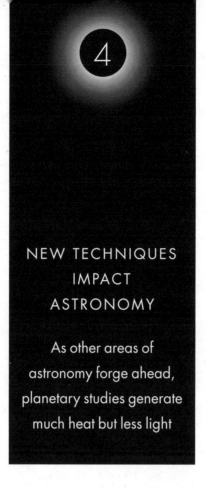

4

NEW TECHNIQUES
IMPACT
ASTRONOMY

As other areas of
astronomy forge ahead,
planetary studies generate
much heat but less light

During the latter part of the nineteenth century astronomy changed as dramatically as in the decades immediately following the invention of the telescope. Spectroscopy, photography, and photometry not only contributed to advances in our knowledge of the solar system but also revolutionized stellar astronomy.[1] No longer limited to using only the human eye to record direct views through the telescope, astronomers could now hope to understand the true physical natures of celestial bodies. They could go beyond the limited and laborious tasks of measuring the positions of objects in the sky, predicting their motions, and drawing their images as seen through a telescope. As part of the field of astronomy, planetary science played a role in these developments, but advances in studies of the solar system turned out to be relatively few compared to the explosion in our knowledge of bodies far beyond the planets.

While broad advances were made in the technical quality of telescopes during the latter half of the nineteenth century, improvements in the re-

Group photograph of part of the Yerkes Observatory staff in the summer of 1959.
Photograph by Joe Tapscott and courtesy Ewen Whitaker

fracting type were the most dramatic. The development of these instruments culminated with the 36-inch refractor at Lick Observatory on Mount Hamilton, California, and the 40-inch telescope at the Yerkes Observatory at Williams Bay, Wisconsin.[2] These two giants remain to this day the largest successful refracting telescopes. Except for special-purpose instruments, the new telescopes were "equatorial mounted," an arrangement that permitted them to follow the nightly paths of celestial objects across the sky with only a single motion around a single axis. Herschel's clumsy mountings were obsolete. These new telescopes were driven by clockwork powered by slowly falling weights, mechanisms similar to those in old-fashioned grandfather clocks, except on a much bigger scale. Their ability to track an object accurately for hours on end proved vital for the development of the new techniques of spectroscopy and photography in astronomy.

Spectrum analysis—that is, the determination of the physical properties of bodies by studying the light and other radiant energy waves that they emit—now offered astronomers the opportunity to understand the true natures of celestial objects. Early studies of astronomical spectra, except in the case of the Sun, were all done by eye, for photography was still a very "slow" process. Spectroscopy has the serious drawback that the same amount of light from a star or planet that is concentrated in a point or small area on the retina of the eye or on a photographic plate in a direct view is instead spread out in a spectrum. There is a second problem as well. When viewed through a spectroscope attached to a telescope at the place where an eyepiece for direct viewing normally would be, the spectrum of a bright star, for example, looks like a sparkling needle of light, with red at one end and blue at the other, and this line is so narrow that few if any details can be discerned.

One solution is to place a cylindrical lens in front of the slit of the spectroscope, so that the spectrum is widened to resemble a slim rectangle. This setup was first used by Fraunhofer, but it too has a drawback because the limited light is now spread out in a second direction, making the surface brightness of the spectrum even lower and limiting visual or photographic recording to the brightest celestial objects. And there was the additional problem that the eye and the photographic plates of the time could record only a relatively small range of wavelengths. That limitation would not be overcome for many decades.

Early astronomical spectroscopes (except those used on the Sun, where there is plenty of light available) generally used prisms to form a spectrum because, among other things, a grating as introduced by Fraunhofer forms not one but many spectra of a object and thus reduces the brightness of any single rainbow.[3] To lengthen the spectrum and reveal finer details, observers usually used several prisms—commonly two to five. These were arranged as a "train" in which light passed through one element after another. However, each prism absorbs some light and reflects a little at its surfaces, and these losses conspire to reduce the brightness of the spectrum. Despite their disadvantages, prisms continued to hold sway until well into the twentieth century. But the winds of change began to stir after the 1880s, when the American scientist Henry A. Rowland began producing much improved metal-on-glass gratings that would gradually come to dominate astronomical spectroscopy.[4]

Telescopes used for spectroscopic work need relatively large apertures to collect a lot of light. Furthermore, in the beginning observers could only detect spectral lines by eye and then measure or draw their positions. These were laborious and time consuming tasks, demanding that the object under study be followed precisely by a telescope for a long time.[5] Such requirements limited work in the field to that by astronomers with relatively large, equatorial-mounted, and "clock-driven" (literally moved by clockwork) instruments.[6]

Late in 1862 Lewis M. Rutherford (who was a lawyer by trade) published the first positive results in the new field of astronomical spectroscopy. Early the next year the English amateur astronomer William Huggins and his colleague William A. Miller presented their first report to the public, and other observers joined in at about the same time. In 1864, Huggins and Miller's second article using spectroscopic analyses reported the surprising results that many stars contained some of the same elements found on Earth and in the Sun.[7]

In the same year Huggins solved a long-standing dispute among astronomers with a mere "spectroscopic glance." He turned his instruments onto a bright, greenish nebula in the constellation Draco, and to his astonishment saw not a rainbow but only a single bright line of green light. Thus, this nebula, at least, is a glowing cloud of rarefied gas and not an unresolved cluster of stars. Further observations showed that greenish looking nebulae (those known as planetary, annular, and irregular from their appearances) are *all* gaseous. The others, the so-called "white" nebulae, showed only a continuous spectrum.[8] We now know that they do display dark lines that Huggins could not see. Some of these objects are distant star clusters, but most of them, including the famous example in Andromeda, are vastly remote and enormous aggregations of billions of stars— galaxies like our Milky Way.

In the 1870s Huggins suggested and tried a method of measuring the motion of a celestial body along the line of sight. He noted that a phenomenon known as the Doppler shift could cause a slight change in the position of lines in a spectrum—in other words, a wavelength shift—toward the blue if a body is approaching us, or toward the red if it is moving away.[9] The Doppler method gives the velocity in the line of sight right away, without waiting years or centuries. In addition it does not depend on distance, provided that the object observed is bright enough for its spectrum to be recorded.

In 1868, Huggins announced that Sirius was moving away from us at a speed of some 29 miles per second, which was reduced to 20 miles per second in 1872. Huggins' early result was quite close to modern estimates. Unfortunately his equipment was such that even for the brightest stars in the sky his results were largely unreliable.[10] It fell to others to refine the method by using bigger telescopes, better spectroscopes, and above all photography to record spectra.[11] Now astronomers could find the true motions of objects in three dimensions, not just those across the line of sight.[12]

Scientists soon found that Doppler shifts of spectral lines could reveal many things. Before the end of the century the phenomenon was being used to discover and study the motions of double stars too close together for these properties to be resolved with any telescope.[13] On another front some variable stars behaved in a puzzling manner, and toward the end of the nineteenth century observers noted cases in which their line-of-sight velocities varied periodically. However, not until early the twentieth century did scientists determine that some of these objects are not double stars revolving about a common center of gravity but instead single bodies that pulsate, their surfaces moving toward and then away from us as the bodies periodically swell and shrink.[14]

In addition to compositions and line-of-sight motions, the study of line and continuous spectra eventually revealed such properties as the temperatures, pressures, and even approximate distances of celestial bodies, possibilities that had not been dreamed of before the introduction of the spectroscope. But note that most of the early successes with spectroscopy were in stellar and nebular studies, not those concerning the solar system.

By the end of the nineteenth century the study of spectra—unknown a century before—had opened up enormous new fields for astronomers to explore. Now there were so many possibilities, so many bodies to observe, and so many things to explain beyond the solar system. Stellar astronomy got yet another boon and again widened its horizons when photography became a useful tool for studying the heavens. Planetary astronomy began to languish as studies of stars and nebulae revealed fascinating new knowledge about the distant heavens.

ASTRONOMICAL PHOTOGRAPHY

As we have seen, astronomical photography did not become practical until after the development of dry plates in the 1870s. At first, these were about ten times faster than the earlier wet variety.[15] Another big advantage was that the new-style plates could simply be taken out of a box when needed and used with no further ado, whereas the older type had to be coated evenly with a gelatinous light-sensitive emulsion immediately before use, and then exposed while still wet—a real barrier to achieving the long exposures then needed for almost every astronomical study.[16] In contrast, the only liquid chemistry and manual dexterity needed with dry plates was at the very end of the whole process, when the pictures were developed.

Dry plates came into astronomical use slowly as their speed increased; they had come into wide use for direct photography of the sky by the late 1880s.[17] Most early celestial photographs were taken with telescopes having relatively narrow fields of view that showed only small regions of the sky. The properties of these instruments were holdovers from the previous two centuries of visual observing and illustrated just how firmly many astronomers still held to the idea that the precise determination of positions was the highest form of observing. The epitome of this way of thinking was the ill-fated *Carte du Ciel* project, organized at an international congress in 1887. This scheme was nothing less than an attempt to chart the whole sky with specially designed photographic refractors. The plan was wildly overambitious and never completed, but for decades it vainly consumed the energies of astronomers around the world.

Some observers, however, had other—and newer—ideas. Isaac Roberts in England was one of the first. In 1885 he began observing with a 20-inch silver-on-glass reflector designed solely for photographic use. This instrument produced a superb gallery of nebular images, one of which first showed the spiral structure of the Great Nebula in Andromeda.[18] Roberts's images even now look strikingly modern, unlike the antique appearance of earlier efforts. There were similar efforts across the Atlantic. For example, at Harvard College Observatory plates were taken with an 8-inch portrait lens, a type used by commercial photographers and having a *much* wider field of view than any telescope of the time. Among other things, these images showed that the Great Nebula in Orion was vastly larger than any earlier visual or photographic study had indicated.

But the real revelation came when the American Edward Emerson Barnard began photographing the Milky Way with a relatively cheap (compared to telescope objectives) portrait lens. For the first time, our galaxy's enormously complex structure was revealed; huge star clouds, widely extended nebulosity, enormous clouds of obscuring matter—all were clear to see.[19] As in the case of spectroscopy, photography revealed vast new and unexpected areas for astronomers to explore. Due in large part to these two new techniques, the comfortably limited and well-ordered universe of Laplace, let alone that of Newton, Copernicus, or Ptolemy, was gone.

The influence of photography on the study of spectra was immense and profound. As with direct pictures of the sky, it became possible to produce permanent records of many features at the same time. Moreover, thanks to the ability of photographic emulsion—in contrast to the eye—to store information, it eventually became possible to take spectra of objects far, far fainter than those that the eye alone could record.

In 1863, Huggins and Miller tried to photograph spectra of Sirius and Capella, but the wet collodion plates they used showed none of the expected dark lines. It was not until 1872 that Henry Draper (the son of J. W. Draper) photographed the spectrum of Vega, using a 28-inch reflector in upper New York state. Though the emulsions he used were not sensitive to red light, they were sensitive to ultraviolet light and in that wavelength region he discovered previously unknown dark lines that are due to hydrogen. Draper then photographed the spectra of a number of bright stars.[20] In the late 1870s, Huggins was the first to try the new, faster dry plates to record astronomical spectra. This time he succeeded in photographing the spectra of stars, as he later did for comets and nebulae.[21]

Until late in the 1880s even the new plates were not as sensitive as the eye; most astronomical work continued to rely upon direct observation. However, by the 1890s the increased speed of photographic emulsions, and especially their ability to store up light during long exposures, had improved to the point that visual spectroscopy was outmoded.[22] As a result, spectral analysis (the study of spectra) received yet another stimulus, one that initially benefited stellar and nebular work much more than it contributed to studies of the solar system.

The big advances in spectroscopy and photography produced few advances in planetary studies. In the case of direct photography, the reason was that photographic emulsions of the time still came nowhere near to matching the sensitivity of the eye. The human eye has a short response time and in combination with the brain can catch and remember images made in the short intervals when Earth's atmosphere is uniform and steady—when the "seeing" is good, in astronomical terms. On the other hand, photographs of the planets needed longer exposures, during which moments of good and bad seeing averaged out. The result was a "smearing" of fine planetary detail. This disadvantage was not overcome until the late 1980s, when highly sensitive solid-state electronic detectors known as charge-coupled devices (CCDs) came into use. Ironically, they produced images of the planets that were as good as the best drawings made from visual observation, but only after close-up views from spacecraft had surpassed them in both clarity and resolution of fine detail.

Spectroscopy also met with limitations when it came to planetary studies, and here the barriers were more serious than in the case of stellar astronomy. The problem was that most of the features of interest in the study of the planets are at long wavelengths, particularly in the infrared. For just that reason, to note a practical example, one can see a long way on a clear day on Earth because our atmosphere absorbs so little visible light. However, in other wavelengths, even the clear sky is not clear.

Moreover, the eye can see wavelengths only from blue to red, and for early photographic emulsions the situation was even worse. At first, they were sensitive only to light at the blue end of the spectrum. In the latter half of the nineteenth century there were successful attempts to extend that range into the red and even the infrared by means of organic dyes that had recently been invented.[23] However, these emulsions were very slow at long wavelengths, and detailed infrared spectra were limited to the Sun until well into the twentieth century. So-called "orthochromatic" plates, which record (unevenly) the whole visual spectrum, were slow to improve. As late as World War I, photographs taken in direct sunlight often had much more sensitivity to blue than to red light, and showed dark blue areas as lighter than bright red ones, which resulted in weird depictions of well-known subjects such as national flags.[24]

Thus, planetary research in the last half of the nineteenth century suffered from severe handicaps when it came to the two new and vitally important observing techniques of the era. Still, the field retained its wide popular appeal and remained a respected, though no longer dominant field of astronomy.

NEW THOUGHTS ON THE SOLAR SYSTEM

VERMIN OF THE SKIES

As better and better star maps appeared, and as more and more observers scanned the skies, discoveries of asteroids climbed steadily. By 1891, no less than 322 had been discovered, all of them through the laborious visual method. The star field in a telescope would be compared with a celestial chart, and if an "extra" starlike object was spotted, it was marked as a suspect. Observations on later nights then revealed whether or not the faint spark of light had the motion through the background stars that identified it as a minor planet. Further position measurements provided the data needed to calculate an orbit around the Sun, and then the new body entered the formal list of our star's family. But 1891 saw a sea change in the method of discovering asteroids. In that year, Max Wolf at Heidelberg, Germany, began to use wide-field photography in the hunt.[25] On December 22, he discovered the first asteroid ever found by photography—323 Brucia.[26] Other observers soon took up the quest.

In the new method, a camera is mounted and driven so that it smoothly follows the motion of the stars across the sky. After a relatively long exposure, the stars appear as tiny dots on the developed photographic plate, but asteroids often show up as short streaks due to their orbital motion around the Sun. This technique, still used today, is easier and simpler than the one it replaced, and in addition provides a permanent record right from the start. As a result, the number of asteroid discoveries climbed rapidly, and it became a real problem to find workers with the time and expertise to calculate their orbits and keep them from being lost to observers.

It soon developed that there was more to the study of asteroids than their mere discovery. As early as 1866, the American astronomer Daniel Kirkwood noticed that there were significant gaps in their orbits. Few or none of these "planetoids" had orbits with periods that were simple fractions of Jupiter's. The gravitational influence of the giant planet gradually forced them out of those paths, much as small pushes at the proper time can make a child's swing arc ever higher.[27]

Astronomers realized that the combined mass of even a host of asteroids—whether discovered or yet to be recorded—could not be large; less than that of the Earth or the Moon were popular estimates. Eventually, the incomparable observer Edward E. Barnard used the Yerkes 40-inch refractor to measure the minuscule apparent diameters of the largest minor planets and thus confirmed their small sizes and masses. In the meantime, there had been a claim of spectroscopic evidence for an atmosphere around the asteroid Vesta. However, advances in the physics of gases soon showed that the feeble gravity of even the largest minor planet could not retain such an envelope for long. The asteroids were, after all, mere barren, airless rocks.[28]

In 1898 astronomers discovered Eros, an asteroid that came closer to Earth than any body then known except the Moon. Eros attracted attention not only because its light varied in a complicated way, presumably due to its rotation and irregular shape, but also because it offered a chance to improve the value of the solar parallax. This tiny body's starlike appearance aided the making of precise measurements of its position with respect to the background stars. In 1900–1901, astronomers mounted a major campaign to take advantage of the opportunity and the result was a more precise value of the solar parallax.[29]

METEORS

At one time the term *meteor* meant any changeable phenomenon in the sky. By the middle of the nineteenth century, use of the term had become restricted to identifying those brief streaks of light that now and then sear the clear night sky as small bits of matter plunge into our atmosphere at high speeds. There had been some earlier suggestions that meteors and comets were somehow related, but those proposals took on new life in 1866, when the Italian astronomer Giovanni Schiaparelli published orbits for members of the Perseid shower. Immediately, several astronomers realized that the orbits were the same as that of a recently discovered comet, Swift-Tuttle (or 1862 III, the third such object to pass perihelion that year). This was the first direct—and most unexpected—connection between meteor showers and comets. A few more identifications of meteor showers and comets soon followed, and the conviction spread that meteor showers simply marked Earth's passage through debris strewn along a comet's orbit.[30]

There were too few known comets to account for all the known meteor showers, but the difference might be due to leftovers from disintegrated comets that were no longer visible. This explanation was confirmed in no uncertain terms in the case of Biela's comet, which, as we have seen, was last observed in 1852. In 1872 Earth passed through the "lost" comet's orbital path, and the result was a spectacular shower.[31] Unfortunately for skywatchers, Jupiter's influence on the survivors gradually disturbed their orbits so that today few, if any, can be seen.[32]

In addition to the obvious difference in their abilities to survive passage through Earth's atmosphere, there was another indication that meteorites differ from shower meteors. Increasing numbers of meteorite orbits were calculated. Almost all showed that the bodies had moved in direct orbits, that is, in the same sense as the planets. On the other hand, shower and many sporadic (not connected with any shower) meteors are not so limited.[33]

Sadly, the nineteenth century ended with a worldwide debacle for meteor astronomy. The Leonid displays of 1833 and 1866 had been magnificent, and there was intense public anticipation of the expected fireworks in November, 1899, despite the cautions of several astronomers. The time came, but due to the disturbing gravitational effects of the planets, few meteors appeared, and as a result the study of these bodies declined sharply.[34]

COMETS

The appearances of several great comets, such as Donati's of 1858 and Tebbutt's of 1861, spurred public and astronomical interest in the subject.[35] The "Great Southern Comet" of 1880 in particular posed a new puzzle, for its orbit was the same as that of a comet that had appeared in 1843. They both passed very close to the Sun's surface, had similar orbits, and were, in fact, the first two known examples of what now are called "sungrazers." Could the two really be the same body, returning after only thirty-seven years? Astronomers found that hard to believe.[36]

The mystery deepened the following year, when Tebbutt's comet of 1881 appeared, for this body had the same orbit as a comet seen in 1807! Now there were two sets of coincidences to explain, and scientists, with the recent breakup of Biela's comet in mind, realized that both were cases of the disrupted fragments of larger primitive bodies moving in the same path.

Popular and scientific interest got a shot in the arm when there were no less than five conspicuous comets visible in 1880–82. The last of them, the "Great September Comet of 1882" was yet another sungrazer, and one that passed directly across the face of the Sun. During that transit there was no trace of the visitor, showing that the vast bulk of the comet was extremely tenuous, and that any possible solid nucleus was extremely small. The number of sungrazers reached five by 1887, and their orbits were studied by Heinrich Carl Friedrich Kreutz toward the end of the century. He suggested that they were all remnants of a primordial object that had been torn apart during a close approach to the Sun. New members of this of this group are still being discovered and are known as Kreutz sungrazers in his honor.[37]

Wet-plate images of Donati's comet taken in 1858 by an English photographer confusingly named England Usherwood showed the visitor's brightest portions, but only the introduction of dry plates made it possible to record substantial portions of the much fainter comet tails. Henry Draper in New York City and Pierre Jules César Janssen of France both captured images of Tebbutt's comet of 1881, and soon photography was in regular use for the study and eventually the discovery of comets. In 1892 Barnard, working with a wide-field lens at Lick Observatory, accidentally recorded the first comet ever discovered by photography alone.[38] To this day, photography has remained an effective means to discover comets, both accidentally and in the course of dedicated search programs.

The French scientist Dominique François Jean Arago had shown in 1819 that some of the light coming from the tail of a comet seen that year was polarized. This implied that at least some of the glow was reflected sunlight, probably from many small bodies such as particles of dust. Later observations supported this view, and it became generally accepted.[39] But the spectroscope would reveal a more complex tale.

Giovanni Battista Donati of Florence was the first to succeed with comet Tempel in 1864. His visual observations revealed that that body's spectrum was made up of three broad bright bands separated by dark spaces (the bands are the signatures of molecules made up of two or more atoms; such bands are really sets of many fine lines, but the primitive spectroscopes of the day did not resolve the individual members). So here was a case where a comet's light came from glowing gas! The next development came in 1866 when Huggins and Angelo Secchi in Rome observed that the light of the periodic comet Tempel-Tuttle showed both bright bands *and* a fainter bright continuous spectrum, pointing to the presence of both glowing gas and reflected sunlight. Further observations by other observers revealed that different comets, or even the same ones at different times, have different spectra.[40] Cometary spectra were first photographed in 1881, when Huggins and Draper recorded that of comet Tebbutt. This body's spectrum showed a number of bright bands along with a continuous spectrum crossed by some of the strongest dark Fraunhofer lines, confirming that the comet shone partly from reflected sunlight and partly from glowing gas.[41]

In 1868, Huggins scored another breakthrough by making the first correct identification of a substance in a comet's spectrum. The comet was Winnecke's, and the substance was the C_2 molecule, composed of two carbon atoms. However, that was a lucky break. In subsequent decades astronomers discerned little new information about the chemical compositions of comets.[42]

Two bright comets in 1882 both passed relatively close to the Sun, and to the surprise of observers each showed a pair of narrow, closely spaced bright lines in the yellow region of the spectrum. These were due to hot vapor of atomic sodium. One of these bodies, the Great September Comet, was a sungrazer, and it provided a real surprise, for in its spectrum Ralph Copeland and J. G. Lohse, working in Ireland, detected *iron* lines! Features due to other metals were reported, but over the following years astronomers gradually discounted all these observations, until they were spectacularly confirmed almost a century later.[43]

By the latter part of the nineteenth century, the connection between comets and shower meteors was well established, as was the impression that comets are only loosely held together—Biela's split being the most famous demonstration of their fragility. Astronomers generally accepted that a cometary nucleus was not a single body but instead resembled a dense swarm of meteorites. This "flying sandbank" or "flying gravelbank" theory remained a popular one until well into the twentieth century.[44]

Phenomena connected with comets' tails puzzled nineteenth-century scientists, and the then current vague "electrical" explanations were of little help. However, in the 1870s and 1880s, Russian astronomer Fedor Aleksandrovitch Bredikhin developed a theory originally suggested by Olbers and improved by Bessell. Bredikhin sorted comets into three classes depending on how sharply their tails were curved. In the first, the repulsive force—whatever it is—from the Sun appeared to be fifteen or twenty times stronger than the attraction of solar gravity, and so the tail is fairly narrow and straight. In the second, repulsion is only a few times stronger than attraction, producing a broader, more curved tail. In the third, repulsion is only slightly greater than attraction and the tail is short and stubby. Bredikhin suggested that the three classes had different chemical compositions: hydrogen, hydrocarbons, and iron respectively. He was wrong about the compositions—spectra soon indicated that—but his work did explain some features of comet tails.[45]

The subject was bedeviled by the fact that, as the scientists of that era could not know, most comets have two kinds of tails. In reality, the curved variety is made of dust, while the straight type is composed of ionized gas, molecules of which are electrically charged because they have been stripped of one or more electrons by the Sun's ultraviolet light.[46] Another stumbling block was that the nature of the repulsive force was a mystery.

In 1873, the Scottish physicist James Clerk Maxwell provided the first piece for the solution of this puzzle in his monumental *Treatise on Electricity and Magnetism,* in which he showed that light exerts a force on material objects. By the end of the century scientists were proposing theories that used this "radiation pressure" to shape comet tails.[47] This is the correct explanation in the case of dust tails but fails miserably for the ion variety.

As to where comets fit in the origin and history of the solar system, there were many theories but little in the way of hard facts. There was a consensus that comets were members of the Sun's family, though wayward and "different" ones. To give one example, Agnes Clerke, the nineteenth century's most popular historian of astronomy, wrote that comets were "almost certainly so far strangers to our system that they had no part in the long process of development by which its [the solar system's] present condition was attained. They are, perhaps, survivals of an earlier, and by us scarcely and dimly conceivable state of things, when the swirling chaos from which the sun and planets were, by a supreme edict, to emerge, had not separately begun to be."[48] Her words echo the nebular hypothesis, which soon was to go into eclipse, only to reemerge in our own day.

By the latter part of the nineteenth century astronomers had begun the wholesale discovery of asteroids. While almost all were safely out beyond the orbit of Mars, the discovery of Eros showed that at least one of them came rather uncomfortably close to Earth. Astronomers had long known that there was a real chance of a comet hitting our planet with possibly disastrous effect.[49] Moreover, scientists of the time generally accepted the reality that extraterrestrial bodies do indeed land on Earth in the form of meteorites. In the light of this knowledge it is surprising that so few people gave serious attention to the possibility of cosmic collisions affecting solar system bodies in a major way, or looked around for evidence that such catastrophes might leave behind. There had long been those who argued that cosmic impacts played an important role in the history of the solar system, but the contrary opinion of one man overrode those voices.

Grove Karl Gilbert was the chief geologist of the U.S. Geological Survey. In 1896, he published a study of what we now call Meteor Crater, in Arizona. Though originally he held that this unusual geologic feature was the result of a meteorite impact, he finally came down on the side of a steam explosion. The case was a difficult one, because while nickel-iron fragments of the impacting small asteroid were at that time scattered all over the area (many remain to this day), an extensive field of recent volcanic activity—volcanos, cinder cones, and the like—is clearly visible just to the northwest of the site. Gilbert's conclusion was that the meteorites represented merely a chance fall on an igneous structure. So great was his prestige that his pronouncement "had a devastating effect on research into impact phenomena," as Ursula B. Marvin put it. As a result, the possibility of impact craters on Earth (or anywhere else in the solar system, for that matter) was not taken seriously by most scientists until well into the twentieth century.[50]

MOON MAPS AND SPECULATIONS

Lunar studies waned in the late nineteenth century. Professional astronomers showed little interest in studying the craters, plains, and mountains of our satellite, and there seemed little hope of ever learning much about the physical nature of our nearest celestial neighbor. The Moon remained, as it does to this day, a popular object to "show off the telescope" to visitors, but only a few workers labored in the vineyard of lunar studies.

One who did was Johann Friedrich Julius Schmidt, longtime director of the Athens Observatory. In 1878 he published *Charte der Gebirges des*

Mondes (*Chart of the Mountains of the Moon*), a series of twenty-five maps covering the side of the Moon visible from Earth.[51] Other observers continued drawing lunar features, but photography was the wave of the future, except for studies of the finest details. In the late nineteenth and early twentieth century, photographs of the Moon were taken with a number of large telescopes having long focal lengths that provided a large image scale. Perhaps the finest result of this work was the photographic lunar atlas produced at the Paris Observatory by M. Leowy and P. Puiseux. Other series of lunar photographs were made at Lick and Yerkes observatories, among other places, but increasingly, professional astronomers lost interest in our satellite's barren, unchanging surface.[52]

But *was* it absolutely unchanging? Though various observers still kept reporting indications of at least a tenuous atmosphere, accumulating evidence strongly indicated that our satellite was airless. In addition, ever better maps made it easier to check the constancy of lunar features. In 1866 Schmidt created a sensation by claiming that the crater Linné had disappeared. The case depended on early drawings, and a dispute about the reality of this change ran on for a century (as it turned out, there was no change.) Despite this and other doubtful claims, astronomers by the end of the nineteenth century generally agreed that no certain alteration of the Moon's surface had ever been observed.[53]

All through the nineteenth century scientists generally believed that the Moon's craters had a volcanic origin. There were obvious problems with this explanation, such as the tremendous sizes of some lunar craters compared to any terrestrial volcano and the differences in the shapes of the two kinds of features on the two bodies. Such difficulties were usually explained away in some vague manner as the result of the Moon's lower surface gravity compared to that of Earth, or as arising from some difference in the nature of volcanic activity due to our satellite's smaller size, mass, and density. Ironically, Gilbert strongly championed an impact origin for lunar craters in an 1893 article and later held to this view. His prestige and influence were not as great in astronomy as in geology, however, and he could not reverse the entrenched thinking of the day, even though in this case he was right.[54]

Lord Rosse made the first effective measurements of the Moon's far-infrared emission in 1869–72, using a 36-inch reflector. In 1884 the same equipment revealed that the lunar surface cooled rapidly during an eclipse of the Moon, behavior confirmed by the American Samuel P. Langley (the longtime secretary of the Smithsonian Institution, who is perhaps unfortunately best known for his failed efforts to fly an airplane before the Wright brothers). These observations demonstrated that solar heating does not penetrate far beneath our satellite's surface, which thus must be a good insulator. In particular, the results indicated that dust or soil, not solid rock, formed most of the Moon's surface.[55]

"Lunar theory," the prediction of the Moon's future position, was refined greatly by mathematicians such as the American Ernest W. Brown, but perhaps the most noticed development shed light on the past.

"Tidal friction" was not a new concept in the second half of the nineteenth century, but its effects then took on new importance. Scientists had long realized that tides could act as a friction brake on Earth's daily rotation, but there was a new appreciation of the fact that there are not only the familiar ocean tides but also so-called "body" tides, due to the fact that the bulk of our planet is not perfectly rigid but instead reshapes itself continuously in response to gravitational forces. According to theory, body tides raised on the Moon by Earth long ago forced our satellite to slow its spin so that the lunar day became equal to the month, and from then on the same side of the Moon always faced Earth. Tidal effects are causing Earth's day to lengthen and the Moon to recede from us—that is, the month will grow longer. But the day is growing longer faster than the increase of the month, and far in the future the two should coincide. Then the day will be equal to the month, and both bodies will always present the same faces to each other. However, there will still be tides provoked by the Sun. These will cause the terrestrial day to become longer than the month, resulting in the resurrected lunar tides opposing the solar ones, and eventually bringing the moon closer and closer to Earth. Scientists have since learned that the situation is more complicated than that (atmospheric tides, for one thing, were not known, let alone taken into account), and that other events might intervene (the Sun might well turn into a red giant and then a white dwarf before tidal friction runs its course).[56]

But what of the past? Beginning with an 1879 paper, the English scientist George H. Darwin (son of the naturalist Charles Darwin) attacked the problem and reached an astounding conclusion. He suggested that many tens of millions of years in the past, the day and the month were equal, and Earth and the Moon both rotated and orbited each other almost in contact with a period of 2 to 4 hours! Strikingly, that is about as fast as a body like Earth can rotate without breaking up. From this situation it was only a short step to the notion that a larger, "proto-Earth" *did* break up due to too-rapid rotation, forming the Earth-Moon system.[57] This "fission" theory had great scientific and popular support for many years (the Pacific Ocean was a popular choice for the original site of our satellite), though we now know that the Moon was not formed in that way.

CLOSER OBSERVATION OF PLANETS

MERCURY

Early spectroscopic observations of Mercury gave possible hints but no proof that the planet had an atmosphere, and by the end of the century there had been no confirmed dark spectral lines due to an atmosphere around the planet. Photometry did better, for in 1874 Zöllner revealed that the changes in Mercury's brightness with phase closely resemble those of the Moon, and that the planet's albedo is low and similar to that of our satellite. Both findings suggest that Mercury, like the Moon, is airless and has a rough surface on a small scale.[58]

It is possible to see markings on Mercury from Earth, but doing so requires a good telescope and a steady atmosphere. Beginning in 1882, Schiaparelli began observing Mercury during the day, when the planet is much higher in the sky than at twilight, and views of it are much better than those seen through longer paths of air. He was also able to study the planet for hour after hour, instead of during only a short interval each twilight period. This ingenious new technique, along with plenty of observing time, revealed that Mercury's day was apparently equal to its year and that the planet, like the Moon, always keeps the same face toward the body it orbits. This "synchronous rotation" was confirmed in 1896–97 by the Boston Brahmin turned astronomer, Percival Lowell. These reported findings meshed nicely with the theory of tidal friction, for the Sun should produce strong effects on Mercury. Lowell also reported long and narrow features that might be cooling cracks.[59] We now know that Lowell's linear markings were not there, but it is more surprising that the synchronous rotation was not there either. This is true even though Schiaparelli's observations, and probably some of Lowell's, might have been correct, for they erred in the interpretation of their results. For generations, astronomers generally accepted the mistaken belief that Mercury rotated synchronously.

If scientists in the later part of the nineteenth century felt certain about Mercury's rotation period, they also worried about details of the planet's motion. The point of Mercury's elliptical orbit closest to the Sun (perihelion) was itself making a slow revolution around our star; in effect the entire orbit was slowly turning about the Sun. This motion is slow, but only a portion of it could be accounted for by known gravitational effects. The difference between theory and observation is tiny—less than 1 arc minute per century—but the predictions of theoretical astronomy had become so precise that the discrepancy posed a serious problem. Were we finally coming upon a flaw in Newton's laws? Indeed we were, as the next century revealed in an unexpected way, but for the time being astronomers looked for less radical explanations.

In 1869, Leverrier announced that theory and observation would agree if there were an unknown body or bodies revolving inside the orbit of Mercury. Such objects could exist and yet escape notice, for they would be visible from Earth only during a total solar eclipse or perhaps during a transit across the Sun's disk. The idea was all the more reasonable because a similar suggestion had led to the discovery of Neptune.

Sure enough, detections of Vulcan, as Leverrier dubbed it, came from both transit and eclipse observations, but none of these "discoveries" was ever confirmed. By the end of the century many negative searches had convinced most astronomers that there was no such planet, and that Mercury's motion was still a puzzle.[60]

VENUS

In 1890, Schiaparelli announced that Venus, like Mercury, rotated synchronously, and visual observations for and against this possibility piled up. Spectroscopy was called in to assist, but again the first results were inconclusive. As the century ended, astronomers still had two main candidates for the rotation period of Venus: Schiaparelli's and the competing estimate of about 24 hours.[61] Neither is correct.

Venus was known to have an appreciable atmosphere, and extensive or even total cloud cover, but the composition of that atmosphere was unknown. Spectroscopic observations, directed especially at detecting water vapor and oxygen, produced only inconclusive results until well into the twentieth century. There were dissenters of a sort, however, and Lowell believed—mistakenly as it turned out—that he could discern permanent surface markings.[62] But even before our century there were those who believed that Venus was a misty, watery planet, perhaps covered with oceans or possibly resembling Earth at a time when our planet supported the vast swamps from which most of our coal beds formed.[63] That view was wildly mistaken, but some scientists held to it as late as the mid–twentieth century.

JUPITER

Many astronomers in the late nineteenth century believed that Jupiter was a body that could be characterized as somewhere between a decaying Sun

Venus as imaged in ultraviolet light by the
Hubble Space Telescope, showing wispy
features of the top of the planet's clouds.
This view is similar to those visible through a
telescope when a deep blue filter is used
and observing conditions are excellent.
Courtesy NASA

and a developing Earth, a Victorian concept that has held up rather well over the years. Scientists of that era debated whether Jupiter shone to some extent by its own light (we now know that it does not in visible rays), and it was widely believed (and later confirmed) that the giant planet had a high internal temperature. The easily visible and rapidly changing features on its disk testified to a substantial and active atmosphere and were probably driven by internal heat because sunlight on Jupiter seems much too weak to cause such extensive activity.[64] (This view remains popular today.)

Huggins, in 1862, and Secchi, perhaps even earlier, found dark absorption lines and bands that seemed to be due to Jupiter's atmosphere. The features were confirmed by the German astronomer Hermann Carl Vogel in 1871–73. Those that corresponded to water vapor were spurious, but the strong signatures at the red end of the spectrum, due to a then unknown substance or substances, stood the test of time.[65]

The Great Red Spot on Jupiter made the headlines in the last part of the nineteenth century. While not a newly detected feature, after 1878 it drew increased attention, and from 1879 to 1882 the Great Red Spot dominated the surface of Jupiter, being visible even through the modest telescopes of amateurs. Residing in the southern hemisphere of the planet,

A typical example of one of the better
Earth-based photographs of Jupiter from
the 1950s. Much detail is visible, but
there are tantalizing hints of much more.
Courtesy McDonald Observatory,
University of Texas

it was as large as Earth from north to south, and three times as large from east to west.[66]

Since then the Red Spot has become prominent and then faded away several times but is still around as of this writing. Theories concerning its nature have been many, varied, and ingenious. Even now the final result is not in, although the concept that it is a gigantic atmospheric vortex is a leading contender. Changes in this and many other complex cloud features in the atmosphere of Jupiter (for that is what the markings seen on the planet's disk are) were observed from time to time by professional astronomers, but more and more the bulk of the work was left to dedicated amateurs.

Jupiter's Galilean satellites were joined by another in 1892 when Edward E. Barnard, using the Lick 36-inch refractor, discovered a minute fifth attendant orbiting inside the other four.[67] Few suspected it then, but the era of visual discoveries was nearing an end.

SATURN

Spectroscopy provided new insights about Saturn. In 1863, Secchi found wide, dark absorption bands in the red end of the spectrum that were due to the atmosphere of the ringed planet. Other observers confirmed the features. But what the gas—or gases—were that caused the spectral features remained unknown.[68]

Compared to that of Jupiter, Saturn's surface is bland, generally show-

A representative photograph of Saturn from the 1950s. The only ring division visible in this image is Cassini's, though several others previously had been glimpsed visually through telescopes. Courtesy McDonald Observatory, University of Texas

ing only a few muted cloud belts and only on rare occasions distinct features. However, in 1876 American astronomer Asaph Hall discovered a well-defined white spot near Saturn's equator, and timings of the passages of this structure across the center of the planet's disk gave an improved value of the rotation period. Other observations of more or less vague features showed that Saturn, like Jupiter and the Sun, has not one rotation period but a variety of them at different latitudes north and south of the equator.[69]

Maxwell's theoretical work strongly indicated that Saturn's rings were composed of myriad separate particles in orbit around the planet in accordance with Kepler's laws, but supporting observational evidence was wanting. James E. Keeler, the outstanding American astronomical spectroscopist of his time, provided that proof. He used the Doppler effect to do so, and this is how.

Consider a planet with an axis of rotation that is in the plane of the sky, presenting us, so to speak, with a "sideways" view. Now if the planet is observed near opposition, when there is little relative line-of-sight motion between it and Earth, spectral lines at the center of its disk will have wavelengths close to those observed in the laboratory. This is so because the rotational motion there is entirely *across* our line of sight and so causes no Doppler shift. But on the equator at the "edges" of the planet the situation is different, for at those locations the rotational motion is entirely *along* the line of sight. Thus lines at the approaching limb will show a blue shift, while those from the receding limb will exhibit a red shift.

Keeler's spectra of Saturn and its rings clearly showed that the planet is rotating (of course this was long known to be true) and that portions of the rings at different distances from Saturn orbit the planet at different speeds in accord with Kepler's Third Law of planetary motion. Thus Maxwell was right. Even though he was only confirming what was already an established theory, Keeler became a celebrity and spectroscopy achieved greater stature among astronomers and the general public alike.[70]

Now and then observers reported ring divisions in addition to Cassini's and Encke's, while some saw faint radial markings. These features were seldom confirmed, and most astronomers dismissed them as spurious, but it turned out that they were real. In fact, they were the first fleeting and delicate indications of the immensely complicated structure that the Voyager space probes would find in Saturn's rings late in the twentieth century.[71]

In 1898 William H. Pickering of Harvard discovered Phoebe, Saturn's ninth satellite, making the first successful use of photographs in such an effort. This object is quite faint and has a number of peculiarities. For one, its orbit lies far outside those of the eight previously known moons, is highly eccentric, and has a considerable tilt with respect to Saturn's equator. Pickering also claimed a tenth satellite, Themis, but this was never confirmed.[72]

URANUS AND NEPTUNE

Neither of the two most distant planets showed any confirmed features on their disks, and estimates of their periods of rotation were indirect and crude. Visual spectroscopic studies of Uranus by Secchi in 1869 revealed broad absorption bands similar to but even more prominent than those of Saturn. Huggins, in 1871, found additional dark features, but the gas or gases responsible remained unknown.[73] Since it was widely believed in the late nineteenth century that the giant planets (Jupiter, Saturn, Uranus, and Neptune) were partly self-luminous, it is not surprising that there prevailed for a few years what now seems a bizarre interpretation of Uranus's spectrum. This view, proposed by the Briton Norman Lockyer, held that the dark bands were not absorptions in the continuous solar spectrum but rather that the bright regions in between the dark gaps were emission features. But Keeler, using the Lick 36-inch refractor in 1889, demolished that idea, demonstrating that the spectrum of Uranus is indeed reflected sunlight interrupted by wide dark absorption bands produced in the planet's atmosphere. In 1895, Vogel's photographic spectra confirmed Keeler's work.[74]

Neptune is farther from the Sun than Uranus, so its surface brightness and thus its spectrum is much fainter. Neptune's dimly recorded spectrum seemed to show its atmosphere to be similar to that of Uranus.[75]

MARS

The red planet probably received more publicity and spawned more controversy than all the rest of the solar system during the last half of the nineteenth century. At the beginning of the era the dark areas on Mars were widely held to be seas, as such long abandoned names such as Dawes Ocean, Kaiser Sea, and Huggins Inlet attest. However, this belief faded gradually due to factors such as the discovery of detail within the dark areas and the observers' failures to detect any bright gleams of reflected sunlight, as would be expected from an open water surface.

Astronomers knew that Mars had some kind of atmosphere, probably thinner than our own, because of its seasonally changing pole caps and the occasional presence of bright, transitory features that appeared to be clouds.[76] First visual and then photographic spectra offered a way to analyze that atmosphere, and many observers took up the challenge. The results were depressing. There were "discoveries" of dark spectral features peculiar to Mars as well as enhancements of terrestrial lines and bands due to gases surrounding the red planet. In particular, the presence of "aqueous vapor" and oxygen—both so important to life as we know it— were announced as definite on more than one occasion. However, better observations never confirmed any of these positive findings, and in fact by the end of the century there was no firm spectral evidence for any gas in the atmosphere of Mars.[77]

In contrast to the rather dry and technical spectral studies, direct visual observations of Mars through telescopes rated many headlines. The planet's orbit is sufficiently eccentric for it to come much closer to Earth at some oppositions than at others. In 1877 Mars made a very favorable approach to our planet. Asaph Hall of the U.S. Naval Observatory—the 26-inch telescope there was the largest refractor in the world at that time— used the opportunity to make a careful search for Martian satellites and found two diminutive moons that he dubbed Phobos and Deimos. As might be expected, other moons were soon "discovered" by other observers, but these were bogus sightings; Mars has only two natural satellites.[78]

But the really big news from the 1877 opposition came from Italy, where Schiaparelli detected a network of long, thin, dark markings crisscrossing the ruddy surface of Mars. He dubbed these features *canali* in Italian, which inevitably became "canals" in English.[79] The canals' bizarre

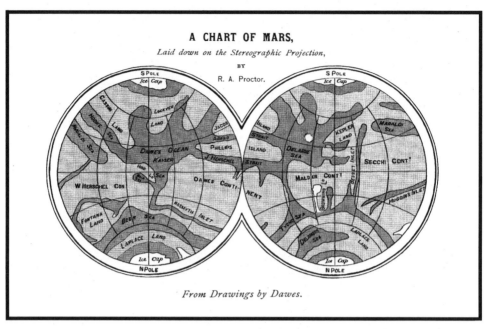

A CHART OF MARS,

Laid down on the Stereographic Projection,

BY

R. A. Proctor.

From Drawings by Dawes.

A map of Mars published about 1873. Some of the features can be identified with ones now known to exist, but the seas, oceans, and other watery features are actually dark rocks or dust. From the author's collection

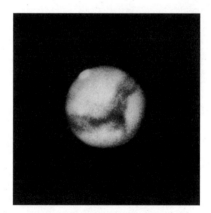

A typical photograph of Mars from the era before the dawn of the Space Age. The southern pole cap is clearly visible, as is the wedge-shaped dark feature known as Syrtis Major, but in general very little detail shows. Courtesy McDonald Observatory, University of Texas

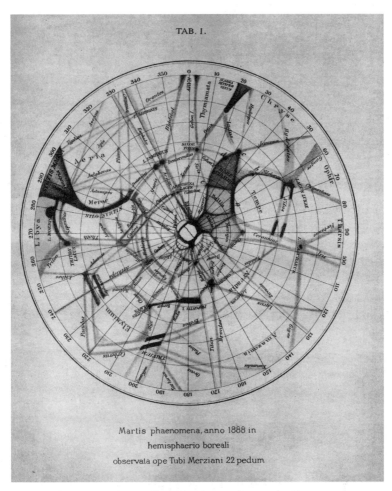

TAB. I.

Martis phaenomena, anno 1888 in
hemisphaerio boreali
observata ope Tubi Merziani 22 pedum

One of Giovanni Schiaparelli's maps of Mars, showing the planet's northern
hemisphere as he saw it in 1888. Note the canals, double canals, oases, and
other features that were widely interpreted as the work of intelligent Martians.
Courtesy Peridier Astronomical Library, University of Texas at Austin

appearance, along with their evocative name, suggested to some scientists
and especially to the general public an artificial origin. Other experienced
observers after Schiaparelli also saw canals, but many did not. In particular, the keen-eyed Barnard, using the mighty 36-inch Lick refractor in
1894, saw no trace of canals at all, but to the contrary glimpsed an enormous amount of tiny, complex detail. The mystery deepened when Schiaparelli also found that many of the canals were actually *double*.[80] The
visibility of the canals did not seem to depend strongly on the size of the

telescope used (Schiaparelli's had a lens not quite 9 inches across), leading some to claim that smaller instruments would show more details than larger ones! While the statement is often valid, this is not the case when Earth's atmosphere is calm and stable above the telescope. Barnard's observations, to cite the best example, showed that a good big telescope is definitely better than a good little telescope for viewing fine planetary detail when the seeing is good.

In the Victorian era it was commonly accepted—though evidence was so scanty as to be almost nonexistent—that life, perhaps even intelligent life, was widespread in the solar system.[81] Mars, with its pole caps, clouds, and "seas" was an obvious target in the search for extraterrestrial life. Moreover, according to the then popular nebular hypothesis, the red planet was older than ours. Thus, according to Charles Darwin's newly developed theory of evolution, Mars's inhabitants should be more advanced than humans. All this speculation was heady stuff and gave rise to much lurid front-page material in the newspapers of the day, when journalistic ethics were often much looser than they are today. A "Mars mania" started building up in the late 1880s, remained popular for several decades, and cannot be said to have left us yet.

While Schiaparelli himself was cautious about interpreting the meaning of his observations, others were not. In the forefront of the to-do was Camille Flammarion, who in 1892 declared the existence of a superior (to us) race of Martians very probable. This French astronomer and popularizer of astronomy wrote well and persuasively and included enough sensational items to make "good copy." Many professional astronomers were much less optimistic about alien life on the red planet.[82]

Today the best known relic of this fad is H. G. Wells's 1898 story *The War of the Worlds,* in which malevolent Martians use heat rays and poison gas to conquer Earth, only to fall victim themselves to terrestrial bacteria against which they have no defense. As we will see, just forty years after it first appeared, this classic of science fiction showed in a striking and sobering way just how widely and deeply the idea of intelligent life on Mars had penetrated the hearts and minds of the general public.

But the excitement about the possibility of life on Mars had yet to reach its peak. In the next chapter we will meet the man who almost single-handedly created a worldwide furor around the topic and whose influence is still felt today.

5

CONTROVERSY AND FRUSTRATION

At the end of the nineteenth century and the beginning of the twentieth, the solar system in general and Mars in particular were much in the headlines, but lack of substantial new discoveries caused scientific interest in the field to ebb as other areas of astronomy made greater advances

Public interest in many areas of theoretical and observational astronomy grew greatly between the close of the nineteenth century and America's entry into World War I, but things were otherwise in the case of solar system research. Although solar system research was often in the news, and even in the headlines, during this time before "the Great War," stellar astronomy eclipsed planetary astronomy in public and especially professional interest. Both this heightened attention to very distant objects and the simultaneous startling and swift demise of planetary studies owed a great deal to the extraordinary actions of a single remarkable man.

THE LOWELL PHENOMENON

Into the midst of the then current excitement about the possibility of extraterrestrial life, and indeed generating a great deal of it all by himself, stepped Percival Lowell. This classic New England Brahmin,[1] born in

1855, was not an astronomer or scientist by training or experience but rather a world traveler, Orientalist, and diplomat, although he did study mathematics at Harvard under the redoubtable Benjamin Peirce. In what seems an unlikely move, in 1893, Lowell suddenly decided to found his own observatory to study Mars, and by the next year it was in operation in the high, clear air just outside Flagstaff, in what was then the Arizona Territory. From that time until his sudden death in 1916, astronomy, especially the study of the solar system—and Mars in particular—was his passion.[2]

There is little hard evidence as to why Lowell suddenly changed careers so dramatically, and he himself never explained that decision for the record. However, the Boston geologist George Russell Agassiz noted that Lowell decided to carry on Schiaparelli's work upon hearing of the Italian observer's failing eyesight.[3] Whatever the reason, Lowell certainly carried on—and far beyond—in the spirit of Schiaparelli.

Lowell located his observatory where the "seeing" (image quality, sharpness, and steadiness) appeared best, as determined by telescopic observations at a number of sites in Arizona. This sort of site testing is standard practice today but was a novelty in those days. The steadiness of the air above Flagstaff, compared to that over other observatories, was to play a significant role in the controversies to come.[4]

The newly fledged astronomer held to the view that because of seeing problems, smaller telescopes were usually better than larger ones for viewing fine planetary detail.[5] As we have seen, this may be true when the seeing is poor but is not so when it is good.[6] Still, Lowell used the "smaller is better" argument as one reason to explain why observers using telescopes larger than his could not see the canals of Mars.

Lowell was definitely not a member of the astronomical establishment. Right from the start of his new career he made some very unconventional statements. For example, as early as 1894, even before he began to observe Mars intensively, he stated publicly that the canals of Mars were probably the works of intelligent beings.[7] Astronomers used to be a generally conservative lot when it comes to announcements, especially *advance* announcements, about their work, and Lowell's well-publicized remarks cannot have made him many friends among professionals in the field.

In setting up his observatory, Lowell at first had the help of William Pickering (the brother of Edward, the powerful director of the Harvard College Observatory), who was already establishing a somewhat bizarre reputation among astronomers. This colorful character is largely forgotten today, but in many ways he was Lowell's immediate predecessor in Martian studies. In 1891 and 1892 Pickering observed Mars from Peru.

When near its most favorable oppositions the red planet is south of the celestial equator and so is best observed from near to or south of Earth's equator. He saw all that Schiaparelli had seen and more: features in the dark areas (making it improbable that they were seas), lakes at the intersections of canals, clouds in the Martian atmosphere, and so forth, all of which were reported widely (and wildly) in the popular press, which then was at the peak of its "yellow journalism" phase. However, many professional astronomers—at Lick, Harvard, and elsewhere—were less than impressed by these sensational results.[8]

Findings equally and more sensational soon after came from the Arizona observatory. During the 1894 opposition of Mars, Lowell and other observers recorded almost two hundred canals, a few of them apparently double. Schiaparelli, it seemed, was vindicated and his findings extended. Among other details, Lowell and his co-workers observed canals lacing cross the planet's dark areas, which once again argued against their being seas.[9]

But Lowell generated even more excitement and controversy 1895, when he produced a series of popular articles and lectures and published his book *Mars,* intended for the general public. Two similar volumes followed, *Mars and Its Canals* in 1906 and *Mars as the Abode of Life* in 1908. These were polished and well-produced works, and even to a modern planetary astronomer give an impression of great scholarship. However, reading them reveals that in general Lowell's theories did not advance but essentially remained the same as they were when he first plunged into astronomy. Mars, in his view, was peopled by an advanced race of intelligent beings (*not* necessarily human, as he often pointed out), who constructed canals to bring irrigation water to the vital fields where they grew the crops that sustained life in a world well advanced in its life cycle, and where water and oxygen were scarce and growing ever scarcer. The dark areas on Mars were vegetation, while the "canals" were actually bands of crops alongside the much narrower—and so unobservable from Earth—true canals.[10]

Not content to rely on visual observations alone, Lowell resorted to photography in an attempt to convince skeptics that the canals and other details he saw were real. This was not an easy task, for in the late nineteenth century it was still considered quite a feat to image one of the Martian polar caps, which often can be seen visually in a mere 3-inch telescope. However, beginning in 1905, Carl O. Lampland, and later Earl C. Slipher, began to take the first photographs of Mars that showed considerable detail. Quick on the draw as always, Lowell announced in 1905 that the canals of Mars had been photographed. The news was a worldwide sensation. This was probably the climax of the Martian furor and perhaps Lowell's finest hour.

Unfortunately for Lowell, the canals are not especially obvious on the original photographic plates, let alone on reproductions. What magazines and newspapers wanted in the worst way were big, clear images of Mars showing sharply defined canals arcing along the planet's surface—and these he could not provide.[11]

Lowell's problems were, in fact, insoluble. Part of the difficulty in taking good images of the red planet is due to the fact that even at the most favorable oppositions, its angular diameter is only about 25 seconds of arc, compared to some 1,800 for our Moon. In other words, Mars looks roughly as big as a single moderately large lunar crater. As a result, even telescopes with long focal lengths produce only tiny images that cover a relatively few "grains" of the photographic emulsion, with the result of losing all fine detail. If a lens is used to magnify that image, the light from the planet is spread out over a greater area, and exposures become longer—and the emulsions of Lowell's time were pitifully slow by modern standards. In turn, these longer exposures made it harder to "beat the seeing"—that is, to take advantage of the rare instants when Earth's atmosphere is steady along the light path between Mars and the telescope. Of course, with the benefit of hindsight, we now know that the overriding reason why neither the astronomers at Lowell Observatory nor those anywhere else were ever able to photograph the canals of Mars is that those features do not exist.

Just what did the early Lowell Observatory images (or any others until a few years ago, for that matter) actually show? Despite having examined thousands of original negative images of Mars taken at a number of observatories, I have never seen a single example of a "classic" canal. True, there were cases of more or less linear features, but they did not appear sharp and did not look narrow, though they did look as if they were on the verge of breaking up into masses of finer detail.[12] When these images were reproduced, and especially when rendered in mass publications such as newspapers and magazines, even more detail was lost. The resulting illustrations merely showed a fuzzy disk with some indistinct dark spots, perhaps one or both of the bright pole caps, depending on the Martian season, and possibly some bright, hazy cloud features. In general, the best photographs of Mars looked like poor drawings of the planet, and such images were certainly not the sort of dramatic evidence that the public had been led to expect.

Martian clouds sometimes appear to project into the dark side of the planet beyond the sunrise or sunset line on the planet. While such events are of relatively little interest astronomically, they were sometimes seized upon by editors eager to increase circulation as examples of attempts by Martians to communicate with Earthlings. This possibility made for some spectacular newspaper headlines, but astronomers did not take the possibility seriously.

Oppositions of Mars were relatively unfavorable in the years just before World War I, and as there was little definite news to report about Martians and their works, public interest in the subject inevitably ebbed. But Lowell's and Schiaparelli's canals already had received some severe body blows from which they would not recover—at least not in the minds of most professional astronomers.

In 1903 astronomer E. Walter Maunder reported that he had set a group of English schoolboys to making copies of an image of Mars and had gotten some very interesting results. When the original was set at such a distance from the viewers that its details were hard to make out, the resulting copies showed disks covered with networks of fine lines *even though the original contained no trace of such lines.* This was a repetition of some similar experiments made by the American theoretical astronomer Simon Newcomb in 1897, in which some of his colleagues drew canals where none existed; but the schoolboy element in Maunder's work lent a tinge of the ludicrous to the whole business of canals, a taint that never really went away.[13]

Direct observations of Mars further challenged Lowell's theories. As noted, the superb observer Barnard had never seen any canals with either the giant 36-inch reflector at Lick or the 40-inch at Yerkes Observatory. At the opposition of 1909, the last relatively favorable one for years, E. M. Antoniadi studied Mars intensely with the 33-inch refractor at Meudon Observatory in France, while George Ellery Hale and others at Mount Wilson in California were able to use the newly completed 60-inch reflector. The results from both telescopes were the same—no canals but lots of fine detail at moments of good seeing.[14]

In spite of this uniform negative evidence from large instruments, the possibility that at least some of the canals might be real hung on stubbornly in some quarters, though Lowell's sudden death in 1916 took a great deal of the heat out of the controversy. Two influential elementary astronomy textbooks published as late as 1945 and 1959 provide revealing examples of how some of Lowell's ideas just would not go away. Both works present the evidence for and against canals and both leave the existence of such features as still considered uncertain.[15] But, after all, the whole wonderful picture of a valiant civilization fighting to live on a dying planet was only a dream. It was the result of the tendency of the human eye and brain combined to "see" fine lines when confronted by a complex mass of detail at or just beyond the limit of visibility.

Some of the features that Lowell and other visual observers saw on Mars *are* real, of course. The pole caps do advance and retreat annually and do so irregularly and nonuniformly. There are darker and brighter areas of the planet, some of which change their appearance with the seasons and some of which change from year to year. But rather than being the results of Lowell saw as the sprouting and dying of crops, these changes—as we now know—are actually the results of windblown dust covering and uncovering different parts of the Mars surface at different times.

Interestingly, there were no confirmed sightings of any high mountains or deep valleys on Mars before spacecraft finally discovered titanic examples. However, there were a few hints, unrecognized until close-up photographs showed their true nature. A few mapped dark spots turned out to be enormous volcanoes, while a sometimes seen white spot once known as Nix Olympica (Snows of Olympus) turned out to be a sometimes cloud-shrouded shield volcano (similar to those on the islands of Hawaii) now dubbed Olympus Mons (Mount Olympus). It is the largest and highest known volcano in the solar system, and still was never detected through any telescope. One, but only one, of the "canals" was revealed as a chasm dwarfing the Grand Canyon. The very modest impressions made on the old-time visual observers by these stupendous structures shows vividly how difficult a job it is for Earth-based observers to detect such features on the red planet.

WATER ON MARS

Lowell was very good indeed at putting his views before the literate public across the world. In addition, his wealth, social standing, education, attainments, and urbanity gave him entrance to many forums.[16] Still, there was much more to his success than that. For one thing, he evidently believed sincerely in what he saw and said and wrote. For another, he put a tremendous amount of effort into amassing an enormous body of systematic observational material concerning Mars, an unprecedented achievement that drew general admiration. Finally, he was a superb speaker and an excellent writer, being most convincing in both roles. His public lectures, articles for highbrow magazines, and scientific publications were widely copied more or less accurately by the popular press. In spite of this popularity, and possibly in part because of it, Lowell was never generally accepted as an equal by the professional astronomers of his day.

This view of Lowell as an outsider by many professional astronomers is something of a puzzle. In his time he had about as good a technical education as a goodly number of "real" astronomers. The modern standard method of becoming an astronomer through conducting research leading to doctoral degree in the subject was just coming into vogue at that time, and quite a few workers in the field held only honorary doctorates (Keeler is an example); many were simply "Mr." in scientific publications.

Whatever the reason, Lowell was ignored, deprecated, or detested by many of his contemporaries. As astronomer and historian Donald E. Osterbrock of Lick Observatory has written, "The professional astronomers of his time never took Lowell seriously. To them he was a rank amateur who did not understand the methods of science."[17] That is a strong statement, but it is all too true. Perhaps the best example of this prejudice against Lowell is contained in the story of spectroscopic attempts to find indications of an atmosphere on Mars, and in particular water vapor.

As mentioned briefly in the previous chapter, visual spectroscopic attempts to detect gases in the atmosphere of Mars were a fiasco. In 1867 Huggins reported that he had seen absorption lines in the spectrum of Mars but concluded "that Mars' atmosphere is unlike ours." The French astronomer Jules Janssen weighed in in 1867. He hauled some sort of equipment up Mt. Etna in Sicily and announced to the world that he had found water vapor in the atmosphere of Mars—and on Saturn for good measure! Some time later the Italian Angelo Secchi claimed to have detected an atmosphere analogous to Earth's, and in 1873 Vogel announced that the red planet had an atmosphere like ours, one rich in water vapor. Maunder chimed in with another positive water detection report in 1877. The case looked good, for these positive results were made by established European astronomers who were true pioneers in spectroscopy.

But the outlook changed in 1894, when a young American at Lick Observatory, William W. Campbell, found no evidence at all for water vapor on Mars, setting a limit of about one quarter as much as in our own air. Further, he found no evidence that Mars had an extensive atmosphere of any kind. It is possible that that senior European scientists of that day did not take kindly to being contradicted by their brash juniors from across the Atlantic, but in any case Huggins (and his wife) and Vogel quickly responded. The Hugginses believed they had found evidence that Mars's atmosphere had gases in it similar to those on Earth and at least one substance that was not. Vogel reported positive results for oxygen and water vapor and also for a different, unknown gas. There were other observers in the field, but these were the major actors in the drama.

Vogel has a certain notoriety among today's planetary astronomers because of an 1895 pronouncement. Referring to the spectroscopic observations of the planets that he began in 1870, he wrote:

> Thanks to the excellent instruments which were at my disposal in the private observatory of Herr von Bülow, and to the extreme sensitiveness of my eye, I was able to see and to measure so many details in the spectra of the principal planets that no observations really subverting my results were to be expected in the future. As a matter of fact, neither the great instruments of modern times, nor the application of photography—so powerful in the field of celestial spectroscopy—has done more in this direction than to confirm the results of these early observations.[18]

In other words, studies of planetary spectra had gone about as far as they could go—ever. As we will see, this mistaken view had a long life.

The first effective attempts to apply photography to the spectroscopic study of Mars's atmosphere had to await the introduction of photographic plates sensitive to the longer wavelengths of light, yellow, orange, and red as opposed to violet and blue, because all the absorption features of oxygen and water vapor then known were in the yellow, orange, and red parts of the spectrum.

In 1895 and 1896 Campbell used some new emulsions sensitized to green, yellow, and orange, and found no difference between the spectra of Mars and of the Moon. In 1896 and 1897 Keeler at Allegheny Observatory made several photographs of Mars's spectrum and found no difference between it and that of the Moon when both were high in the sky. However, Millochau at Meudon, using plates sensitized to red light, where the bands were even stronger, thought that he did have evidence that Mars (and Venus, for good measure) had atmospheres similar to our own, with particular reference to what was then known as "aqueous vapor."[19]

By 1908 Vesto M. Slipher (older brother of Earl C. Slipher) at Lowell was able to use emulsions that were sensitive almost to the infrared (to get ahead of our story, the infrared would prove to be the spectral region that held the key to this quest). He too found evidence for water on Mars—but nothing else. The Lowell results were particularly significant because Frank W. Very made an intensive photometric examination of the spectral plates. This was a pioneering use of a technique that eventually replaced visual estimates of the strengths of spectral bands and lines by quantitative ones. Very found both water and oxygen enhanced in the Martian spectra.[20]

But about then matters took a complicated and somewhat underhanded turn. All the early spectroscopic studies of Mars, and indeed of the rest of the universe except for our Sun, had been done at relatively low dispersion. That is, the measurements were made on spectra where the colors were not spread out much and hence only major features, and not fine details, could be seen. In that case, the right way to look for a gas that occurs on a planet and on Earth is to compare the spectrum of that planet with that of the Moon (which has no atmosphere) at a time when both are at the same height above the horizon, so that Earth's contribution is the same in both cases. But in 1905, Lowell published a new and original way of attacking the problem. He suggested using *high*-dispersion spectra and looking at individual lines in the complex bands of molecular spectra.

There were other novel features to his method as well, for Lowell's technique relied on the Doppler shift. He reasoned that if Earth and a planet were moving toward or away from each other at a relatively high speed at the time of observation, individual spectral lines *of the same gas* formed in the atmospheres of the two planets would be shifted slightly in wavelength with respect to each other. As a result of this shift the lines due to the two planets might be separated, or if not, at least the apparent center of the terrestrial line might be displaced. This situation meant that the best time to observe was not at opposition, when a planet was closest to Earth, but rather at "quadrature," when the planet was 90 degrees away from the Sun in our sky and had the greatest line-of-sight velocity with respect to Earth.[21] This was eventually to become a standard procedure, but at the time it was quite a change from the old ways. Lowell's innovation was out of the ordinary for the astronomy of its day, which still relied heavily on gathering vast amounts of routine data in a routine way, and goes a long way toward showing that his critics were wrong to dismiss him as a mere incompetent amateur in the worst sense of that word.

Unfortunately, Lowell's new technique demanded lots of light, and so needed a telescope of large aperture, which his observatory did not possess. Still, he did have Vesto Slipher try out the method on Mars with the available instruments, and the inconclusive results were published in 1905.[22]

Early in 1908 Slipher tried again, using photographic plates that were bathed in a special solution to make them sensitive to near infrared light. As a result he could examine an absorption band that was more sensitive to the presence of small amounts of water vapor than were the features used by previous workers. Slipher found that this so-called "a" band was stronger in spectra of Mars than in those of the Moon, and this result led him to write that "the spectrograph has revealed the presence of water in the atmosphere of Mars."[23]

Now Campbell reentered the picture. During the opposition of 1909 he observed Mars from the top of Mount Whitney during the summer dry season in central California. He thus got above much of the water vapor in Earth's atmosphere and certainly had less of that gas to contend with than any previous observer. On the negative side, no large telescope could be hauled to the summit, so he had to be content with using the old comparative method with low-dispersion spectra of Mars and the Moon. Nevertheless, his negative results showed that there was much less water vapor in the atmosphere of Mars than above Mount Whitney at the times of observation. Campbell followed the remarkably modern method of first announcing his findings by means of the Associated Press![24]

He followed up by observing Mars in 1910 at high dispersion with the 36-inch telescope at Lick. In passing, his report says something about how at least some science was done in those days. Other persons were responsible for making and adjusting the spectrograph, taking all the exposures, making all the measurements on the photographic plates, and doing all the necessary calculations—but Campbell was the sole author of the resulting paper on the subject.

His conclusions were that "the quantity of water vapor existing above unit area in the equatorial atmosphere of Mars was certainly less than one-fifth that existing above Mount Hamilton under the excellent conditions prevailing on February 2nd," and that "likewise the quantity of oxygen above unit area on Mars must be small in comparison with that in the Earth's atmosphere." As always, Campbell was careful not to claim that there was *no* water vapor or oxygen in the Martian atmosphere but only that there must be less than what he could detect. This distinction was often lost sight of in the popular press, and even among some professional astronomers, but it would stand his scientific reputation in good stead half a century later.

But there was also something in his 1910 paper that would stain Campbell's reputation, for he claimed that in 1896 he had "realized" the advantages of the Doppler-shift method. He had not used it in the past, he explained, because the photographic plates available then were not sensitive to the orange and red regions of the spectrum, where all the prominent water-vapor and oxygen lines lie. Significantly, Campbell made no mention at all of Lowell's earlier paper on the Doppler method or of V. M. Slipher's article describing attempts to use that method on Mars.[25]

Others soon noticed the curious omissions, and Campbell explained in print that he had been out of the country when the Lowell and Slipher papers on the Doppler method appeared, and that both he and his colleague had been unaware of the articles until the oversights in the 1910 paper were called to their attention. If so, Campbell was admitting that he had not read important articles by researchers he knew to be working on the same topic as he was. Lick astronomer and historian Donald R. Osterbrock calls it "a damning indictment of Campbell himself"—a just judgment. The whole sad episode illustrates that there was an unfair prejudice against Lowell on the part of at least one professional astronomer, and that developments in headline-grabbing subjects like water (and, by a wrong but attractive inference, life) on Mars often revealed that scientists, too, are only human.[26] Campbell's results on the upper limits to water vapor and oxygen in the atmosphere of Mars, however, were correct and have stood the test of time.

PROPHET ALMOST FORGOTTEN

Much of the furor over Mars, and indeed about other bodies in the solar system, should never have happened. As early as 1870, G. Johnstone Stoney delivered to the Royal Dublin Society a talk in which he touched on the absence of a lunar atmosphere. He pointed out that the then newly developed "kinetic theory of gases" showed that our satellite's feeble gravity could not hold on to gases, and later showed that Earth could not keep free hydrogen (both of these statements are correct). But then he went on to state that probably no water could remain on Mars and made a strong case that Mars's polar caps, clouds, hazes, and surface frost were made of "dry ice" (frozen carbon dioxide), and that its atmosphere was composed of nitrogen and carbon dioxide. Stoney himself noted that his researches had appeared only imperfectly in printed accounts, and so he prepared a series of articles for the *Astrophysical Journal*.[27]

In these speculations Stoney was partly wrong and partly right. He was dead wrong about the absence of water on Mars and about nitrogen being a substantial component of the red planet's atmosphere. On the other hand, he was dead right about carbon dioxide being a major atmospheric gas, responsible for many of the polar cap, cloud, haze, and frost phenomena. His researches showed all too well the tendency of scientists to attribute too many things to their pet theories, for in fact both H_2O and CO_2 sublimate and fall as snow on Mars, though that dual role would take a long time to be established. Still, Stoney was far ahead of his time, and it is unfortunate that for decades his contributions would be neglected. Only in the 1960s was his work widely resurrected among the reborn fraternity of planetary scientists, and even today his name is often not even mentioned in histories of the subject.

In the early years of the century, E. C. Slipher photographed the spectra of all four giant planets. He found that the mysterious dark bands, none of which corresponded to features due to gases in Earth's atmosphere, grew stronger from Jupiter to Saturn to Uranus to Neptune. He also concluded that there was free hydrogen in the atmospheres of Uranus and Neptune. Curiously that indeed turned out to be true, but Slipher's observations actually were erroneous.[28]

Uranus and Neptune showed no definite spots, but spectroscopy offered the opportunity of using the Doppler shift to find their rotation speeds and thus periods. Uranus was almost "pole-on" to Earth at the turn of the century, but the situation slowly improved, and within a few years Lowell and Slipher had derived a rotation period of somewhat less than 11 hours, compared to the modern value of a little over 17 hours.[29] Neptune, with its fainter spectrum, proved a tougher nut to crack. Not until 1928 did Joseph H. Moore and Donald H. Menzel publish a period of just under 16 hours, close to today's value.[30]

Unfortunately, work in planetary spectroscopy died down after the flurry of activity in the opening years of the twentieth century. Part of the reason for the decline in interest was the lack of positive new results. Scientists of the time knew that Earth's atmosphere produced spectral lines due to oxygen and water vapor, but except for the dark features due to an unknown gas or gases in the atmospheres of the four giant outer planets, there was no spectroscopic evidence for any other gaseous substance on any other planet except our own. This was hardly a situation favorable to generating interest among observers.

Another reason for the lack of progress was the difficulty in producing photographic plates (or any other sort of "detector") that had good sensitivity in the red and especially in the infrared. Astronomers, chemists, and hobbyists alike tried soaking photographic plates in all sorts of solutions in attempts to "sensitize" emulsions to longer and longer wavelengths, but results were discouraging for a long time. Finally, there was a real shortage of large telescopes with spectrographs designed to work at longer wavelengths. Observers were getting good results on stars and nebulae with spectra taken at short wavelengths (mainly in the violet and blue at that time), and few astronomers saw an urgent need to extend the wavelength coverage.

For all these reasons, years would pass before any significant advances would be made in planetary spectroscopy, and in particular it would take a half-century to answer the question of whether there is water on Mars.

104   PLANETARY ASTRONOMY

When these advances finally came, it was because astronomers had better tools to tackle the job, although even then, progress was mainly attributable to the efforts of a few imaginative individuals rather than to the new technology being pressed into use.

A NEW BIRTH OF THE SOLAR SYSTEM

During the nineteenth century the nebular hypothesis held sway among astronomers and the general public as the generally accepted theory of how the Sun and planets came to be. The formation of planetary systems as a natural feature of the formation of their central stars was part of that theory, so that it was widely believed that solar systems, along with life in some form, were common and widespread. But that commonly held opinion was soon to change drastically.

Sometime just before 1900, the American geologist Thomas C. Chamberlain began to have serious doubts about the nebular hypothesis. He noted that, according to that "accepted" theory, planets condensed from a hot nebula and then cooled, along with the Sun (the powering of stars by thermonuclear reactions was then of course unknown), in what was essentially a straight line to a frozen death. This established view seemed plausible when the only terrestrial ice ages known were relatively recent, but Chamberlain began to have his doubts when evidence for very ancient ice ages began to surface. The more he looked into the Kant-Laplace theory, the more difficulties he found in reconciling it with known facts about the solar system, so he created a new theory.[31]

To complement his knowledge of geology, Chamberlain recruited a colleague from the University of Chicago, Forest Ray Moulton, a theoretical astronomer whose specialty was celestial motions. The result of their combined efforts has become known as the Chamberlain-Moulton Planetesimal Hypothesis. In its initial form the theory assumed the previous existence of the Sun and a surrounding nebula, which was a step backward from the nebular hypothesis, wherein our star and its retinue of planets formed at the same time. The Chamberlain-Moulton theory was modified many times over the years by its creators and others as difficulties showed up in earlier versions, but in its many forms it always retains the Sun as older than the rest of the solar system—something we now know is not true.

At first the nebula out of which the solar system formed was taken to be a spiral, but that assumption eventually had to be dropped when the true natures and enormous sizes of spiral galaxies became known. Early on the origin of the nebula was attributed to the chance close encounter of two stars—one of them our Sun. During such an event great tides would be raised on both bodies, reinforcing the luminaries' normal eruptive activity, and if they approached near enough to each other, material could be torn off them and some matter might go into orbit about the stars.[32] Because the near collision of two stars eventually played a large role in this and related explanations, "encounter" theory might be a better name for the whole process than "planetesimal" hypothesis and in fact is often used.

Of course, the initially hot stellar matter would soon cool, but from the first, densities in the nebula were very uneven, with "knots" of higher densities than average, while later there would form small, solid, cold bodies with a wide range of masses—the planetesimals. The more massive of these objects swept up the ones with smaller masses, and the heftiest of all acted as the nuclei of the present planets.[33] For a time, many considered the spiral nebulae as clear examples of the process "caught in the act." From Chamberlain's point of view this collecting together of cold, solid bodies to form planets was important, as it allowed for the possibility of ice ages early in Earth's history.

The planetesimal hypothesis incorporated some up-to-date knowledge. By the end of the nineteenth century, physicists knew that gases are made up of molecules that are in rapid motion. It was determined that speeds of those molecules increase as the temperature does and that in a mixture of gases at the same temperature, lighter molecules such as hydrogen move faster than heavier ones such as oxygen. Thus, a gas molecule at the top of an atmosphere, if moving fast enough, could escape the clutches of gravity and leave the planet forever.

This possibility has important consequences for planetary atmospheres. First, the light gases will be lost before the heavier ones on a particular planet. Second, more massive planets, all else being equal, will be able to hold on to lighter molecules. These discoveries neatly explained the low densities of the giant planets, for they are massive enough to hold on to gases such as hydrogen. It also explained why Mercury had no proven atmosphere, Mars only a tenuous one, and Venus and Earth substantial ones—the different strengths of their surface gravities were responsible. However, none of the inner planets was massive enough to retain substantial amounts of light gases.[34]

As a geologist, Chamberlain naturally tried to use his new theory to explain features on Earth. Unfortunately, one among many problems he faced in this task was his ignorance of continental drift, the movement of large sections of Earth's crust ("plates") with respect to each other and to the body of the planet. He assumed that the present arrangement of

Earth's continents and seas was pretty much as it had been in the distant past and that this arrangement contained valuable clues about our planet's early development. In this he was wrong, as he was in many of his ingenious speculations about our planet's history.[35]

Moulton presented the new theory to his astronomical peers, using the impressive mathematical arguments of celestial mechanics to buttress his case. But he too ran up against the rudimentary state of many other sciences at the time. For example, he assumed that the terrestrial planets, Mercury, Mars, Venus, and especially Earth, had shrunk substantially since they were formed. Such contraction was widely accepted until after the middle of the twentieth century because it seemed the only way to form long mountain chains such as the Appalachians, which appeared to require that some sort of powerful compressive force raise them. Once again, unfamiliarity with continental drift led able scientists astray, for actually the Appalachians were thrown up the last time that Europe and North America crashed into each other.[36]

In just a few years at the beginning of the twentieth century, the nebular hypothesis lost its position as the generally accepted explanation for the origin of the solar system. Its formidable rivals were encounter theories, typified by the Chamberlain-Moulton thesis, which may have owed some of their popularity to the fact that they lent themselves more easily to mathematical calculation of what happened, as opposed to the more qualitative nature of the nebular hypothesis. But there were also severe problems with the nebular theory which the planetesimal hypothesis might overcome. As regards the most serious of these, it looked as if the new theory might offer an explanation as to why the planets, instead of the much more massive Sun, have most of the angular momentum (the kind of momentum a flywheel has) in the solar system. This unusual distribution was a seemingly fatal flaw in the nebular hypothesis. In any case, the encounter theories soon became well respected.

Perhaps the most puzzling aspect of encounter theories in early decades of the twentieth century is how such improbable explanations became so widely popular so quickly when there was no hard evidence for them. Astronomers of the time were well aware of the vast distances between stars in all but a few cases (the centers of globular clusters, for example, are an exception), the relatively slow speeds of stars with respect to each other, and thus the incredibly small chance that *any* two stars in our Milky Way should meet each other in a reasonable time span on such terms as to form a solar system. In addition, over the years the required circumstances of the encounter became ever more restricted due to attempts to answer problems with the theory that kept coming up, and which reduced the probability of such an event to lower and lower levels. As a side effect, this improbability had a drastic effect on the attitude of many scientists and some of the general public toward the always popular topics of other solar systems and possible life in them. From being considered common—perhaps universal—only a few years before, other planetary systems now came to seem more likely to be very rare. Scientists began to wonder whether our solar system might indeed be the only one; in other words, whether our setting might be a "cosmic freak." A lonely thought.[37]

THE AGE PROBLEM

During the late nineteenth and early twentieth centuries, estimates of the age of Earth kept getting larger and larger.[38] Even as early as about 1909, our planet was known to be many tens or hundreds of millions of years old—a far cry from current estimates of about 4.6 billion years but old enough to pose a serious problem.[39] The difficulty was that the Sun apparently had been pouring out energy at roughly its present rate for all that vast stretch of time, for their was no geologic evidence that Earth's surface had ever melted or completely frozen over in that whole long interval. Scientists of the time had absolutely no idea how our star could have done so.

At the turn of the century, the most widely accepted theory of solar energy production was the contraction theory of the German scientist Hermann Helmholtz. In this hypothesis, the Sun was slowly but steadily shrinking and in the process turning gravitational potential energy into heat and light. (A clock driven by falling weights, such as an old-fashioned grandfather clock, is a humble illustration of how gravitational energy can be turned into another form, though in that case the result is the motion of the clock's gears and hands instead of heat and light.) This process could power our star for tens of millions of years, which seemed like plenty of time to scientists of the last half of the nineteenth century, when Earth's age was believed to be a few or a few tens of millions of years. However, the much greater ages revealed by later research dwarfed the Helmholtz time scale. Scientists of the era were completely baffled.[40] It would be decades before it became clear that the fusion of hydrogen nuclei into those of helium at the center of the Sun could power our star for billions of years.

MINOR MATTERS

Though asteroid discoveries continued apace, and the occasional comet made an appearance, pickings were slim when it came to detecting other new solar system objects. Success came with photographic surveys of the sky around Jupiter, which picked up a number of faint satellites orbiting far beyond the moons previously known. Charles D. Perrine found Jupiter VI in 1904 and Jupiter VII the next year, Pierre Melotte discovered Jupiter VIII in 1908, and Seth B. Nicholson rounded out the prewar picture by nabbing Jupiter IX in 1914. Curiously, these satellites remained nameless until the Space Age, when they were dubbed Himalia, Elara, Pasiphae, and Sinope, respectively. All four are only a few miles across, have orbits that are far from circular, and are so distant from Jupiter that the Sun's gravitational influence causes substantial changes in their orbits over the years. The last two proved especially interesting because they move in retrograde paths, opposite to the motions of the previously known satellites and the direction of the planet's rotation.[41]

HALLEYMANIA

The perihelion passage of comet Halley in 1910 was of enormous interest around the world. Astronomers made elaborate preparations to observe the body and tremendous publicity whipped up the public almost to the point of hysteria. There was a special worry that when we passed through the comet's tail, the poison gases in it would kill all life on Earth. Of course the material in the tail was so rarefied that its effect on our planet was nil. Halley passed over the face of the Sun as seen from Earth and, as might be expected, astronomers saw no trace of its passage. These negative observations showed clearly that any solid nucleus must be no more than a few miles across.[42]

Despite all the interest, little new was learned about Halley in particular or comets in general. Once the excitement of the moment died down, some astronomers took their time to analyze and publish their observations. For example, the results of a photographic history of the 1910 apparition did not appear until 1931.[43] In addition to direct images, astronomers took many photographs of the comet's spectrum ("spectrograms") but were still hampered in interpreting these by the undeveloped state of physics at the time. The first real advance came in 1911, when Karl Schwarzschild and Eric Kron proposed that molecules in a comet's tail absorb specific wavelengths of sunlight and then reemit those same—or longer—wavelengths. By this time cyanogen (CN) had been identified in comets, but identifications of more molecules, let alone good estimates of characteristics such as their abundances, still lay in the future.[44]

One bright spot was laboratory confirmation of the pressure of light. This radiation pressure was measured independently by Peter Lebedew in

Moscow and by E. F. Nichols and G. F. Hull at Dartmouth College in the United States.[45] Now there was at least one definite mechanism for forming and shaping comet tails, and scientists were quick to take advantage of the situation. Still, the suspicion lingered that electrical forces of some kind might play some part in cometary phenomena, an idea that turned out to be correct.[46]

The slow progress in our knowledge of comets during the decades just before World War I mirrored the situation of planetary astronomy in general. New knowledge came only rarely, and there seemed little prospect that the situation would change in the foreseeable future. But at the same time, as solar system studies were mired down, stellar astronomy advanced dramatically and soon completely dominated the interests of astronomers and the public alike.

THE WIDER UNIVERSE BECKONS

While solar system research inched forward in the decades just before World War I, things were very different in more distant realms. Astronomers who studied the stars, the Milky Way, and the mysterious nebulae were advancing along roads that would lead to spectacular and unexpected new knowledge.

While there are only a few major planets in the solar system, there are innumerable stars, and in the last half of the nineteenth century astronomers began to record the spectra of these distant suns. The work went slowly as long as visual observations were the rule, but when photographic recording of these stellar rainbows became practical, the number of stars for which spectra were recorded became—astronomical.

The most curious and unexpected thing about stellar spectra was that all but a tiny fraction could be grouped into just a few "classes." Not only that, but most of these classes could be arranged in a single sequence with one type merging smoothly into another. Astronomers of the time did not know just what all this meant, but they suspected that the spectral sequence was an indication of stellar evolution (*aging* is perhaps a better term). In other words, as a star grew older, its spectrum changed. The British astronomer Norman Lockyer (who began as an amateur) was responsible for one temporarily popular theory of stellar evolution. In his view, a star began as a vast, rarefied, and cool nebula. As it contracted under the influence of gravity, its temperature increased to a maximum and then slowly decreased until only a burnt-out cinder remained. Though wrong, schemes of this kind were the best available until the mid-twentieth century.[47]

Early in the twentieth century, another surprising fact about stars emerged. Astronomers had been determining the distances to even more of these luminaries, and eventually it became possible to compare the intrinsic brightnesses of these objects with their spectral types. In a perfect example of how advances in our knowledge are often made simultaneously by several people when the time is ripe, two scientists independently discovered that most stars seemed to be one of two types. A Dane, Ejnar Hertzsprung, and an American, Henry Norris Russell, showed that among stars there are "giants" and "dwarfs" (like the Sun), distinguished by their different intrinsic brightnesses and sizes. The distinction is greatest for yellowish and, especially, reddish objects.[48] At the time no one knew the true cause of this dichotomy, but it seemed to fit well with then popular theories of stellar evolution.

Meanwhile, astronomers had stumbled across a method that provided a means of estimating celestial distances that are vastly greater than those measurable by means of annual stellar parallax. The technique involves a class of variable stars known as Cepheid variables, the brightnesses of which vary periodically. Most important to astronomers is the fact that such a star's period is related to its *absolute* luminosity, and so measurements of the period and the *apparent* brightness yield its distance. Unlike parallax, the Cepheid method is independent of distance, as long as the star in question appears bright enough to register on, for instance, a long-exposure photographic plate. Even in 1913, it was clear that astronomers were no longer limited to the puny tens of light years available from the laboriously derived stellar parallaxes; Cepheids held out the hope of measuring distances of tens of millions of light years.[49] Now scientists had a technique for plumbing truly deep space, and wide new vistas opened to them.

Perhaps the most puzzling astronomical discovery of the early twentieth century was made at Lowell Observatory and did not directly concern the solar system. Percival Lowell was interested in the "white" nebulae, and in particular the mysterious spirals, which some scientists believed were solar systems in the process of formation, and he asked Vesto Slipher to study their spectra. The nebulae were faint and the Lowell 24-inch refractor was ill suited to the task, but by 1910 Slipher had photographed the spectrum of the Great Nebula in Andromeda (the nearest spiral to the Milky way, as we know now). He found that the nebula was approaching us at a speed of some 300 kilometers per second, which was then considered phenomenal. Over the next few years Slipher investigated other, fainter nebulae and found even higher line-of-sight speeds. Curiously, except for a few bright and thus perhaps relatively nearby examples, the rest of the nebulae that he observed were all moving *away* from Earth. Slipher had discovered the expanding universe! The possibility that the universe as a whole was growing ever larger had never even been imagined before, and it would take most scientists some time to believe the straightforward evidence in this case.

In 1913, Slipher's spectrograms showed for the first time that at least some white nebulae were rotating. By 1917 he felt that his nebular work supported the old "island universe" concept, in which the spirals were enormous systems of stars far beyond the Milky Way. Evidence in favor of this view was building up in the first part of the twentieth century, and it indicated a universe vastly larger and more mysterious than astronomers just a few years earlier had ever dreamed of. Once more the studies of the solar system dwindled in importance in the face of awesome revelations about the more distant cosmos.[50]

It is a revealing commentary on the mainstream astronomy of that day that Slipher's advances in our knowledge of objects far beyond the planets—and he made others in addition to those that mentioned here—came from an observatory founded to study the solar system and were encouraged by a man widely thought to be obsessed with the idea of intelligent life on Mars. Part of the explanation of this curious circumstance was that in large part the astronomical institutions of the day were engaged in monumental programs of routine observations: constructing the *Carte du Ciel*, measuring celestial positions, cataloguing stellar spectra, determining line-of-sight velocities, amassing double-star observations, and the like. Then, as before and since, there was room for striking advances on the part of those with the imagination to rise above the routine and try something new.

"MODERN" PHYSICS EMERGES

In 1896, a French physicist, Henri Becquerel, discovered the phenomenon of natural radioactivity, and in the years following his discovery scientists around the world made many intensive studies of this previously unsuspected phenomenon. It soon became clear that the alchemists' ancient dream of transmuting one element into another—a concept that was in disrepute late in the nineteenth century—was not only possible but was going on continuously all around us. The nuclei of radioactive elements spontaneously gave off charged particles (helium nuclei or electrons) or high energy "light" (gamma rays) and in so doing, changed into other elements.[51]

Numerous scientists investigated the obvious possibility that natural radioactivity could provide the energy source for the Sun and other stars, but the results were discouraging. The known radioactive elements at the time were rare in nature and there were just not enough of them to do the job. Another problem with this theory was that the rate at which nuclei disintegrated seemed independent of pressure, temperature, density, or any other physical condition, so that it seemed difficult to explain how radioactivity could account for the vast variety observed among stars.[52] It was only decades later that experiment and theory together showed that when temperatures reach tens of millions of degrees—and even higher—nuclear reactions in relatively dense stellar cores can indeed provide the energy sources that enable stars to shine for billions of years.

But though it was a flop as a source of stellar energy, natural radioactivity was to provide geologists and planetary scientist with priceless information—the actual ages of rocks. Not relative ages, not ages based on the assumed rates at which various rock layers were laid down, not ages derived from estimates of how fast mountain ranges were worn down, but real ages *in years*.

The basic idea behind the method of radioactive dating is that the nucleus of a naturally radioactive atom breaks down into a lighter one of a "daughter" element at a constant rate. Perhaps this daughter breaks down into a "granddaughter," and so on in a chain of decays. Eventually, however, every such sequence ends with a stable nucleus. Thus, the amount of parent nuclei continually decreases, while the amount of "end point" nuclei continually increases. The important feature of this process is that the rate of every step in such a decay chain can be measured in the laboratory.

Now if all the nuclei involved are "locked up" so that none can escape from a body, we can measure the amount of each and then calculate an age. This method works only for certain types of solid rocks and minerals, and even then it only tells us when the rock solidified, or perhaps when it was last at a high temperature or shocked by a collision (some materials can be lost in those circumstances). There are a host of other problems with radioactive dating that had to be dealt with over the following years, but it was clear even early on that at last scientists had found the a key to measuring the age of the Earth and perhaps even that of the solar system.[53]

A later and very different development at first appeared to have little bearing on astronomy. In 1905, Albert Einstein, a Swiss physicist, published what became known as the special theory of relativity. This dealt with the fact that there appeared to be no standard of absolute rest in nature, and in particular, that the speed of light was observed to be the same no matter in what direction the observer was moving. Einstein made the startling assumption that the measured speed of light in empty space was *always* the same, and that any results to the contrary were the result of the observers' measuring rods changing their lengths and the observers' clocks changing their rates.[54]

In 1916, Einstein followed the special theory of relativity with a general theory of relativity. This was an even more startling change from the science of the past, for it connected mass, and thus gravity, with the geometry of space itself. Unfortunately, except for the few scholars who understood what Einstein was saying, "relativity" was wrongly interpreted to mean that "all things are relative." Not so! Actually, general relativity assumed as a basic premise that all physical laws, when properly stated, are absolute and unchanging.[55]

Although special and general relativity seemed initially to hold little interest for astronomers, within a few years they led to spectacular advances in our knowledge of the physical universe and even of the solar system. Curiously, these spectacular advances contributed to the sense that planetary astronomy had become a sort of charming and antique backwater of modern science. The next half-century would be a grim time for planetary studies, which would sink to the level of being barely tolerated by serious astronomers, while stellar, galactic, and extragalactic research went from one astounding triumph to another. This was to be the nadir of solar system research, a long slumber due in part to the lasting influence of Percival Lowell. As Gerard de Vaucouleurs, no mean planetary astronomer himself, often declared to me, "Percival Lowell killed planetary astronomy!" This may exaggerate the matter—but not by much. And when the end of this sorry situation came decades later, it was through developments that only Edgar Allen Poe, Jules Verne, H. G. Wells, and their like could have imagined.

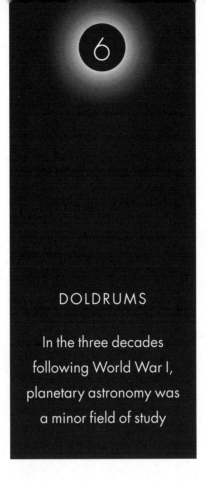

DOLDRUMS

In the three decades
following World War I,
planetary astronomy was
a minor field of study

World War I brought a worldwide disruption of astronomical research. By late 1918 much of Europe was prostrate and, burdened by enormous human, financial, and physical losses, the continent faced hunger and disease. In vivid contrast, the United States of America, largely untouched by the ravages of war, retained a robust economy that could support astronomical research on a large scale. Studies of stars, the Milky Way galaxy, and the vast universe beyond produced a host of amazing and unexpected revelations that captured the interest of scientists and the public alike. During the same period, however, planetary astronomy became a backwater, a relatively barren field of study, despite a few important advances made possible by new and improved equipment, techniques, and knowledge of physics.

The visionary American astronomer George Ellery Hale had shown that really big reflecting telescopes were not only possible but also provided the only practicable way to achieve very large apertures and as a result great light-gathering power. After the 100-inch telescope joined the 60-inch on Mount Wilson in 1917, the pair of California giant telescopes enjoyed a monopoly on many fields of astronomical research for many years. The two large telescopes at Mount Wilson Observatory played a major role in the dominance of American astronomy on the world stage for decades to come. Telescope size alone was not much of a help to solar system researchers, however, and until the advent of the Space Age, only a handful of the advances in astronomy involved the Sun's family. The dry spell would be a long one.

THE NEW "NEW ASTRONOMY"

During the years between the two world wars humanity's concept of the universe outside the solar system changed beyond recognition, and astronomers' interests were drawn farther and farther away from our own star's family. There are some problems in describing this work because there is no universal agreement as to which advances were, are, or will be the most important and long lasting in the history of science, and because it is awkward to attempt to place simultaneous developments in widely different areas of astronomy into strict chronological order. But progress there was, and it came in epic proportions.

Beginning in 1916, Harlow Shapley of Harvard University used Cepheid variables, along with other criteria, to determine the distances of globular star clusters, giant balls of hundreds of thousands of stars. He found that all are relatively far from Earth and was able to plot their three-dimensional positions with respect to the Sun. Curiously, almost all of these objects lie in one half of our sky, and Shapley realized that this peculiar distribution might tell us something important about the Milky Way and our place in it. If the globulars were actually distributed roughly symmetrically about the center of the Milky Way, that circumstance indicated that we were near the edge of the system, off to one side, so to speak, instead of near the center as was generally assumed at the time. Moreover, his studies indicated that we are some 50,000 light years (the distance light travels in a year) from the center of our system, which must be of gigantic size (current distance estimates are about half of Shapley's, but the Milky Way is still considered a relatively large galaxy).[1]

Using Cepheid variables and additional, less reliable types of distance indicators, other astronomers, including Edwin Hubble at Mount Wilson, showed that objects such as the Large and Small Magellanic Clouds and the Great Andromeda Nebula were actually vast collections of stars far removed from the Milky Way. These results firmly reestablished the old "island universe" idea that spiral galaxies (and elliptical and irregular types as well) were vast systems of stars and nebulae like our own Milky Way.[2]

Hubble, along with his colleagues at Mount Wilson, also followed up on V. M. Slipher's earlier discovery that most galaxies appeared to be fleeing from us. With the world's largest telescopes at their disposal, these astronomers demonstrated that, except for some of the Milky Way's immediate neighbors, all galaxies indeed are receding from us. In addition, they confirmed that the more distant a galaxy is, the faster it is fleeing. These findings indicated that, hard though the idea was to accept, three-dimensional space itself was blowing up like the surface of an enormous balloon, only in three dimensions instead of two.[3]

If this concept were true, one could "look backward" in imagination and ask if there had been a time when all galaxies, all matter, and indeed all space had been confined within infinitesimal bounds. If so, that would mean that the universe has a definite age, one measured in billions of years instead of the trillions—or infinity—that generally was assumed at the time. While some theoreticians were enthusiastic about the possibility that the rate of expansion might be able to help us decide among the myriad possibilities of "model universes" allowed by general relativity, other scientists found it hard to accept that inflation. Today, however, its reality is universally accepted.[4]

Advances were not limited to deep space. Developments in physics now enabled astronomers to uncover a vast amount of detail about stellar physical properties. Among these were the chemical compositions, pressures, and temperatures of stars' surface layers. For example, much to astronomers' surprise hydrogen, the lightest and simplest element, turned out to be by far the most common element. Similarly, scientists gained new understanding about gaseous nebulae. Once considered impossible, the study of the physical properties of stars and nebulae now became a matter of hard work at observing and calculating.[5]

Knowledge of stellar interiors improved as well. Scientists made substantial progress toward determining just how the Sun and other stars could pour forth abundant energy for so many years. During the 1920s and 1930s, there was accumulating evidence that the building up of atomic nuclei, or "fusion," rather than their disintegration or the annihilation of matter, provides the primary stellar energy source. Since hydrogen nuclei, which consist of only a single positively charged proton each, are the most common ones in stars, it was natural to look for ways in which hydrogen could be built up into heavier and more complex nuclei.

As early as 1926, British scientist Arthur S. Eddington championed this idea and in its defense penned the classic sentence, "We do not argue with the critic who urges that the stars are not hot enough for this process; we tell him to go and find *a hotter place*."[6] Another pioneer, today unfortunately a largely unsung one, was the British astronomer R. D'E. Atkinson, who as early as 1931 published extensive articles on the subject.[7]

But while numerous scientists had a hand in the development, it was Hans Bethe, a German scientist working in the United States, who made the real breakthrough in 1938. His candidate for the Sun's energy source was the complex "carbon cycle." In this process carbon nuclei act as a sort of catalyst, being changed into the nuclei of other elements but reemerging at the end as carbon. The important net result of the carbon cycle is that four hydrogen nuclei are transmuted into one helium nucleus, and a significant amount of energy is released during this process. We now know that the carbon cycle is the main energy source only for stars more massive than our own, while the so-called "proton-proton" mechanism powers our luminary and other less massive objects. Still, scientists in 1938 for the first time had a specific explanation of how the Sun could have shone at more or less its current brightness for billions of years in the past, and would do so into the future, without greatly changing its size.[8] Of course, few at the time imagined that in the future thermonuclear reactions would become of immense practical importance for good and evil alike.

These are only a few of the many advances made just in the two decades following World War I in our understanding of the universe, but they serve to illustrate how exciting it was to be an astronomer in that era, and how entirely new and previously unimagined areas of research opened up.

STUDIES OF THE SOLAR SYSTEM

While the General Theory of Relativity perhaps had its most important use in investigating the structure of the universe at large, it also had an impact much closer to Earth, for it precisely explained the anomalously large "advance in the perihelion" of Mercury. According to general relativity, a massive and relatively concentrated object such as the Sun distorts the very geometry of space in its vicinity. Thus, for example, in the solar neighborhood the Pythagorean theorem need not hold true, and the interior angles of a triangle need not add up to exactly 180 degrees. In the case of our star the departure from familiar Euclidean geometry is small, but it is sufficient to account for the Mercury's previously unaccounted-for motion. Hence the need for an "intra-Mercurian" planet was buried once and for all. In addition, this success for a long time provided one of the few convincing proofs of the truth of general relativity.

The status of planetary work among mainstream astronomers of this period is well illustrated by a peripheral remark of the American astronomer Theodore Dunham, Jr. Of work he did at Mount Wilson in the 1920s and 1930s, he wrote: "Whenever the seeing was so bad as to make stellar exposures ineffective, the time was devoted to attempts to photograph the spectrum of the planets."[9] In other words, when conditions were hopeless for doing "real" astronomy, the big telescopes would be allowed to turn toward the planets. When the seeing is poor, it is not a good time to do planetary spectroscopy either, but Dunham's statement gives a good indication of the relative importance of planetary studies at the time.[10]

Nevertheless, there were advances in our knowledge of the solar system. Using what telescope time they could get, observers at Mount Wilson took better and better spectra of the planets from time to time during the 1920s and 1930s, first in visible light and later, when improved photographic plates became available, in the near infrared. The results were mixed. In the case of Mars, despite some false alarms, their spectra continued to show no evidence whatever for the presence of water vapor or oxygen, or any other gas for that matter, in the atmosphere of the planet. Clearly, those two substances must be much rarer in the Martian atmosphere than in our own, but all that the observers of the time could do was to set ever more restrictive upper limits for their abundances, leaving the question of actual amounts, if any, in limbo.[11] Thus, by the start of World War II planetary astronomers were still in the frustrating position of not being able to identify a single substance in the atmosphere of Mars, though nitrogen and carbon dioxide were popular candidates.

In the case of Venus, however, there was substantial progress. Spectrograms made in the 1920s showed only a reflected solar spectrum, but improved photographic plates that were especially sensitive in the red and near infrared provided the new tools that changed the situation. In 1932, Walter S. Adams and Theodore Dunham, Jr., working at Mount Wilson Observatory, undertook what turned out to be yet another vain search for water vapor. Unexpectedly they did find two molecular absorption bands (and later a third) in Venus's infrared spectrum. Because the number of known laboratory spectra of different molecules was so small at the time, Adams and Dunham could not identify the mystery bands by simply comparing them with known examples. Instead, they ingeniously measured the positions of the individual lines in each band and then used those quantities to calculate the physical properties of the molecule responsible. The compound turned out to be carbon dioxide. To clinch the case, a long iron pipe was set up on Mount Wilson and filled with carbon dioxide at a pressure ten times that at the surface of Earth. A beam of light was passed twice through the pipe by means of a mirror at one end, and upon emerging it was analyzed by a spectrograph. Faintly, but definitely, one of the "Venus" bands appeared.[12]

Not only was there carbon dioxide in the atmosphere of Venus, but there was a lot of it. The amount was roughly equivalent to a layer of gas as much as two miles deep at a pressure equal to that at Earth's surface. Moreover, this was only the gas above the clouds (the composition of which would not be known for decades) that perpetually shroud Venus; there could be and probably was a lot more below that level. But even the known amount suggested a significant difference between Earth and Venus. Carbon dioxide in the atmosphere acts like an insulating blanket because it absorbs infrared rays and thus blocks those given off by warm bodies. Even though the clouds of Venus reflect much sunlight back into space before it reaches the planet's surface, some gets through. The Sun-warmed surface and the atmosphere near it then emit infrared radiation and consequently lose heat. But if these rays are blocked from escaping, temperatures in the lower regions can get very high indeed. As early as 1937, Arthur Adel at Lowell realized that the temperature at the surface of Venus was probably higher than 50 degrees Centigrade, while by 1939 Rupert Wildt of Princeton argued that the temperature appeared to be higher than the boiling point of water on Earth.[13] Both were eventually proved right and in fact were even conservative in their estimates of the high surface temperature on Venus.

On the other hand there were no traces of oxygen and water vapor in the spectrum of Venus.[14] It should also be noted that no spectra showed any evidence of the planet's rotation, which therefore must be relatively slow—a period of several days at least. But just how many days was unknown.

By 1940 there was good reason to believe that conditions on Venus were harsh and life there was impossible. However, the vision of Venus as a tropical, waterlogged planet similar to Earth in the Carboniferous Age persisted in scientific circles and in science fiction. Despite the failure to find any absorption lines due to water vapor in the spectrum of Venus, it was still possible as late as the 1950s and 1960s for reputable scientists to hold that the clouds of Venus were made of drops of water.[15] As it turns out, there is a small amount of truth in that idea, but taken as a whole we now know that it is wrong.

The giant planets—Jupiter, Saturn, Uranus, and Neptune—presented a different kind of problem. Here the need was not to search for elusive spectral lines but instead to interpret strong and numerous absorption features that had been known for generations. The key was supplied in 1932 by Wildt, who was then still working in Germany. He identified the most prominent bands as due to methane (marsh gas) and ammonia gases present in the atmospheres of Jupiter and Saturn. This suggestion soon was confirmed by Dunham, who used the 100-inch reflector to obtain photographs of high-dispersion spectra on which he could measure the wavelengths of individual absorption lines in the various molecular bands. Line by line the positions of the features exhibited by Jupiter and Saturn matched those measured in the laboratory for methane and ammonia. Again, Dunham could make these observations because he was able to use special new photographic plates with improved sensitivity to near-infrared light.[16]

Dunham was quick to note some important implications of his spectra and the low cloud-top temperatures measured by other workers and suggested that the observed clouds (that is, the topmost layers, the only ones that we can see) on the giant planets might consist in part of frozen crystals of ammonia. He also noted that hydrogen should be abundant on massive planets, the strong gravity of which can hold this light gas, and indeed that "no known substance except hydrogen can exist at the high pressures below the surfaces of the major [giant] planets with a density low enough to explain their mean densities."[17]

Some of this enormous excess of hydrogen would combine with *all* the free carbon, nitrogen, and oxygen present, leaving none of those substances in elemental form. Of all the compounds that hydrogen forms with carbon, only the most volatile, methane, would be expected in the upper atmospheres. Since ammonia freezes at higher temperatures than methane, it is not surprising that while it shows itself on Jupiter, it is barely, if at all, detectable on more distant planets. The most abundant and lightest compound of hydrogen and oxygen, water, must have formed ice crystals and fallen beneath the cloud tops on all the giant planets.[18]

As it turns out, Dunham was right on every point he made. His was an enviable performance, but as we shall see, at the time it possibly helped to foster the idea that the solar system was pretty much "solved." On the other hand, as the years passed, his contributions received less and less attention, and today he is accorded less credit for his work than he deserves.

On other fronts, the increasing strengths of the methane bands from Jupiter to Neptune were generally explained as a result of the increasing thicknesses of the clear atmospheres above the cloud tops. The precipitous decline of ammonia lines (only those in Jupiter's spectrum were securely established) was attributed to lower temperatures in the outer atmospheres of the more distant planets, which resulted in ammonia gas being "frozen out" as crystals that left no traces in spectra. Still, it was worrisome that so few molecules had been identified in the atmospheres of these planets, and there were ingenious attempts to explain this situation based on the enormous preponderance of hydrogen in these objects and the effects of solar ultraviolet light.[19] While both of those influences do indeed affect the situation, much later observations, using improved instrumentation, have detected many other compounds.

There were also advances in our understanding of the interiors of the planets. While the subject is properly a part of planetary geophysics, which is covered more fully elsewhere,[20] it is appropriate to sketch here a significant development in our knowledge of the interior structure of the giant planets, for in that respect they are vastly more different from Earth than are Mercury, Venus, or Mars.

In the early 1920s the general view was that the interiors of the giant planets were hot and mostly gaseous, a view that seemed to be supported by measurements of the infrared radiation emitted by these bodies.[21] However, in 1923 the British theoretician Harold Jeffreys published a different picture of things. In his view the interiors of these planets were solid and not very hot, while their atmospheres were also relatively cool and very deep, comprising a large portion of the planets' volumes.[22]

Wildt provided the next step in our understanding of these bodies when he suggested that the giant planets had a three-layered structure. At their centers were cores resembling the terrestrial planets such as Earth. Above those centers were shells of ice, such as frozen water and solid carbon dioxide, and above these were layers of solid hydrogen, the lowest of which might be so dense that this element, which is a gas on Earth, becomes a metal inside planets as massive as Jupiter and Saturn. Capping everything were gaseous atmospheres, their uppermost cloud layers being all that we can see from Earth.[23]

Thus, in a few years ideas about Jupiter and its cohorts changed completely. Wildt's models were generally accepted by astronomers for decades and were a step in the right direction.[24] Today the three-shell model is outmoded, due to the realization of just how predominant hydrogen is (and after it, helium) in the composition of the giants; how rapidly temperatures increase toward these planets' centers; and other factors. But when all is said and done, Jeffreys and Wildt blazed a trail that led to the acknowledgment that there can be more than one kind of planet, even in the limited confines of our solar system. Future research would show that there are indeed many ways to make a planet.

While important planetary discoveries in the 1920s and 1930s were few, there were actually a fair number of astronomers, especially outside the United States, conducting research in the field. These scientists did the best they could at the time, but that they often had to use equipment and theory totally inadequate for the job at hand. It would be a waste of space to attempt to describe all these investigations, which were often wrong (indications of an atmosphere on Mercury, to name just one example); I mention only a few of the more interesting cases.

Visual observers had long reported seeing vague darkish markings on the bright "surface" of Venus. By the 1920s it was known that these structures seemed to change from day to day, and it was generally accepted that they represented cloud features. Still, it was difficult to conclude more from the sketchy drawings then available. But in 1927 Frank E. Ross changed everything. He used the 60-inch and 100-inch reflectors at Mount Wilson to take photographs of Venus on twenty-five nights, in a series as close to unbroken as possible. Each evening he used different filters to make exposures in various wavelengths.

Ross found that details were *always* visible in ultraviolet light. Blue-light images showed only weak features, and red and infrared photographs showed no details at all. This was a surprising turn of events, because it was known at the time that infrared penetrates clouds and haze much more effectively than does visible light, and ultraviolet does so hardly at all. In fact, the previous year Ross had taken photographs of Mars at different wavelengths, and as expected the planet's surface features showed up best at longer wavelengths, red and infrared, while Martian clouds and haze were best seen at shorter wavelengths, blue and ultraviolet.[25] Thus the two planets were very different indeed.

Evidently the clouds of Venus were opaque enough to obscure the surface even in infrared light, and it took the easily blocked ultraviolet to reveal the subtle structure of the clouds' upper surface. Ross was unable to derive a rotation period for the planet from his images, not only because of the rapid changes in cloud patterns but also because he could observe the planet for only a few hours each evening from just after sunset until Venus sank so low in the west that the seeing became bad.[26] Decades later his findings were confirmed fully by space probes.

There were still other ways to investigate the planets. One of these involved the measurement of very-long-wavelength emissions from these bodies. This far-infrared ("heat," or "thermal") radiation had been known to exist for some time, but the development of new and more sensitive detectors made it possible for astronomers of the twentieth century to study objects much fainter than the Sun or Moon. An important refinement in these studies was to observe objects not only directly but also with a water-filled "cell" placed just in front of the detector. Pure water transmits visible light but absorbs much of the infrared. Comparing the two types of measurements made it possible to separate the contributions of reflected sunlight from those of thermal emission from the planet.

The first such measurements were made by W. W. Coblentz in 1914 at Lick Observatory. Later observations were made at Lowell Observatory by Coblentz and C. O. Lampland, and at Mount Wilson Observatory by Edison Pettit and Seth B. Nicholson, while the young American astronomer Donald H. Menzel developed the theory needed to convert those measurements into planetary temperatures.

The results indicated that the cloud tops of Venus and the surfaces of Mercury and Mars had about the temperatures expected from solar heating. From Jupiter to Saturn to Uranus the temperatures decreased, but they were slightly warmer than those expected from solar heating alone, indicating sources of internal heat in those planets. These results finally demolished the old notion that the cloud tops of the giant planets are at high temperatures. In addition, these investigations showed that the Moon's surface temperature varied widely from day to night, confirming that our satellite is covered with powdery material that acts as a very good insulator, allowing little heat to sink into, or escape from, lower layers. In particular, far-infrared observations during total eclipses of the Moon showed that our satellite's surface cooled off very rapidly. This was a sure sign of an insulating layer, for it demonstrated in dramatic fashion that heat leaked into or out of the Moon only very slowly.[27]

Other techniques involved study of the polarization of light reflected from bodies, and analysis of the relative brightnesses of planetary cloud or surface features on photographs taken in different colors by the use of filters. Such differences in brightness provide clues as to the nature of the visible surfaces, solid or cloud top, and any atmosphere above them. Unfortunately, both of these methods are tricky to use, and results from them were often misleading or just plain wrong.

To consider a single but typical example in detail: Mars is the only planet in the solar system that has both an atmosphere and definite surface features that can be observed from Earth. An obvious question is to ask how much atmosphere the red planet has and, in particular, what is the Martian surface pressure? If Earth's surface pressure is defined as 1 bar (or 1,000 millibars, which is the same thing), early twentieth-century estimates for the same quantity on Mars generally ran in the neighborhood of a few hundred millibars; that is, a few tenths of the surface pressure on Earth, although there were estimates that were well above and below that range.

In the 1920s, Menzel tackled the problem estimating as best he could values of the albedos of various features on Mars as determined visually and from photographs. His aim was "to determine the contribution of a planet's atmosphere to the total light from the planet," and thus to estimate how much atmosphere there was. He concluded that Mars's surface pressure must be less than the estimates current at the time, in fact less than 50 to 60 millibars.[28] Menzel was getting close to the right answer, closer than many other previous (or later) investigators. He was undone by the fact that fine dust, which scatters light much more efficiently that do gas molecules, is abundant in the atmosphere of Mars. This dust mimicked the behavior of a denser atmosphere than the red planet actually has. Had Menzel known how dusty the atmosphere of Mars was, the much lower value that we now know to be correct might have been established long ago.[29]

A few years later, the French astronomer Bernard Lyot attacked the same problem with visual observations of the polarization of sunlight reflected from Mars. He established that both the red planet and the Moon showed similar properties, in spite of the fact that one has an atmosphere and the other does not. Lyot suggested that this was due to the combined effects of the Martian surface and atmosphere, and he derived a surface pressure even lower than Menzel's—less than about 25 millibars. This was getting even closer to the truth.[30]

The ironic part of the story is that in the following decades Menzel's and Lyot's estimates generally were dismissed as too low, even though they were actually too high.[31] This situation arose because of a number of varied studies conducted by French and especially Soviet astronomers. In general, their work indicated surface pressures somewhat above about 100 millibars, or roughly one tenth of that on Earth. The French, Australian, and ultimately Texan astronomer Gerard de Vaucouleurs probably had the best explanation for these high values. As he related to me late one cloudy night at McDonald Observatory in Texas in the 1960s, "They took telescopes this big" (holding his finger and thumb a few centimeters apart), "to get images this big" (holding finger and thumb a few millimeters apart), "and used equations this big" (holding his arms about a meter apart), to get the wrong answer!"[32] There were other problems with the methods as well, but the clumpiness of silver grains on photographic plates, combined with the small sizes of the images, not to mention a myriad of theoretical inadequacies, doomed these efforts from the start. Later, in the 1960s, new and different types of observations proved Menzel's and Lyot's efforts to have been fine examples of brilliant pioneering work. Belatedly, their work received the recognition it deserved.

Much earlier, the versatile American physicist R. W. Wood applied the technique of photographing objects at widely different wavelengths to the Moon and giant planets. Interestingly, his photographs of our satellite taken in the ultraviolet revealed features that could not be seen in visible light. Wood also photographed specimens of volcanic rock, and after comparing these images with lunar ones, suggested that an area near the crater Aristarchus that appeared black in the ultraviolet might be lava or pumice containing sulphur. Unfortunately, many rocks look dark in the ultraviolet, and his work did not settle the question of the Moon's surface composition, though it was a resourceful attempt to do so.[33]

Wood's results on Saturn and Jupiter were more spectacular, but no more informative. He used the 60-inch reflector to take photographs in the ultraviolet, violet, yellow, and infrared. In the case of Saturn, the violet and yellow images looked so different that "were it not for the ring, it would have been difficult to believe that they represented the same object." Jupiter showed differences almost as great as those of Saturn. Wood ingeniously combined the images made in different wavelength to produce "false color" images of Saturn and Jupiter. He correctly pointed out that "the photographs as a whole give us a vivid impression that we are really dealing with great belts of selectively absorbing, and hence colored, vapors or gases." But the substances that caused those colors remained unknown and indeed still remain largely unknown.[34]

COMETS, METEORS, AND THEIR KIN

The study of comets remained popular during the interwar period. The relatively bright examples appeared with little or no advance warning, but it was a widespread practice to reassign telescope time on short notice for spectroscopic and photographic investigations of these objects. The results of these studies peppered the literature of the time and were common even in the august pages of the *Astrophysical Journal*. Part of the explanation for the interest in comets lies in the fact that they provided superb laboratories with physical conditions then unobtainable on Earth for use in advancing the rapidly developing field of molecular spectroscopy, which had not only major scientific but also commercial importance.

One problem with studying comets during this era was that there were few bright ones. Another and more enduring difficulty was that conditions in space are hard to duplicate on Earth. To give just one example, scientists in the 1920s and 1930s could not reproduce the almost pure vacuum of space in which cometary physics takes place. Researchers in that period identified a few more chemical species in comets, but searches for their assumed "parent" molecules (water, for example) continued.[35]

As late as 1942, scientists had definitely identified only seven molecules—in addition to sodium atoms and perhaps iron and other metals that appeared in comets passing close to the Sun—in cometary atmospheres: OH, NH, C, C, C_2, CO^+ (CO missing one electron), and N_2^+.[36] The presence of these compounds was no surprise, for they involve only hydrogen, carbon, nitrogen, and oxygen, which are four of the five most common elements in the universe (the other is helium). Parent molecules were suspected of being simple compounds such as water, carbon dioxide, methane, ammonia, acetylene, and the like, but there was no proof that this was the case. As for just what a comet is—a sublimating iceberg, a flying sand bank, or something else—still no one knew.

Perhaps the most important work on meteors was encouraged by Shapley, who by the early 1930s was the influential director of the prestigious Harvard College Observatory and for some reason was interested in meteors. The brilliant and eccentric Estonian astronomer Ernst J. Öpik visited Harvard during Shapley's tenure, and the two devised the Harvard Meteor Expedition to Arizona, where clear skies were more common than in New England or the Baltic states. One aim of the study was to try to determine whether any "sporadic" meteors (the periodic type, by this time, were recognized as members of the solar system) were arriving from interstellar space. Such interlopers must almost certainly exist, unless either the Sun is the only star surrounded by myriad small orbiting solid bodies or some unknown process prevents interstellar visitors from approaching the Sun's vicinity. Both of these possibilities are highly unlikely, yet there was then no hard evidence for the existence of such callers.

Öpik examined the expedition's records and determined to his satisfaction that many meteorites were moving so fast that they must have come from beyond the solar system. Other workers, however, found no evidence to support that claim. The situation remained undecided until after World War II, when new methods including radio and radar astronomy provided a negative answer. To this day, there has not been even a single confirmed observation of a meteor originating from outside the solar system, though such objects might indeed exist.

But whatever his views on the existence of meteors from beyond the solar system, Öpik's fertile imagination produced an idea that would prove to be prophetic. He conceived that a vast system of comets and meteors was associated with every star, systems that extended far enough to intermingle with each other. This concept of a huge "reservoir" of unobservable comets was to gain general acceptance years later in a different form.[37]

On a related front, the widespread, indeed universal, effects of titanic collisions in the solar system were still unrecognized. At that time there were no generally acknowledged fossil meteorites and there were no generally accepted impact craters on Earth's surface. Lunar features were still widely held to be volcanic in origin, and in the case of other planets, let alone their satellites, the possibility of surface impact craters was seldom even mentioned.

Of course there were some unsung prophets. Perhaps one of the most interesting, colorful, and bizarre characters in the variegated history of astronomy was Thomas Jefferson Jackson See, who held and lost a variety of positions in American astronomy around the turn of the century, was accused of plagiarism on several occasions, and eventually became a pariah among professionals. All the same, many of his views turned out to be no more wide of the mark than others proposed at the time, and several eventually proved correct. See held strongly that the lunar craters were impact features, and that other solar system bodies with solid surfaces (Mercury, Mars, and the satellites of Jupiter and Saturn, for example) also bear the scars of celestial bombardment. Similar features on Earth, he pointed out, would be slowly but surely destroyed by erosion.[38] See even published a drawing of Mercury showing its surface pockmarked with impact craters.[39] Whether or not he could see craters on Mercury is a moot point.[40] But it should be pointed out that T. J. J. See was correct. Mercury, Earth, the Moon, Mars, and all the other bodies of the solar system that have solid surfaces and that have been investigated in a close-up manner by space probes show obvious evidence of meteor bombardment. For all his faults, See should get some credit for this insight.

It is possible that craters have been observed on Mars from Earth through ground-based telescopes. Among planetary observers of the 1960s (and even now in some cases) there was the widespread belief that the keen-eyed E. E. Barnard had seen and drawn craters on Mars but never published his results because these features were so difficult to observe, although he did show the sketches privately to others. Intensive searches of every nook and cranny at Lick and Yerkes observatories, among other places, have not yet turned up a single Barnard drawing showing craters on Mars. Yet the craters, some of them very large—(the Hellas region, which is a huge crater, has long been known as a prominent light, circular feature on the red planet)—truly are there, and Barnard would have been the one visual observer who could have seen them. Perhaps he did, and perhaps we shall know one day.

In the case of the Moon, the awful consequences of World War I shed some unexpected light on the problem of the origin of craters. The awesome artillery bombardments at places such as Verdun and Ypres produced what observers called a lunar landscape. Aerial bombardment was even more enlightening. In 1919, the *Astrophysical Journal* published an article that, in hindsight, demonstrated without a doubt that lunar craters were due to impacts. In this paper, Herbert B. Ives reported on experiments that reproduced the conditions under which lunar craters were formed. Up to this time, proponents of the impact theory had mostly been limited to obviously inappropriate experiments such as dropping pebbles into plaster or paraffin, though T. J. J. See had high velocity naval projectiles fired at targets, which was more like it. Ives, however, studied events that were much closer to the scales of possible meteor or comet collisions. The test objects were craters produced by aerial bombs that fell slowly by comparison with meteorites but were filled with several hundred pounds of TNT. When the projectiles hit and exploded, they produced craters that looked amazingly like those on the Moon.

Ives had it right. He noted that the central peaks found in some of the terrestrial and lunar craters were due to "rebound," which is familiar in high speed photographs of liquid drops hitting a liquid surface. The radial "pits" and "rays" observed around lunar craters were also reproduced. In addition, the amount of material excavated by the explosions matched that in the crater rims and rays.

He also addressed an objection to the impact theory that had been around for generations, namely, why are all the lunar craters circular in outline? Should not grazing impacts produce oblong scars? Not so, Ives answered. He noted that whatever the angles at which the aerial missives came in, circular bomb craters resulted from explosions. And he pointed out that any celestial missile would arrive at such a high speed that when it was stopped by the resistance of a body's solid crust, the energy of motion of the meteor would be converted to heat. This amount of heat would be so great that essentially the entire mass of the incoming body, along with that of a much larger mass of the target, would more or less instantaneously become so hot that they would be converted into gas. That is exactly what happens when one fires a gun—solid gunpowder is converted to gas. In other words there is an explosion, and if the blast happens in the ground the result is a circular crater with material thrown out in a more or less circular pattern, whatever the angle of impact of the incoming projectile. Ives also noted that erosion and weathering would slowly destroy evidence of impact craters on Earth, while the same processes would not happen on the Moon.[41]

Ives was correct in every respect. Still, almost incredibly, the volcanic theory generally held sway, perhaps because it was the more familiar and interesting explanation. Decades would pass before the prevailing opinion changed. But in one case, at least, there was a gradual and significant shift of opinion in the interval between the two world wars. Evidence accumulated that Meteor Crater in Arizona really was just that. For one thing, the fused quartz present at the site would have demanded an extremely high temperature for its production. For another, additional craters in other locations were found that, like Meteor Crater, showed associated meteorite fragments, greatly lengthening the odds against the possibility that features had been produced by volcanic action but in places where a shower of meteorites had happened to fall.[42] By the early 1940s astronomers generally accepted that the Arizona crater is a relic of a meteoritic impact.[43]

A CASE IN POINT

While for the most part celestial objects far more distant than any in the solar system attracted the bulk of astronomers' interest during the 1920s and 1930s, there were some exceptions. For example, in 1925 the Carnegie Institution of Washington, which funded the Mount Wilson Observatory, formed a Committee on Study of the Surface Features of the Moon. This "Moon Committee," although its very existence is almost totally forgotten today, nevertheless kept active until World War II put an end to its endeavors. Committee members were all well-respected scientists connected in some way with the Carnegie Institution: staff members from Mount Wilson (W. S. Adams, F. G. Pease, and E. Petit), a volcanologist, two geologists, a theoretical physicist, and not least the redoubtable astronomer Henry Norris Russell.

Very early on the committee sensibly realized that arguments about the origin of lunar surface features were likely to be a waste of time as long as we knew so little about the structure and composition of the Moon's surface. Thus, they and many other scientists, particularly in France, the Soviet Union, and Great Britain, set out to try to provide the needed information. The results were meager indeed. Infrared temperature measurements, polarization studies, photometric (brightness) observations at different wavelengths, and attempts at the rigorous mapping of our satellite's surface produced little that was new. Instead, results only confirmed already accepted concepts: the Moon has no sensible atmosphere, its dust-covered surface is rough at small scales, steep slopes are rare, and different locations on our satellite show some different properties. There were also statistical studies of the relative frequencies, and the relation between depth and diameter, of craters of different sizes. Such work would eventually produce solid results, but not for a while.

As soon as it began work, the Moon Committee realized that accurate lunar maps were needed. To produce a photographic map required a novel technique. Photographic images of the Moon were projected onto a white sphere, and the illuminated globe was then photographed from any desired position. This procedure has the added benefit of being able to show what the Moon looks like if observed from *somewhere other than Earth*. Thus, craters near the limb (edge) of our satellite that normally look elliptical can be seen in their true circular form. The view of such a globe from a different perspective than we get from our own planet reveals what at first glance looks like an entirely different body than our familiar satellite. The effect is startling to anyone who has any (even just naked-eye) familiarity with what the Moon looks like from Earth.

The Moon Committee also planned to produce a lunar topographic map, which entailed determining the heights of myriad lunar features. To this end, no less than four hundred photographs of the Moon were taken with the 100-inch reflector in 1938. This involved devoting to a solar system project what was for that era a considerable amount of "big telescope" observing time and demonstrates that the committee had considerable influence. Sadly, the project collapsed because it ran short of time and money. It would be decades before good lunar photographic and topographic maps were made.[44]

Nothing done between the two world wars resolved the conflict between the volcanic and impact theories for the origin of lunar craters. Other questions remained unanswered as well. To take just one case, the nature of the bright "rays" that splay out from certain craters was still unknown. These bright streaks are most obvious at full moon, and in fact the ones from the crater Tycho are so prominent that they can be seen with the unaided eye, giving our satellite the familiar appearance of a peeled orange.

Thus despite the best efforts of a group of eminent American scientists, and their colleagues around the world, the celestial body closest to Earth remained largely an enigma as World War II began. Astronomers knew more about the chemical compositions of, and physical conditions in, stars and nebulae thousands of light years away than they did about those of our own satellite. It was a frustrating and depressing situation for planetary scientists, and one that seemed to offer no hope of relief.

Planetary astronomy did have one old-fashioned spectacular triumph during this period—the discovery of Pluto. This event briefly brought solar system research back into the public focus. As we have seen, Percival Lowell had excellent training in celestial mechanics. Stimulated by certain small irregularities in the motion of Uranus, early in the twentieth century he began a concerted, two-pronged attempt to find a planet beyond Neptune. On the theoretical front, he attempted to predict where the so- called Planet X (or Planet X's, should there be more than one) might be seen in the sky, and on the observational side he began a photographic search for the hypothetical orb in 1906, using a telescope with a wide field of view.

The quest continued off and on for decades at Lowell Observatory until an improved telescope—and a tenacious observer, Clyde W. Tombaugh— found such a planet. Tombaugh was an amateur astronomer, in the tradition of William Herschel, and on February 18, 1930, he spotted the images of the sought-after body on a pair of photographic plates. There was little doubt but that this was indeed Planet X, for the body was moving at the right speed for an object beyond Neptune's orbit, and inspection of other photographic plates soon confirmed the discovery. The news gripped the world. The new planet was dubbed Pluto, after the god of the underworld, for both moved in dark and frigid climes. Furthermore, in a nice touch, the first two letters of the name, which would form the internationally recognized symbol of the planet, echo the initials of Percival Lowell.

There is a curious follow-up to this story. Later research showed that the mass of Pluto is far too small to have caused the observed perturbations in the motion of Uranus. Yet, as Tombaugh has pointed out, Planet X was indeed found within 6 degrees of where Lowell had predicted it would be at the time.[45] Was this a case similar to that of Neptune, where coincidences seemed to conspire to produce the right answer from misguided predictions? Perhaps. But it cannot be denied that, in this case at least, Percival Lowell's conviction as an informed astronomer (though he was possessed at times of an overeager imagination) stood the test of time. He was right after all.[46]

ORIGINS

In the decades between the wars, ideas about how stars age also changed. Ejnar Hertzsprung and Russell's demonstration that stars for the most part were divided into giants and dwarfs lent credence to what became a widely accepted version of an old theory of stellar evolution. (As mentioned, *aging* would be a better term, but the terminology is too well established to be changed.) This is how the hypothesis goes. Starting with a huge, rarefied gaseous nebula, such as the one in the sword of the constellation Orion, gravity pulls the widely spaced material together to form an enormous but cool "red giant" star. Continued contraction steadily raises the body's temperature as it passes consecutively through the stages of yellow, white, and blue giant. But inevitably the star reaches a maximum temperature. From then on, as the iron grip of gravity shrinks the object into a dwarf, the star's temperature and luminosity decline as gravitational contraction produces ever less power. As the body cools, its color changes from blue to white, to yellow, to red, and finally to invisibility. At the end, what is left is a slowly cooling cosmic cinder. The view is wrong, but it remained popular for decades.[47]

There was still no consensus as to how the solar system came to be. Increasingly detailed (and ever more improbable) versions of the stellar encounter theory filled many pages of astronomical publications. This hypothesis required that two stars passed close to each other along very specific paths, which eventually became so specific that the chances of a solar system ever being formed became wildly improbable. On the other hand, the older but much less quantitative nebular hypothesis could not be ruled out. As a result, during this period neither theory dominated, and few interested scientists offered strong public opinions on the matter.[48]

The encounter theory was dealt a body blow—which eventually became fatal—by the American astronomer Lyman Spitzer, Jr. In 1939 he showed that a filament of material drawn off during a close passage of two stars is so hot that it will expand to a great extent instead of condensing into planets. The result would be not a solar system but rather "an extended gaseous nebula around one or more of the stars involved."[49] Whether most scientists at the time realized it or not, the encounter theory was dead.

COSMIC STATIC

In the late 1920s Karl Guthe Jansky, a young radio engineer working for the Bell Telephone Laboratories in New Jersey, was assigned to study the interference that was plaguing the then new transoceanic radiotelephone service. He had to design and build his own antenna and receiver, but by the end of 1932 he had enough data to reach a startling conclusion. One of the kinds of static that he detected was a steady hiss in his earphones, and it came come from a fixed direction with respect to the stars throughout the year. Jansky had detected natural, extraterrestrial radio radiation, in particular that from the Milky Way and especially from its central regions in the direction of the constellation Sagittarius. He gave some talks at meetings of professional radio scientists and published several articles in the *Proceedings of the Institute of Radio Engineers*. In addition, he wrote an article for *Popular Astronomy*, the most widely read popular astronomical magazine of the day, appeared on a nationwide radio broadcast, and received a good write-up in the *New York Times*. In short, his results were widely publicized.[50]

However, the response of astronomers to Jansky's breakthrough was less than enthusiastic. Early interest proved fleeting. A few scientists attempted to confirm Jansky's work, and indeed some did, but in very rudimentary ways. Others made vain attempts to come up with a theoretical explanation for how the observed strong emission was produced. Stars probably were not the origin, for in that case our nearby Sun should be a tremendously powerful radio beacon, and it did not appear to be. Hot interstellar dust and gas and other ingenious possibilities were tried and found wanting by factors of tens or thousands. The true cause would remain a mystery for years, but meanwhile the failure to identify the source of the radiation did not inspire enthusiasm about the subject.[51]

Jansky himself either could not or would not follow up his pioneering work, but he did inspire one man to take effective action and follow up the initial discovery.[52] As a result, for several years radio astronomy would be advanced solely by the efforts of Grote Reber, a professional radio engineer who pursued the new science with his own money and as a hobby. He built his own receiving equipment and erected an antenna that was similar in shape to today's ubiquitous "parabolic" home satellite dishes; more than 31 feet in diameter, it was located in the back yard of his home in Wheaton, Illinois. Local gossip had it that Reber's odd-looking contraption was a rainwater collector and a machine for controlling the weather. By 1939, he had begun to confirm Jansky's earlier results and had determined that the radiation was indeed coming from the Milky Way and was particularly strong in the direction of that system's center toward the constellation Sagittarius.[53]

Reber investigated a number of different celestial objects but detected radio waves only from the Milky Way and, just possibly, the Great Andromeda Nebula. Unlike Jansky, he did not have to gain his boss's permission regarding when or where to publish his results, because his work was all done on his own time and with his own funds. Wisely, he decided to go right to the top. He submitted a short article on his findings to the *Astrophysical Journal,* which ran it as a note.[54] A few years later he wrote a longer paper for the same journal. This time he included maps of the radio sky clearly showing that the radiation came from the Milky Way and was strongest toward the center of our galaxy. Also shown, but unrecognized at the time, were a few specific features that were *not* spread over a large area of the sky and that later would be dubbed "discrete radio sources."[55] Eventually the study of these objects would force scientists to realize that the universe is an immeasurably more violent place than the relatively tranquil and well-ordered one it was believed to be by astronomers and other scientists of the 1920s and 1930s.

Reber's publication in the *Astrophysical Journal* ensured that most professional astronomers at least had the opportunity to read about his results, but again the response was less than overwhelming. Part of the explanation for this reaction may have been the lack of common ground between astronomers and radio engineers. By this time the normal training for astronomers included stiff doses of mathematics and physics at both the undergraduate and graduate levels, with no time left for "offbeat" subjects such as electrical engineering courses. Indeed at many, and perhaps most, universities, astronomy and electrical engineering were (and still are) not only taught in different departments but also in different colleges.[56]

Moreover, astronomical research of the time demanded no knowledge of radio techniques. While some observers built their own instruments such as photoelectric photometers, and may have known something about reading circuit diagrams and soldering wires together, knowledge of topics such as antenna theory and radio receivers was essentially nil among professional astronomers. This unfamiliarity no doubt deterred many astronomers from using radio technology. We see a similar phenomenon today, when many people who grew up before the age of personal computers are afraid or unwilling to use them. Moreover, to do radio astronomy in those days one had to build one's own equipment from scratch, and it was difficult for a respected senior scientist to become an apprentice radio technician.

In addition, astronomers of the era, like most people in the 1930s, were short of money, and often the cost of a single photographic plate was a significant expense even at an observatory. Thus few individuals or institutions had the means to buy expensive (by the standards of the day) radio equipment that might or might not contribute to astronomical knowledge.[57]

As a result of these and other factors, when radio astronomy began to make rapid strides after World War II, electrical engineers rather than astronomers made most of the early advances. Significantly, in the United States, which then led the world in research in optical astronomy, radio studies for years lagged behind efforts in other countries. "Classical" astronomers (fortunately with some important exceptions) missed the boat, illustrating how an old, established science and old, established scientists can be tied by habit to the methods of the past. Indeed, as late as the mid-1950s, the most widely used American elementary textbook on astronomy devoted less than six of its more than five hundred pages to the entire field of radio astronomy.[58]

PANIC IN THE STREETS

Astronomy is almost never foremost in the minds of ordinary citizens. However, on those rare occasions when it is, the results can be astounding. The Mars furor in the late nineteenth and early twentieth century is one example, the excitement generated by the 1910 apparition of Halley's comet another. But these crazes are easier to explain than a 1930s episode that provoked a true panic.

The year 1938 was a fateful one, for it seemed to many that the most terrible war in history was about to break out. The crucial event of that year was the infamous "Munich Crisis" in September, which ended when an appeasing England and France effectively handed over Czechoslovakia to Adolph Hitler. Throughout the whole month, the then new medium of radio gave people everywhere a blow-by-blow account of the proceedings. While armies, navies, and air forces mobilized, listeners gathered around their receivers to hear the latest news. In general, the easing of the crisis without open warfare resulted in a feeling of relief tempered with apprehension. But how deeply people were disturbed by these events—and how widespread was the utterly unrelated idea that alien life was common in the universe—were soon to be demonstrated in a spectacular and disturbing way.[59]

On All Hallows Eve, October 30, 1938, Orson Welles and the Mercury Theatre on the Air played over the facilities of the Columbia Broadcasting System what turned out to be a wildly misguided Halloween prank on the American listening public. The nature of the program was clearly announced at the beginning, in the middle, and at the end of the production, as an adaptation of H. G. Wells's novella *The War of the Worlds*. But that mattered not at all. The radio play was presented in a realistic manner that fooled many listeners into believing that they were hearing an actual news broadcast. The public imagination ran riot despite the disclaimers and the obvious impossibilities in the story, such as spaceships traveling from Mars to Earth in a few minutes. Shortly after the broadcast began at 8:00 P.M. Eastern Standard Time, mass hysteria began to break out, radiating from central New Jersey, where the first imaginary Martians landed at the (real) hamlet of Grovers Mill. Fortunately, nobody died or was seriously injured as a result of the uproar, though there were some close calls. But for the next few days many Americans went around wearing somewhat sheepish expressions.[60]

A host of different explanations of the incident soon appeared and indeed have never stopped appearing, but the episode surely showed at least that belief in advanced intelligent life on Mars was widespread in America. The event also gave a generally ridiculous aspect to the topics of Mars and Martians, which only reinforced the earlier impression made by Lowell's unsubstantiated claims on those subjects.[61]

It is important to realize that this was also the heyday of the popular fictional characters Buck Rogers and Flash Gordon. Their disintegrator rays, rocket ships, and the like seemed silly to many (thus describing something as a "a Buck Rogers idea" implies impracticality to this day), and some of this attitude may have rubbed off on solar system studies.[62] Whatever the reasons, planetary astronomy was at a low ebb, with few practitioners and few new discoveries, and the field was held in disdain by many professional astronomers who were working on such exalted topics as the age and size of the universe.

SUMMING UP

Although he was speaking of a slightly later era (the 1950s), American astronomer Andrew T. Young's comments on the state of solar system research apply just as well to the previous decades:

> Newcomers to planetary science can hardly imagine the contempt with which planets were regarded by the English-speaking astronomical Establishment of that time. Planetary observers could not get time on any of the largest telescopes. Physical studies of planetary features and atmospheric phenomena (like dust storms on Mars) were regarded as beneath the dignity of professional astronomers in this country; they were left to the attentions of amateurs and Frenchmen. NASA did not exist; its precursor was mainly concerned with the design of airplane wings. Struve and Zebergs' *Astronomy of the 20th century*, published five years after the first artificial satellite, devoted less than 5% of its contents to the entire solar system.[63]

That may seem harsh, but it accurately reflects the standing of planetary astronomy at the time.

There is some telling evidence for the relatively low standing of planetary work compared to other areas of astronomy in the period between the wars. (The disdain was, of course, seldom written down and almost never published.) One of the most interesting and clear-cut examples is contained in the table of contents of the standard compendium *Source Book in Astronomy: 1900–1950,* edited by Shapley. There are sixty-nine articles in this work, but only nine in the section titled "The Planetary System." The situation is even more one-sided than these numbers indicate, for several of the nine are on topics such as the "wandering" of Earth's North Pole, the solar parallax, and the use of electronic calculators in reproducing observed planetary positions. Others treat of peripheral subjects such as long-enduring meteor trains and using meteors to probe our upper atmosphere. It gives the impression that Shapley had to pad the section with papers of marginal importance to make it look respectable. (An aside: only two articles in the book deal with radio astronomy.)

The four more substantial articles on solar system research deal with the theory of the Moon's motion, lunar infrared radiation and temperatures, the discovery of Pluto, and the 1908 Tunguska meteorite fall in Siberia. Curiously, there is nothing at all about topics such as spectroscopic work concerning the planets and comets or theoretical advances in our knowledge of planetary interiors and the origin of the solar system. In other words, most of the real advances in planetary astronomy simply were not mentioned. In stark contrast to this sparse selection in the planetary field is the panoply of articles relating dramatic gains in our knowledge of the stars, the Milky Way, and other galaxies. The difference is striking, not only in relative numbers of discoveries but also in the vastly more spectacular and fundamental nature of the advances made in fields dealing with objects far beyond the planets.[64]

By comparison, the 1929 work *A Source Book in Astronomy,* edited by Shapley and Helen E. Howarth, contains items ranging in date from the time of Copernicus to about 1900. There planetary studies play an important, and indeed dominant role, in both number and fundamental importance. How times had changed![65]

There seems to have been a feeling among astronomers toward the middle of the twentieth century that for the most part planetary studies had gone about as far as they could go. The American astronomer N. T. Bobrovnikoff, a noted student of comets, exemplified this attitude in 1944, when he wrote: "The identification of methane and ammonia in the atmosphere [sic] of the major planets and of carbon dioxide in the atmosphere of Venus appears to have solved the planetary problem in its entirety." It is not clear exactly what he meant by that remark, for the article in which it appeared is full of references to unsolved problems concerning planetary atmospheres, but it certainly is interesting that Bobrov-nikoff made this claim.

Actually, we knew very little about physical conditions on the planets at that time, and some of what we thought we knew was wrong. A review of our knowledge in 1938 neatly summarizes the situation. Mercury shows no traces of an atmosphere but does have permanent dark features that indicate that it always keeps the same face toward the Sun. Venus is covered with clouds that show changeable structure at short wavelengths (especially in the ultraviolet), has carbon dioxide in its atmosphere, and rotates with a period longer than a few days. Mars is colder than Earth, has variable pole caps and clouds, and has permanent as well as variable surface features. The red planet also has a thin atmosphere of unknown composition. The giant planets are all covered with clouds and have extensive atmospheres that contain methane and, at least in the cases of Jupiter and Saturn, ammonia. The Moon is airless, its craters probably volcanic in origin, and its surface covered with something like pumice or volcanic ash.[66]

Basically, that was it. A sparse harvest indeed, especially when in the same era astronomers were able to perform feats such as determining the chemical compositions and physical conditions in the atmospheres of stars that were hundreds or thousands of light years away.

By the start of World War II it seemed almost impossible that planetary science could ever regain its ancient prestige. Scientists who worked in the field were far from the cutting edge of the astronomical research of the day and used methods that seldom gave clear answers. Lowell Observatory kept up planetary studies, but elsewhere in America it was a case of doing a few things now and then, especially when a new and faster photographic emulsion or some other improvement became available. The solar system was always included in popular works on astronomy, for public interest never flagged, but that was not where professional interests lay.

The situation was even worse than that, for on the eve of World War II there was literally no place in the United States where one could go in order to learn to be a planetary specialist. By this time advanced education in astronomy was effectively limited to graduate departments at a handful of universities, none of which prepared a student for a career in planetary astronomy.

A student could go to Harvard and study comets or meteors (to give one example, the Canadian astronomer Peter M. Millman did this and went on to a distinguished career as an expert on meteors, meteorites, and the like), and there were a number of universities where one could specialize in celestial mechanics, but planets and satellites were another story. In those subjects there were few if any opportunities. And if a one did earn a degree in stellar or galactic astronomy and then wanted to switch research interests toward investigations of the solar system, there were formidable obstacles. Where and how to get a job at a university that wanted a planetary specialist on its faculty? Where and how to get time on the few large telescopes of the day? Where and how to get the money to support planetary research, when the competition was immensely more glamorous? And where and how to get the advice, support, or even criticism of colleagues in the same field, who were pitifully few in number?

Except in the imaginations of a small number of visionaries, it seemed as if we would be forever ignorant of many of the most fundamental facts about even our nearest neighbors in space. What did the "back" of the Moon look like, for example? What was Mars really like? Many wondered, but few believed that they might live to see the answers. The scene looked dark indeed. And yet a spectacular and totally unexpected renaissance of planetary astronomy was only a few years away. Soon to come were were the first faint stirrings, eventually to become an irresistible tide. All in all, it is a remarkable tale.

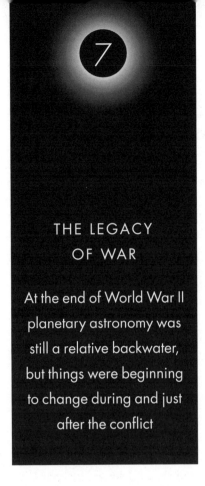

THE LEGACY
OF WAR

At the end of World War II
planetary astronomy was
still a relative backwater,
but things were beginning
to change during and just
after the conflict

During World War II routine astronomical work suffered as many researchers devoted their specialized skills to the more urgent matters of the conflict. The titanic struggle involved science more directly and more intimately than any combat that had gone before, and the enormous technical challenges led to developments that advanced science in general and planetary studies in particular. One of the most important advances in astronomy came from outside the ranks of professional astronomers and resulted from British fears that the Germans had learned how to "jam" Great Britain's radar defenses.

THE RADIO WAR

February, 1942, was not a good time for the British and other Allied Nations. In the middle of that month a powerful German surface fleet sailed boldly right up the English Channel in broad daylight without losing a ship, a feat that not even the Spanish Armada had accomplished.[1] The effort was aided by heavy Nazi electronic jamming, and so when British radars again were disrupted severely just two weeks later, there were genuine fears in London. Had the Germans developed a method of neutralizing radar, upon which the very existence of Great Britain depended?

The British called in James S. Hey, who demonstrated that the Sun, not some Nazi secret weapon, was the culprit. The evidence was clear: the jamming was never observed at night, and bearings and elevations measured at widely separated locations around Great Britain all pointed toward the Sun. The exceptional strength of the interference observed in February appeared to be associated with a large sunspot group that was then at the center of the Sun, though just how our star generated radio radiation was unknown. Wartime secrecy demanded that this result not be published openly at the time, though it was widely distributed among the commands that had "need to know." Thus it was not until four years later that more than a few scientists knew of it.[2] This affair was an enormous boost to the emerging field of radio astronomy, for it demonstrated in no uncertain terms that events far from Earth could be of immense practical importance.

Hey was a radio engineer who played a vital role in the early development of radio astronomy. Not only was he the first to recognize solar radio emission for what it was, but he also, as we shall see, played a major role in several other significant advances in entirely different areas of the field.

Because the obvious importance of electronic warfare in all its forms spurred development of the field across the board, it is not surprising that American and German workers also detected the Sun's emissions during the war, though under less dramatic circumstances than those that Hey investigated. What *is* surprising is that attempts to detect solar radio radiation dated back to the very beginnings of radio itself. As early as 1890, only a few years after radio waves were discovered, Thomas A. Edison and Arthur E. Kennelly proposed, and may have attempted, to detect solar radio waves. Their method was to use a long wire strung around a low grade deposit of iron ore in New Jersey, with the two sharply pointed ends of the strand close to each other, so that any celestial electromagnetic radiation would cause a spark to arc across the gap (this "spark gap" technique was used in all early radio communications). No results were ever announced, but the fact that Edison even thought of the idea shows that he was much more than the "mere practical inventor" of legend. Others made attempts for the next half-century, but all failed to detect the "radio Sun."[3]

After World War II ended, "classical" astronomers began doing astronomy again. But ironically, the field that made the most spectacular, unexpected, and important advances in these years had few astronomers in its ranks. Radio astronomy exploded, but it did so mainly due to the efforts of researchers who had little or no training or experience in astronomy.

The war brought enormous improvements in the sensitivity of radio receivers, the design and construction of large "directional" antennas that were able to pull in radio waves from a relatively narrow range of directions, the analysis of signals, and a host of other developments. Moreover, there were literally thousands of tons of surplus electronic equipment that were free for the asking ("war surplus" was still a major source of gear in the late 1950s), and there were radio engineers who had worked on radar or radio projects during the conflict and wanted to continue working along the same lines. Radio science had proved so useful during the war that several governments decided to fund efforts in that field even as they disbanded the vast bulk of their armed forces.

In the late 1940s, radio astronomers in Australia and England used the new technology to make dramatic strides, while workers in the Netherlands and France were not far behind. One place where radio studies of the universe did not take off was in the United States, where most astronomers, long accustomed to their monopoly of large optical telescopes, sensed little need to venture into this different and rather "grimy" field. But elsewhere, these were the fabled days of yore, when there were "iron radio astronomers and wooden radio telescopes." Practitioners of the art chopped down trees for posts and dug post holes to position them. They strung "liberated" wire to form antennas and soldered together scrounged components to make receivers. For variety, they dug vehicles out of the mud and spent freezing and sweltering nights and days in battered old war-surplus communications trucks taking data, for automation then was only a dream. And because radio observations are seldom bothered by clouds or daylight, researchers seldom got enough sleep. This was an exciting era for radio studies of the universe, and we who experienced it would not have missed it for the world. Their activities were a far cry from the ordered and dignified routines of typical optical observatories of the time, but did they ever produce results!

Despite severe practical problems such as little money and limited interest among the astronomical establishment, radio astronomers racked up one spectacular discovery after another. One revelation came fairly early. The radiation from the Milky Way that Karl Jansky and Grote Reber had studied is spread over a substantial part of the sky, and its intensity changes fairly smoothly from point to point (exceptions actually were in their data, but no one realized that at the time). Then in 1946 observers in Great Britain led by Hey—again—accidentally discovered *variable* radio emission coming from the constellation Cygnus. The intensity of this source, now known as Cygnus A, varied by as much as 15 percent in only a few seconds.[4] We now know that these fluctuations have nothing to do with the source itself (though true variable sources were detected years later) but are due to the effects of Earth's ionosphere, which causes what can be called "radio twinkling" in the case of a source that has a small angular diameter.

Other observers in Great Britain and Australia confirmed the existence of Cygnus A and showed that its apparent angular size was only a few minutes of arc at most. As equipment and methods improved, more of these localized regions of radio emission turned up. At first their locations with respect to the stars were known only roughly, but as determinations of their positions improved, some of these sources were identified with objects known to optical astronomers.

The first few optical identifications included a mixed bag of objects. One turned out to be the Crab nebula, a peculiar cloud of glowing gas that we now know (but did not at the time) is the remnant of a supernova explosion observed on Earth in the year 1054. Another was the Andromeda galaxy, which was not surprising, as it was known to be nearby and to resemble the Milky Way in many respects. Another was Virgo A, which is a giant elliptical galaxy that has a peculiar bright jet projecting from its nucleus. Yet another was Centaurus A, another giant elliptical galaxy with a huge, dark dust lane cutting it in half.

At that time, the most puzzling case of all was Cygnus A, the second brightest (not counting the active Sun—and sometimes Jupiter) object in the radio sky. If the Andromeda galaxy, which is large and nearby, is only a relatively weak radio source as observed from Earth, why is there no prominent optical object corresponding to Cygnus A? It took the light-gathering power of the 200-inch telescope to photograph eventually a closely spaced pair of faint glows at the right location, which were interpreted as two galaxies in collision. The implications were startling. Cygnus A was at a great distance from Earth—it had a huge red shift for the time—and so it must be emitting tremendously more radio energy than a normal galaxy like our own or Andromeda.

However, as we now know, Cygnus A is nowhere near the most energetic of the so-called "active galaxies." It is actually a pretty tame object, belonging to a class known as "radio galaxies." Later, astronomers discovered even stronger radio emitters such as quasars ("quasi-stellar radio sources," which looked starlike in direct photographs) and their ilk, which are vastly more powerful. All these prodigious radio emitters seem to be galaxies that produce immense amounts of energy in very small regions near their centers, the so-called "active galactic nuclei." The cause of this bizarre behavior is currently thought to be connected with massive "black holes," objects that are small on an astronomical scale (the size of our solar system, for example), yet have so much mass (millions or billions of times that of our Sun) that light itself cannot escape from them.

But even though Cygnus A was only the first relatively modest example of the cosmic "monsters" that inhabit our universe, it certainly did open the eyes of astronomers to the existence of objects very different indeed from those we find in our familiar Milky Way and neighboring galaxies. Evidently, the cosmos on a large scale is a much more violent place than anyone had suspected up until that time. As an aside, none of the early optical identifications of radio sources involved a star other than the Sun—that would come, but only decades later—so researchers abandoned the rather appealing early term *radio star*. Instead, they adopted the clumsy designation *discrete radio source*. Progress is not always for the better.[5]

Radio astronomy made other significant advances in the decade following the end of World War II. As one example, an emission line due to interstellar atomic hydrogen was detected, and astronomers used observations of this feature to begin mapping the distribution of interstellar gas in the Milky Way.[6] For another, the source of the cosmic radio waves in most cases was eventually identified as so-called "synchrotron radiation," which is spontaneously emitted by electrons moving at nearly the speed of light as they spiral in a magnetic field. The name came from the fact that this kind of radiation was first observed in a type of particle accelerator, or "atom smasher," called a synchrotron.[7]

RADIO VERSUS OPTICAL

As indicated in the previous chapter, there was a wide gap between radio engineers and astronomers in their training, interests, and techniques. Radio workers mostly learned astronomy on their own, while trained astronomers mostly ignored the "radio technicians." Eventually, however, the spectacular series of completely unexpected and important discoveries made at radio wavelengths forced even the most classical of optical astronomers sit up and take notice.

But we should note that even at the start, there were a few optical astronomers who took a real interest in radio studies. One was Jesse L. Greenstein, who as early as the 1930s tried to account for Jansky's observations, and who in 1947 collaborated with Reber in the first-ever review of radio astronomy. Another was Otto Struve, one of the world's most senior and respected astronomers, who eventually became the director of the United States National Radio Observatory, and by so doing gave radio astronomy instant respectability among the astronomical establishment. Still, these pioneers were in the minority and it was not until the late 1950s that radio and optical astronomy began to mesh on a large scale.[8]

The situation in the United States vividly illustrated this early separation. For example, in January, 1958, the world's first comprehensive survey of radio astronomy in all its facets—observation, theory, and equipment—was published. In fact, an entire thick issue of a highly respected American technical publication was devoted to the subject. But it gives an insight to those times that the journal involved was the *Proceedings of the Institute of Radio Engineers* and not the *Astrophysical Journal* or the *Astronomical Journal,* which were the two premier astronomical publications in America and perhaps the world at the time. Moreover, conspicuous by their absence among the scores of authors represented in this special issue of the *Proceedings* were senior American astronomers.[9] My own first published scientific article likewise underscores the separation then prevailing between radio and optical studies. Addressing radio reflections from ionized meteor trails, that paper appeared in a 1958 issue of the *Proceedings.*[10] I never considered submitting it to an astronomical publication. The merger between radio and optical astronomy still had a way to go.

THE RADIO SOLAR SYSTEM

While there were advances in radio studies of the solar system, these often were overwhelmed in both popular and scientific interest by the flood of staggering revelations about objects in vastly more distant realms. Nevertheless, radio observations did contribute to a better understanding of the solar system.

A special case was that of our the Sun. Because it is a nearby radio emitter, and because that radiation can directly affect radio communications, radar, and even telephone, telegraph, cable, and electrical power networks on Earth, much work was devoted to our own star in this era. We are still learning about the radio Sun, but material on this fascinating subject has become so extensive that we must leave further elaboration to more specialized works.[11]

Meanwhile, there were both expected and unexpected results concerning the Moon and planets. Radio observations of the weak "thermal radiation" (the natural emission from any body at a temperature above absolute zero) from our satellite began in the 1940s.[12] This and later work confirmed the generally accepted idea that the Moon's uppermost layer is a good insulator, consistent with a surface covering of fine dust. But these results did not provide definite answers to specific questions such as how deep the dust is, how firm a surface it forms, and what its chemical composition is, uncertainties that would assume great practical importance in the Space Age.[13]

In contrast, the 1950s brought some surprising revelations about Venus. Radio observations starting in 1956 and made at wavelengths of a few centimeters indicated that the "surface" of Venus had a temperature of almost 600 degrees Kelvin, hot enough to melt metals such as tin and lead.[14] This should not have come as a great surprise, for as we have seen, researchers had already identified enough carbon dioxide *above* the clouds of Venus to cause a high surface temperature, without even considering the added effect of CO_2 lower down in the atmosphere. However, the extremely high temperatures indicated were somewhat disconcerting. There were attempts to explain these results as due to some phenomenon in the planet's atmosphere or ionosphere, but they came to naught. Even at that time, it appeared clear that there was little to prevent centimeter-wavelength radio radiation from passing right through Venus's atmosphere, and that as a result the observed high temperature was that of the actual solid surface.[15]

Radio observations of Mars provided only routine results, merely confirming previous infrared measurements of the surface temperature. The red planet held no surprises in this respect.[16] Jupiter, however, was another story. While studies in the late 1950s at wavelengths of a few centimeters indicated temperatures similar to those measured in the infrared, observations at tens of centimeters pointed to temperatures of thousands and even tens of thousands of degrees. Clearly this radiation could not be coming from anywhere near Jupiter's cold cloud tops, and in 1959 the American astronomer Frank D. Drake suggested that the source was a belt of fast-moving charged particles (electrons, protons, and such) trapped in Jupiter's magnetic field. He was right. This was the first definite indication that the giant planet had both a strong magnetic field and a "Van Allen Belt" of charged particles such as those that early American satellites discovered around Earth.[17]

But the biggest of the solar system's planets held an even greater surprise for radio astronomers. In 1955, the American researchers Bernard F.

Burke and Kenneth L. Franklin detected strong but intermittent bursts of radio noise from Jupiter at meter wavelengths. These bursts generally lasted only a second or so and at times were more intense than any other radio source in the sky except for the Sun in an active phase.[18] This behavior was actually detected as early as 1950 but went unrecognized because it was so "spotty." Further observations showed that the bursts were confined to relatively long wavelengths (and thus to low frequencies). This is a property shared by lightning on Earth, which interferes seriously with AM radio reception but is hardly noticeable on FM radio or in television reception. Although space-probe images have since shown that Jovian lightning does exist, it is not the cause of Jupiter's radio bursts. A Jovian bolt would have to have at least a billion times more energy than a terrestrial one, which seems unlikely, and the intensity of the Jupiter radiation falls off much more rapidly with increasing wavelength than does that of Earthly lightning. Even theoreticians were at a loss to explain the radiation's source, and the answer would come only slowly.

Even more puzzling was the fact that the bursts came with a period that was close to, but not the same as, either of the two generally accepted rotation periods of visible cloud features on Jupiter. Eventually it became clear that this third period was that of the massive interior of the planet. But the situation was complicated by the fact that the bursts did not always occur "on schedule." Something more was involved. As we shall see, it took a long time to sort out all the effects, and even today the total picture is not clear.[19]

During the 1950s Saturn was observed at radio wavelengths, but as was the case with Mars, it provided no surprises. Evidently Saturn's substantial rings suppressed the type of activity that goes on around Jupiter, probably by absorbing the fast-moving charged particles that might otherwise emit radio radiation. The thermal radio radiation, on the other hand, indicated temperatures similar to those derived from infrared measurements.[20]

Radio studies of the solar system in the 1940s and 1950s produced some important results and presented some mystifying puzzles. But on the whole these involved new problems and did little to solve old questions or to advance our knowledge about the nature of the planets and their satellites.

Interestingly, there is no evidence that studies of the Moon and planets in the 1940s and 1950s were looked down upon by radio astronomers, who, as noted, generally did not have classic astronomical backgrounds. And yet, the solar system is a really only a very tiny place compared to the rest of the vast universe. Thus it is no surprise that when the International Astronomical Union held its first symposium on radio astronomy in 1955, there were only nine talks on meteors, the Moon, and the planets, compared to seventy-one on the Sun, the Milky Way, and the then mysterious discrete radio sources.[21] Even in this entirely new field, planetary astronomy had to take a back seat to galactic and extragalactic research.

SHOOTING STARS

Although they did not realize it at the time, radio scientists began to study meteors in the late 1920s. As such a projectile plunges toward Earth, atmospheric friction generates enough heat to knock electrons off (that is, to ionize) atoms and molecules. The result is a short-lived trail of ionized gas, composed of negatively charged electrons and positively charged ions, an expanding cylinder that can act as an efficient reflector of radio waves.

When Guglielmo Marconi unexpectedly demonstrated trans-Atlantic radio communication in 1901, scientists were mystified as to how these signals could be transmitted so far around the curved Earth. One early suggestion was that the radio waves "skipped" off the bottom of an ionized layer high in our atmosphere, and the existence of what we now call the ionosphere was confirmed experimentally in 1925. Before the days of communications satellites, "short-wave" radio communication over great distances was of great practical importance, and many radio scientists and engineers studied its details.[22]

The ionized layers (for there are several of them) are produced by the action of solar ultraviolet light, which obviously cannot have any effects on Earth's dark side. Thus, it was puzzling indeed when as early as 1928 observers detected cases of large and sudden increases in the density of free electrons (which account for the long-distance radio propagation) in the ionosphere *at night*. By the 1930s it was clear that meteors were responsible for at least some of this anomalous ionization. In particular, the Leonid meteor shower had a distinct effect on the nighttime ionosphere.

There are several ways to study this phenomenon. One is to broadcast a short pulse of radio waves straight up and see what, if anything, comes back down (used as early as the 1920s, this was the first application of the radar principle), which gives information about the state of the ionosphere overhead. Another is to listen for a radio station that broadcasts at a frequency so high that "skip" is ineffective. The latter method revealed short but strong "bursts" of signals due to reflection from individual meteor trails.[23]

These trails can reflect radio waves with frequencies much higher than any influenced by the ionosphere, and more important, they offer the promise of increased communications security. The geometry among the transmitter, receiver, and location and orientation of the meteor trail must be just right for reception, so except for the unlikely fluke, enemy listening posts would never detect a signal sent in such a way. "Meteor burst communications" eventually came to be of considerable military importance, and studies of the phenomenon received substantial support in the form of money and workers.[24]

Propelled by theoretical scientific curiosity and practical commercial and military importance, radio meteor studies blossomed after World War II, and for a time in the late 1940s and 1950s significant discoveries came in a torrent. Two technical advances in particular aided this effort. One was the general development of reliable radio transmitters and receivers that operated at frequencies so high that the effects of the normal ionosphere were small. Another was, of course, radar.

Near the end of the war and shortly thereafter, Hey (yet again!) and other workers showed a direct connection between specific radio echoes and visually observed meteors. Researchers also found striking agreement between enhanced numbers of radio echoes and numerous meteor showers long known from visual observations.[25]

In addition, radio observations finally settled the longstanding controversy about the origin of meteors. As we have seen, Ernst Öpik's visual observations suggested that many arrived at Earth with such high velocities that they must have come from beyond the solar system. On the other hand, Fred Whipple's photographic work indicated that such interlopers were rare at best and perhaps nonexistent. Other work was inconclusive.[26] Radio observations over the years changed all that, for they showed that few if any meteors came from outside the Sun's realm.[27] Sadly, there seems to be no organized effort today to look for such objects. While rare, they must almost certainly exist, and it would certainly be exciting to find one.

Radio observations of meteors were responsible for yet another unexpected and spectacular discovery, one concerning daylight meteors and meteor showers. Astronomers had long realized that there must be such things but that the light of the Sun overwhelms all but the very brightest fireballs. Radio methods now provided the first chance to study meteors around the clock, unhampered by daylight or clouds. New annual showers were duly discovered, but it came as a real surprise that the greatest amount of meteoric activity occurs in the daytime. Meteor rates begin to pick up in May and continue at a high level through August. A number of different "streams" with different radiants are involved, and for the strongest, the rate at which meteors were observed (the equipment was adjusted so that the radio rate was about that which a visual observer could see on a clear, dark night) was greater than any annual nighttime shower, excepting only the rare meteor "storms."[28]

THE RADAR SOLAR SYSTEM

In 1946 humans achieved their first "active" contact with a body beyond Earth. Until then we had been only the passive receivers of light rays, charged particles ("cosmic" and "auroral" rays), and meteorites, but in that year there were two separate and successful attempts to detect radar echoes from the Moon. Signals beamed from Fort Monmouth, New Jersey, as well as from Hungary traveled from our planet to its satellite and back and were detected on their return.[29]

Lunar radar studies immediately provided extremely reliable estimates of the distance to our satellite as well as of the line-of-sight velocity between the Earth and the Moon at any given instant. Furthermore, radar research held out the possibility of helping determining the physical properties of our attendant's surface layers.

But then as now, radar studies of objects beyond Earth faced a formidable hurdle, for if a target is moved to twice its former distance and all else is kept the same, the returned "echo" is only *one sixteenth* as strong. Thus it took additional years of effort before radar returns were observed from Venus, the planet that approaches closest to our own. To this day, even the nearest stars appear beyond our reach. Radar research, it seems, is restricted to the solar system.[30]

In spite of its built-in limitations, radar eventually provided substantial gains in our knowledge of the solar system, most spectacularly about the mountains, valleys, and plains of Venus. Andrew J. Butrica's detailed history of the subject provides a full account of this specialized work.[31]

THE ROCKETS' RED GLARE

On September 8, 1944, the first two German V-2 missiles fell on London. The "V" stood for *Vergeltung*, or "vengeance" weapon. The V-2 was the first large, long-range ballistic missile. It was impossible to intercept at the time, landed before the sound of its arrival, and packed a ton of high explosive in its nose, but it was also wildly inaccurate and prone to failure.[32] The V-2 had little influence on the course of the Second World War, but the very existence of a vehicle that could rise above almost all of Earth's atmosphere suggested to some scientists that here was a new tool, the eventual development of which could have a profound effect on astronomy in general and planetary studies in particular. Only a few scientists of the time realized it, but pioneers such as Jesse Greenstein, Fred Whipple, and their like grasped it very clearly indeed. The Space Age had begun in earnest.

After the end of World War II the U.S. Army began an extensive series of test firings of captured V-2 rockets. They were launched at the White Sands Proving Ground in New Mexico. As part of the program, various scientific groups flew experiments that took advantage of the rocket's performance. While the V-2 could carry a hefty 2,000-pound payload above Earth's sensible atmosphere, it left something to be desired as a vehicle for scientific research. Once the engines stopped, the rocket was uncontrollable, spinning and tumbling wildly so that it was impossible to scan the sky in a regular manner, let alone to point instruments at specific targets. In addition, the vehicle spent only a few minutes at high altitudes before plunging back to Earth, where rocket and instruments usually were demolished more or less completely on impact. The last drawback was especially serious, for telemetry, the technique of radioing results back to Earth, was in its infancy. Thus, an otherwise entirely successful flight could be a complete failure in the end if the payload, or at least that part of it containing the data, failed to survive.

Despite these formidable challenges, dedicated scientists and engineers pressed ahead in their attempts to conduct scientific observations, and in some cases succeeded. Studies of Earth's atmosphere were of prime interest, and also there was much to be learned from looking down from above on the surface of our planet. But from the beginning astronomy was not neglected.

Our Sun, being by far the brightest object in the heavens, was the obvious first target for early high-altitude observations. In particular, scientists of many stripes were interested in its ultraviolet spectrum, which is unobservable from Earth's surface and which might provide insights into topics as diverse as radio propagation, atomic spectra, and the physical characteristics of the surface layers of stars. In this case, results were positive if hard won, and the Sun's ultraviolet spectrum was progressively revealed to shorter and shorter wavelengths. By 1947 many new features had been observed, but in general scientific returns came slowly and only with a great deal of hard work and to the accompaniment of many heartbreaking failures.[33]

Meanwhile, it was obvious that the V-2's one-ton payload was far too large for most experiments, even with the relatively bulky and massive electron-tube electronics of the day. Soon a wide variety of more suitable rockets appeared in the United States and elsewhere to advance the business of terrestrial, upper atmosphere, and space exploration. These vehicles were known as "sounding rockets," and were designed to provide a few minutes of observation above Earth's atmosphere. Their performance was far short of that needed to put a satellite into Earth orbit, let alone to send automated "probes" to the Moon or planets. But all the while, improvements in stabilizing and pointing payloads, general progress in electronics and computers, and developments in telemetry and detectors went on apace. However, it would take years before these new technologies could get to the point where they would significantly affect studies of the solar system.[34]

SLOW BUT STEADY PROGRESS

Even during the war some astronomers were able to carry out limited research programs. One important example was observational. In the winter of 1943–44 the American astronomer Gerard P. Kuiper, who had emigrated earlier from the Netherlands and who plays a major role in our story, made a survey of the ten largest satellites in the solar system, using the then new 82-inch reflector at McDonald Observatory in Trans-Pecos Texas. Nine satellites revealed evidence only of reflected sunlight, but Saturn's largest moon, Titan, showed absorption features due to methane, absorption features that were similar to but weaker than those seen on the planet. Kuiper noted that the satellite was orange in color like Mars, and he suggested that in both cases the hue was due to the reaction of an atmosphere on a solid surface. In fact the similar tints have entirely different explanations, though atmospheres are involved in both cases, but that would not be known for some time.

Kuiper also pointed out that atmospheres rich in hydrogen atoms (he noted that every methane molecule has four) previously had been found only around the massive giant planets, their strong gravities keeping relatively light gases from escaping. He reasoned that a similar gaseous mantle around Titan could be present now only if that atmosphere had formed after the satellite had cooled off from any high-temperature phase that it had once had.

Tucked into the short abstract at the beginning of Kuiper's report was the intriguing comment that "Triton and Pluto require further study." He certainly was on the right track, for as we now know, Neptune's large satellite does have a thin atmosphere, while Pluto has a temporary one whenever it is nearest the Sun in its orbit. His predictions have stood the test of time.[35]

Another important example of wartime research was theoretical. In

1944, the German theoretician C. F. von Weizsäcker published a new theory on the origin of the solar system.[36] At the time both the venerable nebular hypothesis and the newer encounter theory in its various forms seemed unable to account for the formation of our planetary system, so the appearance of a fresh stream of thought was not only welcome but was recognized early on as something important.

The new theory assumed that the Sun and the planets formed at the same time from a nebula. As the primitive Sun developed, it remained surrounded by a shell of material some ten times less massive. This shell then collapsed to form a disk in the plane of our star's equator, a disk that had the same chemical composition as the Sun. An important point was the assumption that our star is composed mostly of hydrogen, with most of rest being helium and all the other elements composing only a few percent. There had been earlier indications that this was the case, but now the concept, which is correct, received more support.

Von Weizsäcker's original article was published in Germany in 1944, when the Third Reich was only months from collapse. Amid the chaos surrounding the end of the Nazi regime, scientists in the rest of the world knew nothing of this work at the time. Most American astronomers first learned of it from a short summary that appeared in a 1945 issue of the *Astrophysical Journal*. The authors merely stated that "a reprint of Weizsäcker's paper has become available to the writers."[37]

Where and how was this reprint salvaged from the wreck and ravages of war? We may never know for certain, but some facts are suggestive. Kuiper was then a staff member at Yerkes Observatory, where the editorial offices of the *Astrophysical Journal* were located. He was also a member of the "Alsos" Mission, a top secret American military and scientific unit created to seize all possible information, equipment, and personnel concerned with German efforts on atomic weapons or with any other technical developments of military importance. Alsos teams went into action just behind, along with, and sometimes even ahead of frontline combat troops. One of their prime targets was von Weizsäcker, whom they eventually captured in southern Germany in late April, 1945. Interestingly, Kuiper had the strongest interest in planetary physics of any member of the Alsos team.[38]

In von Weizsäcker's view, most of the nebula was lost to the Sun, carrying away with it the angular momentum that in the original nebular hypothesis would have ended up in an otherwise rapidly rotating star. This neatly disposed of the problem of why the Sun is not rotating much more rapidly than it now does. As it turned out, the situation probably is not that simple, for current thinking is that a typical "proto"-star starts out rotating rapidly and is "braked" by the interaction of its magnetic field with the dissipating nebula. Still, this was a step forward.

In this theory, the atoms and stray small solid particles in the nebula originally orbit the Sun individually. However, some small condensations inevitably form, much as in the old planetesimal hypothesis. However, von Weizsäcker assumed that planets would form only at certain special locations. In effect, rings of "vortices" would form at specific distances from the Sun, and planets would form in "whirlpools" between them. Satellite systems such as those of Jupiter and Saturn were explained simply as smaller versions of the solar system itself.

The new theory strongly suggested that planetary systems are common, as had been widely believed a century before, that they should exist in wide variety, and that they might well be forming today. It would take the introduction of high-speed electronic computers to provide confirmation of this theory by filling in more details to the picture, but the general idea has stood the test of time and in a much refined form is generally accepted today. The solar system did indeed form from a nebula, and the process did not need an unlikely second star passing by on an improbable orbit as required by encounter theories. Furthermore, the new theory of origin required that the Sun and its attendant planets formed at the same time, a situation to which advances in many sciences were pointing.

During the 1950s a small group of astronomers, physicists, meteorologists, and other scientists interested in the red planet formed the Mars Committee. This was an informal organization that met every year or so for members to present their latest research results and to plan and coordinate observational programs during oppositions of Mars. Usually about a score of people would gather somewhere like Lowell Observatory and others would send in written communications.[39]

Even for that era, research on Mars was definitely "small science." For example, to insure continuous photographic coverage of the red planet during the 1954 opposition, the committee provided photographic plates, color filters, lenses, and the like to foreign observatories that were too poor to afford even these relatively inexpensive items. The grand total spent on these gifts (including some secretarial expenses) came to a munificent $669.30! This was less than half the price of an inexpensive automobile at the time but nevertheless presented the committee with a considerable financial problem. The committee decided to approach the U.S. National Science Foundation for a grant to be administered by Lowell Observatory.[40] The story has a happy ending, for NSF did provide two thousand dollars—to coordinate a year-long, worldwide research effort.[41] This incident vividly illustrates that planetary scientists of the time thought and planned in exceedingly modest terms. They were fascinated by their topic but the field was very much a backwater.

We have already met Gerard P. Kuiper, but it is now time to focus on the pioneering contributions of the man who may have done more to advance planetary science than any other individual. Born and schooled in the Netherlands, Kuiper emigrated to the United States in the early 1930s, and by the 1950s was the director of the combined Yerkes and McDonald observatories.

In his early research Kuiper concentrated on double stars. In particular, he investigated the question of whether the relative numbers of stars with very low mass companions could throw some light on the possible number of planetary systems like our own. As discussed earlier, Kuiper began to observe solar system objects in the early 1940s. Following his service for the government with the Alsos mission, he turned almost full-time to planetary research.[42] Kuiper had an intense interest in the solar system as early as the 1920s, and in the 1940s and 1950s he was able to carry out further studies in this area. Because other, more distant fields of astronomy beckoned so strongly, he had to work mostly alone in these efforts, with only a few collaborators. Nevertheless, he made an impressive list of discoveries about our Sun's family.[43]

His efforts were helped considerably by a knowledge of recent German advances in infrared technology that he had acquired in Europe during and just after the war. In 1946 he and his colleagues designed and built a spectrometer, an instrument similar to a spectrograph but which records the data electrically instead of on a photographic plate. The instrument was designed specifically to study infrared radiation. A key item was the use of a "lead-sulfide cell" (which was then a new development) to detect the long-wavelength emission. At the time photographic emulsions were effective only to about 7000 Ångstroms, except in the cases of very bright objects such as the Sun and Venus.[44] The new instrument covered the range from this long-wavelength limit out to approximately 2.5 microns (25,000 Ångstroms). From that point on absorption from atmospheric water vapor becomes very strong and, except for a few "windows," prohibits observations of celestial objects until the radio region is reached.[45]

Kuiper wasted no time in using the new instrument at Yerkes and McDonald observatories and soon reported on the infrared spectra of Venus, Jupiter, and Saturn. Several new carbon dioxide bands were found in the spectrum of Venus and a number of new methane and ammonia bands in the spectrum of Jupiter. Saturn's spectrum was, in the main, similar to that of Jupiter. The interpretation of all these spectra was complicated by the fact that there were few laboratory studies of these features. Still, a beginning had been made in the investigation of a wavelength region that would later supply much information about the universe in general and the solar system in particular.[46]

Kuiper had a habit of initializing the constant stream of memos that poured from his desk and thus acquired the nickname of "GPK." Carl Sagan once described him as "the only practicing planetary astrophysicist in the 1950s," and when that description was criticized, his answer was, "I said it because it's true."[47] Kuiper's lonely position and the moribund state of planetary astronomy at the time are highlighted by an experience he had in 1955. At a meeting of the International Astronomical Union, Kuiper passed out a memorandum to all the members of the union's Commission 16 ("Physical Observations of Planets and Satellites," of which he was president) urging the need for a better photographic atlas of the Moon. He asked for "comments, criticisms, alternate suggestions, or any other advice," but even from this select and presumably interested group, he received only a single reply. In the 1950s, planetary studies were quite low even on these astronomers' lists of priorities, and for Kuiper and a small scattering of other enthusiasts, waiting for a change in the situation was a lonely vigil.[48]

THE PLANETS

Kuiper obtained a number of spectra of Venus which were analyzed by his Yerkes co-worker Joseph W. Chamberlain. The relative strengths of the individual lines in several absorption bands of carbon dioxide indicated a temperature at the cloud tops of Venus of just under 300 degrees Kelvin, which pointed toward a surface temperature much higher than that. This estimate turned out to be too high but continued the trend toward ever lower cloud-top temperatures.

Venus's rotation period and the tilt of its axis were still unknown. As we have seen, earlier spectroscopic studies had already shown that the planet must rotate slowly, but how just slowly was still anybody's guess. In the 1950s Kuiper took a number of photographs to try to determine the axial tilt. He estimated this quantity at about 32 degrees, which is a bit more than Earth's. He was wrong here, as the actual value is almost nil.[49]

Using his new infrared spectrometer, by 1948 Kuiper was able to confirm the presence of carbon dioxide gas in the atmosphere of Mars.[50] This was a landmark discovery, for it was the first detection of *any* gas in the atmosphere of the red planet. Kuiper could not know it then, but he had essentially found the composition of the Martian atmosphere, for CO_2 comprises almost all of it.

In this era, it was generally accepted that the atmospheric surface pressure on Mars was about 100 millibars or roughly 10 percent of that on Earth, and that most of that was due to nitrogen.[51] In fact, the then standard work on Mars stated that "the result cannot be far from" 85 millibars.[52] These estimates were actually 10 times greater than reality, and the mistaken impression would cause severe practical problems for space-probe designers in the not so distant future. From today's perspective, it is clear that many of these estimates were flawed by a failure to realize what a dusty planet Mars is, for a relatively small number of tiny dust particles can mimic the properties of a much denser clear atmosphere.

Progress on the giant planets was slow, in particular because it was difficult to photograph spectra of these distant objects with their relatively low surface brightnesses. Still, it was becoming clear that they were composed primarily of hydrogen and helium, the two lightest elements, a view that would prove correct.

SMALL BODIES

Observational work on comets proceeded at a modest level during this era. One solid accomplishment was the publication of an atlas of cometary spectra by the Belgian astronomers P. Swings and L. Haser. They collected hundreds of spectra from scores of comets and gave identifications for features due to more than a dozen kinds of atoms, molecules, and ions.[53]

There were few bright comets in this period, and public interest in them was low. On the other hand, there were important theoretical advances in our knowledge of the origin and nature of these bodies. In 1950 the Dutch astronomer Jan H. Oort suggested that comets came from a huge spherical reservoir surrounding the Sun. In his view, some 100 billion quiescent comets orbit our star at distances from 30,000 to 100,000 astronomical units. The gravitational influences of passing stars affect the orbits of these bodies, and from time to time cause some of them to pass close enough to the Sun to be visible to us.[54] Though there is still no direct proof for the existence of this "Oort cloud," its reality is widely accepted today.

In the same year Fred L. Whipple published a fundamentally new model of a comet's nucleus. He proposed that a typical comet is an old member of the solar system, and that a comet begins as a frozen conglomerate of "ices" such as water ice, dry ice, and the like that are volatile at room temperature, mixed with substances such as minerals and metal grains that stay solid at that temperature. For obvious reasons this concept became known as the "dirty snowball" theory.

When a "primitive" comet (one that has never been heated) passes close to the Sun, solar radiation vaporizes the surface volatiles, leaving behind an insulating layer of "meteoric" material. The body would resemble an old pile of snow, with a dark crust over a mostly icy interior. From then on, vaporization takes place mainly from relatively small regions where the surface layer has been cracked or punctured in some way, resulting in jets or fountains of escaping material like those often seen emanating from cometary nuclei. These jets would act exactly like rocket engines and could neatly account for otherwise unexplained orbital changes such as those shown by Enke's comet.[55] Whipple's theory was triumphantly confirmed by close-up images of the nucleus of Halley's comet made decades later. The nucleus turned out to be a solid, potato-shaped body covered for the most part with a dark crust. From a few small areas, jets of bright volatile material erupted into space.

There was less progress in the case of asteroids. In 1949 Kuiper began a systematic study of the brightness variations of these objects at various wavelengths. His aims were to estimate how many of these tiny planets there are, their rotation periods, their shapes, and the orientations of their axes in space. These efforts were helped considerably by the introduction of the revolutionary 1P21 photomultiplier tube. This device could measure the intensities of very faint light sources and offered much more sensitivity and precision than the old photographic methods.[56]

In addition to the impetus to meteor studies provided by radio and radar techniques, our knowledge of meteorites received a boost from the technique of radioactive dating. There are in fact several ages that can be estimated in this way: when the original nuclei were forged in the interiors of stars, when the meteorite's parent body melted shortly after formation, when that body cooled, when the parent broke up, and when the meteorite fell to Earth. These methods were tried as early as 1928 but for years gave conflicting results because of many complicating factors: daughter nuclei may escape, "extra" daughter nuclei may be produced by cosmic rays, and so forth. But, by the 1950s, it was clear that no meteorites solidified before about 4.6 billion years ago, which seemed to be the age of the solar system.[57]

Radio astronomy, radar, and spectroscopy introduced exciting new dimensions into planetary astronomy. Few anticipated, however, the revolutionary implications that began to emerge in 1957 with the unfolding revelations that machines made on Earth, and humans themselves, could leave the confines of the planet and fly in space—even to other bodies in the solar system and beyond. Planetary astronomy and humankind itself would never be the same again.

FOUR BOOKS THAT MADE A DIFFERENCE

In the decade following the end of World War II, interest in space exploration mushroomed among the general public, if not in the minds of all the scientists who should have been concerned with the possibility. Science fiction magazines (some pretty good) and movies (some pretty awful) abounded, and the better efforts provoked some readers and viewers—I was one—to look to the heavens for a career.

A quartet of widely popular volumes that appeared between 1949 and 1956 played a significant role in this increased interest and showcased the amazingly prescient paintings of the incomparable space artist Chesley Bonestell. First came *The Conquest of Space,* written by Willy Ley. This was a general survey of our then current knowledge of the solar system and how we might explore it in the not so distant future. It was one of the first serious books on space exploration that had wide popular appeal.[58]

Across the Space Frontier was an entirely different book, featuring contributions by such noted technical experts as the German-American rocket designer Wernher von Braun and astronomer Fred Whipple. This 1952 work was edited by Cornelius Ryan of *Collier's* magazine and is an extended version of the series of articles that appeared in that publication under the general title of "Man Will Conquer Space Soon." It was the outgrowth of a meeting on space travel held at New York's Hayden Planetarium in 1951 and proved an eye-opener to many.

Within this amazing book are predicted the three-stage rocket to orbit; a winged, reusable orbital vehicle that lands on runways like an airplane (this took material form as the Space Shuttle); the tremendous opportunities that observations from space opened to astronomy (the Hubble Space Telescope has fulfilled this prophecy); and the wheel-shaped, rotating space station. In little more than four decades, only the large space station has not become a reality. Perhaps the word *conquer* was unduly optimistic in the title of the *Collier's* series, for after all we have not yet conquered the sea, let alone the air, even on our own planet, but that term did sound a positive and confident note that inspired many and ultimately had some influence on the public mind, American taxpayers, and politically powerful figures.

Perhaps even more significant for the advancement of space exploration in general and planetary astronomy in particular was that senior, well-respected, and hardheaded scientists and engineers such as Whipple and von Braun, to mention just two, would not only lend their names to such a work but would actually take part in writing it. Suddenly, the close-up exploration of the Moon and planets seemed to many not only possible but also imminent.[59]

The book had an interesting genesis. In 1952 the U.S. Air Force sponsored a meeting on the upper atmosphere. At a dinner during that meeting, von Braun, Whipple, and senior scientist Joseph Kaplan sat with Ryan, who gave the impression of being "highly suspicious" of any success in space ventures. However, by the end of a long night the trio had "sold" Ryan on the idea of a *Collier's* series of articles.[60]

A companion book, *Conquest of the Moon,* appeared in 1953. This too originated as a series of articles in *Collier's,* and the same team of experts spelled out in detail just how manned lunar exploration would happen "within our lifetime." Though the hypothetical expedition departed from a permanent space station and comprised three large spaceships, many technical details were duplicated in the actual Apollo 11 mission that landed men on the Moon and returned them safely to Earth just nineteen years later.[61]

The last of the four books was *The Exploration of Mars* by Ley and von Braun. The authors first summarized the advancement of our knowledge of the red planet since antiquity and then described in some detail how a round-trip manned expedition to Mars might take place. This feat, they believed, would happen "within a matter of decades." Their estimate turned out to be hopelessly optimistic, but the voyage might well have been made before the end of the twentieth century if the money for the effort had been available. As proved to be the case with lunar exploration, no scientific or technological barriers appear to stand in the way of such an endeavor.[62]

TURN OF THE TIDE

The launching of the first
artificial satellite, followed
soon after by the first
deep space probes, thrust
planetary astronomy into
the spotlight of intense
worldwide interest

The world emerged from World War II on the threshold of space. The work of astronomers for the past two thousand years or more provided a great reservoir of knowledge about space, the Moon, and the planets. Now that information would become essential to the American effort in space. Moreover, the participation of planetary astronomers in the efforts of what would become the National Aeronautics and Space Administration revolutionized the science itself. Within a matter of decades, planetary astronomers crossed an important threshold and began to acquire a more detailed understanding of the solar system as funding increased, instrumentation improved, and spaceflights provided close-up observations.

In 1949, a two-stage rocket with a V-2 as its first stage lifted off from the White Sands Proving Ground in New Mexico and soared to an altitude of some 250 miles. Significantly, as early as the mid-1950s scientists and engineers had a basic understanding of how to build and launch artificial

Earth satellites. There were no fundamental theoretical barriers involved, but there were practical, and very difficult, engineering tasks such as building reliable rocket engines, lightweight fuel tanks, sophisticated guidance systems, and the like. Nonetheless, it had become reasonable to believe that advancing technology would provide the means to overcome these difficulties and indeed would do so in the near future.[1] By that time many scientists and engineers had come to the conclusion that artificial Earth satellites, human travel through space, and probes of the Moon and neighboring planets were coming within their grasp.

However, the opinions of scientists, engineers, and other enthusiasts would have meant nothing but for the fact that the American public—taxpayers—became committed to the exploration of space. Planetary science not only provided a pool of knowledge but also represented the long-standing human tradition of fascination with the planets and other celestial bodies. Everyone on Earth knew the Moon. Earth's satellite, along with Venus, Mars, Jupiter, and Saturn can be easily observed on clear dark nights with the naked eye, for they are among the brightest objects in the heavens. Americans related the exploration of nearby heavenly bodies in the twentieth century to the exploration of other continents on Earth in earlier ages, and it is probably true that the prospects of discovering and perhaps claiming new territories appealed to people more than did the scientific progress in itself.

Americans could more readily associate space with planetary astronomy than with sciences such as physics and chemistry. While many people had personal knowledge of the Moon and planets, nobody has ever seen an atom, a radio wave, or a chemical bond, to mention just a few scientific topics that would have immense practical importance to the exploration of space. In addition, the legacy of Percival Lowell, H. G. Wells, and Orson Welles lived on. Moreover, the existence of some form of life on Mars and perhaps other planets—perhaps even on the Moon—was considered a serious possibility by many scientists and was the subject of intense speculation by the general public.

Comparing the speculations and anticipations of the 1950s with the realities of the 1990s helps set the historical context in which the United States began its journey into space. Many of the early optimistic predictions about the practical benefits of Earth satellites became the new realities. Maps of our planet are much more precise, as is our knowledge of its shape. Images of weather patterns as seen from space are now routine on television broadcasts and can be viewed directly in individual homes; no more is there the threat of a dangerous hurricane striking unexpectedly anywhere in the world. In the field of communications, worldwide television broadcasts are now common, telephone conversations over vast distances are much improved, and long-distance calls are made routinely from automobiles, ships, planes, or trains by means of satellite links. Navigation has been transformed. Today, ships, airplanes, automobiles, and even individual hikers can locate their positions, via specially designed satellites, to within less than fifty feet anywhere on Earth merely by pushing a few buttons on a hand-held device. Reconnaissance from space has become the backbone of government intelligence work for many nations and in addition has vital applications for environmental studies and economic development. (As one example, the Gulf War demonstrated the ability of satellites to deliver timely warnings of hostile missile launches.) The "back" of the Moon has been revealed and the entire lunar surface mapped; a dozen Americans have walked on the surface of our satellite. Space probes have flown by or to Mars, Venus, Mercury, Jupiter, and all the rest of the major planets except Pluto, and some bodies have been visited several times. Probes from Earth have orbited and landed on Venus and Mars. The Moons of Jupiter, Saturn, Uranus, and Neptune have been closely observed, as have a number of comets and asteroids. In short, in the past forty years we have learned a vast amount about the solar system that could have never been learned from ground-based observations alone.

However, many of the things that came to be happened on very different timetables than those imagined in the 1950s. Some things came much more slowly than was anticipated. For example, NASA first considered an Orbiting Astronomical Observatory (OAO) in the late 1950s, but the first one was not launched until 1966. Unfortunately its electrical and communications systems failed after twenty-two orbits. OAO 2, launched in 1968, successfully reported ultraviolet, gamma ray, x-ray, and infrared radiation and other interstellar information. Also first seriously envisioned in the decade of the 1950s, a much larger telescope in orbit took almost forty years to achieve reality in the form of the sophisticated Hubble Space Telescope.

In the 1950s, manned lunar and planetary missions were expected to follow the development of manned space stations and reusable Earth-to-orbit spaceflight vehicles. Instead, lunar landings preceded the space station and the Space Shuttle.

Few could have anticipated the extent of the revolution in communications engendered by space exploration. Author Arthur C. Clarke was one of the few—or perhaps the only person—who clearly saw the early, widespread, and fundamental changes that communications satellites were almost certain to bring about, changes that would directly affect literally billions of people. He addressed this prospect in considerable detail in *The*

Exploration of Space, published in 1951. Few then could have imagined that by the end of the twentieth century small and relatively inexpensive satellite antennas would be scattered across our planet, bringing hundreds of television channels into individual homes around the entire world and providing easy and reliable communications between most points on Earth. Another unforeseen advance, a development driven in part by the needs of the space program, was the rapid miniaturization of electronic components, which made possible the development of lightweight computers of tremendous power.

Some early predictions did not come to be, or at least not in the form expected. Manned expeditions to Mars, for example, were once thought to be imminent, but today seem as far in the future as ever. On the other hand, unmanned space probes can now perform operations so complex that it has become less urgent to use humans in dangerous interplanetary or deep space missions.[2]

The practical beginnings of the Space Age lay in the first dozen years following World War II, and planetary astronomy played a large part in that inception. When space exploration did became a reality, it opened an entirely new dimension for planetary sciences and astronomical studies in general, for our knowledge of the solar system and of regions beyond exploded. For some, planetary studies became a hands-on experience. In the critical decade of the 1960s, planetary astronomy came to be space-based as well as Earth-based. This is the story of how planetary science fits into this new epoch in human history, and how, in turn, the study of astronomy and our knowledge of the solar system and the universe have been changed.

GROUND-BASED ASTRONOMY, 1946–1957

As in the past, Mars and the Moon were principal objects of interest to planetary astronomers in the postwar years. Not coincidentally, these two bodies would become primary targets for the physical exploration of space. As early as 1950, Dean B. McLaughlin (who, it should be noted, was primarily a stellar astronomer), published an explanation for the observed changes in the face of Mars. His suggestions ignored the more popular and current notions that those variations were due to the life cycle of Martian vegetation. He suggested, on the contrary, that there are now active volcanos on Mars, spewing forth large amounts of dark ash. In his view fluctuating seasonal winds would redistribute this fine material, giving rise to the changes observed from Earth.[3]

McLaughlin was closer to the mark than he knew, for close-up images from space probes have since shown that changes of the red planet's surface appearance are indeed due to seasonal winds blowing fine material around. Then too, we now know that Mars does have many volcanos that have been active "recently" on a geological timescale, though whether any are in that state presently is still unknown. On the other hand, the dark spots that he believed to be volcanos generally were not. In fact, the largest volcano in the solar system, Olympus Mons, had long been known as a sometimes bright spot on Mars, due to the clouds and snows that often crowned it. But McLaughlin cannot be faulted for this particular misidentification. Indeed, the fact that as seen from Earth, the more or less permanent bright and dark areas on Mars do not systematically correspond to either high or low regions has remained a puzzle, though more and more pieces of the puzzle are being collected.

About 1950, C. C. Kiess and his associates decided that they could photograph high-dispersion spectra of the planets *without* using a large telescope. Instead they used relatively small mirrors to collect light for a spectrograph and thus, figuratively following in Campbell's footsteps, hauled their equipment high up the slopes of the Mauna Loa volcano on the island of Hawaii, a very dry site that reduced the confusing effects of absorption features due to water vapor in Earth's atmosphere.

While it may seem against reason to be able to use small collecting areas to get spectra with dispersions equal to those possible with large telescopes, it can work. The key lies in the fact that, as long as the optical equipment is capable of resolving an object into a disk—in contrast to a mere point of light—the useful dispersion is limited only by the planet's surface brightness and the sensitivity of the detector, in this case a photographic plate. But there are drawbacks to the method, for of course a smaller primary mirror collects a smaller amount of light. If this light is spread out greatly along the spectrum, that spectrum must be narrow for that limited amount of light to make an impression on the plate.

In 1956 Kiess and his co-workers used this method to search for water vapor on Mars. They found no evidence for any and set an upper limit of 80 microns for the average abundance of H_2O in the atmosphere of the red planet.[4] Their upper limit has held up, but as we know now, the "grainy" emulsions that they used made it impossible for them to detect the very weak Martian water vapor lines that do exist.

Because they were unable to detect any H_2O lines, and because they did believe that features due to the oxides of nitrogen were visible on their plates, Kiess and his colleagues made the novel suggestion that the latter substances were abundant on Mars and responsible for many observed phenomena on that planet: the behavior of the polar caps, clouds, and the

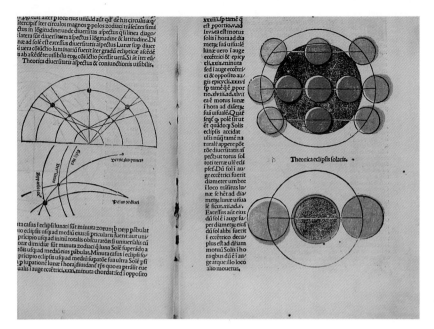

Drawings illustrating the causes of lunar (*top*) and solar (*bottom*) eclipses, from *Sphaera mundi,* published in Venice in 1490. Note that these explanations are correct, even though they assume the erroneous Earth-centered system of Ptolemy. Courtesy Texas A&M University Archives

Mars as it looks from far away.

This image made by the Hubble Space Telescope shows how the planet appears from Earth when viewed directly through a large telescope during rare moments of superb atmospheric conditions. Unfortunately, those moments have always been too short to permit terrestrial observers to record all the myriad details visible. The south polar cap is prominent at the top, and the dark area just below it is Mare Acidalium. The bright areas are too red in this image; they should actually be a dirty yellow. Courtesy NASA

Mars as it looks from orbit, a Viking 1 image. Note that the planet is not red but instead a dirty yellow, and that the contrast between bright and dark regions is much less than that displayed on many "enhanced" views. Courtesy NASA

A Martian afternoon as seen from the Viking 2 lander. As in the case of the Painted Desert of Arizona, our neighbor planet's surface looks quite colorful in the light of the lowering Sun. Courtesy NASA

As seen from a Voyager spacecraft, the giant planet Jupiter shows a wealth of detail, including the Great Red Spot at lower left. Spacecraft images with higher resolution showed even more detail, and the end is not in sight. The colors in this image have been enhanced, as the actual planet is much blander overall, though small areas actually show a good deal of color. Courtesy NASA

The Voyager 1 spacecraft revealed incredible detail in the rings of Saturn. Observations of radio signals as the probe passed beyond them as seen from Earth showed that the individual rings number in the thousands. NASA image

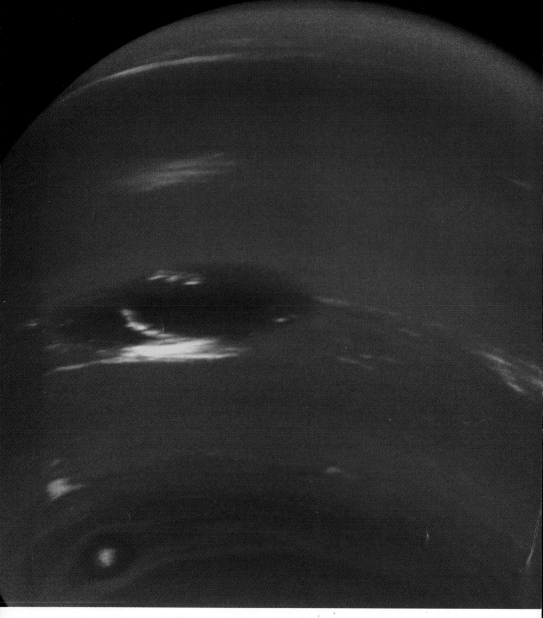

Voyager 2 unexpectedly revealed striking atmospheric structure on Neptune, such as the Great Dark Spot and brilliant high level white clouds, presumably composed of methane ice. NASA image

Opposite page, top: The Hubble Space Telescope unexpectedly revealed that major changes in the upper atmosphere of Neptune can happen in a very short time. These false color images were taken in 1994 on October 10 (*upper left*), October 18 (*upper right*), and November 2 (*lower center*). Courtesy Heidi Hammel and NASA

Opposite page, bottom: Voyager 2 revealed that Neptune's satellite Triton, one of the largest in the solar system, has a weird past. Contrary to what was expected for an object so far from the Sun, this body has had a complicated geologic history and appears to be active to this day. NASA image

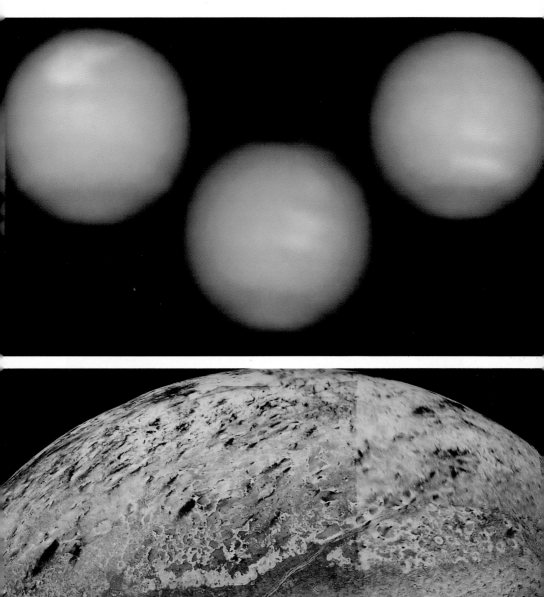
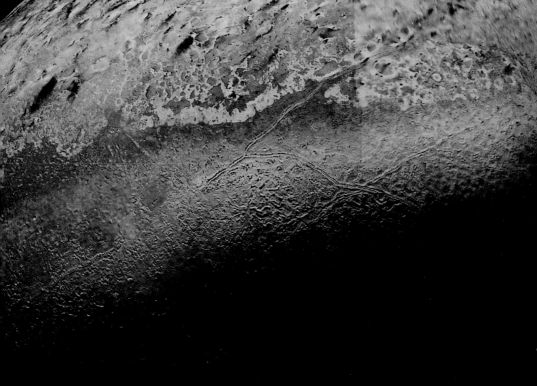

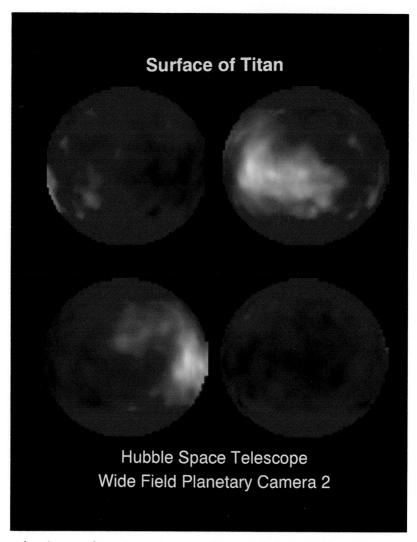

Surface of Titan

Hubble Space Telescope
Wide Field Planetary Camera 2

Infrared images of Titan, Saturn's largest satellite, made by the Hubble Space Telescope, showed that it was not completely uniform (covered by an ocean of some liquid, for example) but instead has a varied surface, and a surface still unknown. Courtesy Space Telescope Science Institute

A "string of pearls." The separated fragments of Comet Shoemaker-Levy 9 in May, 1993, just two months before they collided with Jupiter. Courtesy McDonald Observatory, University of Texas at Austin

This ordinary looking rock picked up in Antarctica is a piece of Mars and may hold evidence that primitive life existed on that planet in the distant past. NASA photograph

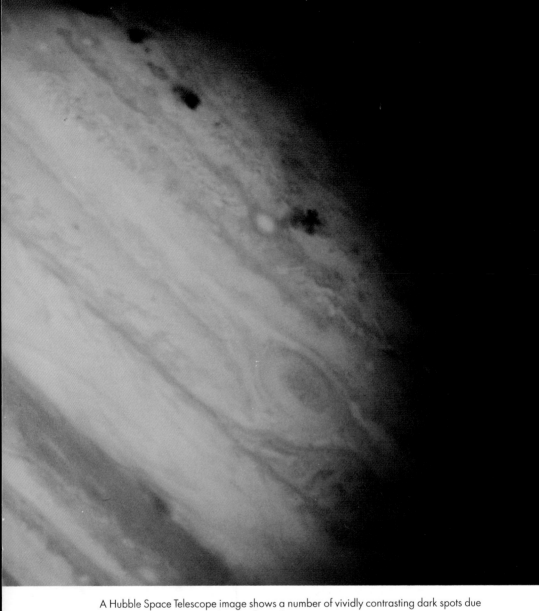

A Hubble Space Telescope image shows a number of vividly contrasting dark spots due to impacts of fragments on Jupiter of Comet Shoemaker-Levy 9. Courtesy NASA

like.[5] Clearly the existence of substantial amounts of the oxides of nitrogen on Mars would mean that life as we know it was impossible on that planet, for such substances are deadly poison to terrestrial organisms. However, observations by other workers showed no trace of any spectral features due to the oxides of nitrogen.[6] Thus, the possibility of life on Mars was still alive.

Kiess and his colleagues had better success when they used the same method on Jupiter in 1957. The giant planet has a substantially larger apparent diameter than does Mars and thus the spectra were wider, permitting the recognition of finer details. These observations provided the first direct evidence for the presence of molecular hydrogen (H_2) on Jupiter. Because of its low density, scientists at the time generally believed that hydrogen was a major constituent of the planet, but spectroscopic confirmation was bedeviled by the fact that the strongest lines of this substance lie far in the ultraviolet and cannot be observed from the surface of the Earth. However, there are some intrinsically weak lines in the near infrared and Kiess and his co-workers found four of them. They succeeded because of the high quality of their spectra and because sunlight passes through a great deal of molecular hydrogen in Jupiter's atmosphere above the cloud tops.[7]

The most sensational and seemingly significant event for planetary astronomy in this period was the announcement in 1957 of what seemed to be definite proof that there was organic life on Mars similar to that on Earth. This startling revelation came from observations made by William M. Sinton, who used the 61-inch Harvard Observatory telescope to take infrared spectra of Mars. These spectra showed infrared absorption bands on Mars near a wavelength of 3.4 microns that were not there in spectra of the Sun. That circumstance seemed to clinch the case for the features being due to some substance on the red planet. Suggestively, organic substances generally show such absorptions, which are due to the presence of the pairings of carbon and hydrogen atoms in such molecules.[8]

Moreover, the spectra showed a similarity to those of terrestrial lichens, low and weird forms of life that combine fungi with algae. Lichens inhabit some of the highest, driest, and coldest places on Earth, and of all forms of life on our planet are perhaps the best adapted for survival on a cold, dry Mars, where oxygen was known to be scarce and carbon dioxide abundant. Sinton was careful to point out that his observations did not prove that there were lichens growing on Mars, but he did feel that his results supported the possibility that there was some sort of plant life there.[9]

Sinton made further observations with the 200-inch telescope on

Mount Palomar, which showed the telltale bands in spectra taken of the dark areas of Mars (which presumably were dark because they were covered with vegetation) but not in spectra of the bright orange regions (which presumably were barren desert).[10] As might be expected, this news provided a sensation. It also convinced many astronomers—I was among these—that there actually was life on Mars, even if it was only in a primitive form. But, alas, things were not what they seemed.

The absorption features were real, all right, but they were actually due to heavy water in *Earth's* atmosphere. Heavy water (HDO) is normal water (HOH or H_2O) in which one hydrogen atom has been replaced by one of deuterium. Deuterium, in its turn, is an isotope of hydrogen, in which the normal atomic nucleus of a single positively charged proton has an added neutron with no charge whatever. Heavy water occurs naturally on Earth, though it is relatively rare. By a perverse turn of fate Sinton's equipment, simply because it was so good, sometimes was able to detect the tiny concentrations of that substance in our planet's atmosphere.

The actual reason for the misidentification was a particularly insidious one. Sinton had been careful to take precautions such as obtaining comparison spectra of the Sun and Moon, for if the bands appeared in them the substance responsible would clearly have been in Earth's atmosphere, as our star is much too hot to contain complex organic molecules and our satellite was generally believed to contain little or none. But what Sinton did not reckon with was the fact that the amount of water vapor (including "heavy water vapor") in our atmosphere varies with time. As it turned out, when the humidity was high, he detected the bands, but when it was low, he did not. Chance determined that he would observe Mars, and the dark areas in particular, when the humidity was high.[11] The whole chain of events was so improbable that it cast a long shadow on planetary astronomy, and as a result, some workers in the field were rather conservative in their claims, at least for the next few years. Nevertheless, scientific discussions of the possibilities of life, an atmosphere, and active volcanoes on Mars heightened public interest in space exploration.

LUNAR OBSERVATIONS

The Moon received substantial attention as well, with results as mixed as in the case of Mars. In 1949, Ralph B. Baldwin published *The Face of the Moon*. In it he showed that there was a relation between the diameters and depths of lunar craters (at least those that were not affected by later events such as flooding by lava) and between the diameters and the heights of the crater rims above the surrounding plains. He also showed that terrestrial meteor craters, as well as those formed by bombs and shells, obey the same relations.[12]

At the time lunar craters generally were still generally believed to be volcanic in origin, but as the years passed and more and more impact craters were recognized on Earth, opinions gradually changed. By 1963, when Baldwin published a second book on the same subject, the impact origin of lunar craters was a hypothesis that was hale and hearty. In this connection, it should be pointed out that Baldwin never fell into the all too common trap of ascribing every feature on the Moon to a single process. While he believed that the craters and the initial cavities that became the maria were due to impacts, he realized that the maria surfaces themselves were probably due to lava flows that followed the collisions.[13] Time revealed that he was correct in all his main points. Yet in the early 1960s, no one was certain just how much either vulcanism or impacts had contributed to the shaping of our satellite's surface features. The arguments about which process was responsible for which features might have raged much longer were it not for the fact that direct exploration was to resolve many of these questions within a very short time.

In 1955, Thomas Gold proposed an unusual explanation for the lunar maria; these, he contended, were not lava flows as was generally assumed but consisted of deep layers of dust. In his view erosive processes of some sort (meteoric bombardment, for example) produced the dust, which then migrated to low areas produced by the impact of relatively large bodies.[14]

Gold's theory produced a great deal of heated argument but was never widely accepted. Even before lunar landers showed in no uncertain terms that he was wrong, other scientists had pointed out serious flaws in his argument.[15] As we have seen, astronomers had long known that the Moon is covered with dust, the question being only how deep that dust is. However, no one could be absolutely certain that the dust was *not* very deep, and the possibility of an expensive space probe or a manned exploration vehicle sinking helplessly out of sight immediately after landing could not be ignored. In the end, of course, no such thing happened.

A startling observational development occurred in late 1958. The Soviet astronomer N. A. Kozyrev was taking spectrograms of the central peak of the prominent crater Alphonsus, and one of them showed emission bands! Was there still some sort of volcanic activity on the Moon, or at the least some gentle emission of gas from the interior of our satellite, which otherwise appeared to be geologically dead? Even more surprising was the fact that Kozyrev identified the features as coming from molecular carbon (C_2 and perhaps C_3), for few scientists believed that there were substantial amounts of organic molecules on the Moon.[16]

Kozyrev's observation favorably impressed some scientists, especially as he made copies of the spectra public and answered criticisms effectively. His case seemed fairly solid at the time.[17] However nothing similar has been observed since. In addition, direct measurements on the Moon have found neither traces of atmospheric gases that might have been emitted from its interior nor significant amounts of organic molecules. Of course these negative results do not prove that rare transient venting might not still be occurring, but they make the possibility unlikely. There are many pitfalls in obtaining and interpreting spectra, and Kozyrev may have stumbled into one of them, but it will probably take direct exploration of Alphonsus to settle the matter. That prospect of human exploration of the lunar surface, to be sure, had by 1958 become much closer to reality.

During the late 1950s and early 1960s a number of scientists, both theoretical and observational, attacked the unsolved problems of the solar system. But as in previous decades, their theories and instruments simply were not up to the job. Studies of the photographic appearances, light variations at different wavelengths, polarization properties, and the like often failed to produce significant advances. We still did not know for sure the answers to such hoary old questions as what the maria of the Moon were, what the dark areas on Mars represented, what caused the colors in the clouds of Jupiter, and so on—uncertainties seemingly without end. It was, in part, because of a broad-based interest in resolving those uncertainties and learning more about the universe, the solar system, and our own planet Earth, that the United States initiated an effort to send scientific instruments into space.

SPACE EXPLORATION BECOMES OFFICIAL

On the afternoon of July 29, 1955, the White House announced that the United States would attempt to orbit a small satellite during the International Geophysical Year, which meant sometime in the period from late 1957 into 1958. Not to be left behind, the Soviet Union made a similar public statement the next day. Both announcements were prominently featured in stories that appeared on the front page of the July 30, 1955, issue of the *New York Times*. For some years, the Soviets had made no secret of their interest in space exploration, and in particular, of their intent to orbit a satellite, but the West generally regarded Soviet claims as pretentious and their statements about space flight and space studies were widely discounted.

Unlike the Soviet work, the American effort to launch a space satellite, dubbed Project Vanguard, was intentionally designed to be an "open," primarily civilian effort, in stark contrast to the competing program, which was shrouded in secrecy. The U.S. approach undoubtedly had its advantages, especially in the long run, but in the short term it resulted in a propaganda setback of staggering proportions for America.

The proposed Vanguard satellites were to be small spheres, only somewhat larger than a basketball, light in weight (about 20 pounds), and relatively simple in construction, carrying a few instruments, power sources, and radio transmitters to send data back to Earth. However, those with vision were well aware that future payloads would be larger, heavier, and more complex. Besides scientific data about the upper atmosphere and space, satellites promised eventually to provide profound advances in fields with important practical applications such as geodesy (the shape of the Earth), weather forecasting, communications, navigation, and of course military reconnaissance.[18]

The announcements of the intent to launch artificial satellites quickened public and scientific interest in space exploration. To be sure, not everyone, not even all astronomers, let alone all other scientists, were enthusiastic about the prospect of such "Buck Rogers" programs, and some of these doubters were very influential indeed. For example, in January, 1956, the newly appointed Astronomer Royal, Richard van der Riet Woolley, was asked by reporters about his opinions on the prospects for interplanetary travel. He replied: "It's utter bilge. I don't think anybody will ever put up enough money to do such a thing. . . . What good would it do us? If we spent the same amount of money on preparing first-class astronomical equipment we would learn much more about the universe. . . . It is all rather rot."[19] In Woolley's defense, it is important to note that he was asked for his opinion on *manned* space exploration, not space exploration in general. Still, it is clear that in the press and hence in the public mind, Woolley's comments could easily be taken as a condemnation of all space exploration. As it turned out, the designation "utter bilge" haunted space exploration in general and planetary astronomy in particular for some time.

Woolley was not alone in his opinion. To mention just one other example, on February 25, 1957, a senior scientist, Lee De Forest, stated that "man would never be able to reach the Moon."[20] Many physical scientists, who should have been better informed, one would think, were unaware that the current state of engineering and technology were poised for some truly remarkable feats.

What surprised the world was not so much that humankind crossed the threshold into space but that Soviet rocket scientists were the first to do so. Remarkably, the excitement and anticipation created earlier by the announcement of the American artificial satellite program was soon transformed by an underlying sense of alarm and even desperation. That sense of shock served to reinvigorate and redirect American efforts in space.

SPUTNIK!

The launch of Sputnik I by the Soviet Union on October 4, 1957, stunned the world.[21] At the time, relatively few people were aware of the fact that current technology was perfectly capable of lofting an object into an orbit around Earth, and so for most, the achievement came as an amazing revelation. Even more astounding was the fact that the feat had been accomplished by the U.S.S.R. and not by the United States. The orbiting of the much heavier Sputnik II the following month was an additional surprise. Both spacecraft dwarfed the proposed Vanguard satellites. Around the world, the question was: What would the Soviets do next?

There was much communist bragging about the triumphs of the new socialist society, and even though the scientific findings were minimal, the technical accomplishments were real and impressive. The effects on world and American public opinion were staggering and long lasting. Soviet scientists and policymakers were ecstatic. A 1960 English translation of an account by V. Petrov exclaims:

> It is not surprising that the successful launching of the artificial satellites of the earth by the U.S.S.R. has aroused the most lively interest throughout the world as the biggest scientific event of all times. The Soviet people feel immense satisfaction at the achievement of its scientists, technologists and industrialists. Truly, Soviet science, technology and industry may be said to have now reached a stage where it can expect to resolve successfully the most complicated technical problems, which had hitherto baffled man's efforts. No wonder that many journals are emphasizing the fact that the U.S.S.R. has gone ahead of the U.S.A so far as progress in the scientific field is concerned.[22]

Although such statements may seem unreasonable now that the U.S.S.R. has disintegrated and international communism has been discredited, at the time the words seemed prophetic. The public perception that the United States was far behind the Soviets in the "space race," coupled with the existing widespread interest in space that had already been kindled by such efforts as the American Vanguard rocket program, and the "X" series of supersonic rocket test aircraft, created in depth actions and reactions in the United States. By the first anniversary of Sputnik, the

United States was effectively going through a peacetime mobilization that would lead it into space. The impact of this effort would be broad and pervasive, affecting education at every level and most prominently in mathematics, the physical sciences, and engineering, and extending even to the way the government conducted its business. It was clear that planetary astronomy would be critical to the mobilization for space, and in turn it was one of the many fields of endeavor forever altered by the ensuing tide of events.

PROJECT VANGUARD

The inception of Project Vanguard preceded Sputnik, but after the first Soviet launches American attention began to focus on Vanguard as a "response" to Sputnik. The U.S. Naval Research Laboratory, which managed the Vanguard project, had a proven record of successful upper atmosphere and astronomical research that included the extensive use of sounding rockets. Unfortunately, on December 6, 1957, Vanguard's first attempt to put a payload into orbit ended in ignominious failure—on nationwide television. The slender three-stage rocket slowly rose a few feet from its launch pad and then just as slowly sank to become a flaming inferno. The first U.S. attempt to launch a satellite was perceived worldwide as a technological disaster and by the Soviets and others as a prime example of American incompetence.[23]

Vanguard's failure was all the more bitter because the tiny 4-pound "grapefruit" payload (a mere "test sphere" and not one of the more heavily instrumented payloads that were to follow) was dwarfed by Sputnik I's weight of almost 200 pounds. Compounding the evidence of the Soviet success, the last stage of the rocket that lofted Sputnik I into orbit was bigger than a boxcar and easily visible to the unaided eye under the right conditions. Millions of people around the world saw it for themselves.

Moreover, the American satellite was to have broadcast its radio signals at the then relatively high frequency of 108 megacycles, which would have provided for more precise "tracking" of the payload (determining its orbit and position in orbit; later Vanguard satellites did achieve this). American telemetry was then at the cutting edge of radio engineering. But the Soviet satellite transmitted at the lower frequencies of 20 and 40 megacycles, which enabled amateur radio enthusiasts around the world to hear the haunting *beep-beep* signals for themselves. Several weeks before the first successful Sputnik launching, as the Soviets publicly announced the radio frequencies that their satellites would use, it was widely assumed that the appropriate U.S. agencies had receivers set up to monitor the Sputniks.[24] However, this did not happen. The antennas, receivers, and recorders hastily assembled were for the most part put together by amateurs.

Sputnik II reinforced this impression of Soviet prowess. On November 3, the USSR launched an 1,100-pound capsule containing a dog named Laika into an Earth orbit. The two Soviet triumphs and the American Vanguard failure had immediate repercussions. Around the world the prestige of the United States plummeted. The capabilities of America's scientists and engineers, its political and educational systems, and even its ability to defend itself and the other Western democracies were questioned.[25] One may wonder what the public reaction would have been if America had succeeded in orbiting the first satellite? The history of planetary science, including planetary astronomy, might have been very different indeed, for to a considerable extent the "Sputnik crisis" drove the United States to a higher pitch of scientific and technical achievement.

THE AMERICAN RESPONSE

Americans accepted Sputnik as a "come from behind challenge." The Unites States effected a peacetime mobilization of its technical and scientific resources and applicable elements of industry—particularly the aeronautical industry. That field, within a matter of years, experienced a change into the "aerospace" industry. The first positive result was the lofting into orbit of Explorer I, on January 31, 1958. The launch was performed by a team combining the efforts of the Army Ballistic Missile Agency at Huntsville, Alabama, under the former German rocket expert Wernher von Braun, who provided a reliable Redstone missile as the first stage booster, and the California Institute of Technology's Jet Propulsion Laboratory, which provided the three solid-fueled upper stages, including the payload attached permanently to the fourth stage, which become the actual satellite. The entire multistage assembly was known as a Jupiter-C.[26] This was a bittersweet victory, as essentially the same vehicle configuration could have launched a satellite as early as September, 1956, when a Jupiter-C assembly (with an inert fourth stage) did indeed send a payload 3,300 miles down the Atlantic Missile range from Florida to the southeast.[27]

Despite a seemingly late start, the United States achieved the first important scientific finding of the space age when data from Explorers revealed a belt of charged particles (negative electrons and positive protons) girding the Earth. Named after its discoverer, James A. Van Allen, this radiation belt raised serious worries about the possible grave effects of the energetic particles it contained on equipment in Earth orbit and, looking down the road, on humans.[28] But, as serious as it seemed at first, this potential problem was eventually worked around (one answer was to not stay in the region for too long a time; another was to use "shielding" of some sort). As time went on, the scientific yield of American space missions, once they began, far exceeded that of the Soviet ones.

The Sputniks caused a widespread concern in the United States about the country's educational system, its competence in science and engineering, its determination and will, interservice rivalries, and a host of other subjects. Space became a national crisis and Congress began to act. The House and Senate appointed a Select Committee on Astronautics and Space Exploration, which began hearings on April 15, 1958.[29]

At the onset of the hearings the committee considered a message from President Dwight D. Eisenhower, recommending that "space science activities sponsored by the United States be conducted under the direction of a civilian agency, except for those projects primarily associated with military requirements."[30]

The first witness on that first day of hearings was Wernher von Braun. Committee members bombarded him with questions such as how soon the United States could launch a Moon probe.[31] This was not an isolated incident, for the hearings, which extended into May, were peppered with references to early and extensive exploration of the solar system. Moreover, the interest continued. The Select Committee on Astronautics and Space Exploration prepared a symposium on space technology in late 1958, in which direct exploration of the Moon and planets—especially Mars and Venus—played a large part. Some of the predictions were far too rosy, as in "Is it fantasy to say that man may set foot upon the Moon in 1965? Upon Mars and Venus three years later?" Optimistic predictions in those days ran riot: travel near the speed of light within forty years, lunar bases, "death rays" (which, as lasers, are now a fact), probes to Jupiter (now accomplished), and even the exploration of possible planetary systems around other stars were all topics seriously mentioned.[32] However over-optimistic these statements may have been, they certainly reflected the popular enthusiasm for space.

What was responsible for this support of lunar and planetary exploration? It is hard to say exactly, but that interest certainly must have had deep roots, for it was there from the beginning of the Space Age. Public interest in the heavenly bodies had been whetted, at intervals, by advances in observational and theoretical astronomy since the days of ancient Greece. In addition, equating space exploration with the earlier exploration and development of the American frontier provided additional incentive and inspiration. Chairman John W. McCormack of the Select Committee on Astronautics and Space Exploration on April 15, 1958, probably reflected the general mood of the public when he said:

> What else space holds for us is beyond the threshold. What we will learn from the moon, and probably the other planets, no man can rightly say. On the basis of what we already know, we can predict that advances will be literally beyond our present understanding. They are giving this country a new frontier. I need not remind you how our American democracy grew great on the older, limited frontier of the past. The worlds of outer space are the greatest challenge to dynamic thought and deed that our pioneer spirit has ever received.[33]

While there are other proposed explanations for the surge of American support for direct lunar and planetary exploration, McCormack's connection of space exploration with the American frontier experience was, and remains, eye-opening.

Swept up in the growing public consternation on the one hand, and the enthusiasm that surrounded the prospects for opening a new frontier in space on the other, L. Eugene Root, a missile systems expert for Lockheed Aircraft, was one of many who anticipated that space exploration could contribute to an explosion in knowledge and technology. "In the next decade," he said before a Congressional Committee hearing held in 1958, "communications systems capable of spanning planetary distances of several hundred million miles, such as will be involved in planetary probes, solar probes and artificial asteroids, will be developed for the transmission of complex data, including pictures." Astronomy, he suggested, would greatly benefit from new developments. Within the decade "astronomical observations from space vehicles will be an accomplished fact [and] will revolutionize conventional astronomy."[34]

Root believed, as did noted British radio astronomer Bernard Lovell, that radio-telescopes and new technologies being used by astronomers might bring answers regarding the evolution of the universe. "Lovell suggests that any telescope, if carried in an Earth satellite, will reach space-time distances of much greater magnitude than is possible today, and thus obtain information of the state of the universe as it existed billions of years ago."[35]

Whipple, by then director of the Smithsonian Astrophysical Laboratory, predicted at the 1958 hearings that during the next decade, "equipment will have been safely landed on the Moon to set up a remote-controlled observatory" and that "the back side of the Moon will have become as well known as the near side." But the age-old dream of leaving the confines of the Earth had "not been limited to the Moon" he said.[36]

> Ever since astronomers first reported "canals" and polar snow caps upon Mars, man has speculated about it. Is it a dead planet? Is it strewn with the remnants of ancient civilizations? Does life exist upon this world? For the first time now, a positive answer to this age-old riddle may lie ahead. . . . As for Venus, what mysteries lie behind its swirling clouds? Does it hide a lush tropical climate, as some believe, is it a watery waste, or is it a desert swept by duststorms?[37]

Scientists in growing numbers discussed manned landings on the Moon and circumnavigation of Mars and Venus; interplanetary space probes to Mars, Venus, Mercury, and Jupiter and the acquisition of reliable data about the composition of the planets; the nature of meteoritic material; and the quest for information about interplanetary gas and electric and magnetic phenomena. Astronomers anticipated that space flight would finally enable them to escape the constraints of the Earth's atmosphere inherent in ground-based studies. As a result, radiation throughout the entire spectrum including ultraviolet, infrared, and radio waves could be used for astronomical studies in ways previously impossible. Rich and rewarding applications of the new knowledge could be expected in the areas of reconnaissance, communications, meteorology, and navigation.[38]

NASA

As recommended by President Eisenhower, Congress supported a civilian as opposed to a military response to the Soviet challenge in space, and accordingly created the National Aeronautics and Space Administration (NASA). NASA was to have a crucial effect on the progress of solar system studies in the United States.

President Eisenhower approved the law establishing NASA on July 29, 1958, and the agency began business on October 1 of that year.[39] At its core was the forty-three-year-old National Advisory Committee for Aeronautics (NACA), which formally ceased to exist at the close of business the day before.[40] NACA had three research centers and two field stations that were incorporated into the new agency at its birth, along with the experienced cadre of scientists and engineers who staffed those facilities. The facilities included Langley Aeronautical Laboratory in Virginia with its associated Pilotless Aircraft Research Station on Wallops Island and the High Speed Flight Station at Edwards, California; Ames Aeronautical

Laboratory in California; and Lewis Flight Propulsion Laboratory in Ohio. But while it provided NASA with a solid base to build on, NACA also brought along some less than useful baggage, including defects basic to the nature of any committee-based organization. The old NACA was a conservative and collegial group of appointees from industry, academia, and government, and in the past it had naturally tended to promote aeronautical projects of interest to committee members while neglecting others. Perhaps the most famous example of the organization's shortsightedness was its failure to anticipate the influence of jet propulsion in aeronautics. Thus, while NACA brought along substantial technical experience, some questioned NACA as the best choice to lead the United States to preeminence in the new field of space exploration. Many at the time thought the Atomic Energy Commission or the Air Force, to cite just two possibilities, might be better selections.[41]

On December 3, 1958, the Jet Propulsion Laboratory (JPL), owned by the U.S. government but operated by the California Institute of Technology, was transferred from the jurisdiction of the U.S. Army to NASA. At the time, the laboratory's expertise was largely in fields such as rockets, radio communications, and tracking systems.[42] However, that emphasis would shift as JPL became the leading NASA facility dealing with lunar and planetary probes. In a few years JPL would become an important center for planetary studies. In addition, it had a unique status, for while legally it was not a NASA space flight center, it was treated as such by NASA Headquarters, for all practical purposes. This situation would cause problems in the future.

NASA staffing proceeded rapidly. Homer Newell and many of his Naval Research Laboratory upper atmosphere research staff transferred to NASA, as did John P. Hagan and his NRL Vanguard staff. A Space Task Group, organized within the Langley Research Center, recruited dozens of Canadian and British aeronautical engineers suddenly unemployed in February, 1959, as a result of Canada's suspension of its jet fighter program. In October, 1959, President Eisenhower transferred Wernher von Braun and the Army Ballistic Missile Agency's Development Operations Division to NASA. The Huntsville facility became NASA's George C. Marshall Space Flight Center. The Goddard Space Flight Center was built in Beltsville, Maryland; and in 1961 NASA began construction of the Manned Spacecraft Center (later renamed the Johnson Space Center) near Houston, Texas.[43]

Meanwhile, the Soviet Union kept up the pressure. In January, 1959, the Soviets launched Luna I, the first craft to fly into interplanetary space. Luna II reached the Moon in September of the same year, while Luna III flew behind and around the Moon in October. To cap this spectacular run of Soviet successes, on April 12, 1961, Major Yuri A. Gagarin became the first person to "leave this planet, enter the void of space, and return."[44]

At the start, NASA planners anticipated a decade of steady and orderly growth, and possible manned expeditions to the Moon and planets were considered to lie far in the future. This relatively cautious approach was in stark contrast to the more optimistic visions of many scientists and engineers, especially the engineers, who believed that there were no insuperable technical problems to hold back a faster-paced and much more vigorous space program.[45] Unexpected events would soon change NASA's plans, resulting in a speeding up of the agency's agenda and the increased budgets to do the job. This metamorphosis affected planetary astronomy as well, for timely, specific, and reliable data concerning the Moon and planets became ever more critical to NASA's mission.

Newell became NASA's assistant administrator for Space Sciences—*all* of space sciences. His concerns thus ranged from the Earth to the most distant galaxies. A former teacher and a widely respected researcher of the upper atmosphere in his own right, Newell contributed greatly to giving the new agency scientific credibility. Upon its formation NASA was subject to considerable criticism from astronomers and planetary researchers, who complained that the agency was dominated by engineers and those who wanted only essentially useless "spectaculars." Some critics argued that NASA budgets could be much better spent on "real" science, and Newell was an effective answer to these critics. He remained in essentially the same position for many years, giving the American space science program much needed stability and direction. Newell fought valiantly and often successfully to see that scientific concerns received the emphasis they deserved at NASA's highest levels and has not received all the credit that is his due.

NASA entered the field of manned space flight in October, 1958, with the creation of Project Mercury, aimed at putting a manned space capsule into Earth orbit and then safely recovering it.[46] Manned missions were and still are extremely popular with the public, and especially in those early days, these received deep and widespread support, which probably spilled over into increased backing for space exploration in general. However, Mercury and following manned programs needed massive amounts of money to keep them moving forward. At first there seemed to be ample funds for both manned space programs and scientific studies. But in the late 1960s, as budgets became tighter, science programs and solar system research in particular became more susceptible to being reduced or eliminated.

At the time, however, compared to the amounts budgeted for scientific research through traditional academic structures, NASA funds seemed more than adequate to provide the science and engineering required for space exploration. Moreover, Congress was anxious to facilitate space exploration and the public wanted to win the space race. At a congressional hearing in 1959, for example, Congressman George F. Miller asked then NASA Administrator T. Keith Glennan, "Is [sic] there enough funds for next year?" In essence, Glennan replied that there probably were.[47]

FUNDING ASTRONOMICAL RESEARCH

Organization of NASA had an immediate and lasting impact upon planetary sciences. It should be remembered that before World War II astronomical research, both in the United States and abroad, was almost exclusively the preserve of academia, private philanthropy, and national observatories largely concerned with time keeping, navigation, and the like. After the war until the 1960s, a substantial amount of astronomical research was funded by the U.S. Department of Defense. In particular, the navy, in which senior personnel had been impressed by the general usefulness of astronomers in the war effort, supported research in a wide variety of fields, particularly those emphasizing navigation and communications technology. The air force, with equally practical but different aims in mind, emphasized efforts in the lunar and planetary fields and especially supported studies of atmospheres, ionospheres, and radar technologies. The amounts of money involved were tiny by today's standards, but to researchers accustomed to small or nonexistent research budgets, these grants and contracts were bountiful. This is not the place to give a complete history of DOD support of solar system studies, but it some examples show how surprisingly early that support developed and how widespread it came to be.

The air force, for instance, funded a comprehensive program called "The Study of Planetary Atmospheres" at Lowell Observatory, which began in 1949 and extended until late 1952.[48] The study contributed materially to the design and development of exploratory planetary vehicles, manned spacecraft, and flight planning. It provided the best summary of the field that had ever been assembled and was particularly timely. Earlier, our knowledge had been too fragmentary for such a work to be written, and later, with the explosion of information generated by space exploration and enhanced ground-based observations, succinct reviews of the field became much more difficult.

The navy also became active in supporting planetary astronomy. A U.S.

Navy grant, for example, supported Sinton's doctoral thesis on the "Distribution of Temperatures and Spectra of Venus and the Other Planets."[49] DOD money also went to a number of aerospace companies, which enthusiastically embraced planetary studies. For example, the General Electric Company in 1959 produced a lunar map which it mailed to all interested parties at a low cost.[50] I was supported by so-called "blue money" from the air force for doctoral research in astronomy at the University of Illinois, a study of radiation pressure effects on Earth satellite orbits. Incongruously, funds from the National Science Foundation and other traditional sources of support for astronomers still were very limited, and as a result money supplied by NASA had much to do with the changing fortunes of planetary astronomy. Within a handful of years planetary astronomy would make the transition from a field struggling to survive to one that became a central component of space exploration, its reputation greatly rejuvenated in academia.

GERARD P. KUIPER AND THE LUNAR AND PLANETARY LABORATORY

There were only a few hundred practicing astronomers of all kinds in the United States in the 1950s. Everybody knew everybody else, and in particular there were few full-time planetary scientists. Among the fifty-six contributors to a study compiled by the staff of the congressional Select Committee on Astronautics and Space Exploration in 1958, for example, only one, Fred L. Whipple, was a recognized solar system astronomer.[51] The American space program, in effect, galvanized the field of planetary astronomy, revitalized it, and reformed it. One of the critical moments in that revitalization came with the establishment of the Lunar and Planetary Laboratory under the direction of Gerard P. Kuiper at the University of Arizona. It was funded by grants from NASA, with some financial support from the air force.

In the late 1940s Kuiper had formed an ambitious plan to publish a systematic summary of our knowledge of the entire solar system. Four massive volumes eventually appeared from 1953 to 1963. The first dealt with the Sun; the second with Earth "as a planet"; the third with planets and satellites; and the fourth with the Moon, meteorites, and comets.[52] Unfortunately, a proposed fifth volume on planets and the interplanetary medium never appeared.

Kuiper's compendium had some curious omissions. There was nothing at all in it concerning planetary spectra, about which plenty could have been written even then, nor was there any unified listing of the known

Gerard P. Kuiper, founder of the University of Arizona's Lunar and Planetary Laboratory, on a visit to Stonehenge in 1970. Fred Whipple on right. Courtesy Ewen Whitaker

physical properties of the planets and their satellites (masses, diameters, densities, orbits, and so forth). Nevertheless, these books form the best available benchmark of our knowledge of the solar system at the dawn of the Space Age, and as such still serve the role their originator intended for them.

In addition, Kuiper assembled a photographic lunar atlas based on the best images available. Significantly, some of the photographic plates he chose dated from the early part of the twentieth century, when observers were still able to use large amounts of observing time on big telescopes to make images of our satellite. This massive compilation was published in 1960 and eclipsed everything that had previously appeared in the field. To support this work, Kuiper first received money from the National Science Foundation and later from the U.S. Air Force, which by the late 1950s considered mapping the Moon a matter of practical importance.[53]

Kuiper, by the late 1950s, had become something of a conduit for the extant knowledge of planetary astronomy. He had assembled what was for the time a substantial staff to work on these and other projects. He was at the same time director of the McDonald and Yerkes observatories. There were, however, problems at Yerkes. Space was limited, time on large telescopes was hard to schedule, and there were rumors of personal problems among the staff. There is no documentation as to what caused the strife. Speculation ran rampant—then and even now. Kuiper was a dynamic and forceful person who could be a most loyal and faithful friend and colleague but also a formidable enemy. In any event, whatever did happen at the Yerkes Observatory had a significant impact on planetary astronomy.

During late 1959 and early 1960, in a sudden whirlwind of activity, Kuiper arranged for the transfer of himself and his staff of scientists to the University of Arizona in Tucson. In fact, on his first brief visit to Tucson in the spring of 1960, before there were any specific arrangements as to the transfer, Kuiper selected a home in town. During that summer, the entire Yerkes lunar and planetary operation transferred to Tucson. His unexpected arrival was greeted with unbridled enthusiasm by the University of Arizona and the people of Tucson.

The move marked the beginning of the Lunar and Planetary Laboratory, an organization heavily funded by NASA's Lunar and Planetary Science program and destined to play a large role in the future development of planetary astronomy. It was to be a new and vibrant institution dedicated to investigating the solar system with the very latest instruments, techniques, and theoretical work.[54] In a sense, it marked the rebirth of the field of planetary astronomy, and its creation would not have come about but for the financial support provided by NASA and the new U.S. program of space exploration in the 1960s. Among other sources, Kuiper received money from the Air Force Chart and Information Center, NASA's Lunar and Planetary Sciences Division, the Army Map Service, and the U.S. Geologic Survey.

Oran Nicks, who was then the director of Lunar and Planetary Programs at NASA Headquarters, explained that the USGS Astrogeology Center in Flagstaff, Arizona, developed under the leadership of geologist Eugene M. Shoemaker who had been loaned to NASA Headquarters, was started upon the initiative of Nicks and Vince McKelvey, director of USGS.[55] Thus NASA influenced the study of planetary astronomy in many direct and indirect ways. It subsidized graduate studies, hired astronomers, created laboratories and study groups, provided technical and financial support for both university- and NASA-operated ground-based telescopes, and through "Requests for Proposals" generated space-based planetary science experiments and observations.

INTO DEEP SPACE

The launches of the first artificial satellites not only demonstrated that the age of space exploration had dawned but also foreshadowed the direct exploration of the solar system. As astronomers had known since Sir Isaac

Planetary astronomy goes big time—the almost completed Space Sciences Building
of the University of Arizona in 1966. This structure was built with NASA funds and
occupied in large part by the Lunar and Planetary Laboratory. Courtesy Ewen Whitaker

Newton's time, the energy needed to put an object into a low Earth orbit is actually most of that needed to send the same object to an infinite distance from our planet. In fact, this "escape velocity" of some 25,000 miles per hour is only 41 percent greater than the velocity necessary to place an object in a low circular orbit (it is precisely the square root of two, or 1.41, times the velocity in a circular orbit close to Earth's surface).[56] This relation was no mystery, for after all it had been known for centuries and, more to the point, was described in daily newspapers in the 1950s.[57] Nonetheless, the swift progress from satellites orbiting a few hundreds of miles above Earth's surface to space probes traveling millions of miles away from our planet came as a major surprise to many people.

Perhaps even more surprising to scientists was the widespread public interest in and support for lunar and planetary probes. It was difficult to argue that people on Earth could expect practical benefits to be gained from going to the Moon, Venus, and Mars, let alone to more distant planets such as Jupiter and Saturn. Scientists, for the foreseeable future, expected that the only benefits from such efforts would be gains in scientific knowledge and the satisfaction of human curiosity about the unknown. But public perception went beyond that. The American public thought of the Moon, and possibly Mars, as "real estate," much as the New World

Oran W. Nicks in the 1960s, when he was
director of NASA's Office of Lunar and
Planetary Programs. Courtesy Phyllis Nicks

explorers viewed the Americas. There were claims to be made, opportunities to be had, and at the least the perceived necessity of thwarting claims
of other nations to the Moon or Mars. In effect, public enthusiasm for
space tended to override doubts or uncertainties regarding benefits and
returns. American taxpayers and their elected representatives in Congress,
for at least a decade, stood strongly behind the U.S. initiatives in the
space sciences.

Though beaten in the race to launch an Earth satellite, the United States
led the way in attempts to launch deep space probes. The first try came on
August 17, 1958. The payload was targeted for the Moon but after only a
mere seventy-seven seconds of flight the first stage exploded. A number of
similar efforts were made through the end of 1960, but none reached our
natural satellite. But one probe, Pioneer III, launched on December 6,
1958, made a significant discovery when it found a second Van Allen
radiation belt outside the previously known one.[58] Another, Pioneer IV,
launched on March 3, 1959, did achieve escape velocity and became an
artificial planet orbiting the Sun.[59] In contrast to the rather dismal record
of the U.S. lunar program, one American probe during this period that
was *not* aimed at Moon was a success. Pioneer V, the first true interplanetary probe, began as an intended Venus probe. Due to technical

difficulties, Pioneer V missed the relatively short launch "window" for Venus, when that planet and Earth were aligned so that the flight could be made with a minimum of energy. Instead, it was launched on March 11, 1960, to explore conditions in interplanetary space between the orbits of Earth and Venus. It did just that, reporting on radiation levels and magnetic fields for months and from distances as far as 22 million miles from our planet.[60] The early Pioneer space probes were begun as projects of the U.S. Air Force and Army but were carried out under the management of the fledgling NASA.[61]

Meanwhile, the Soviet Union scored a number of successes in lunar exploration. As we have seen, Luna I missed the Moon but did achieve escape velocity and thus became the first artificial planet.[62] The Soviets followed up that feat with Luna II, which carried a Soviet medallion to the surface of the Moon but produced nothing in the way of scientific results. It did, however, mark the first time that a man-made object had ever made direct physical contact with another celestial body.[63]

Luna III, however, was another story. This payload looped around the Moon before returning to the vicinity of Earth, and in the process photographed a substantial portion of the "back" of the Moon, the part that we can never see from our planet. These images were then radioed back to Earth. The Luna III images themselves were of poor quality, but they were good enough to show that our satellite's far side is mostly mountainous, with few of the dark, relatively smooth maria that are so prominent on the near side.[64] The Luna II and Luna III missions coincided with the first visit of Soviet Premier Nikita Khrushchev to the United States and provided him with a splendid propaganda opportunity.[65] Khrushchev at one time said that "we will bury you" (referring to the United States and capitalist countries in general), and in late 1959 many observers wondered if they would.

The Soviets were able to accomplish impressive firsts in the early days of the space race because they had powerful booster rockets at their disposal. Paradoxically, this situation came about because the Soviets had not been able to reduce the weight of their nuclear warheads, as had the Americans. As a result, their engineers focused on the development of a reasonably reliable vehicle (about as reliable as American ones) that had the ability to loft payloads considerably heavier than any that the United States could launch at the time.[66] This was an important advantage in an era when electronics, computers, and the like were still tremendously heavy and bulky by present standards. However, improved and more powerful American rockets, along with the commanding U.S. lead in the miniaturization of equipment of all kinds, eventually tipped the balance the other way. But for what seemed a very long time to those who experienced it, the space race was a "stern chase" for America, and a stern chase is always a long chase.

Although Soviet achievements seemed significant, and performance remarkable, in fact their space program experienced as many problems as the American one. Despite the secrecy shrouding much of the effort, the Soviet Union was unable to hide the failures of many missions, especially those that reached Earth orbit or escape velocity. For example, Sputnik IV was launched on February 4, 1961, and Soviet sources announced that all equipment was functioning normally. Actually, it was a failed Venus probe that remained stuck in Earth orbit. A short time later, on February 12, Sputnik V successfully launched a probe toward Venus, but after a few days radio communication with the payload was lost and never regained.[67] The probe sped on in the grip of the iron laws of celestial mechanics, but it was only an inert hunk of metal. Such attempts could not be kept from view as easily as could an explosion on a launch pad in Kazakhstan, for instance. (Even for these sorts of failures the United States gathered fairly reliable information by using high altitude reconnaissance flights, long-range radars, and other means—though for reasons of national security such information could not be released publicly. However, rumors circulated widely in the aerospace community.)

In 1961 the U.S.S.R. launched two probes intended for Mars, though neither made it to Earth orbit. These attempts coincided with the visit of Premier Khrushchev to United Nations Headquarters in New York and demonstrated that the Soviets certainly appreciated the enormous propaganda value of spectacular space achievements.[68] The aggressive Russian effort continued in 1962 with no less than three Venus attempts and three Mars attempts, all of which failed.[69] By contrast, as we will see later, Mariner II flew by Venus in 1962 returning data about its environment and atmosphere, and Mariner IV returned some striking pictures from Mars in 1965.

Thus, despite a truly enormous push, the Soviets' initial interplanetary efforts produced total failure—at least ten launches (possibly more) and not a single success. The main cause of this dismal record was the poor reliability of their mechanical and especially electronic equipment. This difficulty was to prove a severe problem for the Soviets, particularly on space missions of long duration, and it was a problem they never fully solved. However, these failures did reemphasize the sobering fact that, no matter who made the attempt, the direct exploration of the solar system was a hazardous and costly business.

Sending an automated probe to another planet is far more difficult than

Earth satellite operations. Among the problems are much longer flight times, communications over much greater distances, longer time delays between the transmission and reception of commands (affecting their execution and receipt of knowledge of their execution), large changes in the amount of solar heating during a mission, provision of adequate long-life power sources, and much more rigorous navigation, guidance, and control standards. All of these intimidating obstacles had to be overcome before lunar and planetary probes could perform effectively.

Following the launches of the first generation of space probes inherited from the Department of Defense in the late 1950s, NASA began planning additional deep space missions. Key programs included the Ranger, Lunar Orbiter, Surveyor, and Mariner programs. NASA coupled the development of a new generation of advanced scientific payloads with improvements in launch vehicles. In addition, NASA managers attempted to integrate a diverse and massive program of unmanned probes with the launch of Earth orbital satellites, and a man-in-space program. Spacecraft development also had to be carefully coordinated with launch windows. Launches to Venus, for example, could only be made during a window that opened for a relatively short time every nineteen months, and Mars launches could be made only every twenty-six months. While the window was open, there was time to attempt only two launches with the facilities available at Cape Canaveral.[70]

The Ranger program, conceived at JPL during 1959, was designed to take scientific instruments to the Moon. It suffered from all sorts of problems, for among other things the spacecraft had to be redesigned to match a different launch vehicle than was originally planned. The projected Rangers included three different types of spacecraft; two interplanetary probes to serve as test vehicles and to obtain data between the Earth and the Moon; three "rough " landers designed to make scientific measurements, including gamma-ray spectrometry, and to deposit working payloads on the lunar surface, including seismometers and scanning television cameras; and four vehicles carrying TV cameras designed to take high-resolution images of our satellite in the last few minutes before crashing. Although none of the three capsule landers successfully landed on the Moon, "the attempt was brave and technically interesting, paving the way for future successes." Three of the final four probes—Rangers 7, 8, and 9—worked as planned, providing by far the most detailed images of the Moon ever made, and "produced brilliant successes and represented a maturity in planning that comes with experience."[71]

The Surveyor program was initially intended to use a basic spacecraft "bus" for both lunar orbital and landing missions, but with different retro rockets and payloads. It suffered from a number of substantial design changes, in part forced by delays in producing the new, hydrogen-fueled Centaur upper stage for the Atlas booster rocket. Eventually Surveyor was built only as a vehicle designed to land a scientific payload gently on the Moon. A completely separate effort was begun to photograph the entire lunar surface from orbit using the less powerful Atlas Agena rocket assembly. Although the Surveyor orbiter was initially a JPL project, the new Lunar Orbiter was assigned to the Langley Research Center, a former NACA facility. Nicks, who had primary responsibility for the Ranger, Lunar Orbiter, Surveyor, and Mariner missions, wrote that "despite its unexciting title, the Lunar Orbiter project became a sweeping success, accomplishing all its primary goals and then some."[72]

Surveyor continued as a JPL program intended to soft-land a payload on the Moon in a controlled manner and then take photographs of, and perform experiments on, the lunar surface. This was an ambitious project for the time. Not surprisingly, Surveyor suffered delay after vexing delay.[73] As noted, it relied on a high-energy Centaur upper stage for launch, and the then unproven and hard-to-handle liquid hydrogen fuel proved most difficult to tame. The high performance retro rocket, radar landing system, and throttlable "vernier" rocket engines to control the final descent also presented major technical challenges. In fact, serious difficulties with the vernier engines on the Surveyor almost brought the project to a close at one time. As the development of Centaur fell far behind schedule, so too did the Surveyor program. Nevertheless, on May 30, 1966, Surveyor 1 left the launch pad at Cape Kennedy and a few days later made a successful soft landing north of the crater Flamsteed in Oceanus Procellarum. "Within a few hours we knew a lot about the Moon," reported Nicks. Five of seven Surveyors completed their missions.[74] This was an amazingly successful performance considering the great complexity of these landers compared to all previous space probes. However, probably of much greater importance in the long run was the fact that it was clear that productive voyages to the surfaces of the Moon and other bodies in the solar system were indeed possible. The heavenly bodies that for thousands of years had been so alluring, yet so elusive, were now within reach.

Perhaps surprisingly, during the first years of NASA, planetary probes or interplanetary probes were not high on the agency's agenda. In early 1960 NASA had no immediate designs for planetary missions beyond Pioneer V. When Nicks joined Newell in the Space Sciences Division at headquarters in 1960 and was given the principal responsibility for Lunar Flight Systems, he asked the natural question of why planetary missions were not being developed. In response, he was told, to put it in his own words, that "planets were excluded for the present, until activities already begun were moving toward success."[75]

Fortunately, opinions soon changed, and by the latter part of 1960, NASA embarked on the Mariner program designed to send unmanned exploratory craft to Venus and Mars. The original plan was to send two probes to Venus in 1962 and two to Mars a few months later. Unfortunately, all of the intended scientific payloads relied for launching on the same Centaur upper stage as Surveyor used. In what was becoming an all too familiar story, the Mariner spacecraft had to be redesigned for less powerful vehicles and launch attempts were postponed frequently.

Boosted by Atlas Agena rockets, Mariners 1 (1962) and 3 (1964) were destroyed. But Mariner 2, launched on August 27, 1962, returned data on the interplanetary medium, flew by Venus, and returned forty-two minutes of data about the atmosphere and the surface of that planet. In particular, the probe confirmed the high surface temperature of Venus. Mariner 4, launched in 1964, reached Mars after a 228-day flight and sent back more than twenty televised shots of the planet's surface. The mystery of Mars began to unravel, though slowly. There seemed to be no evidence of life (nor was any expected due to the relatively low resolution of the images), no evidence of frozen or ancient rivers or ocean basins. However, there was a major surprise for almost all planetary astronomers, for the Martian landscape was covered with craters and seemed much more Moonlike than Earthlike in appearance. Impressions of the red planet would change, but Mariner 5 was a start. Mariners 6 and 7 revisited Mars in 1969, while Mariner 9 orbited the red planet in 1971. To look ahead somewhat, by the close of the Mariner program the concept of Mars had changed yet again, to conform more closely to classical astronomers' images. Rather than a "barren, Moon-like planet that appeared lifeless," it was indeed more Earthlike, "having many types of terrain, clouds, variations in atmosphere, and evidence of erosion, strongly suggesting that water had once been abundant."[76] Perhaps there had been, or even is now, life on Mars. Perhaps. At any rate, between 1957 and 1969, when the last Mariner visited Mars, the data derived both from ground-based observations and from space probes began to build a more accurate image of the red planet.

Each planetary mission brought step-by-step improvements both in the hardware used and in the scientific results produced. During the earliest period of exploration the United States simply did not have rockets with enough thrust to launch heavy enough payloads to the planets to do the jobs scientists wanted to do.[77] It took several years of difficult and costly development work to perfect the new boosters. Yet again, progress in increasing our knowledge of the solar system was held up by the need for improved technology, and planetary astronomy leapt ahead when more powerful rockets did appear. The rocket, in effect, joined the long list of devices—telescope, spectroscope, photographic plate, and infrared detectors—that had produced singular advances in planetary astronomy in the past. To be sure, the early planetary explorations did not signal the displacement of traditional ground-based astronomical observations but instead provided new and productive ways to "field test" astronomical observations and theories. As will be seen in the following chapters, space-based results eventually resolved many—but by no means all—long-standing issues in planetary studies and raised new questions about the nature of the solar system and its members.

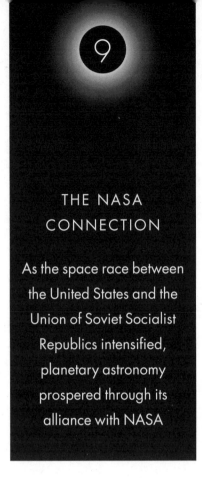

9

THE NASA CONNECTION

As the space race between the United States and the Union of Soviet Socialist Republics intensified, planetary astronomy prospered through its alliance with NASA

The forging of an association between planetary astronomy and NASA transformed the field within a decade. The ranks of American planetary astronomers grew rapidly. Young graduates fresh from completing their doctoral studies and scientists transferring from fields such as physics, geology, meteorology, and upper atmosphere research, attracted in part by the imminent possibility of planetary exploration, joined the small original number of planetary astronomers. At the same time, the powerful influence of the American space program began to change the practice of planetary astronomy drastically. Rather than the traditional, individual "lone astronomer" peering intently through a telescope, or guiding light to a spectrograph or other instrument, expensive and complicated planetary missions required teams of interactive, interdisciplinary scientists, among them planetary astronomers.

Nowhere was this change more evident than in the case of lunar and planetary missions. These missions were so complex, demanded so much time and effort, and produced such enormous amounts of data that individual scientists could not possibly handle things on their own. Instead, driven by a practical need to get things done, NASA organized "science teams." At first, only a few scientists were involved in any specific flight, but as space probes became steadily more complex, and as mission durations grew longer, scores of scientists became involved with each project. Moreover, these researchers were of diverse backgrounds, for planetary research had changed to the point where a wide variety of expertise was needed to work on even a single problem.

It may be difficult for one who did not experience the days before NASA to realize just what a significant change the introduction of scientific teams involved for planetary scientists. Previously, astronomers had usually worked alone. Collaborations among several workers were exceptions to the rule. Even when there was substantial collaboration, often only a single person's name appeared as the author of the published article giving the results of an investigation, although a generous researcher might devote a short paragraph at the end to mentioning the names of other contributors to the project and what they had accomplished. A graduate student might have a faculty adviser as a co-author ("for suggesting this line of research" was a common reason), or an established scientist might give a student's career a boost by adding the junior worker's name to a paper.

Times were changing. Especially after World War II, although theorists still preferred to work alone, experiments in nuclear physics, for instance, often involved enormous particle accelerators and complicated detectors. Gradually the numbers of authors on articles describing new results began to rise. This trend has continued, and currently it is not unusual for the number of names attached to a paper on high energy "particle physics" (which is a step beyond the nuclear variety) to reach into the hundreds. The situation so far has not grown that extreme in the planetary sciences, but the trend is the same.

The science teams for the Viking Mars probes provide a good example of how planetary science has changed since the advent of the space age. There were no less than thirteen such teams involving a formal total of seventy-eight scientists—a far cry from Galileo alone or from William Herschel and his sister Caroline at work. Each team had a leader, but all the members were fully involved. Among the areas of responsibility for the different teams were imaging from the orbiting vehicles, imaging from the landers, biology, thermal mapping from orbit, water vapor mapping from orbit, scientific results obtained during atmospheric entry, molecular analysis on the surface of the red planet, inorganic chemistry, meteorology, seismology, physical properties of Mars, magnetic properties (here, by exception, there was only a single scientist), and radio science. Things had gotten very complicated indeed. But on the positive side, this very complexity reveals clearly how sophisticated planetary probes had become. The "orbiting imaging" team was the largest, with fourteen members, distributed across a wide variety of specialties. To mention a just few names, there were geologists such as Michael E. Carr (the team leader), Harold Masursky, and Lawrence A. Soderblom; planetary astronomers like Bradford A. Smith and Joseph Veverka; and even "classical" astronomers like William A. Baum (originally an expert on globular star clusters, but who had been involved in planetary work for years at Lowell Observatory).[1]

Perhaps the most interesting aspect of NASA's introduction of science teams was that the concept worked so well. While there were the expected number of gripes about this or that person, on the whole things went smoothly. One can only speculate that this result may have been due in part to the fact that this was a radically new field of endeavor and not one encrusted with centuries of outmoded tradition.

In the early 1960s planetary scientists faced the interesting and exciting—and perhaps to some, threatening—possibility that their research results might soon be proved or disproved by ground-based or space probe observations and measurements. In those days many young men and women became planetary astronomers because the field seemed to be on the cusp of space exploration, and because now, unlike in the preceding decades, there truly were jobs for planetary astronomers. Many found employment with NASA and others with institutions or programs supported financially by NASA contracts and grants. Some universities with no direct relationship to NASA found their programs in planetary astronomy stimulated by the general national interest in space, science, and astronomy. Although the monetary support for planetary astronomy and science may have been small compared to the amounts spent on space hardware in the 1960s, science generally, including planetary astronomy, flourished.

As the number of astronomers and the opportunities for research grew, so did the annual number of discoveries and publications. While in the previous few decades a typical year might see only a few significant articles on solar system topics in scientific journals, or perhaps none, during the 1960s the numbers reached into the hundreds. What had once been a paucity of new information became a deluge. In fact, the world acquired more knowledge of its solar system within a few decades than had been accumulated over the previous millennia. This meant, for example, that even tasks such as writing a history of planetary astronomy required greater selectivity. Astronomers produced not only more information but more reliable information as well, which as time passed could be verified by lunar and planetary exploring missions. Much that had been speculation became knowledge, and on the other side of the coin, much that had been unknown became matter for speculation. The former was particularly true in the field of planetary astronomy; the latter applied more to stellar astronomy. All in all, the early NASA years were truly astronomical times.

FROM THE EARTH TO THE MOON

John F. Kennedy became president in 1961, and that was not a good year for a newly inaugurated president of the United States. As we have seen, on April 12 the Soviets launched Yuri Gagarin into space, and after a single orbit his spaceship, Vostok I, returned him safely to Earth. It represented yet another tremendous propaganda triumph for the U.S.S.R. as well as a practical demonstration that the Soviet Union had scientists, engineers, rockets, and technology in general that rivaled or exceeded those of the United States. Only a few days later a rebel force, embarking from the United States with the blessings of the American government, landed in Cuba with the aim of overthrowing the communist government of Fidel Castro. The attempt failed and resulted in the so-called Bay of Pigs fiasco. On both counts the United States seemingly had suffered an irreversible loss of world leadership. President Kennedy selected space exploration as a prominent part of his "New Frontier" program, which he hoped would restore American purpose and American prestige.

On May 25, 1961, in a major address to Congress, the president announced that the United States should set a firm goal of landing a man on the Moon and safely returning him to Earth "before this decade is out." This bold program was proposed only after studies by scientists and engineers had indicated that it could be done. Moreover, the inclusion of humans in the lunar expeditions was expected to, and did, generate vastly more public interest and support than if only unmanned probes were involved. The promise of a manned landing on the Moon sharpened the definition of space exploration and whetted public excitement. The public warmed to the idea and with little debate Congress voted substantial additional funds. Project Apollo became the centerpiece of NASA programs.[2]

The Soviets provided yet a further stimulus to the American manned spaceflight program when on August 6, 1961, they launched Major Gherman S. Titov and recovered him safely the next day after seventeen orbits of Earth. The sense of competition with the Soviet Union became more intense. On August 16, Soviet-occupied East Germany closed its border with West Berlin and began to erect the Berlin Wall. The danger of the

Cold War becoming a hot one became greater. Americans accepted the Apollo lunar program as one of the few bright spots of 1961.

The proposed Moon landing would require the United States to develop much larger and more powerful launch vehicles than any currently available either in the United States or in the Soviet Union. In part, the psychology of the lunar program was conditioned by the "missile gap," and a first manned lunar landing by the Americans would signify the close of that gap (the U.S. was widely believed to be far behind the Soviets in the field of ballistic missiles, while actually it was far ahead). Although the announced lunar expedition was to be a civilian effort, at the time it had strong implications for national security.

However, not everyone applauded President Kennedy's accelerated space program. In particular, some senior scientists, including some astronomers, objected vigorously. For the most part those astronomers who opposed the Apollo lunar program came from the ranks of those who specialized in such areas as stars, galaxies, interplanetary magnetic fields, and charged particles (which was only natural, as planetary astronomers were still few and far between). Some of them no doubt believed that funding for their own research might suffer as a result of increased emphasis on the Moon and planets. Lunar and planetary astronomers, understandably, generally favored expanded planetary exploration.

As early as July 31, 1961, Senator Paul H. Douglas released the results of a poll of 381 members of the American Astronomical Society, comprising professional scientists representing all areas of astronomy. Some 36 percent believed that a manned expedition to the Moon would be of great scientific value, 29 percent considered it of moderate value, and 35 percent reckoned it of little value. Thus a hefty majority of the scientists were cool or lukewarm toward the proposed Apollo lunar landing. To be sure, science was not the primary objective behind the program to land a man on the Moon and return him safely to Earth.[3] Yet, as a matter of hard fact, NASA science projects were often contingent upon the development of an engineering and technological base sufficient to support stronger scientific initiatives. Scientists with a narrow view tended to think that expensive, piloted spacecraft programs diverted money from space science, perhaps ignoring the possibility that the public support generated by such missions benefited all of space exploration.

But to be fair, AAS members held markedly different attitudes when it came to "the exploration of space by automatic devices with the ultimate aim of manned journeys." In this case 66 percent thought it would be of great value, 23 percent of moderate value, and only 11 percent of little value.[4] The manned space initiative, in other words, seemed to many astronomers to divert resources and attention from science to theatrics, but as a group they were more or less behind the space program in general.

The debate over the scientific and practical value of the Apollo lunar exploration program became more rancorous as time passed. On April 19, 1963, Philip H. Abelson, editor of the influential journal *Science,* published an editorial summing up the case against Apollo, the scientific value of which he deemed minimal.[5] It is important to note that his criticism was directed against an accelerated *manned* lunar program, but it is easy to see that such comments might be misconstrued as a wider condemnation of space exploration in general.

The controversy led to congressional hearings on June 10 and 11, which concentrated on "(a) the overall goals of our space exploration effort in comparison with scientific aspects of other national goals, and (b) the relative emphasis on the various projects within the space program."[6] Abelson, with solid scientific credentials as a distinguished nuclear chemist, told the congressional committee: "The practical consequences that may stem from space exploration principally involve regions near the Earth." He dismissed lunar and planetary exploration by automated probes in a mere thirteen lines of testimony, which included the statement that "the chemical constitution of the Moon and Mars will not be strikingly different from that of the rocks at the surface of the earth." Assessment of his position all depends on the meaning of "strikingly different," but in the event he was wrong, as they did turn out to be significantly different. Perhaps one of his most questionable statements was the assertion that the majority of important scientific questions related to the Moon and planets could be answered relatively soon from Earth-based studies. More than three decades of effort since then have shown that such is not the case, but his remark is perhaps a good example of a feeling among at least some senior scientists at the time that lunar and planetary problems were relatively few, comparatively simple, and rather unimportant.[7] In contrast, most of the other witnesses at the hearings thought otherwise. Still, comments such as Abelson's illustrate that at the time planetary research still had a long way to go before it was generally accepted as a "real" science. The stigma attached to the field over the past decades evidently had not yet been removed.

Even at this time, after some years of hard-won experience had shown how difficult space exploration was, many scientists and engineers made some amazingly optimistic predictions. Congressional committee witnesses spoke of manned orbiting laboratories (that is, space stations) in the 1968–75 period, a manned lunar base perhaps as early as 1972, and expeditions to Mars by the time of America's Bicentennial. While these dreams did not come to be, the anticipation and the speculation alone helped make planetary research for the first time a matter of immediate practical concern and popular interest.

In addition to the broader controversy over Apollo's scientific merits, there developed a general, deep-seated, and long-lasting clash between some academic scientists at universities, on the one side, and NASA managers on the other. Basically, the problem was who was boss—NASA or the scientists? Should science issues determine missions and programs, or did missions and programs direct the nature of scientific research? Because of his position as head of space sciences at NASA, Homer E. Newell became the lightning rod for much of the criticism from the scientific community directed toward the agency. Newell, always a decisive but never a demonstrative man, later commented in no uncertain terms on the carping he heard from some of the academic community:

> The complacent assumption of the superiority of academic research, the presumption of a natural right to be supported in their researches, the instant readiness to criticize, and the disdain which many if not most of the scientists accorded the government manager, particularly the scientist manager, were hard to stomach at times. . . . Especially frustrating was the apparent unwillingness, or perhaps inability, of outside scientists to appreciate the problems with which NASA scientists had to wrestle.[8]

In stark contrast, many scientists got along well with NASA, a particular example closely related to the theme of this book being Gerard P. Kuiper. But Newell's comments and the dissension within the scientific community are indicative of significant problems.

In the early days of its existence, NASA created space science groups organized to perform research in areas and on topics of special interest to NASA. Such groups were established early on at the Jet Propulsion Laboratory and Ames Research Center in California and the Goddard Space Flight Center in Maryland. Some university scientists opposed these moves, believing that space research should be confined solely to academia, and concomitantly that NASA funding for research should be directed to academic institutions alone. However, performance and the passage of time proved the worth of these and other "in-house" groups, which not only survived but are still flourishing today—prominently at Goddard, JPL, Ames, and Johnson Space Center. Kuiper's NASA-oriented space science group, on the other hand, successfully integrated itself with the University of Arizona in Tucson.

What all this activity meant, in part, is that the NASA space science program had begun to penetrate and to alter the traditional institutional structures of science. Not only did the techniques of science and astronomy change greatly within only a few decades, but so did the accomplishments. Moreover, the applications of planetary science in human affairs became more direct, immediate, and pronounced. It might matter a good deal that there might be water on Mars, or that the surface of Venus might be a scene out of Dante's *Inferno,* for this knowledge might give us information needed to preserve life on Earth. Planetary astronomy, it seemed, might be a highly practical science.

VENUS UNVEILED — PARTIALLY

By the early 1960s advancing technology provided methods of studying the planets that astronomers of even a decade or two before could only have dreamed of, if they thought of these techniques at all. Venus, because it approaches Earth more closely than any other planet, provided some striking examples of the power of these new methods.

Radar now employed antennas so large, transmitters so powerful, and receivers so sensitive that it appeared reasonable to try to detect pulses of electromagnetic radiation sent from Earth and reflected back here from the surface of Venus, especially when Venus came closest to Earth at its inferior conjunction. And try astronomers did. Once again, more than one scientist independently made the same discovery. During the inferior conjunction of 1962, groups in various countries accomplished no less than *six* successful radar echo detections, five of which contacts were reported in the same issue of the *Astronomical Journal!*[9]

While the radar contacts were in themselves significant, they also revealed some startling new information about Venus. To their surprise, astronomers learned that the actual rotation period of Venus was neither around 24 hours, nor synchronous with respect to the Sun (almost 225 days), the two most popular guesses for almost a century. Instead, the early data indicated that the rotation period was probably some 250 days, and that it was *retrograde.* That is, though Venus revolves around the Sun in the same direction as Earth, it rotates from east to west, instead of from west to east as our planet and most of the others do. Scientists were at a loss to explain how two bodies so similar in size, mass, density, and location in the solar system as Earth and Venus could be so different in their rotation.[10]

The radar technique depends on the Doppler effect. Radio pulses sent from Earth are not only of short duration but also contain only a very "narrow" range of frequencies or, equivalently, wavelengths. If Venus were not rotating (or if its axis of rotation were pointed squarely at us), all "visible" parts of its surface would have the same line-of-sight velocity with respect to Earth. The echo would then come back as narrow as it went out, though it might be shifted in frequency due to the relative line-of-sight motion of the two bodies. However, if the veiled planet were rotating, and its pole were not aimed at us, the situation would be different. Ignoring orbital motion, some parts of Venus would be approaching us, producing a blue shift, and some would be receding, causing a red shift. The result would be that the return echo would have a wider frequency spread than that of the originally transmitted pulse. All other things being equal, the faster the spin, the wider the echo. The initial surprise to observers was that the echo was so extremely narrow.[11]

Even more surprising was that it appeared that the slow "backward" rotation of Venus caused it to present essentially the same "face" to Earth at every inferior conjunction. In effect, Venus has a weird variety of "synchronous" (for lack of a better word) rotation with respect to our planet, a result that no one had ever imagined. This curious coincidence is apparently due to subtle tidal effects, but its discovery was an important early step in convincing many scientists that "solving the solar system" might prove to be a long, hard job.

These pioneering planetary radar studies had an additional important impact on astronomy beyond the solar system, for they provided a way to determine the value of the astronomical unit by an entirely new method. Once again, there was a direct connection between ancient and modern astronomy, as a problem that was thousands of years old—the distance from the Earth to the Sun—was addressed yet again by the latest techniques.

Because of its proximity, Venus was the obvious first choice as a target for deep space probes venturing beyond the Moon. When NASA began a serious program of planetary exploration, the initial plan was to launch pairs of probes toward Mars and Venus (Mariners A and B, respectively) during launch opportunities in the period 1962–68. These would be heavy spacecraft for the time, weighing over half a ton each. As we have seen, development problems with the booster rocket made these missions impossible. However, in August, 1961, the Jet Propulsion Laboratory determined that it might be possible to conduct a modest planetary mission with the air force Agena upper stage, which was well along in development. Because an Atlas Agena could send much less weight toward Venus than could an Atlas Centaur, JPL was asked to prepare a lighter spacecraft (about 400 pounds) based on the Ranger series of lunar probes. Scientists were invited to propose scientific experiments for the mission, and JPL swiftly developed two so-called Mariner R spacecraft ("R" for Ranger, since these were taken from the Ranger series of spacecraft already under construction) for launches toward Venus during the period from July to September in 1962.[12] Because of the necessary changes in the spacecraft and the launch vehicle, NASA scrambled to salvage something from this Venus launch window, when the probes could be sent on their way with a minimum amount of energy. Of course, it was widely hoped that the United States would beat the Soviets to the spectacular goal of launching the first successful planetary mission.

The first launch, on July 22, 1962, ended only 236 seconds after liftoff, when the range safety officer destroyed the launch vehicle. The failure occurred because of two separate problems, the more critical one being the lack of a *hyphen* in the guidance program stored in the Atlas's onboard computer! This was perhaps the most extreme case ever of a minuscule error causing a major setback.[13]

The second try a month later succeeded. Launched on August 27, 1962, the probe that became known as Mariner II worked well, despite annoying problems that at times appeared serious but were eventually overcome. After coasting through space for 109 days, Mariner II passed less than 22,000 miles from the surface of Venus on December 14 with its experiments in working order. Contact with the probe continued until January 3, 1963, when it was almost 63 million miles from Earth.[14]

Thus, the United States won the race to be the first to observe another planet from close up. But Soviet scientists competed hotly. In 1962 the Soviet Union attempted at least four missions to Venus and three to Mars. As we have seen, all failed.[15]

For planetary astronomers the success of Mariner II held special importance, for it demonstrated that direct exploration of other planets in the solar system was indeed possible. Mariner was able to examine Venus with a modest instrument payload that was capable of providing substantial scientific results. This was true science, not a stunt. Mariner also pioneered many of the features that would become standard on future missions. For example, the probe could either hold a desired stable orientation in space with respect to the stars or change it on command. It successfully performed a rocket firing en route to refine its orbit. During the long voyage through interplanetary space, Mariner II instruments provided useful information about solar radiation, the meteoroid or cosmic dust environment, and the interplanetary magnetic field—information that ground-based observations could not obtain. The instruments reported on conditions such as the number of hits by small meteors, the strength and direction of magnetic fields, and the abundance and energies of cosmic rays and other charged particles, data that provided the basis for some interesting hypotheses about the galaxy.[16]

Perhaps the most important findings by Mariner II concerned Venus's atmosphere. Instruments operating at infrared and millimeter wavelengths confirmed the high surface temperature indicated earlier by radio observations from Earth and found little temperature difference between daytime and nighttime areas of the planet. The possibilities of oceans or life on our "sister" planet were finally put to rest, for the body that looks so beautiful in our twilight skies was confirmed to be a hellishly hot and hideous place. In addition, the probe found no indication of a magnetic field for Venus and no radiation belts.

The fact that the gravitational pull of Venus strongly affected Mariner II's orbit during its close approach to the planet provided a means of determining that body's mass, which early analysis of the tracking data gave as about 81 percent that of Earth. This result was especially significant. Since it has no natural satellite of its own, planetary scientists previously had been able to make only rough estimates of Venus's mass. Tracking data also provided confirmation of the improved values of the astronomical unit determined by Earth-based radar observations of Venus. Thus, this single space probe advanced our knowledge of the solar system in a wide variety of areas and addressed and answered questions both very old and very new.[17]

Yet Mariner II left a host of questions about Venus unanswered. Astronomers had long debated the nature of the planet's clouds. Guesses as to their possible composition involved a bewildering variety of possible substances but no one had an answer, let alone definitive evidence for any candidate material. As late as 1969, astronomer Carl Sagan could review the subject and come to no clear conclusion, and neither could anyone else.[18] As we shall see, the eventual solution to this problem came from Earth observations rather than via spacecraft. In fact, one of the scientists who finally solved the problem attended the meeting where Sagan delivered his Venus summary, but at the time even she had absolutely no clue as to the answer.

THE MOON PROBES: MURPHY'S LAW STRIKES AGAIN

Mariner II's successes provided a needed stimulus for American exploration of deep space. As noted, the Mariner accomplishments came at a time when the American unmanned lunar program was experiencing numerous setbacks.[19] Despite the fact that the first relatively sophisticated probes, dubbed Project Ranger, used essentially the same spacecraft as the successful Mariner II, and the same Atlas Agena launch vehicle, the Ranger program experienced continuing difficulties. It seemed that if something could go wrong with the lunar exploratory program, it would.

NASA intended to launch the first two Ranger test missions into orbits some one million miles above Earth. But Ranger 1, launched on August 23, 1961, became stranded in a near Earth orbit, as did Ranger 2, launched on November 18 of the same year. In both cases malfunctions in the Agena upper stage caused the failure. Rangers 3, 4, and 5 were intended to "rough land" (described as something between a feather-soft touchdown and a catastrophic collision) on the Moon's surface carrying seismometers to measure seismic activity and to take rudimentary images of the lunar crust. Launched on January 26, 1962, April 23, 1962, and October 18, 1962, all failed to complete the mission objectives, although one spacecraft did fly past the orbit of the Moon.[20]

NASA designed the next four Rangers to take high resolution photographs of the lunar surface. Ranger 6, launched on January 30, 1964, failed, if such can be the case, even more cruelly than the previous missions. All appeared to go well during launch and into the later parts of the mission, but as Ranger 6 approached the Moon and mission control issued the command to turn on the TV cameras—nothing happened. Ranger 6 crashed into the Moon close to its intended destination but returned no data. Later analysis of engineering instrumentation data showed that an inadvertent high voltage electrical discharge during the early launch phase had apparently triggered the TV cameras prematurely and "burned them out."

Ranger 6 bitterly disappointed everyone connected with the project: scientists, managers, engineers, technicians—all those responsible for the creation and operation of these spacecraft. It affected more adversely, if possible, the small team of lunar scientists for whom the direct exploration of our satellite seemed to offer an immediate opportunity to answer questions that seemed insoluble from Earth observations. The Moon, it appeared, would only yield its secrets reluctantly, if at all.

Not surprisingly, the repeated Ranger failures led to a congressional hearing during which the unique relations between NASA and the Jet Propulsion Laboratory came in for special attention.[21] JPL was an anomaly in the NASA organization. Created in 1944, the laboratory had begun as an army rocket research facility, managed under contract by California Institute of Technology (CalTech). The management agreement gave CalTech some policy control, in that projects to be undertaken were to be of "mutual interest" to the army and the university. Second, the laboratory had broad authority and independence, including the authority (and concomitant funding) to build and launch spacecraft. After its transfer to NASA the issue arose of whether it retained that independence. As Arnold Levine commented in his management history of NASA, "Although JPL was a major acquisition for NASA, its ambiguous status was to lead to serious difficulties over the next six years."[22]

The Ranger problems highlighted those difficulties. Investigations by the House, and an internal NASA board of inquiry, resulted in some seemingly minor yet essentially substantial contract changes. JPL became more like other NASA centers—under management control of NASA Headquarters. The new contract also clarified the right of NASA to assign projects without the so-called "mutuality" clause, but JPL retained its status as an independent contractor managed by CalTech.[23]

Despite the turmoil, NASA and JPL pressed on and finally achieved a stunning success with Ranger 7, which lifted off on July 28, 1964, and hit the Moon three days later. This time everything worked properly and 4,316 close-up photos of our satellite were sent back to Earth before impact. Perhaps the most surprising and yet reassuring thing about these images was that they contained few surprises. The photos showed areas where concentrations of small craters might make a lunar landing difficult, but most of the area surveyed, a low, flat region near Mare Nubium, had level or gently rolling terrain with some low ridges and many small craters with softly rounded rims.[24]

NASA launched the next (and last) two Rangers in 1965. They performed as planned and generally confirmed the earlier results. However, these probes could not and did not settle such questions as the relative importance of vulcanism, if any, on the Moon; the firmness of the lunar surface; or the true ages of particular features. Those problems required "soft" landers, and perhaps samples returned to earth, for their solution.

As we have seen, the Surveyor spacecraft, America's first soft landers, relied on a large rocket retro motor and vernier rocket engines to slow their plunge toward the Moon and deposit their payloads gently on the lunar surface. Surveyors, developed by Hughes Aircraft under contract to JPL, were much more complicated vehicles than Rangers and a host of problems plagued their development. In addition, as we have seen, delays due to the Centaur upper stage also bedeviled Surveyor.[25]

The delays enabled the U.S.S.R. to "beat" the U.S.A. to yet another first. After at least seven failures in a row, Luna 9 finally made a rough lunar landing on January 31, 1966. The touchdown was not as gentle as Surveyor's was designed to be, but the speed at impact was slow enough to enable a rugged, well-cushioned payload to survive in working order. A television camera aboard took twenty-seven pictures of the lunar surface.[26] Although the mission produced relatively modest scientific information as compared to that expected from the Surveyor, the Luna 9 mission reflected continuing Soviet progress in space.

The Soviet photos showed a surface much like that seen in the best Ranger images—a relatively flat, gently rolling surface with scattered craters and rocks of various sizes. The fact that these rocks, not to mention Luna 9 itself, rested on the surface, and did not sink beneath it, seemed to dispose of the "deep dust" explanation for maria once and for all. However, the actual firmness ("bearing strength") of the Moon's topmost layer still remained unknown.

NASA launched the first of seven Surveyors on May 30, 1966, from Cape Kennedy, Florida. To the amazement of most people involved, the very first one successfully landed on the Moon. Surveyor I touched down on a mare known as Oceanus Procellarum on June 2, 1966, and shortly began transmitting back to Earth the first of thousands of photographs. The first image showed that one of three landing pads had penetrated the lunar surface but only to a depth of a few centimeters, providing evidence that the lunar surface could indeed support the planned Apollo landings. Additional photos seemed to confirm what was already known of the character of the lunar mare surface—generally flat or gently rolling with scattered craters and rocks of various sizes. The photos hinted that some rocks might be volcanic, but definite proof of this only came later.[27]

Later Surveyors carried a mechanical arm that could dig trenches, turn over small rocks, and the like. Taken together, these automated exploring machines showed that the lunar surface was composed of particles of a wide variety of sizes, including rocks of very different textures. Physical analysis of lunar soil showed that the material of several different maria were similar, but somewhat different from highland material. The compositions were similar to those of terrestrial basalts, which are volcanic rocks, and substantially different from those of most meteorites falling on Earth.[28] The U.S. lunar program, it appeared, was going well.

The original Surveyor program had included an orbiting version that would image the entire Moon at high resolution as well as supplying detailed information about the nature of the Moon's gravitational field, data vital to the Apollo project. NASA decided to provide these results through a separate program managed by the Langley Research Center utilizing a new spacecraft to be built by Boeing Company.

The resulting program, known by the rather unimaginative name of Lunar Orbiter, may have been one of NASA's most successful but unheralded projects. Between August 10, 1966, and August 1, 1967, NASA launched five Orbiters to the Moon. Amazingly, all of these vehicles returned useful photographs. The images revealed no insurmountable handicaps to manned lunar landings and yielded no surprises on the Moon's far side. The Orbiters confirmed that our satellite's far side contained far fewer maria than the near side and, in particular, showed no trace of what the U.S.S.R. had dubbed the "Soviet Mountains."[29]

In the light of the spectacular images returned by Rangers, Surveyors, and Orbiters, not to mention other lunar and planetary missions, it is surprising that the scientists involved in these early missions initially hesitated to fly cameras as part of the payloads. In fact, many of them believed photography represented cheap and tawdry science, and that NASA's interest in photography had more to do with publicity than with science. To give a revealing example, at a 1961 meeting of what was then most of the planetary science "community," the question of whether to include on spacecraft instruments to record images came up. Scores of the most senior scientists in the United States were in attendance, but incredibly there was only a single vote in favor of images! The lone holdout was Gerard Kuiper, who was arguably the only planetary scientist present.

Of course, the spectacular images that mission after mission returned from the Moon and planets eventually changed those views, though it took some time.[30] With the wisdom of hindsight, we know today that direct images have produced more important advances in our knowledge of the solar system than any other single type of data. Still, this initial reluctance to rely on photos shows that even competent scientists, who should be ready, willing, and able to use every technique at their disposal to investigate a problem, can be closed-minded and slaves to convention. Then too, some may have remembered the media handling of and the controversy surrounding Percival Lowell, Orson Welles, and the like. Many planetary scientists, and astronomers in general, preferred relative anonymity and seclusion. The prospect of spectacular landscapes on other celestial bodies may have threatened that traditional isolation.[31]

MARS AGAIN

As had been the case for almost a century, the red planet and the possibility of some form of life on its surface attracted intense interest. Mars frustrated astronomers, who still knew little about it despite the immense efforts devoted to observations and theoretical studies of that body. Inability to decipher the Martian atmosphere proved particularly irksome. Some carbon dioxide existed in its atmosphere, which was thought to consist mostly of nitrogen. That conjecture probably derived from a weak analogy to Earth's atmosphere, and seemed to be supported by the fact that nitrogen gas has no absorption features that are readily observed from Earth's surface. Astronomers had no certain evidence for any other atmospheric gas and, in particular, no evidence for water vapor on Mars, without which life as we know it would be impossible.

As the exploration of Mars by automated and eventually by manned spacecraft became a real possibility, planetary astronomers once again returned to the search for water in the Martian atmosphere. In 1963 the French astronomer Adouin Dollfus concluded that Mars's atmosphere held an average of 200 microns, or 0.2 of a millimeter, of "precipitable water vapor" (in effect, how much there would be on the ground if it all rained out) across the planet's disk.[32] Dollfus hypothesized a water content substantially above earlier estimates. He later lowered this estimate to 45 microns, still too high an average value according to later determinations made from Earth. Although he was an experienced observer working in the infrared at a high and dry mountain site, it is unclear to this day whether or not he actually detected water. In any case, his results were generally discounted at the time because of the high values he reported.

Meanwhile, Hyron Spinrad, a newly minted Ph.D. astronomer in JPL's newly formed planetary science group, finally reached an answer to the hoary riddle of water on Mars. He specialized in taking spectra, but he faced a severe problem because he could not get observing time on the large telescopes with large spectrographs, the only instruments that offered a realistic chance of success. He even made a forlorn attempt using the 48-inch reflector at Victoria, British Columbia, a usually sodden site that is probably not the best place in the world to try and detect water vapor in the atmosphere of another planet.[33] But while trying to obtain telescope time, Spinrad made an unexpected discovery that would have a vital bearing on his quest.

So called "fine-grained" infrared-sensitive emulsions, which could capture very faint absorption lines, had generally been considered much too "slow," or insensitive, for useful astronomical work. However, Spinrad found that when bathed in a cold and dilute ammonia solution, their sensitivity improved dramatically. That innovation could have been found many years earlier, but no one had thought to try it out. The discovery was more a product of hard work and happy accident than of new technology.

Armed with this technical advance, Spinrad finally obtained some time on the Mount Wilson 100-inch reflector. He did this through the good offices of astronomer Guido Munch, then a JPL consultant, who worked with Louis Kaplan, Spinrad's immediate superior at JPL, and thus created a fortunate happenstance in solving the mystery of Mars. On the night of

Hyron Spinrad (*left*) and Lewis Kaplan in 1962. Courtesy Hyron Spinrad

April 12–13, 1963, this team obtained a good photographic plate of the near-infrared spectrum of Mars in the region of the 8200 Ångstrom band of water vapor. The red planet was then near quadrature, with its line-of-sight velocity with respect to Earth at its greatest, helping to separate Martian absorption features from their terrestrial counterparts. Faintly, but definitely, Mars water vapor lines appeared, nestled against the much stronger ones due to our own atmosphere.[34] The mystery was finally solved! There really was water on Mars, and Percival Lowell's method of detecting it was vindicated after more than a half-century of effort.

The amount of water present was tiny, the first estimate of 5 to 10 microns of precipitable vapor later being refined to about 15. However, many scientists remained unconvinced by the available evidence. The thin, faint Martian absorption lines could be detected on the original photographic plate only because of the superb pattern recognition ability of the human eye and brain combination. The lines were impossible to reproduce on a paper print, let alone in a publication. Thus, the debate about water on Mars continued to rage for several years. The presence or absence of water had a direct bearing on the possibility of some form of life on the red planet, though most astronomers, to be sure, argued about the water, not life, even if the latter possibility was in everyone's thoughts.[35]

In addition to the discovery of water, Spinrad's spectroscopic plate contained another startling surprise. Near a wavelength of 8700 Ångstroms appeared the regularly spaced absorption lines of a carbon dioxide band. This feature was well known in spectra of Venus, where it was prominent because of the enormous amount of CO_2 in that planet's atmosphere. However, it is a weak band in relative terms, and Spinrad realized at once that its presence in this Martian spectrum meant that there was a *lot* more carbon dioxide in the red planet's atmosphere than anyone had realized until then.

Spinrad also realized something else. If carbon dioxide, rather than nitrogen, was the main constituent of Mars's atmosphere, the amount indicated by the strength of the 8700 Ångstrom band pointed to a surface pressure of 35 millibars or so, instead of the roughly 85 generally assumed at the time. The actual abundance of CO_2 could not be obtained from the stronger and previously known features farther in the infrared because these are "saturated." That is, their strength does not depend much on the amount of gas present. The effect is analogous to looking into a mature field of corn—one cannot tell if the crop is only a few rows deep or extends back for miles. The newly discovered band, on the other hand, did not have this drawback.

The drastically lower estimate of the Martian surface pressure was a bombshell that immediately posed severe headaches for engineers pondering the design of probes meant to land softly on the surface of the red planet. If the lower value was correct, a payload using a parachute designed for an 85 millibar atmosphere simply would crash into Mars's surface at such a speed that it would be reduced to a pile of useless junk. As a result, I set up a meeting in Washington to discuss the matter.

The score or so scientists working in the field at the time came up with estimates that ranged from about 100 down to 8 millibars, hardly a reassuring situation. Kaplan half-jokingly suggested the 8 millibar estimate at the end of the day-long session, "in case the Martian atmosphere turns out to be all CO_2." There was general laughter, shared in by Kaplan, at this suggestion, but he turned out to be a prophet indeed.[36]

The debate over the Mars atmosphere took a new turn in 1965. Late in the previous year, the United States launched two Atlas Agena—boosted spacecraft toward the red planet. The first, Mariner III, failed because a composite-materials shroud that protected it during its ascent through Earth's atmosphere failed to deploy. The second, Mariner IV, with a hurriedly made metal shroud, worked. After an eight month coast through interplanetary space, Mariner IV flew by Mars on July 15, 1965, getting as close as about 6,000 miles and taking twenty-two pictures as it did so.

These could not compare in quality with, for example, lunar images obtained with terrestrial telescopes, yet some of them far surpassed any Martian views that ever had been obtained from Earth.[37]

The images provided the most startling result of the entire mission by revealing that a substantial part of Mars's surface was liberally sprinkled with craters resembling those on the Moon. This apparently came as a complete surprise to scientists, although as we have seen, some workers in the past had argued that Mars must have impact craters, and E. E. Barnard may have seen such features. (A Mars liberally cratered, and with some mountains that look like volcanos, had even been depicted in *Wonder Woman* comics early in the 1940s.)[38]

In addition to craters, the Mariner IV images showed only a few vague features, the true nature of which was uncertain. There were no signs of structures such as volcanos, mountain ranges, canyons, and the like, and in particular no traces of any of the classical canals. Thus, Mariner IV disproved Percival Lowell's theories of intelligent canal builders on Mars. Further, the effect of the Martian atmosphere on radio signals from the probe as it passed behind the planet enabled researchers to estimate that the surface pressure on Mars was even lower than Spinrad's estimate. Astronomers revived G. Jonestone Stoney's old suggestion that the polar caps, clouds, and related phenomena were composed of frozen carbon dioxide. Mars now seemed to some to be a waterless, almost airless body, more like the Moon than the Earth. The chance of life, or even of any recent geological activity on the red planet, appeared small indeed.[39] However, it is important to note that in the actual project reports, the scientists involved carefully declined to pronounce a final verdict as to the character of the Martian world.

Space probes could do many things impossible to accomplish from Earth, but these vehicles were relatively few. Rather, they tended to supplement and extend the traditional ground-based research of planetary observers. Astronomers continued to work on the riddle of Mars's atmosphere from observatories on Earth. For example, in 1969, some colleagues and I, in addition to other observers, obtained reasonably convincing spectroscopic confirmation that there was water vapor in Mars's atmosphere.[40] To the surprise of those of us involved, this work possibly created more of a public stir than did Spinrad's original detection.

Still, many scientists remained skeptical, and in a front page story, the *New York Times* put the word "proof" of water in quotation marks.[41] Similarly, a senior scientist, commenting on slightly earlier work on the same topic by some of the same researchers, referred to the "debatable claim that on many occasions the H_2O amount is just above the detectable limit."[42] Despite these less than enthusiastic comments, the estimates turned out to be reasonably accurate, much to the satisfaction of the workers who produced them. In addition to providing more solid evidence for the existence of H_2O, the spectra produced by the 1969 work showed that the water vapor abundance varied with the season on Mars and with location on the planet. These findings at least kept alive the slim hope that some primitive form of life existed there.[43] The value of the evidence seemed to diminish, however, as results came in from the next pair of American-launched Mars probes.

Mariners 6 and 7 (NASA had switched from Roman to Arabic numerals) carried more advanced payloads than their predecessors because the Centaur upper stage was at last available and could send considerably heavier payloads to Mars. NASA launched the two Mars Mariners on February 24 and March 27, 1969. Both spacecraft and payloads worked well, flying past Mars on July 30 and August 5, respectively.[44] Between them, they took synoptic pictures of the entire disk of Mars during approach and then photographed a substantial part of the red planet's surface close up, revealing a few surprises but also missing much. Remarkably, these two Mars probes failed to receive the publicity accorded the earlier and later ones, probably because they were not were not the first probes to Mars and they did not have the capability (or the good luck) to discover some of Mars's most spectacular features. In addition, by 1969, a manned lunar landing rather than probes of Mars preoccupied public attention.

The area of Mars surveyed by the Mariners revealed a host of craters and curious terrain features of uncertain origin. The existence of craterless regions indicated that there must be a process, or processes, that could erase rugged features, while a briefly famous type of "chaotic terrain" seen from the probes created new mysteries about the red planet. Still, many scientists of the time pictured Mars as a planet that had been effectively waterless, airless, and geologically dead almost since its formation. Only rare impacts appeared to have altered its terrain, and it seemed to be a long inert relic.[45]

Once again, later space missions forced a revision of our views about Mars. The evidence suggested by Mariners 6 and 7 basically corroborated that from Mariner 4, but actually these missions had created a "mistaken identity." Three spacecraft in a row had photographed Mars from close up, and by cruel chance had missed the planet's most striking geological structures.

The solar system's largest known canyon, to take one case, was not in the area surveyed by the three Mariners. For another, Nix Olympica was seen on approach images and identified as a "white rimmed crater some

500 miles in diameter, with a bright spot in the center."[46] The "white rim" turned out to be a ring of clouds banked against the titanic clifflike base of the largest known volcano in the solar system, while the "bright spot in the center" was the summit of a lofty mountain capped with snow. Christopher Columbus, who originally thought he had found the east coast of Asia when he reached North America, might have appreciated these misguided interpretations. Soon, the conception of Mars derived from the Mariner voyages was to change drastically.

The Mariners carried other, less glamorous experiments than photography, which in general confirmed the traditional image of Mars developed from extensive ground-based observations. The surface pressure was low (just under Kaplan's earlier estimate) and variable over the planet, depending upon the altitude of the underlying ground. Such a thin atmosphere held "no room" for any major atmospheric constituents other than carbon dioxide. The atmosphere contained a small amount of water vapor, and there was no evidence of molecular nitrogen, argon, ozone, or any other gas.[47]

EARTHBOUND ASTRONOMY

While planetary probes provided insights previously unobtainable into the nature of the Moon and planets, many astronomers collaborated with NASA in Earth-based explorations of the solar system. As one example, Gerard Kuiper's astronomical team at the University of Arizona provided close support for space science projects. When Kuiper moved his lunar project to the University of Arizona late in 1960, the entire staff numbered only nine, although this was an impressive number by the standards of the time. After some fleeting name changes, Kuiper settled on the name Lunar and Planetary Laboratory for his creation, and by the beginning of 1962, the number of personnel at the institute had tripled. Supported in large part by NASA funding, the laboratory grew steadily until it peaked at 119 employees in 1967. The laboratory engaged in a wide variety of research on solar system topics.[48]

Kuiper's contributions to the development of planetary astronomy went far beyond the confines of LPL. He trained a significant number of graduate students, who in turn became solar system researchers. Perhaps the most famous of these was Carl Sagan. Sagan in turn became an ombudsman for astronomy. His writings and television appearances captured the public imagination and attracted many young scientists into the field. Thus, Kuiper's influence spread like the ripples created when a stone is thrown in a pond. In more specific terms, for example, Sagan inspired

Spinrad to enter the field.[49] Spinrad, in turn, introduced me to planetary astronomy. Numerous similar personal "chain reactions" may have done more to advance planetary astronomy than any other single factor.

Another aspect of Kuiper's efforts benefited not only planetary studies but astronomy in general. He strongly advocated placing observatories on high mountains that were above much of earth's water vapor and where the seeing might be very good indeed. In the past, astronomical observatories had tended to be located with the convenience and proximity of the astronomer in mind, rather than the clarity of the view. Kuiper was the first astronomer to stress the advantages of Mauna Kea ("White Mountain") on the island of Hawaii as an ideal site for an astronomical observatory. His dream of building a large reflector on the site was eventually to come true, but sadly he was to have no part in it.[50]

Given the great increase in the number of astronomers and the growing demands being made for viewing time on already scarce large telescopes, astronomers faced something of a technological crisis in the 1960s. As noted, Spinrad encountered severe difficulties in getting observing time on large telescopes with spectrographs good enough to do useful work on the planets. A combination of interesting people and conditions, along with vital financial support by NASA, was needed to resolve the telescope crisis. Eventually, by the late 1960s, a number of observers could use dramatically greater amounts of big telescope time for planetary research, and much of the credit for this vastly improved situation goes to one man, Harlan J. Smith.

HARLAN J. SMITH AND MCDONALD OBSERVATORY

Founded in the 1930s, McDonald Observatory began as a unique, hybrid institution. The University of Texas owned the site and the telescopes, including an 82-inch reflector, but as there was no astronomy department in Austin, the University of Chicago and its Yerkes Observatory ran the facility. Completed just before the beginning of World War II, the 82-inch reflector was at the time the second largest telescope in the world.[51]

This unusual joint arrangement was scheduled to end in 1962. As the deadline approached, the University of Chicago began decreasing its financial support of McDonald, while the University of Texas slowly began to build an astronomy department. In 1963, Yerkes relinquished control, and Harlan J. Smith became the director of McDonald Observatory and at the same time the chairman of the newly created astronomy department in Austin.[52]

Smith had big plans for development of the observatory, and among

The entire faculty of the astronomy department of the University of Texas in 1963. *Left to right:* Harlan J. Smith, department chairman and director of the McDonald Observatory, Gerard de Vaucouleurs, Robert G. Tull, Terrence J. Deeming, and Frank N. Edmonds. Courtesy Robert G. Tull

them was to encourage planetary observing. Beginning late in 1964, he made large amounts of observing time available on the 82-inch for solar system studies, compared to the leftovers with which observers had previously had to make do. It should be noted that this was a time when planetary astronomy was not only not popular but not even safe. As Spinrad has exclaimed, the change was "like night and day."[53]

Planetary spectroscopy in those days required extensive telescope time because not only were clear skies required, but observers also needed low humidity for water vapor studies, for example, and "good seeing" to detect possible variations across the faces of planets. Such conditions varied hourly and large blocks of time were thus required. In addition, the photographic emulsions of the day demanded long exposures: four, six, or even eight hours were commonplace. Some observations were made in the infrared, which meant, for example, that Mars could be investigated at night and Venus during the day, so that little usable time was wasted. Still, the telescope time available was less than was needed by the constantly increasing number of planetary observers. The shift of emphasis at McDonald toward planetary observations helped, but in addition, NASA took some rather extraordinary steps to provide further relief.

NASA'S TELESCOPES

Almost from the beginning NASA supported individual scientists working on ground-based lunar and planetary studies that might be useful in space exploration. As time passed it became more and more evident that such research would become increasingly important "down the road." Support for astronomy came under Newell's "space science" umbrella, and the office of Lunar and Planetary Programs, with Nicks in charge, became particularly active in the work to rehabilitate planetary astronomy.

In 1962 Nicks, an early and effective supporter of planetary research, put Roger C. Moore in charge of "ground and balloon-based [planetary] astronomy."[54] Though his work went largely unheralded, Moore was primarily responsible for getting NASA's ground-based planetary astronomy program under way. Unfortunately, neither Moore nor Raymond L. Newburn of JPL, his counterpart and a vigorous champion of ground-based planetary astronomy, had the "union card" of a Ph.D. in astronomy. This irrational prejudice by the "scientific establishment" against rational arguments did little to help NASA in its efforts to explore the planets.

Nicks sought to recruit a professional astronomer with acceptable credentials for NASA, and in July, 1963, I was selected, on detail from JPL, to serve as "Acting Program Chief, Planetary Astronomy."[55] Significantly, a reorganization placed the program chief for planetary astronomy at a higher level in the hierarchy than Moore's previous position. But now, for the first time, NASA had someone specifically in charge of ground-based planetary astronomy, a daunting task for a newly minted Ph.D. On the morning of my second day at NASA Headquarters, I met with Moore, agreed with him that our aims were identical, and then went around meeting various members of "Code SL"—Nicks's office—and other relevant players.

As the planetary research program grew, it soon became obvious that a shortage of suitable large telescopes severely restricted that work. Moore had already seen the need and indeed had already funded several projects intended to break the bottleneck. NASA, for example, financed a substantial improvement to McDonald's 82-inch reflector, aimed specifically at making that telescope a better instrument to do planetary astronomy, and the upgrade was substantially completed by late 1963.[56] These improvements had a great positive impact on ground-based planetary observations during the 1960s.

In addition, the Lunar and Planetary Laboratory's 61-inch telescope near Tucson, the Texas 107-inch at McDonald, and the University of Hawaii's 88-inch on Mauna Kea were built with NASA money and all contributed significantly to the enhancement of ground-based planetary astronomy in support of NASA's space explorations.

The LPL 61-inch reflector was NASA's first venture in funding a large (for the time) telescope. When he first arrived in Tucson, Kuiper had no substantial instrument under his control. The University of Arizona did have a modest 36-inch telescope, but it was part of the Steward Observatory, which was independent of Kuiper's LPL and located in what had become the middle of the city of Tucson. Relatively small amounts of observing time could be scheduled on occasion at the nearby Kitt Peak National Observatory, the McDonald Observatory, and other facilities, but Kuiper and his team did not have access to the large amounts of observing time, nor to the large instruments required for the wide-ranging and long-duration lunar and planetary programs he desired to establish.[57]

Prior to leaving Yerkes Observatory, Kuiper had urged NASA to fund large telescopes to be used primarily for solar system studies. He argued soundly that because ground-based research is so much cheaper than that done by sounding rockets, satellites, or probes, as much research as possible should be done from terrestrial observatories. He also noted that ground-based studies can be extended over long periods of time to study changes in planetary properties. Perhaps most important of all, he stressed that almost all major observatories in the United States were designed for stellar work and devoted only a small portion of their time to studies of the solar system.[58] Now at Tucson, Kuiper continued to press NASA on the importance of ground-based lunar and planetary observation to planetary exploration. In late 1965 NASA approved funding for a 61-inch reflector to be located at a site high in the Catalina Mountains just north of Tucson, to be operated by the LPL Laboratory.[59]

However, a single 61-inch telescope would not solve the problem of enough observing time for the increasing number of planetary astronomers. The difficulty was to find the money to build other instruments, for although NASA's budget increased year by year, more and more funds went to the Apollo program, leaving science programs, and in particular ground-based planetary astronomy, in tight financial straits. Fortunately, the cost of ground-based telescopes paled compared to the costs of lunar and planetary missions. NASA's Lunar and Planetary office located a small in-house surplus and with it took a major step toward encouraging research in planetary astronomy. This is how it came about.

Early in 1964, Moore came to me and explained that there would be several million dollars left over in the Code SL research funds for the current fiscal year. The reason for this curious situation cannot be documented, but the simplest explanation is that there were too few scientists interested in the solar system to apply for the available money! ("They're all busy," as the saying went in those days at NASA Headquarters.) We both realized that the best use for this money would be to build sizable telescopes dedicated to providing NASA with the information that it badly needed for upcoming flight missions. As it turned out, NASA funded two instruments that did exactly this.

Even after the decision to support the construction of ground-based telescopes for lunar and planetary observation, and after the appropriate public request for proposals, few individuals or institutions responded positively. There were many expressions of strong interest but few definite proposals. A big part of the problem was that NASA could only pay for the telescope, while the other institution involved had to match that expense in some way, such as funding the observatory dome or building a dormitory, roads, or the like. Then too, the obvious candidates—that is, universities with astronomy departments—were almost universally concerned with matters far beyond the solar system. Despite the surge in public interest in the solar system caused by NASA's space program, relatively few astronomers wanted to focus their studies on the Moon and planets.

One strong exception was the University of Texas. Smith leapt at the chance to gain a bigger telescope at McDonald Observatory and had no prejudice whatever against doing planetary astronomy or taking NASA money to do the job. Details of how the 107-inch telescope (originally proposed as an 84-inch) was funded shed an interesting sidelight on how NASA has changed over the years. The 1964 proposal submitted by the University of Texas was only eight pages long (plus a cover page); today even a NASA *request* for proposals can easily run to thirty pages or more.[60] Despite the usual setbacks that seem to bedevil many large telescope project, the 107-inch reflector was dedicated late in 1968 and has provided NASA much needed and basically inexpensive data. Concurrently, the telescope helped the University of Texas astronomy department to build a world class research program.[61] To this day the McDonald telescope is still the largest instrument of its kind ever funded by NASA.

Its dedication on November 26, 1968, provided some Texas-sized misadventures appropriate for a state renowned for its tall tales. The skies were clouding over the evening before the ceremonies and then rain began to fall, changing eventually into sleet. On the day itself an unseasonable snowstorm developed, which turned into an incredible "thundersnow" (the effect of a vivid lightning flash on a mountain top in the midst of a blizzard has to be seen to be appreciated). By the end of the ceremonies, things were getting rather difficult. The chartered bus carrying many of the more important dignitaries backed off a road and came within a few feet of plunging a good fraction of a mile down the slopes of Mount Locke. Valiant work on the part of some expert "mountain men" winched the vehicle back on the road, but the problems did not end there. Although the bus made it safely to the airfield in Marfa, Texas, some forty miles away, the snow by then was so deep that the pilot of the chartered airplane wandered off the runway and stuck the craft hub deep in the sodden soil that lay below the beautiful white blanket. The passengers finally made it back to Austin by train, while those who stayed behind at McDonald were snowed in for three days.[62]

The Jet Propulsion Laboratory, already deeply involved in space exploration under the NASA mantle, submitted a proposal in late 1963 for a 60-inch reflector to be sited in the mountains well north of Los Angeles. Raymond L. Newburn, Hyron Spinrad, and I, three classical optical planetary astronomers, helped write the JPL proposal.[63] Moore and I supported and encouraged the JPL and McDonald projects in parallel. Newell approved them both, saying in no uncertain terms that he was firmly committed to obtaining the needed scientific results in the most economical and speediest way, and emphatically adding that he would cancel a space mission if the results could be gotten in good time from the ground.[64]

That, we was thought, was that. But unfortunately, while the Texas telescope would be built and would prosper, JPL's never saw the light of day. The problem was the California Institute of Technology, which felt that it should take all the time it needed to design and to build a really superb instrument. Considering that CalTech already had 60-, 100-, and 200-inch telescopes, it is all too understandable that they might have been reluctant to spend their one (that was all NASA allowed) chance of a possible facility grant on what was to them a small instrument devoted to a field far removed from that institution's emphasis on the distant reaches of the universe. In any event, in 1964 JPL canceled its proposal.[65]

Now NASA still had the money and the need for a telescope but no place to locate it. Kuiper, while constructing the 61-inch near Tucson, also had long advocated placing major telescopes at high, dry sites, especially when infrared research was involved. He became interested in the possibilities offered by Mauna Kea, an extinct volcano. Supported by NASA, Kuiper supervised site tests, which indicated that the mountain was possibly the best place in the world to place a large telescope. Moreover, the state of Hawaii agreed to perform some preliminary improvements on the site, such as grading a rough road to the summit.[66] Although NASA did

William Brunk, longtime chief
of planetary astronomy for NASA.
Courtesy William Brunk

soon support the construction of a large telescope on Mauna Kea, the observatory was not to be under the supervision of Kuiper's Lunar and Planetary Laboratory despite his initiatives in establishing it.

NASA liked the idea of an observatory on Mauna Kea, but the agency for some reason decided that if a telescope were built there, it should be operated by the University of Hawaii rather than by the University of Arizona. While the decision was pending, Kuiper's stream of proposals supporting the Mauna Kea observatory were tabled. NASA (or other authorities) thought that giving Kuiper authority over a telescope in Hawaii might "overextend" the LPL director.

In the midst of the Mauna Kea deliberations, I transferred back from NASA Headquarters to JPL with the aim of getting directly involved in planetary observations. My successor, William E. Brunk, right from the start of his tenure confronted some very difficult conditions. By now planetary studies were becoming popular among professional astronomers, and of course they had never lost the attention of the public. Numerous institutions sent in bids to take on the new telescope and there were some interesting and attractive options, but Mauna Kea loomed large in the perspective of things, thanks largely to the groundwork laid by Kuiper.

Eventually, Brunk went out on a limb with Hawaii. It was a difficult decision, especially because the University of Hawaii then had no astronomy department.[67] That, in fact, may have affected the decision. In those days few astronomy departments—except Texas and LPL, which was not really an astronomy department—devoted any substantial effort to solar system studies. A new organization could be molded to solar system research. Brunk made a wise and courageous choice. Eventually an 88-inch reflector was built on Mauna Kea, smaller than the McDonald instrument because of the higher construction costs at such a remote location. But precisely because of that location, it was particularly suited to solar system work. In the years since Kuiper's enthusiastic early appraisals, the superior properties of the site have been amply confirmed, and many more telescopes have joined the 88-inch on the White Mountain.

Undoubtedly, "territoriality" played a part in the final decision by NASA to locate a telescope at Mauna Kea, and to place it under the authority of the University of Hawaii. In addition, NASA had a policy or preference to disperse its centers and facilities as broadly as possible across the United States. Although the University of Hawaii had no astronomy department, part of the NASA mission was to build up those areas which enhanced NASA's and the nation's technology base. In any event, Kuiper ceased having any role in the further development of a superb observing site that he had done much to develop and publicize.[68]

Although NASA had now helped create pockets of research in planetary astronomy, as at the University of Arizona, the University of Hawaii, the Jet Propulsion Laboratory, and in some of the NASA centers, planetary astronomy still held secondary interest among the broad range of practicing astronomers. As an illustration of this situation, in 1964 the National Academy of Sciences published a study of the prospects for ground-based astronomy for the next ten years. In the table of contents to that report, "A Solar Radar System" is the only item that relates to bodies nearer than another star. And indeed, lunar and planetary studies are dismissed in only a few lines.[69] For the most part astronomers continued to look beyond the solar system. But in spite of their lack of recognition for the remainder of the 1960s, planetary astronomers working under the aegis of NASA probed Earth's nearest neighbors more deeply. Mars (the red planet) and Venus (the most popular evening and morning star) began to reveal their elusive identities. And before the decade was out, men walked on the Moon.

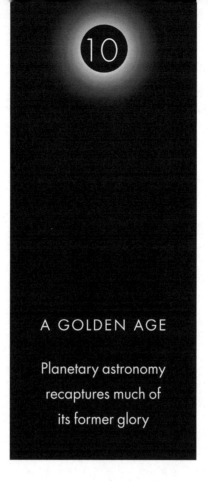

A GOLDEN AGE

Planetary astronomy
recaptures much of
its former glory

Our knowledge of the solar system grew by leaps and bounds during the late 1960s and early 1970s, and the advances were particularly spectacular as regards our close neighbors the Moon, Venus, Mars, and Mercury.

In great part these accomplishments were made possible by direct exploration with automated space probes, and in the case of the Moon, with manned expeditions. The lunar and planetary missions produced a host of fascinating and in many cases unexpected discoveries that were totally beyond the grasp of ground-based observers. However, astronomers working at terrestrial observatories played a significant role, especially involving objects not yet visited by exploring machines. Meanwhile, NASA-sponsored research began to alter the traditional basic structures of American astronomy in general and of planetary astronomy in particular.

New tools, new techniques, new knowledge, the effects of scientists "teaming" on projects, and an influx of new workers changed planetary astronomy vastly from what it had been in the past. The field was no longer a purely observational and theoretical science but, in a sense, an applied one. Scientists involved could "get their hands on" the bodies they studied in ways that they never could before—sometimes literally. Many began to refer to the study of the solar system as *planetary science*, reserving the term *planetary astronomy* for research done with telescopes based on Earth. In practice both descriptions are often used interchangeably, though, for example, geologists analyzing lunar rock samples probably would not call themselves astronomers.

Now disciplines such as geology, geophysics, cartography, and the like became an important part of the expanding field of planetary science, though of course they long been involved in the field. In a broader sense, planetary astronomers now studied—as practical problems and not as abstract or philosophical subjects—such topics as atmospheric compositions, pressures, motions, and changes of all kinds; surrounding environments such as radiation belts; body properties such as internal mass distributions; the topography and the mineral and chemical compositions of planetary and satellite surfaces; and the origin and development of the different solar system bodies.

However, while in the 1960s the nature of planetary astronomy changed in many ways, in one essential feature it had not changed very much at all. Decades earlier astronomer Henry Norris Russell had written that there was "no sharp boundary between astronomy and the other physical sciences." He mentioned in particular physics, mathematics, geology, and chemistry as elements of astronomy. Russell also noted that even biology, which in his day was considered a "natural" rather than a "physical" science, overlaps with astronomy.[1] My own view is that as planetary research in related fields such as geology or biology becomes more abundant, detailed, and narrowly focused, those fields may stand alone as "geology" or "biology," but the results of such investigations often bear on important questions related to planetary astronomy. Indeed, human understanding of the solar system is necessarily based in large part on our knowledge and understanding of Earth.

The enormous expansion of solar system studies after 1960 was fueled overwhelmingly by money from NASA. Without exception astronomers contacted during research for this book confirmed that NASA support, far more than any other factor, accelerated and expanded planetary studies.

Previously, planetary astronomy had been funded on a modest basis by universities and philanthropic organizations. By comparison, the NASA era was a time of relative opulence for astronomers.

Garnering funding for individual projects was nevertheless highly competitive, and projects in planetary astronomy competed with scientific research for Earth-related and stellar topics. In addition, with the adoption of more advanced and more complex new technology, planetary astronomy became a much more expensive endeavor. Telescopes had always been relatively expensive instruments to build, but they could and often did soldier on for generations if given proper care (the Mount Wilson 60- and 100-inch reflectors, for example, are approaching a century of service). However, the auxiliary equipment attached to those telescopes was another story. Over the years the human eye had been almost entirely replaced by apparatus such as the photographic plate, the visual spectroscope and then the photographic spectrograph, visual and later photoelectric photometers, infrared detectors, and the like. As their sensitivity and precision increased, these items not only became more expensive to build but also cost more to maintain in proper working order. Up-to-date observatories now needed a full crew of skilled technicians to keep them operating, and replacement parts were becoming ever more costly.

Moreover, planetary research necessarily focused on only a small number of planets (plus, of course, some satellites, asteroids, and occasional comets), in stark contrast to the hundreds of billions of stars in the Milky Way, not to mention the yet unknown number of galaxies beyond ours. A stellar astronomer, for example, might use outdated equipment to study an unusual star that no one else had yet examined, and obtain significant results. Not so the planetary counterpart. After all, there is only one Jupiter, and the "easy stuff" had already been done on that body.

But observers were not the only ones with problems in the Space Age. By the 1960s theoretical astronomers of all kinds found themselves in awkward financial straits. For thousands of years, these researchers had needed nothing more to do their work than a writing instrument—a stylus, a pen, or a pencil—and something to write on—a clay tablet, a waxed board, a roll of papyrus, a sheet of parchment, or a pad of paper. However, the widespread use of electronic computers changed all that. Advanced modern computers cost considerably more to buy and maintain than pencils, and theoreticians now had the same problem that their observational counterparts had had to face somewhat earlier but enjoyed fewer financial resources.

There was another cloud on the horizon as well. In the past astronomers generally had been supported by rich patrons—emperors, kings, princes, or other wealthy persons, government observatories (largely concerned with practical matters such as navigation, lunar and planetary motions, and stellar positions), and universities. Their salaries and research budgets might be small, but they were usually stable. By now, however, a substantial portion of astronomers in general and planetary workers in particular were supported by so-called "soft" money, which was mainly dependent on annual appropriations from the U.S. Congress. Thus, these scientists not only had to seek financial support for their occasional equipment purchases, as in the past, but also for their basic salaries. For the three decades between 1960 and 1990 the vast majority of that support in the case of planetary researchers came through only a single source—NASA. As we shall see, this dependence was to be the cause of severe problems when the agency began reducing programs and cutting budgets. Meanwhile, the expanding opportunities created for planetary astronomers by the space program and the broadening scope of planetary science resulted in a much wider and larger participation in the traditional professional organizations of astronomy. In turn those organizations, and prominently the American Astronomical Society, began to change.

GETTING REORGANIZED

During the more than half a century since its founding, the American Astronomical Society had held first one and then two general meetings a year. These gatherings were small, numbering a few score of researchers; everybody knew everybody else, and all attended the presentations of their colleagues' research. All facets of astronomy were represented and often mixed in haphazardly: planetary motions, solar system research, solar studies, stellar positions and motions, the physics of the stars, the structure of the Milky Way, investigations of other galaxies, and the large-scale structure and evolution of the universe.

By the 1960s, hundreds of astronomers were attending every meeting and the AAS, with much misgiving, began to schedule several sessions at the same time.[2] But even with their own "mini meetings," planetary researchers felt restricted. Their numbers had grown until they formed a substantial fraction of the AAS membership, and they were looking for something more. They got it in 1968, when the American Astronomical Society approved the formation of a Division for Planetary Sciences (DPS).

Most of the future DPS's members were surprised at the ease with which the proposal for creating a subunit of the AAS was accepted. However, the real reason for the prompt acceptance was actually simple and none too flattering. At the time, the newest and most glamorous field in astronomy had to do with "high-energy astrophysics," the study of cosmic objects by means of highly energetic cosmic rays, x-rays, and gamma rays. As was explained by Joseph W. Chamberlain, who played a substantial part in the creation of the Division for Planetary Sciences, "the formation of the planetary division was never a big issue. . . . Astronomers . . . could have cared less what happened to the planetary people." The high-energy scientists wanted their own division (there were rumors that they would defect as a body to the American Geophysical Union) and they got it. To quote Chamberlain again, "And so the formation of a committee to study the ways and means of instituting a division of high-energy astronomy also brought with it the separate planetary [people]."[3] The creation of the DPS was thus an afterthought of the movement to create what was at the time considered the more significant Division of High-Energy Astrophysics. Following the precedent set by the High-Energy Astronomy and Planetary Sciences divisions, the AAS soon created other divisions, such as Dynamical Astronomy and Solar Physics. These changing structures of professional astronomy were the result of significant growth and vitality in astronomy and its related fields, nourished in large part by America's ventures and interests in space. The Division for Planetary Sciences in particular became a going and growing concern. It held its organizational meeting, not quite yet as an official AAS division, in Austin, Texas, in December, 1968. Harlan J. Smith had the pleasant task of hosting the gathering.

At first, membership in the DPS was limited to members of the AAS, who were then primarily astronomers. However, it was soon glaringly apparent that many presentations by geologists, meteorologists, chemists, physicists, and the like really belonged at DPS meetings. But many of these scientists did not want to pay the fairly hefty subscription cost for either the *Astronomical Journal* or the *Astrophysical Journal,* then a condition of AAS membership. So, in 1973, the DPS instituted a less expensive affiliate membership, which solved the problem and has worked well to the present day.

The massive influx of non-astronomers into the DPS was the cause of some amusing incidents. At one meeting, Smith gave a slide talk about a recent trip to astronomical facilities in what was then the Soviet Union. At the end of his presentation, he asked for questions, and someone asked, "Was there any astronomy in Russia before the revolution?" Smith and the other astronomically trained members of the audience were speechless, for we well knew that F. G. William Struve more than a century earlier had established Russia as one of the leading countries in the world as regards astronomical research. Finally, someone in the audience yelled

"Harlan! Struve!" and then Smith related the history of early Russian astronomy.[4] This incident had a happy ending, for as a result the DPS soon established a Historical Section, dedicated to providing members with a not too pompous exposure to the long history of their field. This was the first organized attempt within the AAS to help preserve the "corporate" memory of astronomy and give history its due. As an aside, the Historical Section of the DPS set the precedent for the later creation of a full-fledged Historical Astronomy Division in the AAS.

In the years since its origin, the DPS has continued to flourish despite later years of difficult financial circumstances for the profession. Its relations with the parent AAS have remained close and friendly, helped a great deal by the favorable publicity that discoveries in planetary fields generate for astronomy in general. Over time, researchers on the solar system seem finally to have become accepted by other astronomers as equal partners.

A JOURNAL FOR PLANETARY STUDIES

Planetary astronomers had professional problems other than organizational ones. An important dilemma involved where to publish their work. Articles on solar system studies appeared in all sorts of journals: astronomical, physical, geophysical, geological, meteorological, and even biological. Each publication might have at best one or a few articles per issue on solar system studies. With the great majority of articles on planetary science thinly scattered among scores of periodicals, solar system researchers faced the boring yet necessary task of hunting through many pages of irrelevant material in order to find the few items that interested them. And if one did not have access to a library at an institution with a large budget for journal subscriptions, the cost of subscribing to all of them was ruinous. Clearly, planetary astronomers needed a journal of their own. There were some such publications already, but they did not have high reputations among astronomers in general. In the view of many astronomers in the United States at least, the *Astrophysical Journal* and the *Astronomical Journal* were the only periodicals worthy of mention, and often only articles published in these journals were considered when the time came for decisions by a university concerning the promotion or tenure of an individual astronomer.[5] On the other hand, there was a distinct feeling among some planetary scientists that those two journals were not particularly interested in publishing articles on solar system research (studies of the Sun, because of George Ellery Hale's interest in our star, was a conspicuous exception, as was work on comets, meteors, and the like).[6] The answer to the publication dilemma ultimately appeared from an unlikely and unexpected quarter.

In 1962 the journal *Icarus* had been founded by the British astronomer Zdenek Kopal and the American Albert G. Wilson, with a Dutch publisher. This periodical was dedicated to publishing articles on all phases of solar system research. However, for the first few years of its existence, the articles that appeared were concentrated in the field of celestial mechanics. *Icarus* back then was just another "minor" journal, and many scientists working in spectroscopy or photometry, for example, went elsewhere. Few "real" astronomers ever glanced at it.

Circumstances began to change radically when Carl Sagan became editor in 1969. He actively began to solicit submissions from scientists studying the widest possible variety of topics in planetary astronomy, going so far as to buttonhole potential authors on the street and invite them to submit their articles to *Icarus*.[7] At the same time, Sagan made sure that all papers submitted would receive intensive review by competent referees, to thwart any possible charges of "second-rate" research, and he worked hard to ensure that the process would be timely. This eminently sensible strategy worked, and within a few years *Icarus* became *the* journal in which planetary scientists published.

At this stage most planetary research was being conducted in the United States, almost all of it by DPS members, and a good portion of their results appeared in *Icarus*. Thus it was only natural that there was substantial interest within the DPS in making that journal its official organ. The division enthusiastically adopted *Icarus* as its official journal at a March, 1963, general meeting.[8]

The connection between the DPS and *Icarus* has lasted to the present day, to the mutual advantage of both. The journal became and has remained the premier place in which to publish research results in planetary astronomy. To be sure, work in the field has often been published elsewhere, and in particular the custom grew up of sending the first substantive results of a particular space mission to *Science* (and perhaps, later, to the *Journal of Geophysical Research*), in part because as a weekly it can get articles into print much more quickly than monthly journals can and also because it has a wide circulation among scientists of all varieties. It also became customary to announce the very first results at well-attended and publicized press conferences, as well as in press releases, tactics that would have been scorned by scientists not too many years before but that have since remained standard.

Still, if one wants a single source in which to read about the advance of planetary astronomy since the 1960s, *Icarus* is the place to go. Its rise was due in large part to the efforts of the scientists who took a chance on their careers and sent their articles to that journal. But in a special sense the credit belongs to Sagan, whose work in this area is well known to planetary scientists old enough to remember it but is largely unknown in other quarters. In my opinion, it is one of Sagan's most important and lasting contributions to the advance of planetary science.

A BENCHMARK MEETING: MARFA, TEXAS

Late October of 1969 witnessed a meeting that had great importance for planetary scientists all over the Earth. The International Astronomical Union, which is the umbrella organization for astronomers around the world, decided to sponsor a symposium on planetary atmospheres. As a measure of the standing of planetary research in the minds of at least some of the classical astronomers at the time, this meeting, which was the fortieth of those the IAU had sponsored on particular subjects, was the first dedicated to what could be called mainstream solar system research.[9]

A good proportion, perhaps even most, of the world's active planetary scientists attended the meeting in Marfa, Texas, and although the official topic was atmospheres, other areas were covered as well. The scientific presentations given at the symposium, later published in book form, provide an illuminating and convenient snapshot of what astronomers did and did not know about the other planets late in 1969.[10] Interestingly, it was possibly the last occasion when most of the latest research on the planets could be contained between the covers of a single volume, for the accumulated information soon became too great for that to happen again. Here are some highlights.

At the time of the Marfa meeting the Soviet Union had succeeded in putting three entry probes into the atmosphere of Venus. The first, Venera 4, entered on October 18, 1967, and stopped transmitting at a time when the atmospheric pressure surrounding it was about eighteen times that on Earth and the temperature about 280 degrees Celsius. The Soviets initially claimed that their vehicle had landed on the surface of Venus, but even then both terrestrial observations and Mariner results indicated that the surface pressure and temperature were substantially higher (roughly 100 atmospheres and some 400 to 500 degrees, depending on the location).

Later probes, Venera 5 and 6, in July, 1969, penetrated more deeply than their predecessor and survived the hellish conditions around them long enough to suggest surface pressures and temperatures more in line with earlier estimates. Thus, by the time of the Marfa meeting, spacecraft and ground-based research agreed that the surface temperature and atmospheric pressure of Venus were both very high compared to those found on Earth, and that carbon dioxide was the dominant gas (previously nitrogen had been a popular candidate for the major constituent).[11]

On the other hand, it was still possible for respected senior scientists to propose that there were polar seas (even ice caps had been proposed just a few years earlier!) on Venus or that some form of life might exist on that planet.[12] Both suggestions were distinctly not the majority view at the time and, as we now know, both were wrong.

The composition of the clouds of Venus was still unknown, but there were a number of popular suppositions: water drops, ice crystals, hydrocarbon smog, dust (silicate or volcanic), ammonium chloride, and ferrous chloride, to name just a few.[13] In addition, the abundance or in some cases merely the presence of minor constituents in the atmosphere such as nitrogen, water vapor, carbon monoxide, and the like were unknown. Moreover, while radar observations from Earth were beginning to show features on the planet's surface, it was not clear what those features represented—were they mountains, rough spots, or what? No one then knew for certain, but Venus certainly did not look like a nice place to visit.

Mars appeared more promising, and in the case of that planet observers usually could see its solid surface. The presence of carbon dioxide was well established and there were attempts to see if the Martian abundance of that gas varied with the seasons. There were also attempts to determine elevation differences by looking at the relative strengths of carbon dioxide absorption features at various places on the planet, although these efforts were hampered severely by a wide variety of practical problems, such as poor seeing on Earth and the relative insensitivity of infrared detectors then available.[14]

On the other hand, the presence of water vapor in the red planet's atmosphere was generally accepted by then, along with variations in its abundance depending on the season and location on Mars, though the existence of *liquid* water—probably absolutely necessary for the existence of life as we know it—seemed very improbable.[15] The possibility that there might be, or had been in the past, liquid water on the surface was one significant factor that kept up both public and scientific interest in the search for Martian life. This was an important question because, as previously described, the results from the first three United Stated flyby probes had been discouraging in that respect.[16]

As might be expected, there was much less said at the Marfa symposium about the outer planets compared to Venus and Mars, because of the difficulties that their low surface brightnesses posed for observers and the fact that no space probes had visited them as yet. One such report offered a new estimate of the amount of molecular hydrogen in the atmosphere of Uranus,[17] but clearly the outer planets would not be giving up their secrets easily.

Scattered throughout the presentations at the Marfa meeting were mentions of new observing techniques that had been brought into use in the past few years. As always in the long history of astronomy, substantial improvements in observational instruments produced significant discoveries. Space probes were the most spectacular example, but others were important as well. As the 1960s gave way to the 1970s, Earth-based radar observations improved to the point where they could not only give information about variations in "surface roughness" and dielectric constant (electrical properties) of our nearest neighbors but also determine true elevation differences on the Moon, then Venus, and then Mars. The topic has been treated extensively elsewhere and is only briefly mentioned here.[18]

One of the most surprising of the radar results concerned Mercury. In the early 1960s several groups succeeded in receiving echoes from the planet, and by 1965 its rotation was shown to be about fifty-nine days, and not synchronous as astronomers had believed for generations.[19] This period is two-thirds of the eighty-eight-day period of revolution around the Sun, so that Mercury spins three times on its axis as it orbits the Sun twice. The effect of this rotation, combined with the planet's eccentric orbit, produces some bizarre effects, such as multiple sunrises and sunsets in a single Mercurian "day" (if it can be called that).[20]

In 1967 Kuiper had pioneered the use of a high-flying jet transport for astronomical observations. The original aircraft was a small Learjet, so only small telescopes could be carried aboard. As a result, the airborne observations did not have the angular resolution of ground-based instruments at good sites. However, for infrared observations they were a godsend, for at high altitudes they were above practically all of the absorbing water vapor in the terrestrial atmosphere. Bigger airplanes and bigger telescopes would follow, and today such observations continue. It is an expensive method of research compared to ground-based telescopes, but cheap compared to spacecraft.

Another new (and yet old) technique involved the use of electronic detectors that might provide better and more sensitive ways of recording brightness, spectra, and images in general than the traditional photographic plate alone. Progress was slow for decades, but in 1967 observatories began to receive what was arguably the first electronic image intensifier capable of routine day-to-day use at the telescope. This was the RCA-Carnegie "image tube" (named for the builder and the foundation that paid for most of the development), which had a distant relation to television cameras. Such a "tube" (overall it was a cylinder about a foot in diameter and a bit longer) received an image on a photosensitive faceplate at its front end and projected an electronically intensified image on a photographic plate at the back.

Although the wavelength range of a spectrum that could be photographed at once with this image tube was small compared to the usual range of a photographic plate alone, the improvement in sensitivity was so great that exposures that formerly took hours were reduced to minutes. The infrared version of this instrument in particular was a boon to observers, for it transformed the incoming radiation into visible light. This eliminated the need for any tedious, delicate, time-consuming, and sometimes dangerous sensitizing procedures needed to record infrared radiation.

When the first such tube arrived at McDonald, the observatory director, Harlan J. Smith, advised me to drop all previous plans and take as many spectra as possible with the new detector, for it might last only a few days, weeks, or at best months (such was the doleful track record of previous image intensifiers). To everyone's surprise, these tubes soldiered on for years, becoming a mainstay of infrared planetary astronomy. The Carnegie tubes would eventually be replaced by even better and more sensitive detectors, but they showed the way, and for many astronomers of the era, both planetary and otherwise, they provided the first taste of what the future would bring.[21]

In connection with the Marfa symposium, most of the participants attended the "scientific" dedication (formal dedication having already occurred) of the 107-inch telescope at McDonald Observatory. Remarks Kuiper made at that time seem to sum up keenly the situation in those days. Perhaps his most important point was that "much of planetary astronomy in the last decade has been the clearing away of incorrect ghosts left by earlier publications." He then went on to mention some of these mistaken ideas that had been proven wrong: the surface temperature and rotation of Venus, the rotation of Mercury, the presence of canals and vegetation on Mars, the existence of ice and deep layers of dust on the Moon, and others.[22] Kuiper's words seemed appropriate to the audience at the time, and the passage of decades has not changed that opinion. The decks had been cleared, much excess baggage had been thrown over the side, and now planetary astronomy was once again sailing ahead.

That a major focus of the research and writings of planetary scientists in the 1960s and 1970s had to do with celestial mechanics and the motion of Earth's satellite, the Moon, was not, of course, purely coincidental. Celestial mechanics was intimately related to the navigation of space probes in the solar system, and unmanned missions to Mars, Venus, and more distant planets as well as manned voyages to the Moon had become NASA's most glamorous missions.

"O, SWEAR NOT BY THE MOON, TH' INCONSTANT MOON" [23]

As we have seen, exploration of the Moon by automated spacecraft of the United States began in earnest in the 1960s and became a matter of great practical importance when President John F. Kennedy announced that a manned lunar expedition was to be America's goal before the decade was out. Project Apollo was by any measure the most significant space adventure of its era.

This is not the place to tell the story of Apollo, for it was not primarily concerned with planetary astronomy, though Apollo explorations made significant contributions to human knowledge of the Moon and of the solar system in general. While there are many books and articles about NASA and the American space program, one of the most relevant to this overview of the history of planetary astronomy is William David Compton's *Where No Man Has Gone Before: A History of Apollo Lunar Exploration Missions*, published in 1989.[24] Compton explains that it "is an attempt to show how scientists interested in the moon and engineers interested in landing people on the moon worked out their differences and conducted a program that was a major contribution to science as well as a stunning engineering accomplishment."[25]

The Apollo program, initiated by President Kennedy in 1963, reached a budgetary peak in 1965 ($5.25 billion), achieved a resounding technological triumph by landing the first men on the Moon in 1969, and followed with five technical and scientific expeditions on the lunar surface between 1970 and 1973. An issue arising during the Apollo program was the question of whether scientists should be included among the astronauts or whether, instead, astronauts should be trained to serve as surrogates for scientists on Earth. Although trained scientists, one of whom was an geologist, did fly in later Apollo missions, the point of contention was never fully resolved.

One important product of the Apollo missions was the Lunar Receiving Laboratory, which was primarily responsible for the storage, distribution, and preservation of lunar samples. Compton addresses the question, "Do we understand more about the origin and history of the moon and the solar system as a result of Apollo's six voyages?" Remarkably, despite the hands-on, "hard" science made possible by Apollo, that important question is still not fully answered.[26]

We must remember that the Ranger, Surveyor, and Lunar Orbiter projects were but preludes to the Apollo lunar landings. These explorations produced solid results demonstrating that indeed a lunar landing was possible. In addition, there were some unexpected scientific dividends from the automated explorer vehicles. Perhaps the most interesting and unexpected discovery came from the Lunar Orbiters. These were the first true satellites of our satellite. Their low orbits, designed to give the on-board cameras good resolution of lunar surface features, permitted scientists on Earth to map out the details of the Moon's internal mass distribution.

Surprisingly, it turned out that the Orbiters' paths were disturbed slightly by small irregularities in our satellite's gravitational field. This finding was of immense importance for calculating descent paths for manned exploring vehicles, but it also posed a puzzle for scientists interested in the nature of the Moon. Up until this time, researchers had assumed that our satellite was either more or less homogeneous or else was composed of a series of spherical shells of different density. That assumption was no longer valid. In fact the nature of the lunar "mascons" (mass concentrations) is still uncertain.

Under the direction of George Mueller, NASA's associate administrator for Manned Space Flight, the agency first planned Apollo scientific projects through its Apollo Applications Program Office. But as lunar exploration took precedence over other Apollo-related projects, and as funding began to decline under the duress of the Vietnam War and Great Society programs, Mueller decided to separate lunar exploration from the Apollo Applications Program and in December, 1967, created an independent Lunar Exploration Program Office, since lunar exploration had indeed become the primary focus of the NASA effort. Lee R. Scherer, who had directed the Lunar Orbiter program, only recently concluded, became director of the new office under the Apollo Program Office. He established two divisions within the Lunar Exploration Program Office, one styled Flight Systems Development, and the other Lunar Science. The Lunar Science Division reported to the Office of Space Science and Applications for science planning for Apollo missions.[27]

Other inputs into Apollo mission planning for science came from the President's Science Advisory Committee, which in 1966 completed an intensive study and evaluation of NASA's post-Apollo plans and potential scientific applications for Apollo programs. The committee at that time advised NASA that unless Apollo missions incorporated greater mobility for the landing parties, and remained on the surface for longer periods of time than the few days planned, Apollo flights would not provide justifiable scientific returns.[28] One result of those warnings was the development of a lunar rover vehicle, giving scientists and astronauts a 75-mile exploring range on the lunar surface; another, if indirectly, was the organization of an Office of Science and Applications at the Manned Spacecraft Center in Houston.

"The status of science within MSC rose measurably as the understanding of the Apollo program began to go beyond a physical landing on the Moon," notes Henry Dethloff in his history of the Johnson Space Center.[29] Center Director Robert Gilruth established a Science and Applications Directorate at the Manned Spacecraft Center in January, 1967, under the interim leadership of Robert O. Piland, who had previously headed the Experiment Program Office under the Engineering Directorate. In February, 1967, Gilruth appointed Dr. Wilmot N. Hess (whom Homer Newell had sent to the Manned Spacecraft Center to provide scientific leadership) to head the Science and Applications Directorate. A nuclear physicist from the University of California, Hess had headed the Lawrence Radiation Laboratory at Livermore, California, before joining NASA's Goddard Space Flight Center as chief of the Laboratory for Theoretical Studies. "His reputation came largely from his work in high-energy physics, neutron scattering, cosmic ray neutrons, and studies of the Van Allen radiation belts."[30]

Hess turned to lunar scientists for advice in planning the scientific exploration of the Moon. Beginning on July 31, 1967, the Manned Spacecraft Center hosted a gathering of more than 150 scientists and NASA officials at Santa Cruz, California, to discuss lunar exploration. As reported by Compton, the purpose of the gathering was to establish "an order of priority for lunar investigations," to prepare detailed scientific plans, and to "recommend instrumental and technological support." The conference was organized into eight working groups, including one on astronomy, headed by Lawrence W. Frederick of the University of Virginia, and others on bioscience, geochemistry, geodesy and cartography (chaired by Charles Lundquist of the Smithsonian Astrophysical Laboratory), geology, geophysics, lunar atmospheres, and particles and fields.[31]

The conference produced remarkably detailed and significant recommendations relating to such things as extending lunar surface travel, the use of expendable supplies and scientific instruments, the management of lunar samples, and the improvement of communications between engineers and scientists by having a project scientist assigned for each experiment on an Apollo mission. The conference also recommended strongly that Apollo astronauts should be "scientists first and pilots second." Following the conference, Hess established a permanent advisory group called the Group for Lunar Exploration Planning to monitor and advise Apollo operations and program planning.

In addition to the President's Science Advisory Committee and the Santa Cruz conference and its Group for Lunar Exploration Planning, NASA's Office of Space Science and Applications Lunar and Planetary Missions Board shaped Apollo scientific planning. This board advised NASA management on the "overall balance between lunar and planetary programs" and met periodically in Houston to review Apollo lunar exploration plans.

When Hess reviewed the recommendations of the Santa Cruz conference, according to David Compton, Lunar and Planetary Missions Board members "were clearly uneasy." Following preliminary reviews by Newell's staff in the Office of Space Science and Applications, the Lunar and Planetary Missions Board found the Santa Cruz recommendations "acceptable in principle" but asked for extensive reviews and revisions of the proposed scientific projects "in light of the severe fiscal constraints currently in effect." [32] By 1967, budget realities had begun emasculating NASA programs, including Apollo. In the end, the result of those realities would be to cancel the three most sharply defined Apollo scientific missions, Apollo 18, 19, and 20.

Nevertheless, despite budgetary pressures, by all external appearances NASA continued to expand and achieve success. The manned lunar program pressed on, aided by the results of the unmanned program, to peak when Apollo 11 made a successful landing on the Moon on July 20, 1969. Preparatory to that first human contact with another body in the solar system, in 1966 Manned Spacecraft Center Director Gilruth initiated construction of a Lunar Receiving Laboratory to process lunar samples before they were distributed to individual researchers. The "processing" of these samples included quarantine procedures established by the U.S. Public Health Service (and they applied to astronauts as well as Moon rocks). Design came under the bailiwick of Newell's Office of Space Science and Applications. Although the laboratory was completed in June 1967, staffing became a controversial and complex problem as competitive scientific, political, budgetary, and quarantine interests intervened.

With the return to Earth of the first known Moon rocks, planetary astronomy changed from an observational to a laboratory science. Following the arrival at the Lunar Receiving Laboratory of the first lunar samples from Apollo 11, the Moon rocks became a matter of intense public interest. When the first lunar sample was displayed at the Smithsonian in September, Compton records, thousands of people queued up glimpse of a moon rock; many found it "disappointingly ordinary."

Prior to their release to the Smithsonian and 142 authorized researchers, the lunar samples were first sterilized by ultraviolet light, treated with peracetic acid, rinsed in sterile water, and dried under nitrogen gas. Two teams of scientists, known as the lunar sample preliminary examination team and the lunar sample analysis team, worked in the vacuum chambers of the Lunar Laboratory. Initial analyses indicated the rock specimens were igneous (formed by volcanic activity) and contained three common minerals: feldspar, pyroxene, and olivine. Significantly, the samples were similar to those examined by Surveyor V two years earlier. The first specimens contained abnormally high quantities of titanium and very little carbon.

Weeks later, more detailed analyses of samples indicated that they were of fine and medium-grained crystalline igneous origin, probably deposited by lava flows, and some were breccias (heterogeneous crystalline rocks compacted from smaller particles, possibly by impact events). There was no evidence of water or of organic material to the level of less than one part per million. While there were certain similarities, the lunar rocks were definitely different from terrestrial rocks and meteorites (so much for Philip Abelson's confident predictions to the contrary). The rocks clearly were not of terrestrial origin, and some were as old as if not older than any so far found on Earth. "Sketchy as these results were, they clearly showed that Apollo would revolutionize scientific thought about the moon and its relations to the earth."[33]

Apollo did demonstrate that many lunar craters were due to impacts, while the maria were enormous lava flows. Thus, both centuries-old explanations of the Moon's surface features were partially correct. With hindsight, this seems quite reasonable, as it is unlikely that every feature of any planet's surface is due to exactly the same process, but it took the returned lunar samples to prove the point.

Radioactive dating of lunar rocks showed that some of them, unlike any known terrestrial examples, date back to the earliest days of the solar system. Moreover, things did not happen all at once on the Moon. Early periods of intense bombardment were followed by several billion years of widespread igneous activity that gradually tapered off. The past few billion years of our satellite's life seem to have been tranquil, with little activity except for the occasional impact of an asteroid or comet. Still, it remains an open question whether some residual activity, such as the rare escape of gas from the Moon's interior, for example, may sometimes happen even now.

Studies of lunar rocks brought back by Apollo missions showed that water, and other "volatile" substances (those with low boiling points) were never abundant on the Moon. In addition, the relative proportions of various elements and their different isotopes did not match those of Earth. These findings seemed to dispose of the theory that our satellite split off from Earth at some early time. The other "traditional" possibility, that the Moon was originally a separate planet captured by ours, suffers, among other things, from some of the same problems as did the old encounter theories of the origin of the solar system—it is highly improbable. There is a possibility that our satellite originated from the collision of a now defunct body with the young Earth, but as of this writing, despite all the hard facts provided by the Apollo missions, there is still no generally accepted explanation for the origin of the Moon. Obvious questions often do not have obvious answers.

After the spectacular success of Apollo 11, much of the initiative left the American space effort. We had beaten the Soviets, no other competitor was in sight, and there were other problems to attend to. NASA's budget, which peaked in fiscal year 1965, thereafter declined steadily in amounts and in terms of actual purchasing power, as double-digit inflation racked the country. Domestic social programs and the war in Vietnam had higher priority, and as early as the fiscal year 1967 there was a particularly severe crunch in NASA funding. Although the Apollo program maintained an adequate level of support, sustaining that funding came at the expense of other parts of the space program, such as Mars exploration, larger booster rockets, and the space sciences, including planetary astronomy.

As might be expected, after the first few successful lunar expeditions, they began to seem routine to many, and public support waned. A result, as noted, was that scheduled Apollo missions 18 through 20 were canceled. The lunar landing missions actually launched included Apollo 11 through 17 (13 never made it to the surface of the Moon). Apollo 12 aimed for the Surveyor III landing site, and it carried an Apollo lunar surface experiments package (ALSEP) with more sophisticated equipment for geological observations and sample collection. Despite the fact that a group of scientist-astronauts had been recruited by NASA, and despite growing pressures from the scientific community, the flight carried no scientists.

In essence, there was strong disagreement (just one apect of the long-standing battle) between scientists on one side, who believed that engineers and managers in NASA were using scientific efforts only as a smoke screen to promote "hardware" projects, and on the other side the "hands-on" types, who considered scientists to be impractical dreamers with no idea of the real practical problems involved in space exploration.[34]

Nevertheless, Apollo 12 did achieve its major objective, to locate and land near a specific target site, in this case Surveyor III. And despite threatening equipment failures, Apollo 12 returned with 75 pounds of samples for the Lunar Receiving Laboratory plus a camera and other parts from the Surveyor III. Preliminary analyses of the samples indicated that they differed in significant characteristics from those gathered by Apollo 11, as regards titanium and olivine content, for example. The first Lunar Science Conference held at the Manned Spacecraft Center in January, 1970, concluded that the surface of the Moon varied in composition and age and that it was therefore of great scientific importance to obtain materials from a variety of terrains and sites.

Following Apollo 12, Apollo planners began to give more attention to scientific objectives. Apollo 13 was scheduled to land near the Fra Mauro Formation, one of the largest impact basins on the Moon. But following its launch in April, 1970, an oxygen tank aboard the service module exploded. Only through heroic measures was the crew able to return to Earth, without accomplishing a lunar landing. Under budgetary duress, NASA meanwhile had canceled Apollo 18, 19, and 20. Apollo 14, intended to land on the Littrow site, was diverted to the Apollo 13 Fra Mauro target. Astronauts Alan Shepard and lunar module pilot Edgar Mitchell spent over 33 hours on the Moon, mapping, sampling and photographing their surroundings. Apollo 15 astronauts Jim Irwin and Dave Scott, landing near Hadley Rille in July, 1971, spent 67 hours on the surface. They rode a lunar rover, took surface and core samples (170 pounds of materials), and found anorthosite, which scientists believed to be the first material that solidified as a crust from our satellite's once molten surface.

Apollo 16 left Cape Kennedy on April 16, 1972, and landed astronauts John Young and Charles Duke on the plain at Descartes on April 20. The mission primarily proved that the area was not volcanic as expected. The last Apollo flight, 17, set scientist-astronaut Harrison H. (Jack) Schmitt and mission commander Eugene A. Cernan on the Moon at the Taurus-Littrow area. These were the last men to walk on the Moon. In time, as we have seen, these lunar explorations at least proved that the Moon was never a part of the Earth, but scientists still could not determine its origins. Furthermore, while our satellite had been intermittently heated and cooled by internal or external forces for billions of years, it seemed to have been essentially inactive for at least the last three billion years.

Unfortunately, the canceled Apollo flights were scheduled to investigate three of the most intriguing spots on the Moon: the prominent and probably fairly youthful crater Copernicus, the enigmatic Hadley "rill" region, and Tycho, a crater so spectacular that its ray system can be seen from Earth with the unaided eye. In addition to canceling the Apollo program, NASA also stopped construction of additional Saturn V rockets, leaving the United States without a booster capable of launching massive payloads into space. By the end of 1971, budget cuts and reductions in force (rifs) had considerably reduced NASA programs, with corresponding reductions in planetary astronomy programs.[35]

Looking back at all this, it is only fair to say that NASA probably did all that it could do to ensure the greatest possible scientific return from the Apollo missions. The stray carping critics perhaps did not realize just how difficult it was to return hundreds of pounds of selected rock samples from the Moon, but in the end the job was done, and well done at that.

Among the projected programs for planetary exploration that failed to receive funding was a manned mission to Mars. Shortly after his inauguration President Richard M. Nixon created a special Space Task Group to study and recommend alternatives for the post-Apollo space program. The committee recommended a balanced program of manned and unmanned projects and urged the adoption of a major program for planetary exploration including a landing on Mars.

As Compton describes, three options were proposed: an all-out effort, including the establishment of a fifty-man Earth-orbiting space station and a lunar base, culminating with a Mars landing in the mid-1980s; a less ambitious program providing for evaluation of an unmanned Mars landing before setting a date for the manned mission; and a minimum program that would develop a space station and a shuttle vehicle but would defer the Mars landing to some unspecified time before the end of the century.

Costs, the Vietnam War, and opposition from science groups such as the American Association for the Advancement of Science, which doubted the scientific value of a Mars mission, forced the rejection of the planetary exploration options. Congress instead opted for the Earth orbital Space Shuttle, and (tentatively) an orbiting space station.[36] Dismissals of Mars as an always lifeless and relatively uninteresting body were based in large part on results from the early Mariner missions and would in due course come back to haunt those who put forth these views.

Despite the ending of substantial efforts directed toward manned exploration of Mars, the red planet continued to hold considerable public and scientific interest. There were, in fact, dramatic advances in our knowledge of the planet due to results from both automated probes and ground-based observations.

RED PLANET REVEALED

American space programs rekindled the human and scientific fascination for Mars. In the 1960s and 1970s NASA sponsored both ground-based and space-probe explorations of the planets, and the red planet was given particular attention. As we have seen, extensive Soviet efforts at direct Martian exploration were all failures, while the first successful U.S. flyby probe, Mariner 4, showed only a cratered planet, along with white caps at the poles and elsewhere a variegated surface with patches of different brightness. The last two types of features, of course, had long been known from ground-based work, and the early close-up observations did not reveal what the caps were made of or why the reflectivity of the surface varied as it did. Of mountains, valleys, or other Earthlike features there was no recognizable trace. In addition, the failure to detect any evidence of Martians or their works certainly had a depressing effect on public and congressional support for the exploration of Mars.

Still, NASA pressed ahead, although with some false starts. As early as 1962 the agency had begun studies of a program dubbed Voyager, which involved a series of complex and massive payloads that would both orbit the planet and soft-land on its surface starting in the early 1970s, performing a wide array of observations. The initial concept envisaged an early version of the Saturn rocket as the launch vehicle, but eventually the decision was made to use the Saturn V, the same vehicle employed in the manned Apollo program. Each enormous booster would carry two orbiters, two landers with surface science laboratories, and all the needed equipment to deliver them safely to their destinations. The combined weight of all this gear was estimated at over 30 tons per launch!

Of course the cost of such a program was also enormous, and in 1967, Congress simply eliminated it from NASA's budget. With the war in Vietnam becoming more and more expensive, a massive effort to explore what appeared to be a "dead" planet was an obvious target. Thus, for neither the first nor the last time, events entirely outside planetary science had a dramatic influence on the field.[37] As the Mars Voyager program literally never got off the ground, memory of it has faded. Today it is almost forgotten except by those who worked on it. The Mars Voyager program disappeared from view in part because a later and very successful program involving probes to the outer planets was also called Voyager.

The demise of the original Voyager was a turning point for solar system research, for it marked the beginning of a long, irregular, but eventually substantial decrease in support for planetary missions and in the ground-based research to back them up. From that time to the present, NASA has never had as ambitious a project directed toward planetary exploration.

But even in the days when Mars Voyager was still a "live" project, NASA pressed ahead with more of the relatively smaller, simpler, Mariner-type probes, which were intended to fill the gap until more complex spacecraft became available. When the Mars Voyager was canceled, these Mariners became America's first-line probes.

Thus, the Mars probes Mariners 6 and 7 were in a sense transition types. Like Mariner 4, they were flyby missions, each making only a single short-lived pass close to the red planet. As noted, they flew past Mars on July 31 and August 5, 1969, respectively, and found little to encourage hopes of life on that planet. Because of improvements in electronics, particularly the television cameras, the images returned to Earth had better resolution than those from Mariner 4. More impact craters were identified and clouds were photographed in the Martian atmosphere, and the transient white spot sometimes observed from earth and named Nix Olympica was wrongly identified as a large crater with a wide rim and center spot. However, the one big surprise was discovery of so-called "chaotic terrain." This consisted of large blocks of rock, some many miles on a side, that had the appearance of having been dumped willy-nilly on the surface from some gigantic wheelbarrow. At the time, the origin of this weird landscape was a total mystery.[38]

Even though results from the early probes were not encouraging, interest in the red planet remained intense. Our knowledge of the true nature of Mars took a giant leap forward with Mariner 9, which benefited from improvements in the power of launch vehicles and the miniaturization of electronics (its twin, Mariner 8, ended up on the bottom of the Atlantic Ocean after a launch vehicle failure). This was no mere flyby mission but instead was intended to go into orbit around the red planet, permitting an extended period of observation. After a trip lasting 167 days, the probe arrived at Mars on November 13, 1971. It became the first spacecraft to orbit a major planet other than our own, narrowly beating the Soviet Mars 2 spacecraft to that accomplishment.

The first Martian images from Mariner 9 showed almost no detail, for the entire planet was then enshrouded in a tremendous dust storm. This was no surprise, as telescopic observers on Earth had noted the storm's development, but it certainly was frustrating.[39] About the only features that could be seen were several large and mysterious dark spots. Here the advantage of an orbiter became obvious, for a flyby mission would have revealed only this and no more.

Mariner 9 was not the only space probe targeted for Mars in 1971, for the Soviets had launched several vehicles toward the red planet during the same window of opportunity. Mars 2 and Mars 3 made it to the red planet but ultimately failed in their missions. The first released a lander that crashed on the planet's surface, while the lander of the second made a safe descent but transmitted data for only a few seconds. Both Soviet orbiting vehicles remained in orbit, but they produced little scientific return.

The dust began to settle early in 1972, and Mariner 9's cameras began their task of photographing most of the surface of Mars. The results were spectacular and utterly unexpected. The "dark spots" were revealed as huge volcanoes that had towered above the dust storm, including Olympus Mons (Mount Olympus), still the largest known mountain of its type in the solar system and roughly the size of Texas. As we saw previously, this feature had originally been named Nix Olympica (Snows of Olympus), and the name proved apt, for close-up images revealed that its sometimes white—and variable—appearance was due to white snow or clouds crowning its upper reaches or clouds ringing its base.

But the discoveries had just begun. A vast canyon system, big enough to span the United States, was revealed, while the polar caps showed a curious structure of light and dark layers, which seemed to indicate alternating periods of snow and dust deposits due to some cyclic variation in the climate of Mars. Fields of sand dunes became apparent, which showed that the red planet's atmosphere could move substantial amounts of fine surface material, a finding that was consistent with the supposed dust storms visible from Earth.

Perhaps the most startling revelations of all were numerous indications that there had once been abundant flowing water on Mars. The true nature of the chaotic terrain provided one of these indicators. It appeared that subsurface water in the form of ice or permafrost had suddenly melted, perhaps as the result of underground volcanic activity, and burst out toward lower ground. The overlying rock, deprived of its support, then cracked and collapsed into a jumbled heap of debris. Suggestively, leading away from the chaotic terrains were channels that gave all the appearance of having been carved out and sculpted by enormous fluid flows.

Initial press releases were extremely cautious, merely mentioning the possibility of some sort of fluid and shying away from the mention of water. While water was the obvious candidate, the idea of Mars being more like the Moon than the Earth died hard. But die it did, when further images revealed river *systems,* complete with many tributaries, proceeding from higher to lower ground, and looking just like similar structures in arid or semiarid portions of Earth as seen from a high-flying airplane. Evidently, at one time the red planet had an atmosphere capable of producing abundant rainfall—and for a substantial period of time, for such river systems are not carved out overnight.

After Mariner 9, it was generally accepted that Mars had once had a much denser atmosphere, with a much greater abundance of water vapor, than it does now. The question then became, and remains, just when was this era? Was it early in the planet's history, or later on? Complicating the issue is the fact that evidences of flowing water are not distributed evenly over the planet's surface, a circumstance not yet fully explained. But even if free-flowing water was present only in Mars's early years, that situation still holds out the possibility that some form of primitive life might once have developed there. After all, estimates of the first appearance of simple life on Earth have been constantly pushed back in time until now they approach the ages of the earliest known terrestrial rocks.[40] The process seems to have happened rapidly on our planet. Could it have happened on Mars as well, only to be ended when the atmosphere changed to a cold, thin one? Perhaps with Percival Lowell in mind, planetary scientists did not dwell overlong on the possibility; but, to look ahead, by 1996 the odds suddenly seemed far better.

Mariner 9 served to revive interest in Mars and renewed the dream of a Martian landing. More immediately, the results and questions raised by Mariner 9 served to help convince Congress to fund a new but not too expensive explorer. The Viking program owed its inception in part to the successes achieved by Mariner 9.

VIKINGS TO MARS

The twin Viking missions to Mars represent a landmark in our studies of the red planet. Sadly, they also represent a temporary ending. While their story might be told in the next chapter, where it chronologically belongs, the tale would then be isolated. Here, it assumes its rightful place as the climax of NASA's early efforts in the field.

As described, after the Voyager program was canceled, NASA had to make do with improved Mariner probes, but the agency also cast about for what to do next. It seemed clear that it would take a soft landing on the planet to provide any hard evidence for the presence or absence of life there. Thus during the 1960s a bewildering array of possibilities were studied, proposed, and ultimately rejected, all in the shadow of increasingly severe financial restrictions. Finally, in 1968, the Viking project was approved. This involved a pair of flights that, while not using the enormous Saturn V, did employ a powerful Titan III booster with a liquid hydrogen–fueled Centaur upper stage. The combination was beefy enough to put several tons of payload into orbit around Mars, to permit detailed measurements while an entry probe descended through the Martian atmosphere, and to soft-land a useful package of instruments on the planet's surface.

This was a big project and, not unexpectedly, various NASA centers vied for control of the task. In the end, the agency divided responsibilities between several of its centers: Lewis Research Center looked after the rocket booster, JPL was responsible for the spacecraft designed to deliver the lander to Mars and then remain in orbit around the planet, and Langley Research Center would oversee the entry system and the development of the new lander itself. Interestingly enough, this seemingly complex arrangement worked out very well.[41]

What probably allowed Viking to be born and to live was a combination of widespread scientific and public interest in Mars as the possible abode of life—and the Soviet space program. As we have seen, after several failures, the Russians reached Venus with their probe Venera 4 in 1967. For this part of our story its importance is that at the time, the United States had no firm plans to land *anything* on *any* planet; only Moon landings were planned. Runners in races usually do better when they have stiff competition, and this was no exception.[42]

After the inevitable delays found on any new project, Vikings 1 and 2 were finally launched on August 20 and September 9, 1975. In July of 1976 Viking 1 arrived at Mars, followed shortly thereafter by its twin. While the dual spacecraft orbited the red planet, making television images of possible landing sites, scientists and engineers debated where to land them. The images continued the trend in our knowledge that had begun with Mariner 9, showing that the more we learned about it, the more complex a place Mars appeared to be, with a long and complicated history, very different indeed from the long dead Moon.

There had been plans for an initial landing on July 4, 1976, to celebrate the bicentennial of the American Declaration of Independence, but worry about how dangerous various potential sites were delayed those plans. The situation was complicated because there were two sources of information that often did not agree. Viking images could target specific regions but could not detect rocks that were big enough to demolish a lander, while Earth-based radar observations gave information about small-scale surface slopes but only averaged over a relatively large area on Mars.

The decision as to where to land was thus made with considerable risk and uncertainty. Viking 1 landed safely on July 20, 1976, soon followed by Viking 2 on September 3. Those familiar with the space program's checkered history could scarcely believe it, for, despite the usual array of last minute problems and anomalies, the orbiters, entry capsules, and lander spacecraft components did their jobs extremely well.[43]

Once again the Soviet Union had mounted an enormous effort to beat the United States. They launched no less than four spacecraft—two orbiters and two landers—toward the red planet in 1973. Once again, the result was nothing but failure, with only a few close-up images of Mars to show for all the work.

Books, pamphlets, and popular and scientific articles by the thousands have been written about the results from Viking, and we can do no more than summarize them here. Many topics are still being argued, and time will have to tell who is right. However, there are some highlights. The first eye-catching results were images from the orbiters, which were far better than those provided by Mariner 9, both because of improvements in technology and also because the Martian atmosphere now was relatively clearer of dust, probably because the planet was near the point in its orbit farthest from the Sun, so that solar heating was at a minimum. These images confirmed that sometime in the past the planet had experienced extensive volcanic and tectonic activity, along with episodes of substantial erosion by flowing water. Evidently, many solar system scientists became convinced, Mars was a planet that had once been extremely active, though apparently that activity had largely ceased by now.

Of course, there was intense interest in what the first images of the surface of the red planet, taken from the Viking 1 lander, would show. As it turned out, these photographs were sharp, clear, and in a sense eerie, for they revealed a surface that looked just like the Mars that many of us had expected. There was a cold, arid desert scattered with rocks of various sizes and with drifting sands in between. The prevailing color was reddish, which included not only the surface but also the sky. Mars is a dusty place, and even when the sky is "clear" there is enough airborne dust to mask the deep blue of a really clear Martian atmosphere. Actually, the prevailing color might be described as a dirty yellow or brown.[44] This phenomenon is familiar to those who have visited places like the Painted Desert in Arizona, where the colors are spectacular in the late afternoon. However, this appearance has a lot to do with the low altitude of the Sun and the resulting long path of sunlight through our atmosphere. The hardy few who have ventured into this region at high noon can testify that the true colors of the rocks and sands resemble nothing so much as slightly tinted concrete. Observers on Earth, using only their unaided eyes, can check this fact whenever Mars is near Earth (near opposition); the planet is bright in our skies at those times, and one has only to compare its color to some bright advertising signs—it is definitely not red like a stoplight.

The orbiters and landers made a host of observations and measurements over about five years. Among the results, Mars was confirmed as a cold, dry desert. Besides the few cubic kilometers of water vapor in the atmosphere, any additional H_2O would have to be locked up in solid form, perhaps in the remnant polar caps or permafrost. While the parts of those caps that come and go with the seasons are composed of carbon dioxide, the permanent cores are made of ordinary water ice. The distribution of atmospheric water vapor, as indicated by earlier terrestrial observations, varies with the seasons, migrating from polar regions toward the equator during spring and summer.

As was already known, the Martian atmosphere was essentially composed of carbon dioxide, but there are also small amounts of nitrogen, argon, oxygen (only a tiny amount), and other trace gases. The relative abundances of these gases, and of their various isotopes, pointed to a much denser atmosphere sometime in the planet's past, a situation indicated earlier by the images of extensive erosion by running water. The surface itself consists primarily of rocks, sand, and dust, their composition similar to that of terrestrial basalt, a volcanic rock that can be seen forming even now on the island of Hawaii. The reddish color, as expected, is due to small quantities of oxidized (literally rusted) iron.

The greatest interest among scientists and the general public alike centered on a suite of four miniature laboratories aboard each lander, facilities that held the possibility of answering the question of whether or not there was life on Mars. Improvements in miniaturization of electronics and other equipment allowed the Viking landers to carry a remarkably sophisticated array of equipment to look for life on Mars, perhaps even more extensive that those planned for the earlier, ill-fated Voyager program. The basic idea behind these experiments was to look for evidence of life on a very low level, for while we might miss something like Martian elephants, we would have a good chance of picking up evidence of the more primitive life forms—bacteria, perhaps—associated with them.

To this end, soil samples were dug up and inserted into the lander instruments, and then subjected to a variety of tests. The results were puzzling. On the one hand, there were indications of some sort of chemical activity when, for example, liquid nutrients were added to the samples, but on the other hand, the results of the experiments were not those expected from living, growing cells. Moreover, analysis of Martian soil samples showed no traces of any organic molecules at all, though even a few parts in a *billion* would have been detected. Without organic molecules how can there be any life? The debate lasted for some time, but eventually the consensus was that the chemical reactions observed were due to oxidizing chemicals present on, in, or near the surface of Mars, rather than to life.

This oxidizing environment occurs in the upper atmosphere of Earth, where highly energetic ultraviolet radiation produces an ozone layer with a high concentration of O_3 (three atoms of oxygen instead of the normal two in a molecule of oxygen gas). The resultant layer is in general beneficial for life on Earth, for it shields us from harmful, highly energetic ultraviolet radiation, but when ozone is produced at the surface, as in Los Angeles smog, it can be harmful to life. Evidently, because of Mars's rarefied atmosphere compared to our planet's, similar oxidizing and superoxidizing substances can be produced right on the planet's surface. As a result, any organic molecules originally present will be swiftly destroyed and broken down into simple compounds such as carbon dioxide, water, and the like.[45]

Despite the Vikings' stunning success, they were not soon followed by any greater or even equal efforts. To be sure, there were a few Soviet and American attempts to launch space probes to Mars in the following decades (the Soviet Phobos 1 and 2 and the U.S. Mars Observer) but all failed, and this long draught was not broken until July 4, 1997 (as this book was being edited for publication), by the successful soft landing of the U.S. Mars Pathfinder probe with its Sojourner roving vehicle. As of now, the red planet remains much "the undiscovered country."

VENUS

Interest in our misnamed "sister" planet was never as great as that given to Mars, but there was still a lot of curiosity about what lay under Venus's all-encompassing clouds. As we saw earlier, the United States had carried out the first successful flyby mission to that planet, but then the Soviet Union took the lead in direct exploration with the first three successful entry probes. They scored again with Venera 7, which landed on the surface of Venus on December 15, 1970, and survived for almost half an hour. It fully confirmed that the surface pressure and temperature on Venus were indeed high. It also found evidence for water vapor but none for oxygen or nitrogen.[46] However, the measurements of atmospheric composition were made by rather involved and indirect methods and were subject to a wide variety of interpretations. On the positive side, the high surface temperature of Venus, first seriously proposed in the 1930s, was firmly established.

During the late 1960s the United States, which as yet was not in a position to send entry vehicles to Venus, did manage to launch Mariner 5, which flew by Venus on October 19, 1967.[47] However, this probe, like the Soviet ones, left a lot of important questions unanswered, in particular the matter of the composition of the planet's clouds.

Meanwhile, back on Earth, both theoreticians and observers attacked this and other problems concerning Venus. To take just one example, at the time crystals of water ice were a popular candidate for the cloud particles, so many researchers sought evidence for water vapor in the planet's atmosphere above the clouds. There are a number of ways to do this, but the most straightforward was still the spectroscopic method, which had been tried in various forms for a century, all to no avail.

The results fell into two groups: those that gave evidence for relatively large amounts of water vapor, perhaps 100 microns of precipitable vapor, and those that did not. Arguments went back and forth inconclusively for years, with theoretical studies proving of little or no help in resolving the debate. In this connection, it is important to note that most of the observations were not carried out systematically over long periods. Typically, Venus would be observed for weeks, or days, or even just hours, and a result announced. In large part this was because time on telescopes was hard to get, and because other methods, such as those involving the use of balloons or aircraft, were not only expensive but also difficult to repeat frequently. In addition, there may have been an unconscious feeling by the workers involved that one or at most a few really good observations would solve the problem.

In any event, the question was settled by extensive observing programs carried out by Kuiper and his colleagues at the Lunar and Planetary Laboratory and at McDonald Observatory by workers from the University of Texas and JPL. Here was a clear case where NASA's generous financial support produced results of direct use to the spaceflight program and at a tiny fraction of the cost of determinations by planetary probes. As it turns out, there is a small and variable amount of water vapor in the upper atmosphere of Venus, in amounts never observed to rise above a few tens of precipitable microns. These abundances are similar to those seen on Mars, a coincidence that surprised those of us working in the field at that time. As in the case of the red planet, the amount of water vapor observed on Venus varied with time. However, there were no regular variations such as those caused by the march of the Martian seasons (with hindsight this should not have been surprising, for the tiny axial tilt and almost circular orbit of Venus mean that it has no seasons). To be sure, the low H_2O abundance above the clouds could not rule out the possibility that there could be more water vapor below them, but it dealt a severe blow to the "water ice crystal" theory.[48]

A minor sensation was caused by the announcement that infrared spectra had detected traces of hydrochloric acid (HCl) and hydrofluoric acid (HF) in the atmosphere of Venus.[49] While this caused quite a stir at the time, because it made the planet even more inhospitable to life than had been thought (and gave theoreticians the chance for a field day), it turned out to be of minor importance. To peek ahead somewhat, the minute amounts of these acids are overwhelmed by the much greater amount of yet another acid that is also present.

THE OUTER PLANETS

In contrast, progress in our knowledge of the outer planets was modest indeed during this period, as a summary of what we thought we knew back then shows.[50]

Methane, ammonia, and hydrogen had been positively identified in Jupiter's atmosphere, while it was widely believed that hydrogen and helium must comprise the vast bulk of the planet. Spectroscopic searches for other substances produced no detections. In addition, it appeared that the giant planet was giving off more heat than it absorbed from the Sun, confirming an old nineteenth-century idea. Many long-standing questions were still unanswered. Among them were the composition of the planet's clouds, the agents that colored them, the reason for the planet's differential rotation, the explanation of the complex changes in the cloud structure, the nature of the Red Spot, and the cause of Jupiter's impulsive radio radiation (a steadier radio component, however, was known to come from intense radiation belts similar to Earth's Van Allen belts).

Little was known of Jupiter's tiny, distant, "irregular" satellites. The Galilean satellites, of course, were known always to keep one face toward the planet, but no one had ever observed evidence of an atmosphere for or produced reliable maps of surface features on any of these bodies.

Saturn was also believed to be composed mainly of hydrogen and helium, and hydrogen and methane had been positively identified in its atmosphere. The presence of ammonia was another story, for observations were contradictory (it actually was there, and radio observations even then had picked it up). As in the case of Jupiter, Saturn appeared to be radiating more energy than it absorbed from the Sun. As might be expected, many of the unanswered questions about Jupiter also applied to Saturn. In addition, the mass, thickness of, and particle size in Saturn's rings could only be guessed at. Little was known about the ringed planet's satellites except that Titan's atmosphere contained methane.

About Uranus and Neptune even less was known. Methane and hydrogen were known to exist in their atmospheres, and radio observations indicated the presence of ammonia. No distinct features had ever been seen on these planets, and their spectroscopically determined rotation periods were subject to revision. Of the satellites of these planets, very little was known. As for Pluto, values of even its size and mass were crude estimates, and it showed no evidence of an atmosphere.

This was a bleak picture indeed. Of course there were many measurements of characteristics of these objects, such as of their brightnesses in different colors and at various times, but they gave little clue as to the nature of these bodies. While ground-based observations would advance our knowledge of them in the years ahead, there were few if any clues as to the dramatic findings that future spacecraft would disclose, especially as regards the satellites of the outer planets. We literally had no idea what was in store for us.

DECLINING PROSPECTS

To someone reading the newspapers in the 1970s, it would have appeared that planetary astronomy once again had become the queen of the sciences, for spectacular and unexpected discoveries about the solar system were being reported regularly. In some senses this optimistic view was valid, for the pace of discovery continued to be rapid, and well-trained astronomers and individuals in related fields, many of them taught by the small cadre of earlier researchers, joined the profession. But beneath the running waters lay some jagged rocks, for planetary astronomy and the American space program in general actually were facing a difficult future.

HARD TIMES FOR NASA

As Apollo wound down, the public's interest in many aspects of the space program declined. Vietnam, the environment, and social programs preempted interest in and support for space. NASA's yearly expenditures, justified in large part by the costs of Apollo hardware, peaked in the mid-1960s and then began to decrease. As time passed, it became clear to many working in space-related programs that this trend was not going to be reversed sharply for some time to come—if ever.

At the time, NASA was trying to decide what should come after Apollo. What kind of manned or robotic spaceflight program, if any, should or could the agency undertake after the manned lunar missions? Although the question of possible future manned spaceflights did not directly concern the progress of unmanned planetary exploration or ground-based research on the solar system, the answer would have a significant bearing on the future of planetary astronomy. Even though the general public, and thus the U.S. Congress, had a deep and long-lasting interest in planets, their satellites, comets, and the like, the manned spaceflight program had been receiving the lion's share of public attention and congressional funding. Planetary science and exploration, at best, were widely considered an adjunct to human space flight. Thus, as funding for manned flight programs declined, support for the related scientific fields was affected even more seriously. In general, as went the human spaceflight program, so went the associated sciences.

APOLLO APPLICATIONS AND SKYLAB

NASA proposed several plans that would use the Saturn rockets and other Apollo hardware that had been developed and proven at such great cost. What was originally called the Apollo Applications program was one of these proposals. Eventually it developed into what became the Skylab missions and the cooperative Apollo-Soyuz mission involving the United States and the Soviet Union.

Skylab grew from a number of roots. One had to do with the long-standing interest in developing a permanent orbiting space station, while another involved utilizing the existing and powerful Saturn-IB and Saturn V Apollo rockets developed by the Marshall Space Flight Center. Still another root or precedent was the former U.S. Air Force Manned Orbiting Laboratory program. Then to, there was the need to provide operational programs that would bridge the gap between the end of the Apollo missions and the first launch of the Space Shuttle, scheduled for the 1980s. There would have to be some sort of manned missions during that interval to preserve the launch and operations teams that had been built up and trained over the previous years.[1]

Skylab moved rapidly from its inception to actual flights. As an aside, NASA and the National Science Teachers Association organized an innovative competition among students to propose flight experiments for Skylab, a program that certainly heightened public interest in the program.

On May 14, 1973, NASA launched Skylab 1, the so-called Orbital Workshop, which was a modified version of the third stage of the Saturn V Moon rocket. Shortly thereafter, on May 25, an Apollo spacecraft, dubbed Skylab 2, rendezvoused with the workshop and the crew (including Charles Conrad, Jr., Joseph P. Kerwin, and Paul J. Weitz) transferred to the space station, erected a heat-protective parasol, and freed a stuck solar power array. They spent a total of twenty-eight days conducting a variety of experiments, most of which related to Earth surveillance, many to medical and biophysical tests on the astronauts themselves in order to determine human ability to live and work in space, and some of which sought to "extend the science of solar astronomy beyond the limits of earth-based observation."[2]

Over a period of nine months, three crews visited the orbital laboratory for stays of twenty-eight, fifty-nine, and eighty-four days respectively. The biophysical experiments proved the ability of humans to live and work in space for extended periods, while the solar physics and Earth resources experiments gathered massive amounts of data, including ultraviolet stellar astronomy readings; X-ray, spectrographic, microwave, and infrared observations of the Sun and Earth; and extensive photography of selected terrains on our planet. Student experiments carried aboard included a search for possible objects within Mercury's orbit, a study of possible x-rays from Jupiter, and observations of ultraviolet radiation from quasars. As an unexpected bonus, the Skylab 4 crew had the good fortune to be in orbit during the passage of Comet Kohoutek by the Sun (we will return to this) and succeeded in taking photographs of the comet both before and after perihelion.[3]

The Sun was a special object of study. Skylab's coronograph experiment (in the vacuum of space, this instrument essentially consisted of a simple opaque disk that blocked the direct view of our star's visible surface) observed changes in the form of the Sun's outer atmosphere in greater detail than the best ground-based observation. However, unlike terrestrial studies, the Skylab studies were carried on for months at a time, for it is never cloudy in space. In addition, an X-ray telescope capable of isolating specific wavelengths provided good resolution of details in the corona's structure, which is very different in the light given off from different substances. Moreover, an ultraviolet spectrometer observed temporal changes in the radiation emitted by several different types of solar regions. Further, an instrument designed to work in the ultraviolet made many images of the Sun at selected short wavelengths.

Earth resource work included photographic studies at different wavelengths, photography that provided the means to evaluate the large-scale distribution of such important items as timberline locations, soil erosion, plankton production, fishing productivity, and global drought areas. An infrared spectrometer provided information on visible solar and thermal infrared radiation with the aim of assessing Earth's surface composition and other properties. Farther afield, Skylab carried out studies of the counterglow, or gegenschein, and the zodiacal light (covered in more detail later). Still other experiments involved mapping of x-rays from our Milky Way galaxy and ultraviolet photography of the heavens.[4]

In general terms, Skylab experiments relating to planetary astronomy were marginal at best. Nevertheless, scientists of various stripes received a total of 103,000 photographs and spectra from Skylab observations for evaluation. The Apollo Telescope Mount, designed especially for the orbital observation mission, "proved to be revolutionary for the field of solar physics" but had little bearing on planetary studies.[5] However, it did provide valuable lessons on how to operate a substantial observatory in space. While the Skylab missions brought back no sensational advances in astronomical knowledge, the cumulative information increased the resources available to stellar and planetary astronomy and provided material for long-term studies. In some respects, although it was not considered so at the time, Skylab can be seen as a prototype for a future complex manned or automated laboratory for planetary exploration. Certainly, human knowledge of the Earth and its environment were greatly enhanced by Skylab. And, of course, it sustained public interest in space science.

As its name implies, the Apollo-Soyuz flight in July, 1975, involved a docking and joint exercises by an American Apollo spacecraft and a Soviet Soyuz vehicle. The stress on this mission was on cooperation between the two former Cold War protagonists, and the redesign of the two spacecraft to produce a true union and joint flight proved a daunting task. The scientific results from the nine days of joint exercises were minimal, but the true importance of this mission was that it effectively signaled the end of the Space Race. Until this time the two leading spacefaring nations had challenged each other, a situation that had spurred both sides on to greater efforts but was clearly a wasteful manner of exploring space.[6]

For years after the Apollo-Soyuz joint mission, progress in cooperative space efforts grew only slowly; but more significant, they grew steadily. Recently, that collaborative spirit has flowered into programs such as the joint efforts of the United States and Russia to carry out joint missions with the Space Shuttle and the Mir orbital laboratory. These missions, in turn, are designed to pave the way toward the construction of a true space station, which is planned as a joint effort of many spacefaring nations. Looking into the future, the replacement of the Space Race by united, worldwide efforts has obvious implications for planetary science. Extensive investigation of the solar system, not to mention dreams such as the colonization of the Moon and Mars, are simply too costly for any single nation to undertake, while a worldwide effort may indeed make such ventures possible.

Planning for what would become the Space Shuttle began quite early in NASA's existence, and concepts for an aerospace craft had been around for decades (the series of *Collier's* articles in the 1950s assumed the development of such vehicles). However, the concept of a reusable spacecraft that could take off from Earth, operate in space, and return to land on Earth like an airplane did not receive specific congressional funding until fiscal year 1973. By that time the design of the proposed vehicle had changed from one in which all parts were fully reusable to a partially reusable one that relied on an expendable external fuel tank, along with reusable solid boosters, for its launch. But the main advantage of the design was that the most expensive component, the orbiter, along with its computers, engines, power supplies, and all the rest, could be used time and time again and not junked after every launch, as had been the case with earlier space vehicles. However, by that time the Apollo program was over, and only the concluding Skylab and Apollo-Soyuz flights remained to fill the void in manned American missions.[7] After 1975, NASA's space-based programs, including planetary astronomy, were tied directly to Space Shuttle operations. However, as we shall see, that was to change drastically.

In the meantime, astronomical payoffs continued to arrive in the 1970s and 1980s from NASA programs and projects initiated earlier. Planetary astronomers began to focus greater attention on Mercury, Venus, and the outer planets and less attention, interestingly enough (considering the red planet's magnetic attraction for the past century) on Mars.

DEAD MARS

As described previously, the Viking missions revealed that Mars, contrary to Percival Lowell's views and widespread popular beliefs, was now an apparently cold, arid, and lifeless body. That image put a damper on projects for further exploration of the red planet and effectively discouraged any planning for manned expeditions. Indeed, many scientists, who for one reason or another recoiled from Lowell's widely publicized belief in intelligent life on Mars, probably overreacted to the "dead planet" thesis.

Upon the conclusion of the Viking missions, NASA drastically reduced its support for direct observations of Mars by means of automated probes, and astronomers were faced with reduced allocations of telescope time—and financial support—for observing the red planet.

To be sure, a large number of scientific articles offering new interpretations of data returned from the Viking orbiters and landers kept appearing—and still do to this day—as planetary astronomers and scientists gradually absorbed the new results. Still, this was a kind of "archeology" involving data already collected, and not a search for new information. Thus, for the first time in generations, Mars was in the unfamiliar position of not being relatively frequent front page news. Instead, scientists and the public alike transferred some of their interest to another neighboring planet.

ASSAULT ON VENUS

While there was a general decline of interest in Mars, speculation about Venus increased. Although the hellish conditions on the next planet sunward from Earth ruled out most possibilities of life, there was intense speculation about just what the surface looked like. Radar studies from Earth showed mountainous regions on the planet, which was somewhat of a surprise, as the temperatures were known to be so hot (just short of being hot enough to glow in the dark when seen with human eyes) that the structural strength of rocks might be very low. With the lack of water, and probably low wind speeds, would there be any signs of erosion? Would there be massive rock, boulders, sand, or dust? Would it be pitch black even at noon? Just what would Venus look like? And, for added measure, there was still the question of what the clouds of Venus were made of.

For several reasons, Venus is an easier target than Mars to explore by means of planetary probes. It takes less energy to get there, and so a given booster rocket can be used to launch a heavier, more complex, and more sophisticated payload. The denser atmosphere means that parachutes alone will be enough to ensure a soft landing, so that bulky and complex retro rockets, approach radars, and similar gear can be dispensed with. Finally, it takes less time to get there, which in turn means reduced chances that equipment will fail during the trip.

Reliability was an especially sore point for the Soviets, whose technology in general was far behind that of the United States, and particularly so in electronics. The Soviet Union had only a dismal record of failures to show for their attempts to study Mars by means of space probes, but

Venus was a different story. They made the most of the difference and, despite a number of failures expected in any such program, racked up an impressive series of achievements.

Following the success of Venera 7, which was the first space probe to land softly on another major planet, the Soviets followed up with Venera 8, which settled onto the surface of Venus on July 22, 1972, and from there transmitted data on temperatures, pressures, and light levels for an hour or so.[8]

The next pair of successful probes, Venera 9 and 10, worked beautifully. After landing in October, 1975, they provided the first ever images taken from the surface of another major planet. Indeed, they did so by means of radio relays made through orbiting components of these probes. The photographs turned out to look surprisingly ordinary, showing a terrain that might be some desolate desert region on Earth. Boulders, rocks, and sand were scattered about the landscapes, and in somewhat of a surprise, the light levels were high enough that floodlights provided in case it was too dark for the television cameras to work were not needed. Venus might be shrouded in clouds, but evidently they were not too thick, for light levels were about the same as during a cloudy day on Earth.[9]

Venera 11 and 12, which both arrived at Venus in December, 1978, took atmospheric samples as they descended and landed safely, returning data for some time after they arrived. Unfortunately, the imaging systems on both probes failed. The next pair of Soviet attempts, Venera 13 and 14, worked well and between them provided surface images, atmospheric composition data, and analyses of soil samples, among other results.[10] All in all, the Soviet run of achievements as regards probes to Venus was impressive. However, these results told of conditions only in the immediate area of the vehicles' landing. The next generation of probes was to use very different techniques to provide much wider views.

Because of the tight budgets a free society demanded, the United States could mount only much more modest efforts than the Soviets did toward exploring Venus. Mariner 10 was among those. This probe's main purpose was to explore Mercury, but due to the peculiarities of gravity and celestial mechanics, it was possible to fly by Venus on the way to a Mercury encounter. Moreover, the pass by Venus could use that planet's gravitational pull as an "extra rocket stage" to put the payload on a course for Mercury even though the original launch vehicle did not have the power to do so. This was an early example of the imaginative yet practical use of a so-called "gravity assist" in a space mission, and it was a technique that would see increased use in the future. However, we should point out that this procedure would have been easily understood by astronomers as far back as Isaac Newton and Edmond Halley, providing an example of the continuity in planetary astronomy that extends over centuries.

Mariner 10 took an extensive series of ultraviolet images of Venus as it flew by the planet, and for the first time, these showed the detailed structure of the planet's upper cloud layer. In addition, these pictures showed in no uncertain terms that the major cloud patterns moved completely around Venus in about four days. This behavior had been detected earlier from Earth-based observations but was not generally accepted because the planet's rotation period was known from radar observations to be so much longer. Once again, and not for the last time, a planet had surprised the "experts."

As had become a common practice by now, the first substantial results of the Mariner 10 encounter with Venus were published in a special edition of the magazine *Science,* and therein lies a tale. On the cover of that issue was a beautiful Mariner 10 image of the planet in which the ultraviolet images were rendered in shades of blue and white. Unfortunately, Venus is not Earth (which *does* look blue and white when seen from a distance), and the true colors should have been various tinges of pale yellow. One can easily check this with the unaided eye the next time Venus is a prominent evening or morning star, for the planet is definitely not blue, but creamy white or pale yellow.[11] Later versions of this image were altered to produce the correct color, but the originals are now collectors' items in some quarters. The episode does have a moral, for it shows how easily we can be misled by our preconceived opinions.

Another U.S. effort was a pair of probes dubbed Pioneer Venus 1 and 2. (The names are somewhat confusing, as "Pioneer" initially had been used to designate a series of simple, lightweight *inter*planetary spacecraft designed to investigate conditions in the vast spaces between the planets, not those bodies themselves.) The name may have been chosen because advances in miniaturization of equipment allowed the weights of these probes to be reduced so that they could be launched by relatively small booster rockets, reducing the expense of missions.

These two machines reached Venus in December, 1978. Pioneer Venus 1 went into orbit around the cloud-shrouded planet and then, using on-board radar, proceeded to "map" the entire surface, revealing features that the then current ground-based radar could not, even though the probe observations could only distinguish features 50 miles or so across. This was an important first, for radar is the only feasible way of examining large areas of Venus. Images made from orbit in visible or even infrared light cannot penetrate the clouds. Images taken from landers, while they can show great detail, can cover only a tiny part of the surface. Even a camera in a balloon floating below the lowest cloud layer would be useless, as it could not see the surface. The reason is that even the lower "clear" atmosphere of Venus is so dense that scattering of light rays from molecules of carbon dioxide limits vision to a few miles. As we shall see, better radar maps would provide a series of surprises about Venus.

Pioneer Venus 2 was unique in that it carried no less than four entry probes (one large and three small) targeted for different regions of the planet. All of them made it safely to the surface, and one small probe even managed to transmit data for over an hour after impact.[12]

The effort to explore Venus was not confined to spacecraft, and in the early 1970s American scientists solved one of the oldest and most baffling problems of planetary astronomy: the nature of the clouds of Venus. Amazingly, they did so without the aid of any spacecraft data at all, contrary to what most planetary scientists expected or even believed possible. The essential clue came from ground-based telescopic observations, which gave estimates of the "index of refraction" of whatever it was that made up the particles in the obscuring layer. The index of refraction is a measure of the speed of light in a substance (confusingly, the greater the index, the slower the speed). This quantity has important practical uses, for it tells how much a lens or prism of a particular substance will bend a ray of light of a particular color.

The curious thing about the situation is that even after the index of refraction of the particles in the clouds of Venus was known, it took a while before anyone noticed that the index was close to that of sulfuric acid, a very common substance. Perhaps recognition was hampered somewhat by the fact that one theory at the time held that sulfur and thus all its compounds were rare on Venus.[13] But, as had happened before in different cases, when the connection was made, several persons made it at about the same time.

First to publish the sulfuric acid explanation was Godfrey T. Sill.[14] Next was Andrew T. Young, though he pointed out in no uncertain terms that it was actually his wife, Louise G. D. Young, who had made the initial suggestion.[15] As soon as the actual suggestions had been made, all the pieces fell into place, and droplets of sulfuric acid (along with some contained water) were generally accepted as composing the clouds of Venus. Interestingly, similar droplets occur high in Earth's atmosphere. They are fairly long-lived and, when produced in relatively large quantities (though still small compared to the amounts on Venus) by violent volcanic eruptions, help cause long-lasting and spectacularly colorful twilight phenomena.[16]

This episode provides an interesting example of just how difficult it sometimes is to decide who did what when, even when all the participants are still living. The dates of formal publications are of little help, especially in these days when many months can pass between submitting an article and having it appear in print. Then too, it obviously takes some time to go from a first idea to a manuscript ready to mail, and most planetary scientists did not and do not have the luxury of full-time assistants to document their every inspiration.[17]

POOR MERCURY

As late as the 1970s, astronomers knew little about the closest planet to the Sun. Even the best telescopic views usually showed only a fuzzy blob, though as we have seen, it had been known for a century that Mercury's surface resembled that of the Moon (and thus that it had little if any atmosphere), and some observers claimed to have gotten glimpses of craters on its sun-blasted wastes. Even the planet's mass was poorly known because it had no satellite.

All this changed with Mariner 10. After flying by Venus early in 1974, this probe made no less than three close passes of Mercury in that year and the next. Unfortunately, due to the ironclad laws of celestial mechanics, all three flybys photographed essentially the same sunlit half of the planet. The results were partly expected and partly unexpected. Images showed a body much like the Moon, scarred with impact craters large and small, with some areas covered with vast lava flows. But in contrast to our satellite, on Mercury there were high cliffs of vast extent, which seemed to indicate an era of surface compression sometime in the past. The planet's high density was confirmed, and its magnetic field was shown to be weak, a finding that appeared consistent with its slow rotation. On the other hand, there was a very tenuous atmosphere, about a trillionth as dense as that of Earth, which was much less than some scientists expected but much more than most planetary astronomers believed existed.

All in all, Mercury seemed to be a sort of variation on our own Moon as regards its surface. Even though half of the planet had not been viewed—and has not been to this day—it seemed to be just a battered, geologically dead, essentially airless, and certainly lifeless rock. This view was widespread and probably is the reason that Mariner 10 is the only space probe that has ever visited Mercury. This mission certainly did not get the recognition that it deserved, perhaps because the results were so mundane. Still, in terms of what we knew about Mercury before and after the Mariner 10 flybys, this voyage rates high on the scale of how much an exploratory flight has added to our knowledge.[18]

But, while Mercury might have seemed a dead and relatively uninteresting planet after the flight of Mariner 10, that would not always be the case. Two decades later, as we shall see, evidence would surface to indicate that this body may still hold some surprises.

THE OUTER PLANETS

The gas giants—Jupiter, Saturn, Uranus, and Neptune (not to mention the weird and recalcitrant Pluto, which is an entirely different sort of body)— pose severe difficulties to Earth-based observers because, being far from the Sun, their surface brightnesses are low. These planets are also difficult targets for space probes in that it takes much more energy to reach them compared to Venus, Mars, or Mercury. Moreover, at great distances from the Sun solar cells become useless to supply electrical power, and nuclear power sources must be used. In addition, it takes well-positioned transmitting antennas and sensitive receiving systems on Earth to pick up the faint signals from far out in the solar system. Thus, it is not surprising that direct exploration of these bodies lagged behind that of the terrestrial planets and was even more dependent on the development of improved booster rockets and miniaturized equipment—especially electronics.

Even though the Soviet Union long enjoyed an advantage in the thrust of their launch vehicles, the lead of the United States in miniaturization and reliability essentially left the more distant reaches of the solar system to the Americans. Still, the first probes to the outer planets were not launched until the early 1970s. Pioneer 10 was launched in March of 1972 and Pioneer 11 in April of the following year. These vehicles were simple, lightweight, and spin stabilized (as opposed to vehicles that kept all three axes in a constant orientation with respect to the stars). As mentioned, Pioneers were originally designed to study interplanetary space, and while this duo performed that duty, they were also meant to pass by at least some of the giant planets.

Despite the long flight times to their targets, both probes worked beautifully and, though there had been serious worries on this point, passed through the asteroid belt between Mars and Jupiter without a hitch. The known asteroids themselves were never considered a problem, for while their numbers are many, they are far apart. But at the time many scientists believed that there were so many small but potentially destructive solid particles in the belt that no spacecraft could pass through it safely. As it turned out, there is no greater a concentration of small particles in the asteroid belt than, for example, between the orbits of Earth and Mars. Thus, as far as probe safety went, there was effectively no asteroid belt at all. This was a stellar example of how direct exploration could solve a problem that had been debated vainly for years on the basis of theoretical studies and terrestrial observations alone.

Pioneer 10 flew by Jupiter in December of 1973, and its rudimentary imaging system provided views of that planet that were better than even the best fleeting glimpses that terrestrial observers had ever had. Its mate, Pioneer 11, passed close to Jupiter in December of the next year and, by taking advantage of the effects of the Jovian gravitational field, was able to fly by Saturn in September of 1974.

While there was a deluge of data from both probes, notably information about the magnetic fields and radiation belts of the two giant planets, public and scientific interest alike concentrated on the images of Jupiter and Saturn. The views were spectacular, far better than any ever recorded through Earth-based telescopes. Fortunately, the Great Red Spot was not undergoing one of its episodes of poor visibility but appeared in all its glory, as did a smaller red spot in the opposite (northern) hemisphere of the planet. Also revealed were plumes of white, high-level clouds arising from strong, localized regions of upwelling air on Jupiter. Then there were some relatively clear regions, the so-called "blue festoons," where the view into atmosphere went deep enough for the scattering of sunlight by gas molecules to produce a blue color, much as it does in Earth's own clear atmosphere. Many of these features had been glimpsed previously by visual observers on Earth, but they were much more clearly depicted on the Pioneer images. The turbulent and active nature of the giant planet's upper atmosphere was revealed dramatically. Unfortunately, these images were just shy of showing an enormous variety of phenomena that better views from later probes would disclose.

Images of Jupiter's four large Galilean satellites also fell just short of showing what we now know are many extraordinary features. Observers on Earth had recorded hints of vague markings on all four bodies, but there was no generally agreed-on "map" of any of them, and observers had hardly a clue as to what these features—if indeed they existed—represented. The Pioneer results changed all that, as they definitely showed features on all of the satellites. However, these images gave no hint of the truly bizarre nature of these bodies, which turned out to be very different from the major planets (again, excluding Pluto) and our own Moon.

During Pioneer 11's encounter with Saturn, the ringed planet's atmosphere showed much less (and more muted) detail than had Jupiter's, as was expected from terrestrial observations. Even so, there was much more structure visible than anything ever glimpsed through a telescope. The fabled rings revealed many more details than had ever been recorded before, and a new, faint outer ring was discovered (ground-based observers had shortly before detected two more rings in addition to the well-known A, B, and C, so the Pioneer feature was dubbed the F ring), as were two small new satellites. Astronomers of earlier eras would have given their eye teeth for images like these. And yet, as in the case of Jupiter, they were not quite good enough to show what we now know to be an amazing amount of structure.

As it left Saturn on its outbound voyage, Pioneer 11 snapped some close-up images of the large satellite Titan. This object was known to have an atmosphere, and so scientists were disappointed though not particularly surprised when no surface details were visible and even cloud features were muted. Evidently this body is covered with more or less structureless clouds, though there was no indication as to what they were made of or why they are orange in color.

Despite some "near misses," the Pioneers did the job that they were designed to do and gave us the best views ever of Jupiter and Saturn. But perhaps their greatest contribution to space exploration was to show that it was indeed possible to reach the outer planets and return useful information.[19]

The Pioneers have performed a great number of other tasks, including some that had not even been thought of when they were launched. Here we will only mention that they provided an enormous amount of data on the properties and variations of the solar wind, the changing structure of the interplanetary magnetic field, the effects of violent events on the Sun, the speed of light, the possible existence of gravitational waves, and the like—all data recorded at great distances from our star.

The Pioneers also cleared up some long-standing problems that concerned space closer to Earth. For a long time scientists had speculated about the nature of the zodiacal light, a feeble glow that brightens the dark sky along the ecliptic and becomes brighter near the Sun. The zodiacal light is so faint that the Milky Way is enough to blot it out (as can Venus or Jupiter, and certainly the Moon or street lights) and so is not easy to observe. This glow actually extends faintly all around the ecliptic and exactly opposite the Sun in our sky brightens slightly to form an indefinite feature known as the counterglow or *gegenschein* (which means the same thing in German). The zodiacal light is prominent enough that when conditions are right it is readily visible to a truly "dark adapted" eye, and long ago it was known as the "false dawn" (though it can be seen after sunset as well). The counterglow, on the other hand, is much more difficult to see. Interestingly both phenomena are perhaps most easily detected by the unaided eye.

Planetary astronomers in general had long believed that both the zodiacal light and the counterglow were due to sunlight reflected from dust grains in orbit around the Sun, particles produced by the collisions of asteroids and the evaporation of comets. However, this explanation was not a certainty, particularly in the case of the counterglow, which just might be some sort of "tail" of Earth.[20]

Pioneer observations solved the problem once and for all. The counterglow appeared from Pioneer 10 in different directions than when seen from Earth at the same times, yet always remained opposite the Sun. Thus, it must be due to small particles orbiting our star, and not a tail of our planet. As for the zodiacal light, its brightness gradually dropped the farther the probe went out into the solar system. By the time the asteroid belt was passed, there were virtually no counterglow or zodiacal light. Jupiter's gravity, it appears, sweeps space clean of small particles beyond this limit.[21]

More than these scientific results, Pioneer 10 and 11 have set records for endurance in very deep space that are still unmatched among spacecraft. As this is written, both of these probes are still in working order (Oran Nicks has written that "spinners live forever"). From far beyond the orbits of the most distant known planets, they continue to send back information on conditions as they cruise toward inter*stellar* space. That they have not yet reached that region is somewhat of a surprise, for various "educated guesses" before and during the Pioneer voyages tended to put the boundary of interstellar space (the "heliopause," where the solar wind ends and interstellar particles and magnetic fields take over) closer to the Sun. As might have been expected, estimates of the distance of this boundary from the Sun have increased over the years as the two probes cruise steadily outward from our star.

TELESCOPES STILL WORK

Ground-based observations during this decade were largely devoted to the unspectacular but needed work of determining what could be learned from Earth much more cheaply than from expensive space probes. However, sometimes terrestrial observers struck pay dirt, and before automated probes reached the giant planets, planetary astronomers produced some startling surprises ahead of those that came from flybys.

In one case, spectra of Io, Jupiter's innermost large satellite, revealed *emission lines* of sodium. Evidently Io is immersed in a cloud of softly glowing sodium vapor (if one were standing on that satellite's surface, the glow would appear about as bright as a typical aurora borealis on Earth).[22] Gradually other substances were found in the cloud—sodium was found first because its yellow spectral lines are so very strong—but the reasons for the cloud's existence and the details of its composition were hotly debated. The eventual explanation was to prove even more spectacular than the cloud itself.

Another striking case involved Uranus, about which little had been learned since William Herschel discovered it. The planet's mass was known because it has satellites, and its density also was fairly well known (uncertainties in the measurement of the angular diameter of its faint and tiny apparent disk were the main problem). Uranus was known to have methane and hydrogen in its atmosphere, but little more was known about it. In particular, it seemed that there might be substantially more helium in Uranus than in Jupiter and Saturn, because its density was greater than that of those two planets, even though its gravity was weaker and should not compress any known substances as much.

A chance to examine the upper atmosphere of Uranus came on March 10, 1977, when the green planet passed in front of ("occulted") a star known as SAO 158687. The hope was that the rate at which the star's light dimmed (and later brightened) at different wavelengths would help solve the problem of the planet's upper atmospheric composition and structure. In anticipation, observing teams from around the world prepared to record the event. Their results were completely unexpected.

A few seconds before the occultation, the brightness of the background star dropped dramatically and then rose again after a short interval. This weird behavior happened several times as Uranus passed in front of the star and was repeated, more or less, as the planet moved away from the star. What was going on?

Eventually, it became clear that at least nine narrow rings of small solid particles around Uranus were responsible for momentarily blocking the light of the faraway star. While William Herschel had once thought that he had glimpsed rings around Uranus, these had never been confirmed and indeed still are not obvious features. The rings of Uranus astonished astronomers of the time by their narrowness, for they were typically only a few tens of miles wide as regards the distances of their inner and outer edges from the planet. Even more strangely, some of the rings were not circular but elliptical in outline, and they appeared to be composed of very dark material. Later observations confirmed this situation.[23]

On the whole, the properties of the rings of Uranus were so different from the best known planetary rings of that time (those of Saturn) that planetary astronomers were largely a loss to explain them. Of course, there was an immediate and continuing spate of scientific articles attempting to show how and why such rings should and did come to be. However, it is only fair to point out that as of this writing, there is no generally accepted explanation of their origin and continued existence.

BEGINNINGS

The first decades of the Space Age saw the appearance—and in many cases disappearance—of a bewildering variety of theories as to how the solar system formed. Greatly increased interest in the subject was due to many factors. First of all, of course, was the space program itself, which began to provide hard information on the composition of the Moon, Venus, and ultimately Mars. Another factor was the emergence of a wide variety of techniques for measuring the ages of meteorites by analyzing their chemical and isotopic compositions. In addition, the ever increasing power of electronic computers made it possible for scientists to perform numerical simulations of processes so complicated that there was essentially no hope of ever investigating them by means "classical" means using mathematical analytical equations. As a result, hard numbers began to replace time-honored vague arguments. Then too, there were simply more scientists interested in the field, people who were able to work on the subject because of financial support provided in large part by NASA. One might think that given all these factors, planetary scientists would in relatively short order have come up with a definite answer to the question of the origin of the solar system. However, that was not the case, and there is still no generally accepted theory at the time this book is being written.

Among the hotly debated topics are whether the planets formed "hot" or "cold," and whether they condensed directly from a cloud composed mostly of gas with perhaps a little dust mixed in or instead went through an intermediate stage (the old "planetesimal" scheme). And, if there were small solid grains present at the beginning, are any of them still around, preserved perhaps in meteorites that have never been heated substantially? Another question concerns the composition of the nebula that became the solar system. Most theories assume that it was uniform throughout, but this is not certain.

While it is now generally accepted that the Sun and planets formed more or less at the same time, and probably fairly quickly, it is still not clear whether the formation of planets is a normal stage of ordinary star formation. If so, solar systems should be common or even ubiquitous. On the other hand, if some external "trigger" is needed, extrasolar planets must be rarer. One popular candidate is a supernova—or perhaps several supernovae. An attractive feature of this suggestion is that these titanic explosions can affect such large volumes of space (light years across), that other solar systems may still be fairly common even if this trigger is needed.

There is the still unsolved problem of how small grains or pebbles can collect themselves together and grow into bodies large enough to have substantial gravitational fields. And, once large bodies did form, why did the denser, rocky, less massive terrestrial planets form inside the asteroid belt and the gas giants outside?

Not surprisingly, the old problem of the possible significance of the Titius-Bode "law," which represents the curiously regular spacing of the planets in an uncannily accurate manner, will not go away. Is it telling us something, or is it just a coincidence? Another old question still without a definite answer is how most of the angular momentum of the solar system ended up in the planets instead of the Sun.

In the last half of the twentieth century scientists have made great strides in understanding just how stars are born. On the theoretical side, modern electronic computers have made it feasible for researchers to "model" the collapse of a dusty gas cloud into a star. On the observational front, infrared and radio observations have made it possible for astronomers to peer inside stellar nurseries, which are opaque to visible light.

The results of all this effort point to a star formation process that is much more complicated and much more violent than previously imagined. A cloud, it seems, does not gently contract into a star but rather may exhibit all sorts of activity in the process, such as showing great fluctuations in brightness, spewing out energetic jets of matter, and the like. Whether this tumult aids or hinders the formation of planets is still unknown.

The question of whether solar systems are common, rare, or whether our own is unique still does not have a definite answer. The best hopes of finding one depend on a variety of new techniques that astronomers are developing, which hold out the possibility of discovering planets around stars, if there are any. These methods may provide some interesting information in the decades to come, and it is important to remember that finding even one other solar system will eliminate the currently unique position of our own.

In one area, however, there appears to have been substantial progress: as regards the origin of the Moon, most scientists now at least hold to the same explanation. By the time of the Apollo lunar missions, the fission theory had been more or less abandoned by scientists, though it had not been ruled out for certain. The capture hypothesis, on the other hand was perhaps the most popular explanation. In addition, there was a third conjecture holding that the Moon grew from the same small cloud of particles out of which our own planet was forming at the same time. (This last possibility had a problem—the well-known fact that our satellite's orbit around Earth is tilted substantially with respect to our planet's path around the Sun.)

Thus, the origin of the Moon was very much an unknown, but there was a widespread expectation that intensive laboratory studies of lunar samples that the Apollo missions would bring back to Earth would enable scientists to decide once and for all among the competing theories. The hundreds of pounds of lunar rocks and soil did provide a much more detailed view of the Moon's present state and past history. However, to the disappointment of many, they did not reveal the method by which our satellite came to be. In fact, they fairly ruled out all three possibilities then current. It was a frustrating situation.

Eventually an apparent breakthrough came about because of the increasing appreciation by scientists over the course of the twentieth century of the important role that catastrophic impacts have had on the development of the solar system. If it should be proven that Earth, at some time early in its history but when it was already at about its present mass, had been hit by a body perhaps equivalent to the size of Mars, many problems about the Moon's origin would be solved. Some of the debris from the collision might go into orbit around our planet and eventually form the Moon. The "giant impact" explanation, in various forms, is widely accepted as this is being written. Unfortunately, there are annoying potential problems even with these hypotheses. Only time will tell if the collision theory or yet another is correct.[24]

FIASCO?

During the 1950s, 1960s, and 1970s, research on comets generally made steady but on the whole unspectacular progress. After several bright comets appeared early in the century, research in the field was hampered by a lack of really bright objects. This drought ended with the appearance of Comet Arend-Roland in 1957, and in the following decades several bright objects visible to the naked eye appeared. However, advances were still hindered by the relatively crude state of detectors, especially those for infrared and radio radiation, and by the enormous gaps in our knowledge of the properties of molecules and their behavior in the near vacuum of interplanetary space ("nuclear" physics was all the rage in those days, and as a result other areas suffered by comparison). However, cometary science soon gained prominence.

If measured by the amount of public interest, the apparition of Comet Kohoutek during 1973 and 1974 might be considered the premier astronomical event of the 1970s. Unfortunately, that was not the case. Here is the story, and it certainly has a moral.

On March 7, 1973, the astronomer Lubos Kohoutek noticed a small smudge on a photographic plate of the sky that he had taken at the Hamburg Observatory in Germany. Further observations showed that the faint glow was a comet, and an unusual one at that. When it was discovered, Comet Kohoutek was about as far from the Sun as Jupiter (some 5 astronomical units) and was much brighter at that distance than all but a few of the previously known deep space visitors of a similar type. Calculations soon showed that this object would come within 0.14 astronomical units of the Sun at its closest approach, well within the orbit of Mercury.

If (and this was a most important "if") Kohoutek was a "typical" comet, it should become very bright indeed when it was near the Sun. In fact, early predictions indicated that it might become as bright as Venus or even the Moon. Astronomers were quick to point out that Kohoutek would only reach this brightness when it was very near the Sun in the sky as seen from Earth, and thus it would be difficult to observe as its glow would be greatly diminished by the light of the twilight sky. However, such cautions were generally dismissed by the press, which instead trumpeted the coming appearance of "The Comet of the Century" and predicted spectacular views.

Even if Kohoutek had equaled the brightest comets in recorded history, it would have been visible only with difficulty—if at all—from any large modern city due to the effects of electric lights and air pollution. Yet many people seemed to be looking forward to a spectacle rivaling the sudden appearance of another Sun at midnight (there was some confusion of comets with bright meteors, and the concept of Kohoutek "streaking across the sky" was all too common). Public interest reached a pitch reminiscent of the "Halleymania" that attended the last two visits of that most famous of comets. To give just one example, the Cunard Line arranged a special three-day voyage of the liner *Queen Elizabeth* 2 from New York in December, 1973, just to view Kohoutek in the dark and, promoters hoped, clear early morning skies on the Atlantic Ocean. And, of course, there was no shortage of "prophets" predicting the end of the world. Some things change little over the years.

As Comet Kohoutek approached the Sun late in 1973, it brightened much more slowly than expected, and astronomers were careful to reduce their estimates of how brilliant it might appear to observers on Earth. Unfortunately the publicity machine, once started, proved impossible to stop or even to slow. Finally, early in 1974, when it was very close to the Sun in the sky as seen from Earth, Kohoutek did get about as bright as Jupiter or Mars at its brightest. But it could only be viewed well from space, where the twilight of our planet's atmosphere did not interfere. Astronauts on the Skylab space station, for example, had a fine view. However, for watchers on Earth, the vista was much less impressive. Those at really dark, clear sites saw a faint fuzz (the coma) with about the same surface brightness as the Milky Way, and a short, even fainter tail. While the comet was comfortably visible to the naked eye if one knew just where to look, it was not at all a striking object (a rule of thumb at the time was that if the Milky Way was obvious, you could see Kohoutek), and even from the most favorable locations, the view of it was much better with binoculars.

I was fortunate to have the opportunity to view Kohoutek from the University of Texas McDonald Observatory when the comet was well placed for viewing from Earth. However, even from an altitude of 7,000 feet, and with the advantages of very clear and dark skies, Kohoutek was just a faint glow. Needless to say, for those who lived in or near a city or town, the comet was nearly or totally invisible to the unaided eye. Thus, for many, it was a cosmic media flop. Planetary astronomers had egg on their faces; but, as we shall see, they learned their lesson, and when Comet Halley appeared a decade later, they handled things very differently.

However, there was a bright side to the debacle. Because of the intense public interest, planetary scientists were able to wangle observing time on instruments when they would not otherwise have been able to use these. As a result, there were many significant findings, of which perhaps the most important was the positive identification, by several groups of investigators, of water vapor in the ejecta from the comet. This was a significant discovery, for it was a positive detection of one of the elusive "parent" molecules that astronomers had long believed must exist in solid form on a comet when it is far from the Sun (which in most cases is by far most of the time). Observers had searched vainly for these parent molecules for decades but had been bedeviled by the fact that once these substances evaporate from the surface of a comet, they are soon destroyed by the action of energetic solar ultraviolet radiation.

The finding of water vapor was particularly important, for planetary scientists had long felt that ordinary water ice must make up a significant part of the bulk of most comets. As it turned out, this view was correct for, as Fred Whipple had surmised long before, comets are indeed "dirty snowballs." Thus, for this and other reasons, while Comet Kohoutek was a fiasco as far as public relations were concerned, it was responsible for major advances in our knowledge of comets in general.[25]

Despite the significant discoveries in the decade of the seventies, focusing on Venus, Mercury, and Comet Kohoutek, in some respects this decade comprised a rather sad "glorious evening" for planetary astronomy. The inception of new NASA-inspired programs and projects relating to planetary astronomy almost ceased. NASA funding increasingly was directed to operational and near-Earth projects. Skylab, the Apollo-Soyuz mission, and Space Shuttle design and development absorbed most of NASA's energy and funding during the decade. Research and development work both declined. And the shuttle, by definition, was to be an Earth-orbital vehicle, not a spacecraft capable of interplanetary missions.

Although the inception of the Space Shuttle directly involved the idea of creating a permanent orbiting space station about the Earth (a facility widely held to be capable of being a launch depot for planetary missions), the space station failed to receive adequate support, and the idea of manned and even automated planetary missions faded almost entirely out of the picture. NASA believed that future science and planetary programs would be inextricably linked to the shuttle. In addition, there was a public and political perception that these reusable vehicles would focus on Earth resources and problems rather than on planetary or stellar concerns. As a result, the need for additional efforts in the fields of planetary astronomy and science diminished. This decade saw the cancelation of numerous planned space probes, a trend that hindsight shows began with the deletion of a number of Ranger and Surveyor vehicles—even after some of them were actually under construction.

Thus, the new age of planetary studies that began with Sputnik in 1957 experienced in the 1970s a partial eclipse.

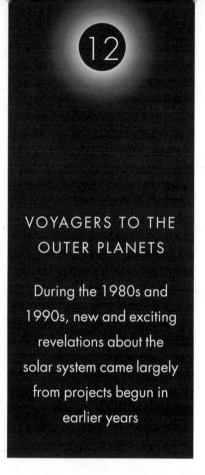

VOYAGERS TO THE OUTER PLANETS

During the 1980s and 1990s, new and exciting revelations about the solar system came largely from projects begun in earlier years

In the 1970s, NASA engineers studying prospective interplanetary trajectories for the Mariner 10 probe recognized that the relative positions of the planets would soon be such that a single spacecraft, using gravity assist, could fly by Jupiter, Saturn, Uranus, Neptune, and perhaps even Pluto! Such an alignment had last occurred almost two centuries earlier, in William Herschel's time. To take advantage of this rare opportunity, NASA planned to develop and launch a set of heavy and complex spacecraft on a "Grand Tour" of the outer planets.

Unfortunately, the design and construction of the spacecraft and equipment for such advanced missions would be very costly, and this was a decade in which the public interest in many aspects of the space program, including planetary astronomy, declined. NASA began to focus on Earth-orbital programs, including the Space Shuttle, which flew its maiden voyage on April 12, 1981, and a space station, projected for construction in space in the last decade of the twentieth century.

NASA budgets declined sharply from the 1964 and 1965 highs of more than $22 billion (in 1992 dollars), to average about $9 billion through the 1970s. Not until 1987 did funding for NASA programs exceed $10 billion, and it averaged $12–13 billion from 1980 through 1995.[1] Much of the increased funding was allocated for shuttle replacements, but physics and astronomy programs also received improved levels of funding after 1980. Although the media and public perception was that NASA's support of planetary studies continued unabated after Apollo, the fact was that the accomplishments and discoveries derived from initiatives begun in previous years. Post-Apollo budgetary pressures resulted in fewer space probes and less funding for ground-based astronomy than had been anticipated. As a result, NASA returned to the less ambitious and less expensive project of sending probes of the well-tried "Mariner class" to Saturn by means of gravity assist from Jupiter. Confusingly, this new project was dubbed Voyager, the same name that had been used for the long defunct project to investigate Mars.[2]

THE VOYAGERS

Many important discoveries during this era were made at terrestrial observatories, but in good measure the public's perception of the good health of planetary sciences stemmed from two remarkable missions named Voyager 1 and Voyager 2. These probes to the outer reaches of the solar system took many years to accomplish their primary missions, and their active careers have exceeded all expectations. The saga of these two amazing exploring machines winds like a thread through the history of planetary astronomy for many years after their launches. However, their very success helped mask serious problems in the field.

Despite their relative simplicity compared to the proposed Grand Tour vehicles, the new Voyagers were nonetheless complex exploring machines that presented severe development challenges. Unlike their predecessors, Pioneers 10 and 11, these probes would be stabilized in all three axes, would carry improved imaging systems capable of much better resolution, would have the capability of aiming many of their instruments toward a specific direction in space independently of the orientation of the main body of the spacecraft, and would be able to radio data back to Earth at much higher rates.

As for the earlier two probes to the far reaches of the solar system, solar cells would not suffice to provide the needed electricity. Developers selected improved generators relying on radioactive isotopes as their power sources. Meanwhile, continuing advances in miniaturization, especially in electronics, and in particular in the capabilities of lightweight computers, eventually meant that even these "substitute" probes could do most of the things that had been planned for the proposed Grand Tour missions. Advances in computers and imaging techniques and better communication rates allowed navigation inputs and mission program updates with precision during the mission, long after the spacecraft hardware had been built. This operational flexibility, plus the long-life power supplies and reliability, greatly extended the usefulness and effectiveness of the aging hardware. The most important advances, however, were in the field of reliability, which was critical to the success of these missions. After years of cruising through the outer solar system, Voyager spacecraft had to perform many complex operations on a precise schedule and, because of the long time delays imposed by the finite speed of light (and radio waves) over vast distances, they would be operating largely "on their own" after receiving information and commands.

Although the basic mission of these probes was to fly by and make close-up observations of Jupiter and Saturn, NASA engineers and scientists continued to design capabilities into the systems that would allow for the possibility that the spacecraft could go on to more distant planets. To take advantage of this prospect, NASA adopted the same engineering and design strategy that had served so well in the cases of Pioneer 10 and 11. The first Voyager was targeted to achieve the basic mission—flying by Saturn by way of Jupiter—while producing the largest possible amount of what was considered the most desirable scientific data, and doing so with the greatest probability of success. If this first spacecraft succeeded, greater risks could be taken or additional scientific objectives addressed with the second. By adjusting its path as it flew past Saturn, researchers could send the craft to Uranus and, they hoped, Neptune. The scientific potential was enormous if the spacecraft and instruments worked as designed. Both missions succeeded brilliantly and many of the results they produced were stunningly unexpected.

VOYAGERS TO JUPITER

Voyagers 1 and 2 were launched on September 5 and August 20, 1977, respectively. Voyager 1 made its closest approach to Jupiter on March 5, 1979, and Voyager 2 on July 9 that year. In both cases, for many weeks both before and after the closest approach, a battery of scientific equipment returned data on the king of the planets and his retinue. The most dramatic results, and arguably the most important from a scientific point of view, came from high resolution images of Jupiter and the Galilean satellites.[3]

In the case of the planet itself, images taken during approach showed ever more detail as the spacecraft neared Jupiter. This was not inevitable, as we can see in the case of clouds in our own sky, which can appear quite sharply defined when seen at a distance but may show indistinct edges when viewed from close up. The cloud features that observers on Earth had long viewed imperfectly broke up into myriad details of incredible complexity, far more intricate than any revealed by Pioneers 10 and 11, indicating violent and energetic weather patterns. The Great Red Spot was revealed as a great spinning eddy in the planet's upper atmosphere, and on the night side of the planet there was lightning in the clouds while auroras glowed near both poles.

A great surprise was that Jupiter had a ring around it. This is a faint, tenuous, and extended feature, not at all like those of Saturn, but a ring it is.[4]

The Voyagers' revelations about Jupiter itself were eclipsed by those concerning the planet's satellite system. Several new, small companions were discovered, but the real surprises came from images of the Galilean satellites, the most spectacular and bizarre case being that of Io. For years, evidence from a variety of ground-based observations had been piling up to the effect that it is a very unusual satellite, but it is fair to say that no one fully expected to see a world as different as this one turned out to be. Io appeared as a dappled disc splattered with riotous shades of yellow and orange, along with white and black. Even more astounding, close-up images revealed a number of active volcanic vents spewing debris high above the surface. Evidently this satellite is much more active volcanically than Earth, so much so that it is entirely resurfaced in a short time on a geological scale. Presumably molten material in these vents, the debris, and the kaleidoscopic colors are due to various forms of sulfur.

As we have seen, unusual coincidences are unexpectedly common in the history of astronomy, and here was another example, for vulcanism on Io had been predicted just a short time before the Voyager 1 flyby. Stanton J. Peale and his colleagues had reasoned that the tides that must be raised on the satellite by the presence of the massive and nearby Jupiter would heat Io's interior and probably melt at least part of it, possibly resulting in active vulcanism at the surface.[5] Over billions of years, and because of the satellite's weak gravity, volatile substances such as methane, ammonia, and water would be lost to space, until by this time only less volatile materials such as sulfur (which is fairly common in the universe) would be left.

Europa, the next satellite outward from Jupiter, was equally strange in a very different way. Its surface appeared to be the smoothest of any known body and to be covered with a sheet of water ice laced by long sinuous features that appeared to be frozen cracks where liquid water once welled up.[6] Apparently, tidal heating, which is not as effective on this satellite as on Io, has not yet removed the water from Europa. However, below this gigantic skating rink may be a thick layer of liquid water, otherwise unexpected this far from the Sun. In fact, there may be geysers of water in some form (*vulcanism* seems the wrong word in this case) active even now.

Ganymede, the next satellite outward from Europa, showed two types of terrain. There were darker patches, evidently older because they sported a greater density of impact craters, separated by brighter bands composed of long, parallel belts of ridges and troughs that appeared to have been squeezed in the past. Callisto's surface, on the other hand, was entirely saturated with impact craters and had very low surface relief. Apparently little had happened on this body for billions of years except for occasional impacts. The flat nature of the terrain is no doubt due to the fact that the water ice composing it flows slowly, as glaciers on Earth demonstrate, and over millions of years that flow fills in craters and lowers crater rims.

The Voyager observations of the Galilean satellites revealed bodies different from any known before. Earlier ground-based observations had indicated that the densities of these bodies grew smaller as the distance from Jupiter increased, and the flybys confirmed this trend. Io and Europa have densities (about four and three times that of water, respectively) consistent with a composition that is basically rocky, despite the latter's outer shells of solid and, presumably, liquid water. Ganymede and Callisto, on the other hand, have much lower densities, about twice that of water, and probably have water ice in some form as a major constituent of their bodily composition. These latter satellites were the first two recognized members of what might be termed "ice worlds." They are large, about the size of Mercury, yet they have densities much less than that of the terrestrial planets.

ENCOUNTERS WITH SATURN

Voyager 1 flew by Saturn on November 12, 1980, and its twin followed on August 25, 1981. As expected from a long history of terrestrial telescopic observation, the upper portion of this planet's atmosphere showed far less detail than that of Jupiter, but in other places there were unexpected surprises in store.[7]

Saturn, it turns out, has literally thousands of rings! Images showed hundreds of them, so that the system resembles an enormous, unreal-looking long-playing record or compact disc. In addition, effects on radio signals when a probe passed behind the rings as seen from Earth indicated the presence of far more even narrower rings. Moreover, there were ephemeral, darker, radial "spokes" on the surface of the ring system.

Interestingly, earlier ground-based observations had given tantalizing indications of this complex structure. Those few observers with access to telescopes adapted to the task, and enough observing time to take advantage of the rare moments of good seeing, recorded a great deal of structure in the Saturnian ring system. For example, as early as the 1890s E. M. Antoniadi had sketched the dark radial spokes, while multiple ring divisions had been recorded for at least as long, and by 1943 Bernard Lyot was able to draw a ring system with at least eleven components and more indicated by brightness variations.[8]

However, such observations were generally ignored or dismissed as illusory by astronomers. The astronomical establishment of those days was perhaps bemused by spectroscopic and photographic studies of the stars and distant galaxies and may have remembered all too well the drawings of canals on Mars and Venus. (Note that both Antoniadi and Lyot worked in France, where they could get the amounts of telescope time that they needed.) In any event, these and other early hints of the complex structure of Saturn's rings were largely forgotten by the time of the Voyager missions, except in the minds of a few planetary astronomers, but the Voyager space probes vindicated the earlier observers in a dramatic way.

What causes the myriad divisions in Saturn's rings, a structure so different from the case of Jupiter? Naturally the gravitational influence of satellites was an obvious candidate, but both planets have a host of attendants, which weakened the argument. Theoretical studies, though, had indicated that relatively small "shepherding" satellites close to the rings might do the job. There was little hope of spotting such objects from Earth, but Voyager images might pick them up. Indeed some were found, in particular two that orbited just inside and just outside the wirelike F ring. However, there did not appear to be enough of these bodies to do the whole job, and as of this writing, the detailed structure of Saturn's rings still has no generally accepted explanation.

The Voyagers revealed much detail about all the rings, but in particular they discovered that the F ring is a complicated structure composed of several very narrow strands that exhibit bizarre kinks and knots and appear to form braids, of all things. It looks weird and unreal, and how it can maintain that structure is still not known. These probes also imaged a D ring, but surprisingly found that it was too faint ever to have been seen from Earth, even though a number of terrestrial observers claimed detection.

As discussed in the previous chapter, terrestrial observations made before any spacecraft visits had found that Saturn had major rings other than the three classical ones known as A, B, and C. The detections of these fainter features came at those times when the ring system is seen edge-on from Earth and the tenuous components are not overwhelmed by the reflected light from the brighter ones, a circumstance that occurs roughly every fifteen years.

Times when the rings are seen edge-on also offer the best opportunities to detect faint satellites, and observers have long used these opportunities to search for possible new attendants of Saturn. The last three of these ring-crossing episodes (there tend to be several in the course of a few months) occurred in 1965–66, 1979–80, and by coincidence in 1995 as this chapter was being written. Over the years many possible satellites have been announced, but far fewer have been confirmed. The story of these observations could fill a book, but here we will only mention that the number of confirmed satellites of Saturn is unknown, because different scientists accept different numbers.[9] While the Voyagers added a number of discoveries, they did not resolve the dispute.

The larger satellites of Saturn differ from those of Jupiter in several ways. There are more of them, but only one, Titan, is in the size class of the Galilean moons. Nevertheless, the Voyagers discovered some surprising features about these bodies.

Images of Titan indicated little evidence of atmospheric activity, and it was uncertain whether or not its surface could be seen. On the other hand, compounds of hydrogen, carbon, and nitrogen were identified, which points to the fascinating possibility that complex organic chemistry is possible even on this cold world. Another interesting result was that the surface pressure was only a little greater larger than that on Earth, far higher than on Mercury or Mars, but much less than on Venus. With the lack of definite information, speculation about what conditions are like on the surface of Titan ran riot. Is it completely covered with an ocean of liquid methane surfaced with a layer of organic material? Are there islands or continents of frozen methane, water, or other substances? All in all, data from the Voyagers generated a great deal of new scientific and astronomical interest in Titan.[10]

The other major satellites of Saturn for the most part were remarkable for their sameness. All of them presumably consist in large part of water ice, and all exhibit impact craters, which had come to be expected, but many also showed unexpected evidence of past geologic activity. The details of these structures properly belong to the field of planetary geophysics, but some features deserve mention here.

First of all, we should note that the icy Saturnian satellites showed variations in elevation—deep craters, high mountains, and the like—that were at first sight surprisingly great. They stand in sharp contrast to the more uniform surfaces of the large, icy subworlds around Jupiter. This difference is probably due to at least two factors. One is that the lesser gravities at the surfaces of the icy satellites of Saturn allow greater elevation differences, and another is that at the lower temperatures found farther from the Sun, water ice is much stiffer.

Mimas, the closest to Saturn of the "major" satellites, is only a few hundred miles in diameter, and so it came as a surprise that it exhibited long, deep grooves, perhaps the result of a gigantic impact sometime in the past. Still, little seems to have happened on this world for billions of years.

Enceladus, the next satellite outward, is drastically different. Even though it too is only a few hundred miles in diameter, it must have undergone extensive geological activity relatively recently, for large areas of its surface show no impact craters at all, and so must be young. The reason why Enceladus and Mimas, similar in size and orbit, are so different is still a fascinating puzzle.

All the rest of Saturn's large satellites show evidence of varying forms of activity and resurfacing to various degrees, but the case of Iapetus presents perhaps the greatest puzzle. Astronomers have long known that the dark "leading" (in its orbit around Saturn) and light "trailing" hemispheres of this satellite differed greatly in brightness, but Voyager images only deepened the mystery. One half is indeed dark, as if it had plowed through some dusky material in its trips around the planet, but the boundary between the two regions turned out to be unexpectedly sharp and irregular. In particular, dark material appears to have encroached into low areas such as crater floors, as if it had flowed there in liquid form. Needless to say, the explanation of this bizarre situation is still unknown.[11]

ON TO URANUS

After its Saturn encounter, Voyager 1 headed out of the solar system toward the depths of interstellar space. On the other hand, Voyager 2, now that its predecessor had accomplished the program's primary mission successfully, had its path by Saturn adjusted so that after its flyby it sped on a path toward Uranus, passing that greenish planet on January 24, 1986.

Several days before the probe's closest approach to the planet, receivers on board detected radio emissions from Uranus. These varied with a period of as little as 17 hours and 24 minutes, and presumably represented the rotation period of the body of the planet, as opposed to that of the upper atmosphere. This was the first determination of that period.[12]

As was expected on the basis of earlier ground-based observations— no definite features had ever been glimpsed from Earth—only a few cloud features appeared in images of the greenish planet, but there were enough to determine rotation periods for at least some latitudes. As in the cases of Jupiter and Saturn, the upper atmosphere of Uranus rotates differentially, with clouds at different latitudes moving at different speeds, a situation that was not unexpected. These periods were much more precise than those measured spectroscopically from Earth.

Images taken at various wavelengths revealed that Uranus has a faintly banded structure, with the bands running parallel to the equator. However, these bands were too subtle ever to have been seen by terrestrial observers, for to human eyes, Uranus even close up looks remarkably bland and uniform. Thus, earlier reports of relatively pronounced banded structure were probably erroneous.[13]

Details of the rings and satellites more than made up for the lack of detail seen on Uranus itself. The nine previously known narrow rings were confirmed, and two more were added to the list. Voyager confirmed that the rings are very dark, reflecting only a small percentage of the light that falls on them, but surprisingly, some are variable in brightness around their circumferences.

The most unexpected discovery came when the rings of Uranus were viewed with the Sun behind them as seen from the probe—in a word, backlighted. Hundreds of rings were visible, and the scene eerily resembled the rings of Saturn when seen by direct reflected sunlight. All these features appear very tenuous, which explains why they did not show up in the occultation observations made from Earth or in the images taken by Voyager in direct light.[14]

Ten new satellites, all small and dark, were discovered. Scientists had hoped that Voyager might reveal "shepherding" satellites that could explain the ring structure around Uranus. However, as in the case of Saturn, few were found. Only one pair, shepherding a single ring, were detected. Thus, the explanation of the detailed structure of this system of rings is also uncertain at present.[15]

The four largest satellites of Uranus all have impact craters. Ariel, Titania, and Oberon show evidence of geological activity: grooves, valleys, cliffs, and flows of some sort—perhaps water that later froze into ice. Umbriel, as earlier terrestrial observations had indicated, is different. This body is darker than its three siblings, and its surface looked as if little had happened there since the intense meteor bombardment shortly after its formation. Why this body should be so different from the other three is unknown.

Miranda, discovered by Gerard P. Kuiper in 1948, is only about 300 miles in diameter. Any internal heat, however generated, would soon be lost from such a small body, and so scientists expected to find it a long dead, cratered object with little or no traces of geological activity. Fortunately, Voyager passed less than 2,000 miles from the satellite and took images of very high resolution. Those images were astounding, revealing a tiny, bizarre world of unbelievable complexity.

Besides having relatively mundane regions studded with impact craters, Miranda had areas covered with grooves composed of parallel valleys and ridges, and more complicated districts that are difficult even to describe. Moreover, these different zones had strangely shaped boundaries, one being basically rectangular. Another facet of this unique satellite was the existence of sheer cliffs many miles high. How this grotesque body came to be what it is now remains one of the great puzzles of the solar system.

However different their histories may be, it seems probable that all the satellites of Uranus are composed mainly of frozen water and other ices. They are additional, relatively small examples of ice worlds.[16]

FAR NEPTUNE

Before the visit of Voyager 2, even less was known about Neptune than about Uranus. Telescopic observations had detected two satellites. The planet's rotation period had been estimated spectroscopically, and methane and hydrogen had been detected in its atmosphere. That was about the extent of our knowledge.

Curiously, while Voyager was in flight to this blue planet, some intriguing if puzzling results began to come from terrestrial observations. For one thing, occultation studies similar to those made on Uranus gave hints that Neptune too might have rings. But there was a disquieting aspect to these studies, for they were not consistent. The number of rings seemed to be different from time to time, and the dimming effect of the same ring would sometimes show up and sometimes not. There was a suggestion that at least some of these rings were actually discontinuous arcs, but to many that idea seemed a faint hope at best.[17]

Meanwhile, as Voyager was nearing Neptune, ground-based images indicated that the planet might have large and prominent atmospheric features that varied rapidly. This came as a surprise to planetary astronomers, for ground-based observations as well as those from the Pioneer and Voyager spacecraft had shown that visible features in the upper atmospheres of the outer planets became steadily more subdued as the distance from the Sun increased. It seemed odd that Neptune would reverse the trend established by Jupiter, Saturn, and Uranus, but by this time planetary scientists had learned to expect the unexpected and frankly did not now know what they would find.[18]

As in the case of Uranus, Voyager's observations of radio radiation from the planet established that the body of Neptune rotated once every 16 hours and 7 minutes. In this case too, it was the first determination of that type of period and was more precise than any estimate of any sort made previously.[19]

As the space probe closed in on Neptune, it became obvious that the planet did indeed exhibit a great deal of structure in its upper atmosphere. The first features detected were bright, white, and variable. Images taken with better resolution showed a surprising variety of cloud forms. The most dramatic and unexpected was dubbed the Great Dark Spot. This was a dark blue oval that bore an uncanny resemblance to Jupiter's Great Red Spot. While Neptune's spot was of course much smaller, its relative size compared to that of the planet was about the same as in the Jovian case. Still, the dark spot was big, about the size of Earth.

Around the spot's edges, bright clouds formed and dissipated. In many respects they resembled the so-called "orographic" clouds that occur on Earth when a strong wind forces air up and over a tall mountain, causing water vapor to condense. However, in the case of Neptune, methane appears to take the place of water vapor.

There were other bright clouds and dark spots as well, some with complex and rapidly changing structure. By measuring the positions of these features at different times, planetary scientists determined that Neptune, just like all the other giant planets, has an atmosphere that rotates differentially.[20]

As for the rings, Voyager confirmed the existence of five of them, three narrow and two relatively broad. All were tenuous and composed of particles that were very dark, as in the case of Uranus. The outermost ring, dubbed Adams, had three separate, brighter areas, but fainter material filled in the rest of its circumference.[21]

Six new, small, dark satellites were discovered in Voyager images. Images of these bodies showed impact craters, and perhaps some hints of geological activity, but the resolution of these pictures was too poor to draw any definite conclusions. No shepherding moons were found, and so yet another ring system was added to the list of those that still await detailed explanation.[22]

Of the previously known satellites of Neptune, Voyager never approached Nereid closely enough take images that showed any significant detail. Large and massive Triton, on the other hand, was a different story. This moon had long been known to be a maverick, for it is the only large satellite in the solar system with a retrograde orbit about its primary.

No one expected Triton to be what it really is. Surprisingly, there were few impact craters, which points to its surface being unexpectedly young compared to the age of the solar system. Even more surprising is that there was a bewildering variety of surface detail. The satellite had a relatively small amount of relief—the highest and lowest spots were not that much different in altitude—and several different terrain types were found. Among others, there was a bright southern polar cap full of weird and unexplained structures, and some regions at first glance looked startlingly like the skin of a ripe cantaloupe. There were also extensive regions that had probably been flooded by some liquid—probably water—that later froze. This may be yet another example of the unusual (by Earth standards) type of "vulcanism" found on cold worlds.

In sharp contrast to everything that planetary scientists expected, this satellite on the outer fringe of the solar system evidently has been active throughout its long history. In fact, it is active today! Voyager images of the southern polar cap showed plumes of dark material rising several miles above the surface and then being born by winds for a hundred miles or so. In addition, there were many dark streaks that appeared to be "fallout" from previous events of this kind.

How can this be? The surface temperature of Triton is the coldest ever measured for any body in the solar system. The atmospheric pressure at its surface is 100,000 times less than that on Earth. One possibility is that these eruptions are geysers of nitrogen in the form of gas and small particles (Triton's atmosphere is probably mostly nitrogen). Whatever the explanation, Triton provides a striking example of the fact that we still have many surprises in store even in the exploration of our own parochial solar system.[23]

After the Neptune encounter, Voyager 2 joined its twin and the two Pioneers in their voyages out to the stars. The Voyager missions were triumphs of reliability, a level of reliability that no other spacefaring nation has yet matched. They discovered, largely by means of superb images, an incredible amount of previously unimagined information about the outer planets and many of their satellites, and thereby finally demolished the mistaken idea that pictures somehow are not "scientific." Observations from these two spacecraft demonstrated decisively that our solar system and its history are far more complicated than scientists had ever imagined, proving yet again that things seem simple when you do not know much about them but get more complicated the more you learn.

Because of the Voyager missions, our view of the solar system changed dramatically in several ways. For one thing, our previous view had been that there were just two kinds of planets: the rocky terrestrial ones like our own and the gas giants such as Jupiter. Now we know that there is at least a third entirely different variety, the ice planets, such as some of the satellites of the outer planets. For another, the Voyagers revealed that even small bodies far from the Sun have had complex histories and may even today harbor vigorous activities of varying kinds, a far cry from the somnolent state that was widely accepted before—a view that may have been colored by the history and present condition of our own Moon. Another surprising finding was the pervasive occurrence of impact craters, even as far from the Sun as the satellites of Neptune. This was somewhat unexpected, as distances in these far reaches of the solar system are so vast that meandering small bodies should be far apart. It appears, however, that they are not, which raises the question of just how many such bodies exist out there.

Perhaps most important of all, the Voyager program showed clearly how interplanetary spacecraft can provide information that could be obtained only after a very long time, or at vast expense, from terrestrial observations or even those from observatories in Earth orbit—if they could be achieved at all. The two probes arguably provided the greatest advances in all history of our knowledge of the solar system.

All in all, the two Voyagers were the most successful space probes ever launched. They showed in a most concrete manner the rewards provided by reliability, proper planning, and superb performance of the terrestrial controllers during a mission. Nothing like them has been seen before or since.

PLUTO

One of the things that the Voyager probes did not do was to visit Pluto, for that possibility faded when the Grand Tour mission was canceled. At the time this seemed a relatively modest loss, as the planet generally was considered to be a small, frozen world where little happened—or had ever happened—and of little interest except for its vast and unusual orbit. However, that view would change as ground-based observations over the years revealed more and more fascinating details about the body, which is evidently not as uninteresting as astronomers once thought.

As we have seen, soon after its discovery astronomers realized that Pluto appeared to be too small and thus too low in mass to cause the slight deviations in the orbits of Uranus and Neptune that, presumably, led to its discovery. Estimates of that mass were no more than educated guesses. One way of making those estimates more realistic was to measure the planet's diameter, but this was a daunting task with terrestrial telescopes. Perhaps the best effort was that of Gerard P. Kuiper, who used the 200-inch telescope to derive a value of a little more than 0.2 of a second of arc.[24]

Over the decades estimates of the planet's mass grew smaller and smaller and there were ingenious (perhaps the word *desperate* might apply) suggestions to explain the situation. One was that the surface of Pluto was very smooth, so that it reflected sunlight from only a small spot on its surface, much like a garden "gazing globe." Depending on just how smooth that surface was, the planet's true diameter and thus its mass might be much larger than the measured value.[25] This was a faint hope and indeed turned out to be a vain one.

Pluto had another curious property as well. In 1954 and 1955 Merle F. Walker and Robert H. Hardie found that the planet's brightness varied regularly over a period of a little more than six days. This result suggested a planet with a spotted or variegated surface that rotated once on its axis in that time. They also found that the brightness change is a little more than a tenth of a magnitude, about that exhibited by Mars (later observations would increase that variation). Here was a tantalizing hint that there was much structure on Pluto's surface, if only we could see it.[26]

However, perhaps the most exciting and important discovery about Pluto occurred in 1978. James W. Christy and Robert S. Harrington were examining images of Pluto taken to refine the planet's orbit, when they noticed that Pluto seemed elongated. Looking at photographs taken years earlier showed that the effect was real and ruled out possibilities such as a faint background star or a plate defect. The only possible conclusion was that Pluto had a satellite!—indeed, a satellite with an orbital period of just a little over six days, the same as that of the planet's light variations.[27]

Further observations confirmed the discovery, and revealed that this is indeed an unusual system. In fact, astronomers' ideas about Pluto underwent a revolution. The satellite, dubbed Charon by its discoverers (after the ferryman who took dead souls over the River Styx into Pluto's dominion of Hades), orbited a mere 10,000 miles or so from its primary. More important, the mass of Pluto itself could now be estimated with some confidence, and it came out to be about one-fifth of 1 percent of that of Earth, while of course Charon's was less. This meant that even the combined system could not have been responsible for the observed perturbations in the orbits of Uranus and Neptune.

Until this discovery, our own Moon had enjoyed the distinction of being the most massive satellite in the solar system compared to the planet it revolved around (its mass is a little more that 1 percent of Earth's), but Charon took the palm, as its mass was estimated at 5 to 10 percent of Pluto's. Thus, there was a second "double planet" added to the Sun's family.

Another result of Charon's discovery was that Pluto's density could be estimated more accurately now that its mass was known with some precision. The value turns out to be about that of water (or water ice) or somewhat lower. Thus, the planet cannot contain a high percentage of metallic or rocky materials and must consist mostly of ices such as water, frozen methane and ammonia, and the like. (Because Pluto's mass is so small it probably long ago lost almost all of its helium and molecular hydrogen.)

Charon performs one orbit around Pluto in the same period as the planet makes one rotation on its axis. Thus, both bodies always present the same faces to each other—only from half of Pluto's surface can Charon ever be seen, and only from half of the satellite's surface can the planet be viewed. Moreover, when seen from either body the other is always in the same place in the sky, though the Sun and stars wheel around the sky every six-plus days. As far as we know, this situation is unique in the solar system.[28]

But there were even more surprises in store concerning Pluto. As the planet is so faint in our sky, decades passed after its discovery before observers obtained any decent spectra of that body. The wait was a long one because many of the possible atmospheric gases absorb most strongly in the infrared, and really sensitive detectors for that portion of the spectrum were developed only after World War II.

Definite progress came in 1976, when Dale P. Cruikshank, Carl B. Pilcher, and David Morrison reported evidence for absorption features due to methane, which were tentatively interpreted as evidence for methane frost.[29] But where there was methane frost, could there also be methane gas above that solid? This possibility was intriguing, because at the time Pluto was nearing the closest point in its orbit of the Sun. Early in 1979 the planet would pass inside the orbit of Neptune, there to remain until 1999 (and thus making Neptune the most distant known planet during that interval). Near perihelion, sunlight would be stronger and might turn into gases a number of substances that ordinarily would lie frozen on the planet's surface. Methane was one candidate that had the correct physical properties. Follow-up observations by other observers indicated the possibility of both gaseous and solid methane and suggested that other substances might be involved as well.[30]

As planetary astronomers have learned more about Pluto (and its satellite), the planet has become much more interesting. The lost opportunities to visit it loom ever larger as the years pass. Even a flyby probe might answer many questions about that body and its history, questions that became all the more intriguing when Voyager 2 showed that even small solid bodies in the outer solar system have had complex histories and can show activity even to this day. However, there is at present no funded mission to that distant planet. This situation is additionally frustrating because Pluto may be the only planet with an atmosphere that regularly comes and goes (comets, we might point out, could be considered miniature Plutos in that respect). But because Pluto is now heading out from the Sun, any space probe not launched in the relatively near future may find a body with its atmosphere lying frozen on the ground.

CLOSER TO HOME

As regards the inner planets, the 1980s brought a mix of successes and failures. Rewarding results came in from projects begun in the 1970s; some new Soviet programs drew blanks; and it became possible to launch planetary probes from the Space Shuttle.

THE VENUS SURFACE AND ATMOSPHERE

The United States had dispatched a pair of probes to Venus in 1978. As we have seen, Pioneer Venus 2 successfully deposited no less than four entry probes at widely separated locations on the planet, one of which survived for over an hour on the surface. Its partner, Pioneer Venus 1, was an entirely different sort of vehicle. It orbited the planet and used an on-board radar system to map surface features with a resolution that detected features as small as 50 miles across.

As Venus is entirely cloud covered, telescopic observations had never revealed any surface features, but, as we have seen, beginning in the early 1960s, terrestrial radar studies provided increasing evidence that the planet's surface was diverse and intriguing. Landing probes could provide surface data other than the small-scale structure of tiny regions surrounding their impact sites, and it was clear that radar observations from low orbit were needed to study the planet as a whole. Pioneer Venus 1 was the first step in that direction.[31]

The next steps were taken by the Soviets. Beginning late in 1983, the orbiting Venera 15 and 16 (the first purely orbital missions to the planet undertaken by the U.S.S.R.) began radar investigations of large areas of the surface of Venus with a resolution as good as a mile or so, revealing complex structures, many resembling nothing known on Earth. The most advanced radar mission to date has been the American Magellan, a Venus orbiter launched by the Space Shuttle *Atlantis* in 1989 and dedicated solely to such studies. It mapped almost the entire surface of the planet with resolution down to a few hundred feet.

These radar studies revealed a different sort of planet. There are impact craters but relatively few of them, indicating that the surface of Venus is young in geological terms. As might be expected, there are no small impact craters due to shielding by the dense atmosphere.

On the other hand, although most of Venus appears to consist of rolling lowlands, there are enormous mountains, vast plateaus, chasms, faults, and features the nature and origin of which can only be guessed at. There is little evidence of plate tectonics similar to that found on Earth but plenty for extensive volcanic activity such as lava flows and perhaps—as indicated by a variety of evidence—even active volcanoes.

Well before the Magellan mission and shortly after Venera 15 and 16, our neighbor planet was visited by a pair of most unusual Soviet probes, Vega 1 and 2. These were primarily intended to encounter and study Halley's comet but were first targeted for the vicinity of Venus to make use of gravity assist. Taking advantage of this opportunity, in June, 1985, each released an entry probe that landed on the surface and performed analyses of soil samples. In addition, each lander released an instrumented, helium-filled balloon of French origin. These novel payloads floated for days in the atmosphere, radioing back to Earth data on cloud and atmospheric properties and wind speeds. These complex, imaginative, and novel missions worked as planned, and were a high point of Soviet planetary exploration.

The visits of the Vegas and Magellan were farewells in a way. Interest in Venus subsided and no other probes to the planet have been launched since then.[32]

FAILURES WITH MARS

After the Viking missions in 1975 and 1976, general interest in Mars tailed off dramatically. For two decades there were a mere three missions to the red planet. The Soviets launched Phobos 1 and 2 in 1988 to study the Martian moon of the same name, but both failed, insuring that the Soviet Union would never have a successful Mars probe. For its part, the

United States launched the Mars Observer in 1992, but radio contact with the probe was lost just before the spacecraft was to have entered orbit around the planet. The failure was particularly disappointing to younger planetary scientists, who had been brought up during the period of the Voyagers' continuous string of successes and so were not prepared for the debacle. On the other hand, older researchers, who remembered all too well the many probe failures during the early days of the Space Age, tended to react with resignation and renewed determination.

HALLEY'S COMET

The passage of Halley's comet near the Sun during 1985 and 1986 had been anticipated for generations. At the time of the 1910 apparition the airplane had been a mere toy, but this time around it would be possible to fly to the comet itself and study that body from close up. Because of this revolutionary new capability, scientists and the general public alike confidently looked forward to exciting new revelations about this comet, at the least, and possibly about comets in general. A fleet of spacecraft did indeed examine this famous visitor, but conspicuously absent was a probe from the United States, the leader in deep space exploration in the 1960s and 1970s.

This omission was not because of lack of planning, for the United States began serious study of possible cometary missions in the 1970s. At first these were conceived of as simple flybys, but by the middle of that decade there were ambitious plans not only to visit Halley's comet but also to rendezvous with that body and to "fly in formation" with it for months, in the hope of gaining the maximum of scientific results.

This was a daunting challenge, for Halley orbits the Sun in the opposite direction from Earth and all the other planets. As a result, any flyby must occur at a very high velocity, and this was the reason that American scientists decided results in the case would be minimal. It also meant that there was no available booster rocket that could put a sufficiently heavy payload in the needed trajectory with enough onboard rocket propellants to achieve a rendezvous (a Saturn V could have done the job, but no more of them were available). Alternative and exotic space propulsion methods such as a "solar sail" (using the pressure of sunlight) and an "ion drive" (shooting individual charged particles out of a rocket's nozzle) were proposed. While enticing—the solar sail, for example, would be visible to the unaided eye for months after launch—these alternatives were untried, and developing them would be very expensive. In the stringent financial atmosphere of the times, the project died in 1979.

Space scientists in the United States then fell back on a flyby mission but were foiled by the fact that they had earlier declared such a probe likely to be of little use. In this case, best was the enemy of better, and the result was that the United States had no Halley probe at all. The fast flyby missions, all of which succeeded, showed that good science could indeed be done with such spacecraft.

In March, 1986, as Halley retreated from the Sun, an international armada of spacecraft intercepted it. Two were launched by Japan (they passed the farthest from the comet's nucleus, and were perhaps the most conservative and best designed to survive the encounter), two were from the Soviet Union (the Vegas mentioned above), and one by the European Space Agency. The latter was the most sophisticated probe of all, came the closest to the nucleus of the comet, and managed to take pictures of the dark gas- and dust-spewing body that was Halley.

The comet's nucleus was revealed as an irregular, potato- shaped solid body covered with a very dark crust. In a few places this outer shell was missing, exposing much brighter material underneath. From these locations arose energetic streams of gas and dust released from the solid nucleus by solar heating. Thus for this comet, at least, Fred L. Whipple's "dirty snowball" theory was proven correct in all particulars.[33]

The international Halley armada marked in an emphatic manner the end of the monopoly of deep space probes previously enjoyed by the United States and the Soviet Union, for Japan and Europe now had the capability of building their own booster rockets.[34] Surprisingly, despite its failure to participate in the Halley fleet, the United States was the first to send a probe to a comet. In 1978 the International Sun-Earth Explorer 3 was launched and placed in an orbit about a million miles from Earth. Much later, it was realized that there was the possibility that, with its onboard propulsion and with the aid of gravity assist, it could pass through the tail of comet Giacobini-Zinner. After a complex flight path that involved no less than five close approaches to the Moon, the probe encountered the comet on September 11, 1985.[35] It was a first, but a poor second to encountering Halley.

GALILEO

The end of the Cold War rivalry, stringent financial times for the entire world, and the failure to find any evidence of present or past life anywhere in the solar system except on Earth caused public interest and governmental support for deep space probes to wane. Since the era of the Halley armada, such missions have been few, and we have already mentioned the abortive Phobos and Mars Observer spacecraft. One important effort involved an American mission to Jupiter.

The U.S. Galileo mission to Jupiter first took form in the 1970s. There are two components to the spacecraft: an entry probe intended to explore the planet's upper atmosphere directly and an orbiting vehicle to make long-term studies of the planet as well as to investigate its larger satellites, particularly the volcanically active Io.[36]

Galileo was planned to be launched out of Earth orbit from a Space Shuttle. However, following the Challenger disaster in 1986, there was a long and unavoidable delay. Sometime and somehow during the delay or the actual launch process, something happened to the "high-gain" directional antenna, and as a result that umbrella-like structure never opened fully after the payload entered space on October 18, 1989. There was a "low-gain" antenna available and in good shape, but it could transmit data only at a much slower rate. Information, and in particular images, could still be transmitted to Earth, but very much more slowly than planned.

Galileo was originally meant to be boosted into a direct orbit to Jupiter by a hydrogen-fueled Centaur stage carried in the shuttle's cargo bay. When this combination was deemed to be too dangerous to use, a solid-fueled rocket stage of lesser performance was substituted. As a result, the probe had to follow a complex and time-consuming trajectory that included close flybys of Earth and Venus to gain gravitational assists. Although compromised by its antenna problem, Galileo has already scored some firsts. It imaged the asteroids Gaspra in late 1991 and Ida in August, 1993, and showed both bodies to be irregular in shape and pockmarked with impact craters, as expected. What was unexpected, however, was that the latter asteroid has a tiny satellite only about a mile across.

To finish up this saga, the entry probe from Galileo successfully entered the atmosphere of Jupiter on December 7, 1995. Unfortunately, the capsule landed in one of the relatively rare, clear areas of downwelling atmosphere (the blue areas long known from terrestrial observations). Perhaps the most important result was that strong atmospheric motions persisted far below the level of the cloud tops, which confirmed what was by then a generally accepted opinion—that the giant planet's atmospheric activity is largely driven by internal heat. Meanwhile, the Galileo's "bus" portion went into orbit around the planet. Data from the orbiter, in particular close-up images of the planet and its large satellites, have been beamed to Earth at a very slow rate due to the failure of the high-gain antenna. With luck, this information should continue to dribble in for years to come.

CLEMENTINE

Another venture was Clementine, a joint venture of NASA, the U.S. Department of Defense, and private industry. This was an innovative project to use a "leftover" Titan missile from the Cold War with "off the shelf" equipment to fly by an asteroid, pausing for a while to orbit the Moon. The primary instruments were four cameras that had different fields of view and worked at different wavelengths, ranging from the ultraviolet to the infrared. Clementine was launched early in 1994 and orbited the Moon for several months, for the first time gathering good information about the polar regions of the Moon. Unfortunately, an error in its software used up all its propellants and prevented any asteroid mission. However, this probe did demonstrate that modern technology can enable deep space probes to be economical as well as productive.[37] In addition, as described in the next chapter, Clementine data could provide a major surprise several years after it was obtained.

THE HUBBLE SPACE TELESCOPE

The inception of the idea of a large telescope in orbit developed early among NASA's scientists and administrators. Such an instrument, many believed, would escape the limitations of Earth-based observatories and would offer clear images and new information about the Moon and future planetary mission targets, such as Mars and Venus, not to mention about the rest of the universe. Fred L. Whipple, then director of the Smithsonian Institution's Astrophysical Observatory in Cambridge, Massachusetts, suggested in congressional hearings held in 1959 that the American space program would within ten years result in "telescopes in space, to observe the solar system in particular as well as the stellar universe in general, [and would] have brought in a wealth of new facts that may well revolutionize our concepts of the cosmos."[38]

NASA began to fund new and expanded programs in the planetary sciences, including the construction of Earth-based telescopes and the design of orbital telescopes, as important adjuncts of space flight programs.

Substantial studies for the design of an orbiting large telescope began during the early 1970s, but budget constraints prevented construction.[39] Finally, in 1978, the administration approved funding for what would become the Hubble telescope, named for Edwin Hubble, an astronomer with the Palomar Observatory who specialized in studies of distant galaxies. The Hubble Space Telescope was designed primarily for stellar, galactic, and extragalactic astronomy. Planetary studies had only a small share

TABLE 12.1

NASA Physics and Astronomy Program Funding, 1978–1993
(millions of dollars)

FY 1978	1979	1980	1981	1982	1983	1984	1985
$233.1	281.8	335.6	320.0	318.2	480.8	558.6	654.7
1986	1987	1988	1989	1990	1991	1992	1993
$554.6	528.5	596.2	712.1	847.1	954.9	1,019.9	1,025.3

Note: Total funding from 1958 to 1977 was $2,196.3 million, or an average of approximately $105 million per year.

of its design and intended purposes, but the initiation of the Hubble project resulted in sharp increases in program funding for NASA physics and astronomy programs (see table 12.1), with most of the increases directed to the Hubble Space Telescope.

In 1981, following a recommendation by the National Academy of Sciences, NASA established the Space Telescope Science Institute. Located on the campus of Johns Hopkins University, the institute was managed by a consortium of universities entitled the Association of Universities for Research in Astronomy, Inc., and funded by NASA with oversight by the Goddard Space Flight Center in Greenbelt, Maryland. Later, NASA entered into an agreement with the European Space Agency, giving European astronomers access to the Hubble Space Telescope. Goddard subsequently managed the construction of the Hubble Space Telescope, which was completed and placed in orbit by the Space Shuttle *Discovery* during a mission launched on April 24, 1990.[40]

Unfortunately, after the successful placement of the Hubble telescope in Earth orbit, it became obvious that there were serious flaws in the optics and other instruments comprising the telescope. Most serious was the fact that the large primary mirror had been precisely ground and polished to the wrong shape! The wide-field planetary camera revealed a number of problems. In addition, thermal distortions of the solar panels and their supporting structures due to passages into and out of Earth's shadow produced oscillations that caused serious problems in pointing the HST and keeping it pointed in a stable manner. A gyroscope failed in November, 1992, leaving three active gyros to control the Hubble Space Telescope (although astronomers concluded that the disability did not impair performance). In mid-February, 1993, one of the three Fine Guidance Sensors showed signs of serious wear and was turned off. A Solar Array Deploy Electronics system also failed, and this and other similar problems limited the electrical energy available to operate the satellite. Yet, despite these handicaps, a status report issued by the Division for Planetary Sciences of the American Astronomical Society concluded that HST had "continued to perform steadily." The society itself noted that the number of papers on HST results "has steadily ramped up to a rate of about 70 new articles per year in refereed journals, and at least as many more in conference proceedings."[41]

NASA, under tremendous public surveillance and media scrutiny, immediately began planning for corrections to HST. By December, 1993, NASA was ready for a Hubble "rescue" mission that would remedy the defects in primary mirror, the wide-field planetary camera, the solar power panels, and other items. A Corrective Optics Space Telescope Replace (COSTAR) package had been developed to provide corrective optics for the faint object spectrograph, the Goddard high resolution spectrograph, and the faint object camera. The repair mission aboard the Shuttle *Endeavor* flew on December 2, 1993, and returned on December 13 after a difficult but highly successful mission.[42]

While HST was primarily intended to study objects far beyond the Sun's family, it turned out that phenomena in the solar system, many of them completely unexpected, provided many of its most spectacular results. The Astronomical Society's Division for Planetary Studies and the Space Telescope Science Institute were able to report significant discoveries by Hubble teams. Astronomers from the United States and Europe competed for time on the HST by submitting proposals to the institute's Science Program Selection Office, which established guidelines and managed the peer review of proposals. Consistent with the modern "team science" approach to problems, proposals usually come from project teams with widely distributed members and facilities. For example, a successful planetary study of the asteroid Vesta included team members from Georgia Southern University (Ben Zellner), the Space Telescope Science Institute in Baltimore (Alex Storrs), the Computer Sciences Corporation in Bethesda (Ed Wells), the European Southern Observatory in Garching bei München, Germany (Rudi Albrecht), and Olivier Hainaut with the European Southern Observatory in Chile.

In November and December, 1994, Vesta team members used Hubble's wide-field and planetary camera 2 (which can resolve objects ten times more clearly than can ground-based telescopes) and the faint object camera to observe Vesta at distances of 146 and 156 million miles from Earth. Vesta, which "has survived essentially intact since the formation of the planets," revealed a "surprisingly diverse world with an exposed mantle, ancient lava flows and impact basins." The findings "contradicted conventional ideas that asteroids essentially are cold, rocky fragments left behind from the early days of planetary formation." The study, Robert Zellner reported, "provides a record of the long and complex evolution of our solar system."[43]

Another astronomical team, headed by Philip James, professor of physics and astronomy at the University of Toledo, has focused on Mars. The Hubble has made possible long-term observation. "Mars," James reports, "is a very, very dynamic planet, characterized by a very active changing weather system." And an associate at the University of Colorado in Boulder, Steve Lee, commented, "Mars does not behave as we thought." The climate of Mars has distinctly changed since the visits by Mariner and Viking explorers in the 1960s and 1970s. The atmosphere is clearer, cooler, and less dusty. "Though Hubble has observed Mars only for four years, the observations are equivalent to 15 years of ground-based observing because Hubble can follow seasonal changes through most of Mars' orbit."[44] The red planet, it is becoming clearer and clearer, is not like our Moon at all.

In an entirely unrelated and unexpected development, Hubble was able to assist in the observation of one of the rarest and most unusual celestial phenomena of the modern era.

JUPITER ASSAILED

On March 25, 1993, David Levy and Carolyn and Eugene Shoemaker discovered a curious, *rectangular* looking feature on a photograph taken of the sky near Jupiter. Images made with better resolution showed more than a dozen separate small cometary objects strung out like beads on a wire. Further observations and some calculations showed that Comet Shoemaker-Levy 9, as it was dubbed, had passed close to Jupiter on July 7, 1992, at which time the giant planet's strong tidal forces disrupted a nucleus that evidently was only weakly held together.

At discovery, the new comet was in an orbit that would take it some 30 million miles from Jupiter, to return in July of 1994 on a collision path with the planet. Would there be spectacular fireballs, or would the fragments simply be swallowed up by the giant planet? Would there be any long-term effects on Jupiter and, if so, what would they be? No one was certain of what would happen. The situation was complicated by the fact that all of the collisions would take place just behind the limb of Jupiter as seen from Earth, though the giant planet's rapid rotation would bring the sites into view in a short time. Remembering all too well the dismal shows put on by Comets Kohoutek and Halley, planetary astronomers were reserved in their public statements.

Fortunately, observers had more than a year to plan their strategies. Ground-based telescopes, instruments flown in high altitude jet planes, Earth satellites, and deep space probes were all pressed into the fray. Astronomers were well prepared, and this time they were not disappointed. The collisions were spectacular. Some of the resultant fireballs were as large as Earth, and could be seen rising above Jupiter's limb. When the collision sites came into view they were marked by dark spots caused by material dredged up from deeper in the planet's atmosphere. Some of the spots were the most obvious features ever seen on Jupiter, and were seen by thousands of observers even in very small telescopes. Over time Jupiter's winds gradually smeared them out in latitude, they gradually faded, and it appears that the planet has suffered no permanent damage.[45]

Had Shoemaker-Levy 9 collided with Earth, however, the results would have been catastrophic, possibly wiping out all life on our planet. That sort of possibility had long been recognized, but the remarkable images of huge fireballs rising above Jupiter made the peril seem much greater and certainly more immediate. The result was a welcome infusion of money for research on methods of finding such dangerous objects (asteroids as well as comets) long before they might collide with our planet, as well as research on means of avoiding the impacts (such as changing a body's orbit, for example). Thus, once again, planetary astronomy came to be seen as a serious and practical matter.

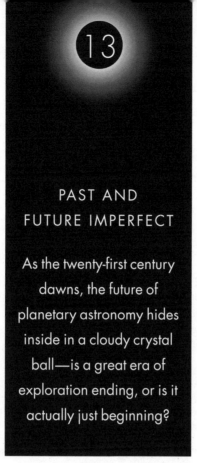

13

PAST AND
FUTURE IMPERFECT

As the twenty-first century
dawns, the future of
planetary astronomy hides
inside in a cloudy crystal
ball—is a great era of
exploration ending, or is it
actually just beginning?

With at least four thousand years of written history behind it, planetary astronomy has a legitimate claim to being by far the oldest science.[1] That long history has featured bursts of substantial and often spectacular advances, interposed with extended intervals when knowledge of the solar system advanced only slowly and painfully, stagnated, or even regressed. The story of planetary astronomy is by no mean an uninterrupted record of triumph. Yet, for all its myriad failures and blind alleys, startling successes and brilliant insights, planetary astronomy has always had one constant—one great, unfailing characteristic: it has enjoyed widespread public interest. Financial support may wax and wane, but the magic and mysteries of the night sky have retained a powerful grip on the public imagination, whether for their force as portents, their applications for navigation, or their status as the next great frontier to conquer.

What of the present? If we become fully convinced that Earth is the only body in the solar system that supports life, will interest in the subject decline? Or will the chances of finding that there might earlier have been life on Venus and perhaps ancient and even current life on Mars and Jupiter's ice-clad satellite Europa, sustain public interest and involvement in planetary studies and exploration? Will our efforts in planetary astronomy be spurred by the prospect of finding the precursors to life in comets and objects in the outer solar system? Will the possibility that our very lives may depend on learning all we can about the solar system—so that we could avoid a calamitous collision with a comet such as that of Comet Shoemaker-Levy 9 with Jupiter in 1994—stimulate a broad reawakening of interest in planetary astronomy?

THE PAST AS PROLOGUE

Whatever the future holds in store, the record of the past offers some perspectives as regards the on again, off again development of planetary astronomy over the millennia.

In the beginning, phenomena such as night and day, the cycle of the Moon's phases, and the annual march of the constellations were the chief contents of the human bank of knowledge about what happened in the sky. Superstition and myth, undoubtedly mingled with fear and awe, abounded. But human memory is imperfect; oral tradition is a poor medium for transmitting precise knowledge of events. The first substantial advances in astronomy came with the invention of methods for recording events in a more or less permanent way—cuts on a stick, paintings on a skin, alignments of natural features or stones erected for the purpose, to mention just a few possibilities. Such indicators served a common and vital purpose, for they could be conveyed from teacher to student.

With the invention of writing, knowledge took a leap forward. Now—besides records of what had happened—opinions, possible explanations, and methods of observational and theoretical procedures could also be conveyed in detail. The Sumerians left us the oldest surviving records of planetary astronomy. In the thousands of years after the flourishing of Ur and other Sumerian city states, there was slow but substantial progress in astronomical observation. Scholars in many places were able to use observations made long before their time to establish and chart many long-period regularities in the motions of celestial bodies.

Significant advances in planetary astronomy and knowledge as a whole came in the classical era, beginning with the Greeks. That era was characterized by theorizing on all possible topics on a scale never seen before or since. (To give one example, Parmenides taught that all change is illusory, while Heraclitus claimed that everything is change. Logically, that stakes out the range of all possible views on the subject.) The views of Greek philosophers such as Aristotle have often been derided as theoretical dreaming and held up as examples of contempt for practicality, experiment, and observation. Ironically, Aristotle himself is considered by many to be the first true natural scientist, and we should remember that all that survives of his teaching are probably his students' class notes.

There was a practical side, however. The descendants of the Greeks who ruled the Hellenistic kingdoms—the successors of Alexander of Macedon, who conquered a good part of the developed world—raised to new heights fields as widely diverse as warfare, architecture, and technology in general, and Hellenistic scholars made dramatic advances in planetary astronomy, culminating in the work of Ptolemy. His theoretical explanations predicted planetary motions to the precision of then current observations, which were restricted to the unaided eye and simple instruments.

Next came the Romans, universally deemed a hardheaded and practical folk. They built superb roads, aqueducts, and basilicas, many of which still stand, in whole or part, and some of them are in use even today. Yet the Romans made few advances in science. Glass, for example, was cheap and common in the later Roman Empire, and the magnifying properties of clear glass beads and globes full of water were well known. Why did not someone, somewhere, at some time in the thousand-year history of the empire, invent something as useful to war, trade, and surveying as the refracting telescope? Why classical Mediterranean civilization failed to do more in the area of science is a fascinating puzzle.

In China there were significant technological advances, but the Chinese did not try to devise any detailed explanation of planetary motions. In the Islamic lands scholars observed the sky and attempted to make improvements on the Ptolemaic system, but their attention was largely devoted to celestial activity as portents; there were few substantial observational or theoretical advances.

In Western Europe, the centuries following Roman withdrawal were troubled times. Barbarian invasions, Islamic assaults, Viking raids, and a fragmented feudal society hardly provided the best climate for scientific research. Knowledge did grow and spread during the Middle Ages—any age that can produce vast, magnificent cathedrals that still stand can hardly be viewed as primitive—yet the process was slow, in part because much of that knowledge (such as how to build a cathedral) was looked upon as "trade secrets." But the medieval era did see a number of developments that eventually affected astronomy. For example, mechanical clocks appeared. Arabic numerals replaced the Roman variety, an enormous gain; the very thought of calculating a planet's orbit using Roman numerals boggles the mind.

Tycho Brahe began the modern era of observational astronomy, enormously improving the precision of astronomical observations, despite having no real boost from a technological breakthrough. His instruments were large and his observations systematic, but a Roman could have done the same. Copernicus and Kepler began the modern area of theoretical astronomy, again working without any great advance as a platform, for in their work they used no mathematics beyond that with which a clever Greek, such as Euclid, would have been familiar. Brahe, Copernicus, and Kepler were unlikely revolutionaries, being rooted in medieval backgrounds and immersed in a Renaissance culture that in large part looked back to the ideals of classical times.

The next advances in planetary astronomy were very different. Invention of the telescope and its astronomical use by Galileo Galilei were a true observational milestone. In short order he made most of the discoveries that could possibly be made with the primitive refractors of the time. Newton made a similar theoretical breakthrough, employing revolutionary (though cumbersome) new mathematics. Thereafter, however, progress in astronomy lagged. Early telescopes improved only slowly, and on the theoretical side, calculating orbits of bodies in the solar system becomes immensely complicated as soon as one attempts to achieve a precision greater than Kepler did.

REVOLUTION—AND STAGNATION

By the beginning of the nineteenth century planetary astronomy could be distinguished from the stellar variety (the mysterious nebulae received relatively little attention), but both fields had in large part settled down to an almost routine state. Observers made long series of ever more precise positions of heavenly bodies on the celestial sphere, while theoreticians used increasingly complicated calculations—still done with pen or pencil—to predict the future positions of those bodies with ever greater precision. On the whole, astronomy seemed doomed to a future limited to adding more numbers behind the decimal point. The work had severely practical aims, such as improved navigation, geodetic studies, and better timekeeping. Stars, as far as anyone knew, would always remain mere points of light, and we could never glimpse more than a few features even on the planets through Earth's unsteady atmosphere.

This dreary prospect gave way to a new era with the invention of photography and spectroscopy, though both took time to make their full impact on astronomy. Early photographic emulsions were excruciatingly "slow," and it took generations of development before they were efficient enough for astronomical use. Spectroscopy produced some exciting results almost from the start, but measuring and drawing features seen in faint, flickering spectra was a long, laborious, and uncertain business at best. Only when it was possible to photograph spectra with the spectrograph did the combined technique become one of the most powerful weapons in the arsenal of astronomers.

The rate of advance of observational astronomy in the two centuries following Newton hinged upon improvements in instruments, notably telescopes and devices for measuring angles precisely, and the discovery and application of novel techniques such as photography and spectroscopy. As far as astronomical theory went, developments depended on new and improved methods based on the concepts that Newton had pioneered, though there were stirrings in the wind of something different ahead.

At the opening of the twentieth century planetary research was still a respectable field of study, but it soon declined into several decades of relative somnolence—even derision. Part of the reason lies in the fact that positive results were so few. To be sure, planetary astronomers did achieve substantial results on planetary temperatures from observations in the infrared, polarization studies, brightness measurements at various wavelengths, and the like, but these failed to throw much light on the broader (and more interesting) issues such whether there is life on Mars, what lies beneath the clouds of Venus, or what the Great Red Spot is.

By contrast, stellar, galactic, and extragalactic astronomy experienced explosive growth in the first half of the twentieth century, scoring triumph after spectacular triumph. The more distant reaches of the universe, beyond the jaded perimeters of the solar system, attracted considerable scientific and public interest. Stars are relatively simple objects compared to planets. Most of them are made primarily of atoms or nuclei of atoms, and can usually be assumed to be composed of "perfect gases"—that is, the simplest and most easily treated kind of vapor. Planets, on the other hand, contain liquids and solids, which are much more difficult to deal with. As an example, there were reasonably accurate estimates of the temperature at the center of the Sun in the nineteenth century, at a time when that at the center of Jupiter—or Earth, for that matter—was anyone's guess. Another problem is that planetary atmospheres, in general, are more complex than those of stars. Opaque clouds are common on planets, and a substantial proportion of their atmospheres are composed of molecules containing several atoms, complicating interpretation problems. To illustrate the point, the spectral features of water vapor are immensely more intricate than those of atomic hydrogen, for instance. As a result, the physics developed during the twentieth century produced far fewer results for planetary than for stellar astronomy.

However, the factors noted cannot explain fully the depressed state of planetary studies from the 1920s through the 1950s. Other fields have gone through long periods of little substantial advance and still held the high regard of scientists. Einstein's general theory of relativity remained in high repute among physicists and mathematicians for decades despite relatively little progress in the field. Something other than the lack of significant new discoveries in planetary astronomy is needed to account for the air of disdain in which some astronomers held planetary research during this peculiar time. That "other" may have been the work of Percival Lowell and Orson Welles. Speculation about canals on Mars and a Martian invasion of Earth provided excitement but also put planetary research in a ludicrous, crackpot light.

It is only fair to note that not all historians of planetary astronomy believe that the field was essentially moribund in the interwar era. For example, Ronald E. Doel, who is completing work on a study of planetary astronomy for the period, has assembled an impressive list of those who worked in the field between 1920 and 1960.[2] Doel, however, includes in his list those researchers who worked in the area of celestial mechanics. Such workers generally demanded little or no telescope time, seldom time on big telescopes especially, and they required little equipment beyond pencils and paper. Few astrophysically trained astronomers (one notable exception being Fred L. Whipple) devoted their energies to planetary research between 1920 and 1960.

All the same this quiet, somewhat notorious period in the recent history of planetary astronomy gave way to one of the most exciting and productive seasons in the field's four-thousand-year history.

TAKING OFF

The reasons for the rapid development of solar system research after 1950 are clear. After World War II, studies of the solar system changed from a relative backwater to a matter of immediate practical concern, for it had become clear to many that the direct exploration of the Moon and planets was now near at hand. Fueled by the mounting Cold War tensions, funding for planetary studies became, by past standards, prodigious. Money for once was not a problem. Initially the U.S. Army, Navy, and Air Force (soon to be unified in the Department of Defense) paid the bills.

Within a few years solar system research and planetary astronomy changed dramatically from a small, low key, subsidiary area of astronomy to become a major field of great practical importance. As a result of the recent decades of obscurity, there were relatively few planetary astronomers at work or being trained by American universities. There was much to be done but few could do it; there were few departments of astronomy offering graduate degrees, and within those departments only a handful of researchers were working in celestial mechanics and other planetary fields. With the advent of space probes the United States needed to produce a great number of space scientists in a relatively short time. Most of them would have to come from outside the ranks of professional astronomers.

Near the end of World War II the American military and the old National Advisory Committee for Aeronautics (NACA) began experimenting with hypersonic flight and high-altitude sounding rockets. Many scientists and engineers, including planetary scientists such as Fred Whipple, began a new era of research under the auspices of army, navy, and air force contracts and grants. The military had found astronomers particularly useful during the war because of their knowledge of celestial mechanics (useful in ballistics), optics, navigation, infrared spectroscopy, radar, and related fields. While many younger space scientists indicate surprise at this, most researchers during World War II and in the years immediately following the war were perfectly content if not delighted to receive funding from the military. Space and astronomical studies for a time came under the bailiwick of national defense.

Inspired in part by the results being achieved in space studies under military auspices, but truly galvanized by the Soviet success in launching Sputnik, the first Earth satellite, in 1958 Congress created the National Aeronautics and Space Administration (NASA) and committed the United States to a developing space program that would include studies of, if not flight to, Earth's neighboring planets. As NASA was being created in Congress, President Dwight D. Eisenhower and congressional leaders decided that all space research should be conducted by a civilian agency, with the military services restricted to missions with direct military aspects (photographic and electronic reconnaissance, early warning of missile launches, secure strategic and tactical communications, and so forth). The inception of NASA resulted in an unparalleled mobilization not unlike that experienced in wartime.

The new space program brought engineers, cosmic-ray physicists, students of Earth's upper atmosphere, and solar astronomers (the Sun was a bright, obvious choice, and it was already known that its upheavals affected our planet directly) into an association with the field of planetary astronomy under the mantle of NASA. Astronomers with widely diverse specialties began working together on exciting new projects. Fred Whipple and other planetary astronomers were joined by Jesse L. Greenstein and others whose careers had largely concerned astrophysics. Teamed together, engineers and scientists rushed to launch sounding rockets, Earth satellites, and space probes. Early efforts often encountered failures and frustration, yet they produced results that could have been gained in no other way. Thus, rocket probes of planetary bodies became another tool in the planetary astronomer's kit.

A paradox of the time was that there was more money available for research, through NASA, than there were scientists to spend the money allocated by the Congress. That funding created the incentive and the academic infrastructure for producing, in time, the planetary astronomers, scientists, and engineers needed to achieve America's goals in space. For a field in which budgets had been minuscule, NASA provided a bonanza. The space program offered unparalleled opportunities for astronomers in particular and for space scientists in general. All too soon, there were more projected space missions than there was funding to support them.

When space probes became practical, the engineers who had to design them were astounded by how little we actually knew about the Moon and planets. Perhaps they were overly impressed by astronomy's long history and widespread reputation as the most exact of all the natural sciences. Given that astronomers had been studying the solar system telescopically since Galileo's time, and spectroscopically and by other means for almost a century, it came as quite a shock to learn that there were still no firm answers to such obvious and important questions as how rough the Moon's surface is or how dense was the atmosphere of Mars. Could astronomers settle question of whether the lunar surface was covered with a thick, quicksandlike dust or had a firm crust? Engineers needed to know in order to design landing vehicles.

Severe problems stood in the way of answering these questions. Besides the lack of planetary astronomers, there was a lack of telescopes. Large ones in the United States were few, and they were used overwhelmingly to study stars, nebulae, and galaxies. Instruments on which a substantial portion of observing time were devoted to the solar system were smaller. It proved impossible to provide all the needed answers in time, but there were just enough answers for the engineers to be able to make intelligent guesses about the rest.

Under NASA program emphasis, the tempo of discovery picked up. Ground-based observations increased with allocation of more time for planetary study at existing observatories and with construction of new observatories in Arizona, California, and Hawaii, some largely dedicated to planetary observation and funded by NASA. Experiments and probes carried by Mariner, Ranger, Lunar Orbiter, and Surveyor spacecraft, and eventually by the manned Apollo spacecraft, added immensely to knowledge of the planets.

The end of the Apollo program, and diversions caused by the Vietnam War and the rising costs of public welfare and assistance programs, began to diminish public interest in and congressional support for space studies and programs. The Space Shuttle, an Earth-orbital vehicle, reflected the growing concern for things of the Earth, rather than preoccupation with the heavens. Moreover, success itself may have contributed to declining interest in planetary studies: the landing vehicles from the two Voyager space probes found no trace of present or past life or even organic molecules on Mars.

It seems that much of the support for exploration of the solar system was and is based on the possibility of finding some sort of life on at least one other body circling the Sun, and on aspirations for human exploration of the planets, Mars in particular. With no signs of life found and finances tightening, support receded until by the close of the 1980s, planetary astronomy, though much more vital than it had ever been, once again faced hard times.

Unlike in the past, when progress in planetary studies seemed to await breakthroughs in technology (telescopes, radar, spectroscopy, rocket vehicles), now progress or lack of it seemed to relate more directly to costs and funding. The technology was there, but the financial wherewithal to use it was often lacking. Planetary astronomy had entered the age of "big science" and concomitantly high costs. The old world of the solitary planetary astronomer had been supplanted by the more complex, expensive—and usually more productive, we should mention—team science fostered by NASA.

SOLDIERING ON

Like the old soldier of song, planetary astronomy of course did not die. But the number of planetary missions did shrink dramatically after the close of the Viking program, as did financial support for those scientists working on space missions and for those observing from and calculating on Earth. In the 1980s the Pioneer and Voyager missions sustained at least a minimal level of effort in planetary astronomy, providing views of the outer solar system that revealed bodies in these distant regions to have had much more complicated histories than scientists had never imagined. Still, the excitement produced by these discoveries was as nothing compared to what might have been generated by finding life anywhere in the solar system beyond our own planet.

Planetary scientists were well aware of the falling off in support for their work, and by the early 1980s were much worried by that trend. Most members of the Division of Planetary Sciences were supported by "soft" money. That is, they depended on annual grants or contracts from NASA (the National Science Foundation and other agencies had effectively withdrawn), and NASA funding dwindled year by year. Few workers had secure and permanent positions as regular faculty members at universities, and most faced an uncertain future. The situation was especially acute because a substantial portion of funding went to relatively large projects such as the Viking missions to Mars and the Voyager explorations of the outer solar system.

By the mid-1990s, even if one was lucky enough to obtain a NASA grant or contract, often the amount of money was just enough to pay part of one's salary, perhaps support a graduate student, and buy a few pieces of equipment. To those who had been in the field long enough to remember the penurious 1930s, 1940s, and 1950s, this situation had a familiar feel. To researchers who entered the field in the 1960s and 1970s, the plunges in funding came as a real shock.

Funding is not all, however. A credo among planetary scientists that is sometimes spoken but seldom appears in print is that they need the excitement, encouragement, and opportunities provided by space probes, substantial research grants, and the like, in order to be attracted to and continue working in the field. But is it not also true that in the long run, it is the individual scientist who must generate the enthusiasm for a project? It is hard to imagine committed researchers basing the future of their research on what amounts to bribery—that their continuing to work in the field is conditional upon society munificently funding and loudly applauding their work.

At a recent Division of Planetary Sciences meeting I asked a planetary astronomer to describe the current situation of the field. She paused a moment and then replied, "There always seem to be plenty of bright-eyed newcomers around, but every year they have different faces." Responses from planetary astronomers and related scientists to my questions over a span of the last four years indicate that all are worried about the future. Tenured faculty members are not as concerned as young holders of temporary postdoctoral positions, but without exception everyone is troubled. With most workers relying on soft money provided by a single governmental agency (NASA), planetary astronomy has a very fragile financial base indeed.

The one saving grace in this predicament is that support from the general public remains strong. Space remains a frontier full of mystery. Anyone can walk outside and easily see planets in the night sky (though all too few do, and fewer yet recognize a planet), which certainly can not be said of atoms or galaxies. Planetary astronomy also enjoys the advantage that we *live* on a planet. After millennia of detailed study, there remain many things about Earth that we still do not know, but we might fill in some of these gaps from studies of other planets. The study of the solar system is a matter of personal interest and importance to us all.

PLANS

In the recent past one thing that has not been in short supply are plans for the future, both for planetary astronomy and for NASA. There have been a bewildering variety of such studies, usually paid for by an assortment of official bodies and almost always devised by a panel of distinguished workers in the field. In fact, it is common for the same people to show up on several different panels.

These plans and recommendations make fascinating reading, especially as regards their changes in emphasis over the years. It is fair to say that the recommendations generally support each other, that they change mainly because of new scientific discoveries and developments in technology, and that they all suffer the common handicap of uncertainty as to the amount of money likely to be available for research in both the near and far future.

In 1983, for example, NASA published a projection for exploration of the planets through the end of the century. *Planetary Exploration through the Year 2000* made it clear that huge, expensive new planetary missions were not possible in the foreseeable future.[3] Instead, the emphasis was on relatively lightweight, low-cost payloads. However, the writers still proposed a fairly extensive program. The initial "core missions" were to be a Venus radar mapper (which did fly), a Mars orbiter (which also flew but failed just before going into orbit around the red planet), a combined comet rendezvous and asteroid flyby (which did not fly), and an entry probe and radar mapper (which has not yet arrived) to study Saturn's large satellite Titan.

Recommendations for additional probes for the inner planets were Mars orbiter and a Mars lander, a Venus entry probe, and a lunar orbiter. For the outer solar system the program proposed a Saturn orbiter, a Saturn entry probe, and a Uranus entry probe. Also included were a mission to return a sample of a comet, and attempts to orbit a typical asteroid as well as to rendezvous with a minor planet that approached Earth closely. In the more distant future a Neptune entry probe and a Pluto flyby were considered to have high priority.

Significantly, this panel put considerable emphasis on the most *economical* means to carry out the proposed tasks. Clearly they realized that money for planetary exploration was becoming dear. From the viewpoint of the mid-1990s even this "reduced" program for planetary exploration seems wildly optimistic, and indeed it turned out to be just that. Yet, at the time the report was put together in 1983, the proposals seemed realistic and achievable to many planetary scientists.

In a different vein, the 1986 report *Pioneering the Space Frontier,* by the National Commission on Space, focused on a much broader space program but did include specific recommendations relating to planetary astronomy. This report was produced by a "blue ribbon" group that included only a few planetary scientists, and it dealt with the future of the entire U.S. space program over the next fifty years. Nevertheless, there is great emphasis in the recommendations concerning the exploration, prospecting, and even settling of the solar system. For example, manned lunar and Martian bases, not to mention ones on Deimos and Phobos, are deemed practical and desirable goals for the time frame covered. In addition, there are suggested probes to comets and asteroids as well as to the outer planets and their satellites.

However, the compilers of this report were well aware that NASA's funding for space research and technology had been declining for decades. Once again the authors were at pains to hammer home the message that they were suggesting relatively inexpensive means of accomplishing their rather optimistic goals.[4]

Two studies relating to the future of solar system exploration appeared in 1994. Sponsored by NASA, *Solar System Exploration: 1995–2000* dealt with the short term.[5] Here one can see the effects of severely reduced budgets. A striking example is that the weights of the proposed spacecraft and thus of the booster rockets needed to launch them are reduced. Gone are the powerful and expensive Atlas- and Titan-based vehicles. In their place are much cheaper boosters based on the venerable Delta. In one form or another the Delta has been around since the late 1950s and has always been considered a "medium-lift" system. What a change from the 1960s, when the mighty Saturn V was seriously considered as a launch vehicle for planetary probes! To be sure, lighter probes are less expensive, but advances in miniaturization, and especially in electronics and in computers, have been so great in recent decades that the retreat from the more ambitious spacecraft designs of the past is not nearly as severe as it might appear from a simple comparison of payload weights. Still, miniaturization can only go so far.

Mars exploration rates a high priority in this 1994 plan, which recommends two orbiter probes to replace the failed Mars Observer and, should funds allow it, a Martian lander. These would be followed early in the twenty-first century by six more landers to explore the most interesting regions of the red planet. Also recommended is a new program dubbed Discovery, to investigate a wide variety of solar system bodies and involving probe launches every year or year and a half during the early years of the new century. And there are vaguely defined proposals for beyond the year 2000 for Venus landers, Jupiter and Saturn probes, and the like.

A unique and distinctive proposal was for a program to investigate Pluto and its satellite Charon. Not only is Pluto the only planet that has never been visited by a spacecraft, but it is also the only one with an atmosphere that comes and goes. Due to Pluto's very elliptical orbit, the planet's surface temperature varies widely. In the 1990s Pluto has an atmosphere, but as the decades pass and the planet recedes from the Sun, that envelope inevitably must freeze out on the surface. The idea is to get there before it does. Interestingly, the Pluto program also would include an Earth-orbiting spacecraft to search for planets around other stars. This is an indication that planetary astronomers are staking a claim in this field and do not intend to leave it entirely in the hands of stellar researchers.

Missions to Pluto and the search for other solar systems have great popular appeal, but the rest of the recommendations are well thought out and much in keeping with the financial climate of the time. It remains to be seen whether even these reduced plans are carried out.

A second study completed in 1994 was *An Integrated Strategy for the Planetary Sciences: 1995 to 2010*, by the U.S. National Research Council. This is a very different sort of document and does not present detailed recommendations for future missions, though it does include short summaries of current and proposed solar system missions. Instead, what it offers is a well-written survey of what we know about the Sun's family, what we would like to know based on current evidence, and how to go about gaining that knowledge. Throughout the report, the influence of ever shrinking budgets is clearly apparent.[6]

A more recent (February, 1995) and a more broadly conceived NASA Strategic Plan is notable for its lack of explicit mention of solar system research.[7]

A drawback all the plans and predictions share is that they can only be based on what is already known, and the solar system keeps revealing surprises, such as rapid changes in the appearance of Neptune, infrared images of Titan showing that its surface is not uniformly covered by an ocean of some sort, the continuing discovery of small solid bodies (perhaps quiescent comet nuclei) orbiting far from the Sun, and the probable existence of planets around stars other than the Sun. And 1996 produced two truly stunning surprises.

Reexamination of data returned from the Clementine mission indicated that there may be deposits of dirty water ice in a deep crater near the Moon's South Pole. If so, this would be a finding of major importance for future manned space exploration, for ice can be melted to drink and split apart to provide oxygen for breathing and oxidizers for rocket propulsion as well as hydrogen for rocket fuel. It is not surprising that ice could exist in a polar crater for long periods of time, as the region involved never sees the Sun, only the cold sky of space, and so ice in it would simply lie there like any other rock. The real puzzle was *where the ice came from* in the first place, for, as we have seen, the Apollo missions had shown that the Moon had always been a waterless planet. In the absence of a better explanation, the impact of a comet sometime in the past seems to be the best bet. At any rate, the news was a sensation.[8]

The real blockbuster, however, was the announcement in August of 1996 by David S. McKay of the Johnson Space Center and a team of co-workers that there may have been life on Mars in the distant past. The story is a curious one, for the evidence came not directly from Mars but instead from a meteorite found in Antarctica and known as Allan Hills 84001.

This ordinary-looking rock has had a complicated past. Evidently it solidified on Mars very early in the planet's history, some 4.5 billion years ago (the isotopic composition matches what we know about Mars from the Viking missions). Later, perhaps 3.6 billion years ago, compounds associated both with the presence of liquid water and life were deposited in cracks in the rock. Then, about 15 million years ago, a titanic impact blasted the rock into interplanetary space until it encountered Earth some 13,000 years ago. But the most tantalizing aspect of the meteorite is that it appears to contain fossils of actual Martian microorganisms. Simple shapes, true, but not too different from those of bacteria on Earth.

The possibility of ancient life on Mars is not improbable, for it is now generally accepted that at one time the red planet had abundant liquid water—we have come a long way from viewing Mars as more like the Moon than like the Earth.[9] Further, it now seems that life on Earth ap-

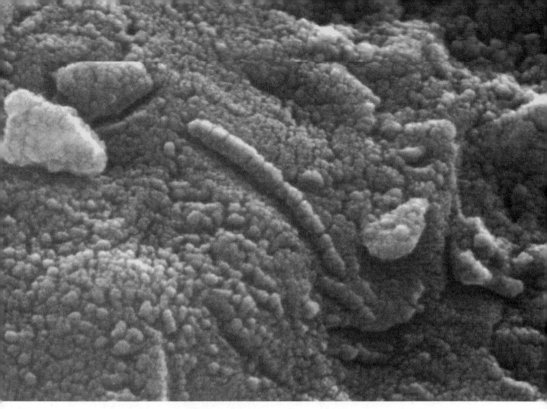

Is the curious structure in the center of this image an actual fossil of primitive life on Mars? It lies in a meteorite discovered near the Allan Hills of Antarctica and may hold the answer to questions asked for thousands of years. Courtesy NASA

peared very early in our planet's history and the same thing could have happened elsewhere.

Is there still life of some form on Mars? Certainly not on or near the surface, as Viking data has told us. But on Earth simple forms of life exist in places as inhospitable as the bottom of the oceans and deep underneath the solid surface of our planet, and perhaps Martian organisms have retreated to havens far undergound. But even proof of past Martian life, no matter how primitive, would be one of the greatest discoveries of all time, for Earth would no longer be unique, and the odds in favor of life existing elsewhere in the universe would increase enormously. In any case, such possibilities made front page headlines around the world, confirming once again that Mars still has a powerful grip on the public.[10]

Whether claims of water on the Moon and life on Mars will hold up only the future can tell. However, the reaction to these claims by planetary astronomers, astronomers in general, and scientists of all kinds was very interesting. Gone were the condescending sneers, knowing looks, and "inside" jokes that would have greeted such announcements a few decades ago.[11] Research in planetary astronomy has come too far, and produced too much, to be dismissed out of hand anymore. It appears that the ghosts of Lowell, Wells, and Welles have finally been laid to rest.

What of the future of planetary astronomy? The rapid progress of the field after World War II was due in great part to the influence of the Cold war and its attendant Space Race, both now but memories. For this and other reasons, funds to support researchers have been drying up. On the other hand, there are vastly more large telescopes than there were a generation ago, so that planetary astronomers (*if* they can find the money to support themselves) no longer have to beg for observing time; the equipment to make their observations has improved dramatically, and there are many more workers in the vineyard. And public interest in the solar system is probably as great as ever.

As this book goes to press, NASA's Mars Global Pathfinder is orbiting the red planet, gradually descending toward the altitudes at which it will begin its task of mapping that body's surface in detail. At the same time the ambitious U.S. Cassini probe is on its way to Saturn's moon Titan by the year 2004, where the plan is to map that moon's surface by radar and deliver the entry capsule Huygens, provided by the European Space Agency. Meanwhile NASA's Near Earth Asteroid Rendezvous mission is also in flight. Whether these missions will succeed is anybody's guess, but if they do, they will no doubt generate a great deal of public interest. At any rate, it is encouraging that planetary space missions are still being launched.

Still, will the results of such new missions, along with practical worries such as the chance of a comet or asteroid impacting Earth or fascinating possibilities such as life on Mars produce enough financial support to prevent planetary astronomy from entering yet another dark age? The queen of sciences has enjoyed a grand past, but as so often in that past, it faces a future imperfect.

NOTES

INTRODUCTION

1. Examples are scattered throughout the bibiliographical essay.

CHAPTER 1. PRIDE OF PLACE

1. Owen Gingerich, *The Great Copernicus Chase and Other Adventures in Astronomical History* (Cambridge, Mass.: Sky Publishing Corporation, 1992), pp. 7–12. This is a clear and concise treatment of the obscure origins of some of the oldest of our present constellations.

2. A. Pannekoek, *A History of Astronomy* (New York: Interscience Publishers, 1961), pp. 33–35. A very useful general history of astronomy.

3. Otto Neugebauer, *Astronomy and History: Selected Essays* (New York: Springer-Verlag, 1983), p. 232.

4. Pannekoek, *History*, pp. 38–47.

5. Neugebauer, *Selected Essays*, pp. 196–203.

6. Gingerich, *Copernicus Chase*, pp. 1–6.

7. Neugebauer, *Selected Essays*, pp. 99–100.

8. Pannekoek, *History*, pp. 86–94.

9. Ibid. pp. 130–32; Gingerich, *Copernicus Chase*, p. 7.

10. G. J. Toomer, *Journal for the History of Astronomy* 15 (1984): 147.

11. Pannekoek, *History*, pp. 49–50, 64.

12. Neugebauer, *Selected Essays*, p. 37.

13. Otto Neugebauer, *A History of Ancient Mathematical Astronomy* (New York: Springer-Verlag, 1975), pp. 2–4.

14. Pannekoek, *History*, p. 81.

15. Ibid. pp. 97–98.

16. J. L. E. Dryer, *A History of Astronomy from Thales to Kepler*, revised by W. H. Stahl, 2nd edition (1906; [New York]: Dover Publications, 1953), p. 12.

17. Dryer, *Thales to Kepler*, pp. 38–52.

18. Ibid., p. 21.

19. Arthur Berry, *A Short History of Astronomy from Earliest Times through the Nineteenth Century* (New York: Dover Publications, 1961), pp. 24–25.

20. Pannekoek, *History*, p. 101. Studies of Socrates, as well as Plato and Aristotle, have been a major scholarly industry for more than two millennia. The citations to them in this work are merely a few taken from reasonably available works on the history of astronomy.

21. Ibid., p. 113.

22. Ibid., pp. 113–14.

23. Berry, *Short History*, pp. 27–29.

24. Ibid., p. 29.

25. Pannekoek, *History*, pp. 111–12.

26. Ibid., pp. 113–16.

27. Ibid., pp. 116–18.

28. Ibid., pp. 118–21.

29. Dryer, *Thales to Kepler*, pp. 174–76; Berry, *Short History*, pp. 39–40.

30. Ibid., pp. 42–43.

31. Pannekoek, *History*, pp. 130–32.

32. Dryer, *Thales to Kepler*, pp. 151–52; Pannekoek, *History*, pp. 134–35.

33. Later writers in classical times, in particular Claudius Ptolemaeus, attributed an enormous amount of original work to Hipparchus, and there is no reason to doubt them. Descriptions of his efforts are in almost every general history of astronomy; here we will only cite Berry, *Short History*, 40–61; Pannekoek, *History*, pp. 124–150; and Dryer, *Thales to Kepler*, 167.

34. Berry, *Short History*, p. 62.

35. A short summary of Ptolemy's work is in Fergus J. Wood, *The Encyclopedia Americana*, 1959 edition (New York: Americana Corporation), vol. 22, pp. 752–53.

36. Dryer, *Thales to Kepler*, pp. 195–96; Berry, *Short History*, p. 67.

37. Liba Chaia Taub, *Ptolemy's Universe: The Natural Philosophical and Ethical Foundations of Ptolemy's Astronomy* (Chicago: Open Court, 1993), p. 152.

38. Pannekoek, *History*, pp. 164–66.

39. Dryer, *Thales to Kepler*, pp. 231–32; Pannekoek, *History*, pp. 174–75; Berry, *Short History*, p. 85.

40. Berry, *Short History*, p. 85; Dryer, *Thales to Kepler*, pp. 272–75.

41. Jan Adamczewski, *Nicolaus Copernicus and His Epoch* (Philadelphia: Copernicus Society of America, no date), pp. 67–103, 114. This work contains extensive background material on Copernicus and his times but little on the technical aspects of his astronomical work.

42. Pannekoek, *History*, pp. 189–193.

43. Berry, *Short History*, pp. 123–24.

44. Ibid., p. 121

45. Ibid., p. 96.

46. Adamczewski, *Copernicus*, pp. 150–54.

47. Ibid., pp. 147–48.

48. Berry, *Short History*, p. 125.

49. Pannekoek, *History*, p. 198.

50. Dryer, *Thales to Kepler*, pp. 345–46.

51. Pannekoek, *History*, p. 198.

52. Dryer, *Thales to Kepler*, pp. 131–32.

53. Berry, *Short History*, pp. 132–34.

54. Victor E. Thoren, in *The General History of Astronomy*, vol. 2: *Planetary Astronomy from the Renaissance to the Rise of Astrophysics, Part A: Tycho Brahe to Newton*, edited by René Taton and Curtis Wilson (Cambridge, England: Cambridge University Press, 1989), pp. 11–12.

55. Pannekoek, *History*, pp. 215–16.

56. Ibid., pp. 209–15; Thoren, in *General History*, 2A:9–19.

57. Christine Schofield, in *General History*, 2A:33–44.

58. Thoren, in *General History*, 2A:19–20.

59. Owen Gingerich, in *General History*, 2A:54.

60. Ibid., p. 58.

61. Ibid., pp. 61–68.

62. Ibid., pp. 68–69.

63. Ibid., pp. 71–73.

64. Ibid., pp. 75–77.

65. Henry C. King, *The History of the Telescope* (London: Charles Griffin, 1955) pp. 30–34.

66. Ibid., pp. 34–36. One can experience vividly the poor view through a Galilean telescope by buying a *really* cheap and shoddy refractor and looking at objects in the sky.

67. Albert Van Helden, in *General History,* 2A:81–84.

68. Ibid., p. 84.

69. Ibid.

70. Ibid., pp. 92–93.

71. Berry, *Short History,* pp. 165–67.

72. There is of course an enormous literature about Galileo. A good summary of his later life is Van Helden, in *General History,* 2A:101–102.

73. Ibid., pp. 102–103.

CHAPTER 2. DISCOVERING THE NATURE OF THE UNIVERSE

1. The origins of modern universities and printing from movable type are relatively popular topics, but the role of the House of Thurn and Taxis in setting up efficient public mails in Europe is known in the main only by advanced stamp collectors. A short description of that service is Franklin R. Bruns, in *Encyclopedia Americana,* 1959 edition, 25:476.

2. Schofield, in *General History,* 2A:38–44.

3. Stephen Pumfrey, in *General History,* 2A:45–49.

4. Ibid., 2A:48–53.

5. Eric J. Aiton, in *General History,* 2A:206–21.

6. Curtis Wilson, in *General History,* 2A:205.

7. Ibid.

8. Astronomical instruments and techniques of the time were not yet able to measure the solar parallax accurately. However, values that were *not* observed kept getting smaller and smaller, which meant that the Sun got farther and farther away.

9. Wilson, in *General History,* 2A:205

10. Ibid., 2A:201–206.

11. Gingerich, in *General History,* 2A:70–71.

12. Van Helden, in *General History,* 2A:103.

13. Suzanne Débarat and Curtis Wilson, in *General History,* 2A:149.

14. Van Helden, in *General History,* 2A:104–105.

15. King, *Telescope,* pp. 67–68.

16. Van Helden, in *General History,* 2A:105.

17. Pannekoek, *History,* pp. 277–78.

18. Van Helden, in *General History* 2A:104, 109–11.

19. Ibid.

20. Débarat and Wilson, in *General History,* 2A:145.

21. Ibid., 2A:145–50.

22. Van Helden, in *General History*, 2A:104.

23. Ewen A. Whitaker, in *General History*, 2A:125–26.

24. Ibid., 2A:127–29.

25. Ibid., 2A:132–34.

26. Ibid., 2A:134.

27. Ibid., 2A:138.

28. Pannekoek, *History*, pp. 254–55; Van Helden, in *General History*, 2A:104–105.

29. King, *Telescope*, p. 97.

30. Van Helden, in *General History*, 2A:105.

31. King, *Telescope*, p. 58.

32. A. F. O'D. Alexander, *The Planet Saturn: A History of Observation, Theory and Discovery* (London: Faber and Faber, 1962), pp. 112–15.

33. Van Helden, in *General History*, 2A:105.

34. Pannekoek, *History*, p. 256.

35. Earl C. Slipher, *The Photographic Story of Mars* (Cambridge, Mass.: Sky Publishing Corporation, 1962), p. 15.

36. Patrick Moore, *The Planet Venus*, 2nd edition (New York: Macmillan, 1959), pp. 133–35. Moore gives a list of 75 of these estimates, along with references.

37. Pannekoek, *History*, pp. 257–58.

38. Débarat and Wilson, in *General History*, 2A:152–54.

39. Ibid., 2A:153.

40. Pannekoek, *History*, p. 251

41. Ibid., pp. 250–51.

42. Ibid., pp. 278–79.

43. Ibid., p. 280.

44. Curtis Wilson, in *General History*, 2A:233. Here is a summary of Newton's life and work in a single paragraph!

45. There are statements and explanation of Newton's Laws of Motion in thousands of books on physics and astronomy. A very clear example is in Stanley P. Wyatt, *Principles of Astronomy*, 3rd edition (Boston: Allyn and Bacon, 1977), pp. 192–94.

46. Ibid., 194–95.

47. *Ibib.* pp. 195–98.

48. Wilson, in *General History*, 2A:233–35.

49. Wyatt, *Principles*, pp. 198–99.

50. Wilson, in *General History*, 2A:255–56.

51. Ibid., pp. 256, 261; Berry, *Short History*, p. 230.

52. Berry, *Short History*, p. 231; Wilson, in *General History*, 2A:261.

53. Wilson, *General History*, 2A:67–68.

54. Ibid., 2A:269–70.

55. Berry, *Short History*, pp. 237–38.

56. Ibid., pp. 247–49.

57. Gingerich, *Copernicus Chase*, pp. 146–51.

58. King, *Telescope*, pp. 67–71.

59. Ibid., pp. 71–74.

60. A. D. Thackeray, *Astronomical Spectroscopy* (New York: Macmillan, 1961), pp. 15–17.

61. George H. Sabine, in *Encyclopedia Americana,* 1959 edition, 17:237.

62. Berry, *Short History,* pp. 249–50.

63. Ibid., p. 256.

64. Pannekoek, *History,* pp. 291–92.

65. Ibid., p. 281.

66. Berry, *Short History,* pp. 258–65.

67. Ibid., pp. 265–69.

68. Moore, *Venus,* p. 64.

69. King, *Telescope,* pp. 144–45.

70. Ibid., pp. 145–48.

71. Ibid., pp. 158–59.

72. Pannekoek, *History,* pp. 282–87.

73. Ibid., pp. 299–300.

74. Forest Ray Moulton, *An Introduction to Celestial Mechanics,* 2nd revised edition, 13th printing (New York: Macmillan, 1959), pp. 363–64.

75. Berry, *Short History,* pp. 294–95.

76. Berry, *Short History,* pp. 304–306.

77. Pannekoek, *History,* p. 305.

78. Berry, *Short History,* pp. 312–13.

79. Pannekoek, *History,* pp. 304–305.

80. Berry, *Short History,* pp. 313–17.

81. Ibid., p. 306.

82. Ibid., pp. 320–22.

83. Pannekoek, *History,* pp. 306–307.

84. A. F. O'D. Alexander, *The Planet Uranus: A History of Observation, Theory, and Discovery* (New York: American Elsevier Publishing Company, 1965), pp. 25–43. Naturally Herschel's discovery touched off a burst of activity by observational and theoretical astronomers, and Alexander gives a host of references for those who might wish to read the original reports of that work.

85. Owen Gingerich, "The Naming of Uranus and Neptune," Astronomical Society of the Pacific, leaflet no. 352, October, 1958. This short but lively account describes the hilarious variety of names proposed for Hershel's new planet, the hot controversy concerning the choice, and the later naming of Neptune.

86. Alexander, *Uranus,* pp. 56–58.

87. King, *Telescope,* pp. 120–26.

88. Alexander, *Uranus,* pp. 58–66.

89. Ibid., pp. 68–72.

90. Ibid., pp. 67–68.

91. Ibid., pp. 74–76.

92. Alexander, *Saturn,* pp. 127–49. Saturn was one of Herschel's favorite objects, so it is no wonder that he made substantial discoveries concerning the planet and its system.

93. Moore, *Venus,* p. 43.

94. Angus Armitage, *William Herschel* (Garden City, N.Y.: Doubleday, 1963), pp. 50–53.

1. A. Pannekoek, *A History of Astronomy* (New York: Interscience Publishers, 1961), p. 320.

2. Ibid., pp. 311–12.

3. Ibid., pp. 314–15.

4. Ibid., pp. 315–16. Solar motion is described in many elementary textbooks on astronomy. A good example is Stanley P. Wyatt, *Principles of Astronomy*, 3rd edition (Boston: Allyn and Bacon, 1977), pp. 392–93.

5. Agnes M. Clerke, *A Popular History of Astronomy during the Nineteenth Century*, 4th edition (London: Adam and Charles Black, 1908), pp. 22–25.

6. Dieter B. Herrmann, *The History of Astronomy from Herschel to Hertzsprung*, translated and revised by Kevin Krisciunas (Cambridge, England: Cambridge University Press, 1984), pp. 10–14.

7. Henry C. King, *The History of the Telescope* (London: Charles Griffin, 1955), pp. 140–41.

8. Because of the many important practical uses of infrared radiation in the 20th century—especially its military applications—there are many descriptions of the field's early development. A typical short survey is in Henry L. Hackforth, *Infrared Radiation* (New York: McGraw-Hill, 1960), pp. 7–13.

9. J. B. Hearnshaw, *The Analysis of Starlight: One Hundred and Fifty Years of Astronomical Spectroscopy* (Cambridge, England: Cambridge University Press, 1986), p. 22.

10. Pannekoek, *History*, pp. 317–19.

11. Arthur Berry, *A Short History of Astronomy from Earliest Times through the Nineteenth Century* (1898; New York: Dover Publications, 1961), 327.

12. Herrmann, *Herschel to Hertzsprung*, p. 30.

13. King, *Telescope*, pp. 135–36; Berry, *Short History*, p. 350.

14. Ewen A. Whitaker, in *General History*, p. 134.

15. Stanley L. Jaki, *Journal for the History of Astronomy* 3 (1972): 136–37.

16. There are many descriptions of "Bode's" Law. One of the best is in Henry Norris Russell, Raymond Smith Dugan, and John Quincy Stewart, *Astronomy: A Revision of Young's Manual of Astronomy*, vol 1: *The Solar System*, revised edition (Boston: Ginn and Company, 1945), pp. 235–37.

17. Jaki, *Journal for the History of Astronomy* 3 (1972): 137–38.

18. King, *Telescope*, p. 136.

19. Günter D. Roth, *The System of Minor Planets* (Princeton, N.J.: D. Van Nostrand Company, 1962), pp. 24–26.

20. Forest Ray Moulton, *An Introduction to Celestial Mechanics*, 2nd revised edition (New York: Macmillan, 1914), p. 259.

21. Roth, *Minor Planets*, p. 25.

22. Berry, *Short History*, pp. 376–77. William Herschel and his son John coined a wide variety of names for new objects and phenomena (as is seen later in this chapter), many of which are still in use.

23. Roth, *Minor Planets*, pp. 28–29.

24. Pannekoek, *History*, p. 357.

25. Charles P. Olivier, *Encyclopedia Americana*, 1959 edition (New York: Americana Corporation), 18:713.

26. Ibid.; Clerke, *Popular History,* pp. 327–28.

27. Olivier, *EA,* 1959 edition, 18:713 f.

28. Clerke, *Popular History.* pp. 329–31.

29. Ibid., pp. 328–32.

30. Ibid., pp. 99–105.

31. Ibid., pp. 90–92.

32. Ibid., pp. 93–94. The "non-gravitational" forces are due to the "rocket effect" of molecules in the comet's nucleus that are turned from solids to gases by the heat of the Sun. A good description is given by Nikolaus B. Richter, *The Nature of Comets,* translated and revised by Arthur Beer (London: Methuen, 1963), pp. 131–34.

33. Clerke, *Popular History,* pp. 95–97.

34. Ibid., p. 107.

35. N. T. Bobrovnikoff, *Astrophysics: A Topical Symposium,* edited by J. A. Hynek (New York: McGraw-Hill,1951), p. 312.

36. Zdenek Kopal, ed., *Physics and Astronomy of the Moon* (New York: Academic Press, 1962), p. 285.

37. Ibid., pp. 285–89.

38. Whitaker, in *General History,* 2A:142.

39. Clerke, *Popular History,* p. 85.

40. Ibid., pp. 85–86.

41. Ibid., pp. 298–99.

42. Pannekoek, *History,* p. 376.

43. A. F. O'D. Alexander, *The Planet Uranus: A History of Observation, Theory, and Discovery* (New York: American Elsevier Publishing Company, 1965), pp. 76–77.

44. Ibid., pp. 114–15.

45. Morton Grosser, *The Discovery of Neptune* (Cambridge, Mass.: Harvard University Press, 1962), pp. 39–49.

46. Alexander, *Uranus,* pp. 97–98.

47. Grosser, *Discovery,* pp. 49–57.

48. Ibid., pp. 102–17.

49. Ibid., pp. 118–43. The tangled strands of the story of Neptune's discovery have never ceased to be a topic for popular and scholarly books and articles. The widely (and wildly) different personalities of the principals involved, the insight that the matter gives into scientific practices of the time, and the astounding result combine to keep the subject fascinating. All in all, the affair goes a long way toward contradicting the widespread but naive view that science advances only in an objective, impersonal, planned, and rational manner.

50. Ibid., pp. 139–41.

51. Clerke, *Popular History,* p. 84.

52. Ibid., pp. 35–38.

53. The drawbacks of speculum metal mirrors are legion. Examples pepper the text of King, *Telescope,* pp. 74–140.

54. King, *Telescope,* pp. 214–16.

55. Ibid., pp. 220–22.

56. Ibid., pp. 261–64, 270–71. There were and are several different "silvering" processes, many involving potentially dangerous and even explosive substances, so

it is no surprise that modern reflectors use an aluminum film that is not deposited chemically. Instead, in a vacuum chamber, the metal is evaporated from electrically heated filaments to cover the front of a glass disk. The inside of a burnt-out incandescent light bulb is a common example of such a mirror, although in that case the metal film is tungsten.

57. Pannekoek, *History*, pp. 384–89.

58. Herrmann, *Herschel to Hertzsprung*, pp. 70–72; Pannekoek, *History*, pp. 384–85.

59. Pannekoek, *History*, p. 385.

60. Ibid., p. 386.

61. Hearnshaw, *Starlight*, pp. 23–24.

62. Ibid., pp. 24–28.

63. King, *Telescope*, p. 186.

64. Ibid., p. 28.

65. Ibid., p. 30.

66. Ibid., p. 44.

67. Kirchhoff's laws of spectral formation appear in myriad elementary books on astronomy and physics. A good presentation is William K. Hartmann, *Astronomy: The Cosmic Journey*, 3rd edition (Belmont, Calif.: Wadsworth Publishing Company, 1982), pp. 238–40.

68. Hearnshaw, *Starlight*, p. 47.

69. Auguste Comte, *Cours de Philosophie Positive*, II, (Paris: Bachelier, 1835), 19th lecture. While Comte's original work is somewhat hard to find, there are a number of modern English translations of the more important parts. One such reference is Stanislav Andreski, ed., and Margaret Clarke, trans., *The Essential Comte: Selected from Cours de Philosophie Positive by August Comte, First Published in Paris 1830–42* (New York: Harper and Row, 1974). The dates of publication and the first deliveries of the lectures are discussed on pp. 239–40, while Comte's views on astronomy begin on p. 74.

70. Ibid.

71. Ibid.

72. The light-sensitive properties of naturally occurring silver chloride, among other minerals, are described in many works on mineralogy. A typical description is in Cornelius S. Hurlbut, Jr., revisor, *Dana's Manual of Mineralogy*, 17th edition (New York: John Wiley, 1959), p. 324. I should mention here that the literature on the history of photography is vastly greater than that of all of astronomy, and it was not possible to read more than a minute fraction of the available material, even though I have been trying my best for decades. Apologies then, to historians of photography, for it seemed best just to cite a few general references of well-attested facts, especially those that relate to astronomy.

73. Because of photography's enormous worldwide popularity, the story of its development has been told many times. A concise summary is given by Glenn E. Mattews, in *EA*, 1959 edition, 22:1–2.

74. Ibid.

75. Ibid., p. 2.

76. King, *Telescope*, p. 203.

77. Ibid., p. 2.

78. Ibid., p. 290.

79. Ibid., p. 224.
80. Ibid., pp. 249–50.
81. Ibid., p. 224.
82. Ibid., pp. 224–226.
83. Ibid., p. 261.

CHAPTER 4. NEW TECHNIQUES IMPACT ASTRONOMY

1. Agnes M. Clerke, *A Popular History of Astronomy during the Nineteenth Century* (London: Adam and Charles Black, 1908), p. 428.

2. Ibid., pp. 429–34. A more detailed discussion is in Henry C. King, *The History of the Telescope* (London: Charles Griffin, 1955), pp. 226–59, 305–18.

3. A. D. Thackeray, *Astronomical Spectroscopy* (New York: Macmillan, 1961), pp. 25–27.

4. King, *Telescope*, p. 352.

5. Ibid., p. 289.

6. Ibid., p. 284.

7. Ibid., p. 285.

8. Clerke, *Popular History*, pp. 402–403.

9. A locomotive whistle on a moving train provides a good example of the Doppler effect, which occurs with sound as well as light waves. To someone standing near the track, the pitch of the whistle will sound higher when the train is approaching (i.e., the frequency will be higher and the wavelength shorter or "bluer"), and then lower when the train is moving away (frequency lower, wavelength longer or "redder").

10. King, *Telescope*, pp. 288–89.

11. Clerke, *Popular History*, pp. 405–406.

12. Ibid., p. 387.

13. Ibid., pp. 387–89.

14. Dieter B. Herrmann, *The History of Astronomy from Herschel to Hertzsprung*, translated and revised by Kevin Krisciunas (Cambridge, England: Cambridge University Press, 1984), p. 111.

15. Glenn E. Matthews, in *Encyclopedia Americana*, 1959 edition (New York: Americana Corporation), 22:2–3.

16. J. B. Hearnshaw, *The Analysis of Starlight: One Hundred and Fifty Years of Astronomical Spectroscopy* (Cambridge, England: Cambridge University Press, 1986), p. 76.

17. King, *Telescope*, p. 305.

18. Ibid., pp. 299–300. Clerke, *Popular History*, pp. 408–11.

19. E. E. Barnard, *Astrophysical Journal* 6 (1897): 446. Donald E. Osterbrock, John R. Gustafson, and W. J. Shiloh Unruh, *Eye on the Sky: Lick Observatory's First Century* (Berkeley: University of California Press, 1988), pp. 79–80. A more lyrical description is in Clerke, *Popular History*, pp. 424–25.

20. Hearnshaw, *Starlight*, pp. 74–75. King, *Telescope*, p. 291.

21. Hearnshaw, *Starlight*, pp. 76–77. King, *Telescope*, pp. 292–93.

22. Osterbrock et al., *Eye*, pp. 73, 115.

23. Clerke, *Popular History*, pp. 438–39. Osterbrock et al., *Eye*, p. 115.

24. Many examples of the blue sensitivity of then current photographic emul-

sions are in *National Geographic,* October, 1917. This was "Our Flag Number," and some of the images of the banners of the United States of America and the United Kingdom look strange indeed.

25. Fletcher G. Watson, *Between the Planets,* (Philadelphia: Blakiston Company, 1945), pp. 10–12.

26. Günter D. Roth, *The System of Minor Planets* (Princeton, N.J.: D. Van Nostrand Company, 1962), pp. 34–35. The name honors Catherine Wolfe Bruce, a rich, reclusive American who provided substantial financial support for diverse projects in astronomy.

27. Clerke, *Popular History,* pp. 286–87.

28. Ibid., pp. 287–88.

29. Ibid., pp. 284–85. Roth, *Minor Planets,* pp. 98–99.

30. A. C. B. Lovell, *Meteor Astronomy* (Oxford: Clarendon Press, 1954), p. 277. Watson, *Between the Planets,* pp. 122–24. Donald K. Yeomans, *Comets: A Chronological History of Observation, Science, Myth, and Folklore* (New York: John Wiley, 1991), pp. 195–99.

31. Clerke, *Popular History,* pp. 334–35. Lovell, *Meteor Astronomy,* pp. 353–54.

32. Watson, *Between the Planets,* p. 128.

33. Clerke, *Popular History,* p. 340.

34. Lovell, *Meteor Astronomy,* pp. 337–38.

35. Clerke, *Popular History,* pp. 323–26.

36. Ibid., pp. 348–49.

37. Ibid., pp. 352–71. Yeomans, *Comets,* pp. 346–52.

38. Ibid., pp. 205–13. Clerke, *Popular History,* pp. 353–54.

39. Yeomans, *Comets,* pp. 213–14. Clerke, *Popular History,* pp. 103, 342.

40. Ibid, pp. 342–44. Yeomans, *Comets,* pp. 214–19.

41. Ibid., pp. 206–207. Clerke, *Popular History,* pp. 354–55.

42. Yeomans, *Comets,* pp. 216–17. Both chemistry and spectroscopy were not far along at this period, so it is no surprise that many wrong spectral identifications were made. A good sampling is found scattered through chapters 10 and 11 of Clerke's *Popular History.*

43. Yeomans, *Comets,* pp. 217–19. Though a "nonfact" cannot be documented, it appears that over the years the existence of the iron lines came to be doubted by astronomers. Then, in 1965, similar features, along with those of many other elements, made spectacular appearances in spectra of the "daylight" comet Ikeya-Seki. Hyron Spinrad told me he was dumbfounded when he saw these lines on spectra that he had taken. Like many astronomers, he had heard of the earlier observations but did not believe them until he saw them again.

44. Ibid., p. 308.

45. Clerke, *Popular History,* pp. 346–48. Yeomans, *Comets,* pp. 231–32.

46. Ibid., pp. 230–31.

47. Ibid., p. 348. Yeomans, *Comets,* pp. 232–33.

48. Clerke, *Popular History,* p. 371.

49. Comets have been considered as prophets of doom by many, probably since before history began. The 19th century saw increased terror from these celestial visitors, in part due to the widespread availability of cheap and widely distributed popular newspapers and magazines—and their circulation wars. There are many

entertaining descriptions of such "comet scares," but one of the best is by Owen Gingerich in *The Great Copernicus Chase and Other Adventures in Astronomical History* (Cambridge, Mass.: Sky Publishing Corporation, 1992), pp. 165–70. Tongue firmly in cheek, Gingerich relates the hilarious but sobering story of "the Great Comet that never came" in 1857. On a more modern note, many readers may remember the lurid prophesies of doom that attended the spectacular flops that were Comets Kohoutek and, more recently, Halley.

50. Ursula B. Marvin, *Journal for the History of Astronomy* 20 (1989): 132–35. Marvin's short review of two books on meteorite craters contains a concise and to-the-point summary of Gilbert's role in the "volcanic versus impact" controversy and of the hard times endured by those who advocated the impact theory during the first half of the 20th century.

51. J. F. Julius Schmidt, *Charte des Gebirges des Mondes* (Berlin: Dietrich Reimer, 1878).

52. H. Percy Wilkins and Patrick Moore, *The Moon: A Complete Description of the Surface of the Moon, Containing the 300-inch Wilkins Lunar Map* (London: Faber and Faber, 1955), pp. 21–22.

53. Clerke, *Popular History*, pp. 267–68.

54. Eugene M. Shoemaker, in Zdenek Kopal, ed., *Physics and Astronomy of the Moon* (New York: Academic Press, 1962), pp. 285–87, gives a short summary of the topic. William Graves Hoyt, *Journal for the History of Astronomy* 13 (1983): 155, contains a lengthier treatment.

55. Clerke, *Popular History*, pp. 269–70.

56. Henry Norris Russell, Raymond Smith Dugan, and John Quincy Stewart, *Astronomy: A Revision of Young's Manual of Astronomy*, vol. 1: *The Solar System*, revised edition (Boston: Ginn and Company, 1945), pp. 299–303. There are many popular descriptions of tidal effects on the Earth-Moon system, but this is one of the best and clearest summaries.

57. Clerke, *Popular History*, pp. 316–18.

58. Ibid., pp. 245–46.

59. Ibid., pp. 247–48.

60. Ibid., pp. 248–50.

61. Ibid., pp. 251–52.

62. Ibid., pp. 254–55.

63. Ibid., p. 256. William Graves Hoyt, *Lowell and Mars* (Tucson: University of Arizona Press, 1976), p. 58.

64. Clerke, *Popular History*, pp. 289–90.

65. Ibid., pp. 290–91.

66. Bertrand M. Peek, *The Planet Jupiter* (London: Faber and Faber, 1958), pp. 130–31. Clerke, *Popular History*, pp. 293–96.

67. Clerke, *Popular History*, p. 293.

68. A. F. O'D. Alexander, *The Planet Saturn: A History of Observation, Theory and Discovery* (London: Faber and Faber, 1962), pp. 195–96.

69. Ibid., pp. 200–209.

70. James E. Keeler, *Astrophysical Journal* 1 (1895): 416. Donald E. Osterbrock, *James E. Keeler: Pioneer American Astrophysicst and the Early Development of American Astrophysics* (Cambridge, England: Cambridge University Press, 1984), pp. 158–65.

71. Alexander, *Saturn*, pp. 255–59. Clerke, *Popular History*, pp. 298–99.

72. Alexander, *Saturn*, pp. 263–68.

73. Ibid., pp. 195–96. Clerke, *Popular History*, pp. 304–305.

74. A. F. O'D Alexander, *The Planet Uranus: A History of Observation, Theory, and Discovery* (New York: American Elsevier Publishing Company, 1965), pp. 151–61.

75. Clerke, *Popular History*, pp. 303–306.

76. Ibid., pp. 276–77.

77. W. W. Campbell, *Lick Observatory Bulletin*, no. 169 (1910): 156–64. This is a comprehensive review of all spectroscopic observations of Mars up to that time.

78. Owen Gingerich, *Journal for the History of Astronomy* 1 (1970): 109.

79. Some commentators have considered that "channels" might be a more accurate translation of *canali,* but a check of several Italian-English dictionaries shows that "canals" is perfectly acceptable. Then too, Schiaparelli was working in northern Italy, where true canals are not unknown.

80. Clerke, *Popular History*, pp. 278–81.

81. A look through almost any astronomy book of the era written for the general public will show how widespread was the notion that life—and pretty advanced life forms at that—is widespread in the solar system. A typical and charming example is Richard A. Proctor, *Other Worlds than Ours: The Plurality of Worlds Studied under the Light of Recent Scientific Researches* (New York: Hurst & Company, no date). It is interesting to note that this book devotes nine chapters to the solar system and only four to stars and nebulae, a ratio indicating the prominent position that planetary studies held for the public of that day.

82. Hoyt, *Lowell*, pp. xiii–11.

CHAPTER 5. CONTROVERSY AND FRUSTRATION

1. Stephen Halpert & Brenda Halpert, *Brahmins and Bullyboys: G. Frank Radway's Boston Album* (Boston: Houghton Mifflin Company, 1973), pp. 2–3. The term *New England Brahmin* was invented by the noted physician and author Oliver Wendell Holmes, who himself was perhaps the best example of that now almost extinct class.

2. William Graves Hoyt, *Lowell and Mars* (Tucson: University of Arizona Press, 1976), pp. 12–27.

3. Ibid., p. 26.

4. Ibid., pp. 39–43.

5. Ibid., pp. 48–49.

6. On a related topic, the argument that large telescopes will never enjoy really superb seeing, and so their optical surfaces need not be very accurate, hung around until well into the 20th century. However, at rare moments the seeing can get very good indeed, and full use can be made of the very finest large telescopes. For example, using the refigured 82-inch reflector at McDonald Observatory in Texas, I have seen the bright and dark areas of Mars "break up" into incredible masses of detail, with no trace of canals—exactly as Barnard described. Large, modern telescopes are located at sites with excellent seeing and have precise optical surfaces, so they can take advantages of these moments of exceptional condi-

tions and, for example, use electronic imaging equipment to capture views of the planets that are as detailed as any visual glimpses.

7. Hoyt, *Lowell,* pp. 57–58.

8. Howard Plotkin, *Journal for the History of Astronomy* 24 (1993): 101–22. By coincidence, the former long-time director of the California Institute of Technology's Jet Propulsion Laboratory, which was the lead center for NASA's lunar and planetary exploration program, was also named William H. Pickering. This situation has led to some amusement on more than one occasion, but I have found no indication that the two are related.

9. Hoyt, *Lowell,* pp. 64–64.

10. Ibid., pp. 71–86.

11. Ibid., pp. 173–86.

12. Readers can make a judgment on the subject by ferreting out a copy of Earl C. Slipher's book *The Photographic Story of Mars* (Cambridge, Mass.: Sky Publishing Corporation, 1962). Plate 47, titled "Photo Evidence of Lines (Canals) on Mars," is particularly interesting as it gives a good selection of the types of images on which Lowell based his claims that the canals had been captured by photography.

13. I. M. Levitt, *A Space Traveler's Guide to Mars* (New York: Henry Holt, 1956), pp. 79–81. Hoyt, *Lowell,* pp. 164–65.

14. Hoyt, *Lowell,* pp. 168–71. Levitt, *Guide,* pp. 76–77.

15. Henry Norris Russell, Raymond Smith Dugan, and John Quincy Stewart, *Astronomy: A Revision of Young's Manual of Astronomy,* vol 1: *The Solar System,* revised edition (Boston: Ginn and Company, 1945), pp. 332–37. Robert H. Baker, *Astronomy: A Textbook for University and College Students,* 7th edition (Princeton, N.J.: D. Van Nostrand Company, 1959), pp. 207–208.

16. Halpert and Halpert, *Brahmins and Bullyboys,* p. 3. A good illustration of a Lowell's pride of place in the New England of those days is in the well-known ditty, "And this is good old Boston, the Home of the bean and the cod, Where the Lowells talk to the Cabots and the Cabots talk only to God." Back then it meant much to be a Lowell (and Percival was a Lawrence to boot—both of which family names were given to industrial cities in Massachusetts). Times have changed greatly in the Bay State, but my experiences for almost five years as president of the Arlington, Massachusetts, Historical Society, testify that things have not changed completely. Lowell's easy assumption of superiority might well have stuck in the craws of astronomers who were "lesser beings."

17. Donald E. Osterbrock, *Journal for the History of Astronomy* 20 (1989): 77.

18. H. C. Vogel, *Astrophysical Journal* 1 (1895): 196.

19. W. W. Campbell, *Lick Observatory Bulletin* no. 169 (1909). The last part of this article is an extensive, detailed, and on the money description of all the early spectroscopic work on Mars. It is the best such review I have ever seen, and I gratefully acknowledge borrowing extensively from it for the current work. Indeed, there has been no need to modify *any* of Campbell's judgments of the early work in the light of generations of scientific advances. This is frankly an amazing testament to his grasp of the subject at the time. On the other hand, reading his comments leaves one with the feeling that he could have been just a bit less sarcastic in tone.

20. Hoyt, *Lowell*, pp. 140–43.

21. Percival Lowell, *Bulletin Lowell Observatory* 1 (1905): 116.

22. Vesto M. Slipher, *Bulletin Lowell Observatory* 1 (1905): 118.

23. V. M. Slipher, *Astrophysical Journal* 28 (1908): 397.

24. W. W. Campbell, *Lick Observatory Bulletin*, no. 169, 1909. Donald E. Osterbrock, *Journal for the History of Astronomy* 20 (1989): 77.

25. W. W. Campbell, *Lick Observatory Bulletin*, no. 180, 1910. Donald E. Osterbrock, *Journal for the History of Astronomy* 20 (1989): 77.

26. W. W. Campbell, *Supplement to Lick Observatory Bulletin* No. 180, 1910, p. 16A. The unusual page number seems to indicate that Campbell's supplement was printed after the main article and the next one had already gone to press, so that page 17 was already assigned. Donald E. Osterbrock, *Journal for the History of Astronomy* 20 (1989): 77–97. Osterbrock, who is no mean spectroscopist himself, here writes the definitive story of this episode. His description well illustrates the current welcome trend to write the history of astronomy accurately, instead of merely stringing together paeans of praise to "great men."

27. G. Johnstone Stoney, *Astrophysical Journal* 7 (1898): 25. Stoney, *Astrophysical Journal*, vol. illustrious and infallible predecessors. 11, 1910, p. 251. Stoney, *Astrophysical Journal* 12 (1900): 201. Stoney, *Astrophysical Journal* 20 (1904): 69.

28. V. M. Slipher, *Astrophysical Journal* 26 (1907): 59.

29. A. F. O'D. Alexander, *The Planet Uranus: A History of Observation, Theory, and Discovery* (New York: American Elsevier Publishing Company, 1965), pp. 218–23.

30. J. H. Moore and D. H. Menzel, *Publications of the Astronomical Society of the Pacific,* vol. 40, 1928, p. 234.

31. Thomas Chrowder Chamberlain, *The Origin of the Earth* (Chicago: University of Chicago Press, 1916), pp. 1–9, 38–71. In the introduction to this popular book, Chamberlain gives a straightforward and concise description of his early belief in the nebular hypothesis, the doubts he found as his geological researches advanced, and the relief he found when his new theory took form. Later in the book he criticizes Laplace's theory in detail.

32. Ibid., p. 81; pp. 101–29.

33. Ibid., pp. 130–58.

34. Ibid., pp. 10–37.

35. Ibid., pp. 159–262. The present author cannot seem to find any few pages in Chamberlain's book that summarize the problems he faced in trying to decipher Earth's history. Perhaps the strongest impression gotten from reading the last part of this work is how many and how severe were the problems that plagued geologists before they recognized the important role played in the history of Earth by continental drift.

36. F. R. Moulton, *Astrophysical Journal* 22 (1905): 165.

37. Stephen G. Brush covers the history of the Chamberlain-Moulton "cosmogony" in detail in two papers in the *Journal for the History of Astronomy.* The first (9 [1978]: 1) describes the origins and first presentations of the hypothesis. The second (9 [1979]: 77) relates the reception that the new theory received, its modifications down through the years, and its eventual demise. Both of these

articles are good reading for anyone interested in the history of theories of solar system astronomy.

38. William Lee Stokes, *Essentials of Earth History: An Introduction to Historical Geology,* 3rd edition (Englewood Cliffs, N.J.: Prentice Hall, 1973), p. 192. Charts showing how estimates of Earth's age increased over the years appear in many popular works and introductory texts on historical geology.

39. Thomas C. Chamberlain and Rollin D. Salisbury, *A College Text Book of Geology* (New York: Henry Holt, 1910), pp. 447, 466–67.

40. Karl Hufbauer, *Exploring the Sun: Solar Science since Galileo* (Baltimore: Johns Hopkins University Press, 1991), pp. 56–57, 62–64, 307.

41. See J. Kelly Beatty, Brian O'Leary, and Andrew Chaikin, eds., *The New Solar System,* 2nd edition (Cambridge, Mass.: Sky Publishing Corporation, 1982), p. 220, for names and orbital elements. Fred L. Whipple, *Earth, Moon and Planets* (Philadelphia: Blakiston Company, 1941), pp. 169–73 gives a brief summary of the Jupiter's satellite system and a diagram of the orbits of the moons known in 1941. Another short summary is in Robert H. Baker, reviser, *Simon Newcomb's Astronomy for Everybody* (New York: New Home Library, 1942), pp. 174–77.

42. Fletcher G. Watson, *Between the Planets* (Philadelphia: Blakiston Company, 1945), p. 84.

43. Bertram Donn, Jürgen Rahe, and John C. Brandt, *Atlas of Comet Halley 1910 II* (Washington, D.C.: National Aeronautics and Space Administration, 1986), p. ix.

44. Donald K. Yeomans, *Comets: A Chronology of Observation, Science, Myth, and Folklore* (New York: John Wiley, 1991), pp. 219–21. George F. Chambers, *The Story of Comets Simply Told for General Readers* (Oxford: Clarendon Press, 1909), pp. 182–91.

45. Peter Lebedew, *Astrophysical Journal* 15 (1902): 60. E. F. Nichols and G. F. Hull, *Astrophysical Journal* 15 (1902): 62.

46. E. F. Nichols and G. F. Hull, *Astrophysical Journal* 17 (1903): 352.

47. J. B. Hearnshaw, *The Analysis of Starlight: One Hundred and Fifty Years of Astronomical Spectroscopy* (Cambridge, England: Cambridge University Press, 1986), pp. 51–131. Hearnshaw gives a comprehensive, well-balanced, and highly readable account of the early development of stellar spectroscopy.

48. See, for example, Ejnar Hertzsprung, *Zeitschrift für wissenschaftliche Photography* 2 (1905): 429–42, and Henry Norris Russell, *Popular Astronomy* 22 (1914): 275–94, 331–51. Abridged versions of these articles were conveniently reprinted in Harlow Shapley, ed., *Source Book in Astronomy: 1900–1950* (Cambridge, Mass.: Harvard University Press, 1960), pp. 248–52, 253–62.

49. Leon Campbell and Luigi Jacchia, *The Story of Variable Stars* (Philadelphia: Blakiston Company, 1946), pp. 62–74.

50. Hoyt, *Lowell,* pp. 147–50.

51. James D. Stranathan, *The "Particles" of Modern Physics* (New York: Blakiston Company, 1952), pp. 315–24. This is perhaps the best book available on early developments in atomic, nuclear, and particle physics, because later works tend to give less space to those advances so as to leave room for later discoveries.

52. Baker, *Simon Newcomb's Astronomy,* pp. 89–90.

53. Stranathan, *"Particles,"* p. 319, gives a diagram of several radioactive

decay chains; see pp. 324–27 for a description of how the number of parent nuclei decreases while that of the daughter builds up. Radioactive dating is discussed in every modern introductory textbook on geology. Many of these works do a fine job of explaining the method without using any mathematics at all. A good example is Stokes, *Earth History*, pp. 21–32.

54. A. Einstein, *Annalen der Physik* 17 (1905): 891.

55. A. Einstein, *Annalen der Physik* 46 (1916): 769. The original article is somewhat hard to find, as it was published in Germany during World War I. Fortunately, it and the previous reference, along with several others relating to the early history of relativity theory, were republished in H. A. Lorentz, A. Einstein, H. Minkowski, and H. Weyl, *The Principle of Relativity: A Collection of Original Memoirs on the Special and General Theory of Relativity*, with notes by A. Sommerfield, translated by W. Perrett and G. B. Jeffery, (New York: Dover Publications, no date, but an unaltered and unabridged republication of the 1923 translation first published by Methuen).

CHAPTER 6. DOLDRUMS

1. Harlow Shapley, in Shapley, ed., *Source Book in Astronomy: 1900–1950* (Cambridge, Mass.: Harvard University Press, 1960), pp. 319–34. This is a handy summary of work Shapley published in 1918. Bart J. Bok and Priscilla F. Bok, in *The Milky Way*, 2nd edition, (Philadelphia: Blakiston Company, 1946), pp. 81–91, present a masterful survey of how the true extent of our galaxy was revealed.

2. Harlow Shapley, *Galaxies* (Philadelphia: Blakiston Company, 1947), pp. 52–84, 117–49.

3. Edwin Hubble, in Shapley, ed., *Source Book*, pp. 330–34. Edwin Hubble and Milton L. Humason, in Shapley, ed., *Source Book*, pp. 335–39.

4. Shapley, *Galaxies*, pp. 202–14.

5. Leo Goldberg and Lawrence H. Aller, *Atoms, Stars, and Nebulae* (Philadelphia: Blakiston Company, 1950). The entire book is devoted to the development of modern astrophysics and much of the text to advances in the 1920s and 1930s.

6. Arthur S. Eddington, *The Internal Constitution of the Stars* (New York: Dover Publications, 1959), p. 301.

7. R. D'E. Atkinson, *Astrophysical Journal* 73 (1931): 250, 308.

8. Karl Hufbauer, *Exploring the Sun*, pp. 107–12.

9. Theodore Dunham, Jr., in Gerard P. Kuiper, ed., *The Atmospheres of the Earth and Planets*, revised edition (Chicago: University of Chicago Press, 1952), p. 288, gives a review of the studies of planetary spectra at Mount Wilson during the 1920s and 1930s.

10. A number of tales about verbal condemnations of planetary astronomy are well known to many scientists in the field. In particular, there were widespread rumors of a "10-percent rule" that limited planetary observing to that amount at many observatories. Whether it existed or not is a moot point, because except at a few institutions such as Lowell Observatory, planetary work never approached that limit. It is significant that the present day solar system researchers whom I have interviewed, and who are old enough to remember "the good old days," *with-*

out exception believe that planetary astronomy was once considered to be second rate science.

11. Walter S. Adams and Charles E. St. John, *Astrophysical Journal* 63 (1926): 133; Theodore Dunham, Jr., *Publications of the Astronomical Society of the Pacific* 45 (1933): 202 (hereafter *PASP*); Walter S. Adams and Theodore Dunham, Jr., *Astrophysical Journal* 79 (1934): 308; Walter S. Adams, *Astrophysical Journal* 93 (1941): 11; Dunham, in Kuiper, ed., *Atmospheres*, p. 288.

12. Dunham, in Kuiper, ed., *Atmospheres*, p. 288.

13. Arthur Adel, *Astrophysical Journal* 86 (1937): 337; Rupert Wildt, *Astrophysical Journal* 91 (1940): 266.

14. Charles E. St. John and Seth B. Nicholson, *Astrophysical Journal* 56 (1922): 380; Dunham, in Kuiper, ed. *Atmospheres*, p. 288.

15. For an example, see Donald. H. Menzel and Fred L. Whipple, *PASP* 67 (1955): 161. It is only fair to admit that I was guilty of that same error as late as the 1960s, along with such distinguished planetary scientists as Carl Sagan and David Morrison, to name just two other examples. We all should have known better.

16. Theodore H. Dunham, Jr., *PASP* 45 (1933): 42.

17. Theodore H. Dunham, Jr., *PASP* 46 (1934): 231.

18. Ibid.

19. Articles on planetary spectroscopy in the 1920s and 1930s are scattered among what is for that era a surprisingly large number of journals, both professional and popular. However, there are several reviews of the subject that neatly cover developments and which, among them, give all the original references. I have already cited Dunham, in Kuiper, ed., *Atmospheres*, p. 288–305. This work gives a very full list of references. On a more popular level is Theodore Dunham, Jr., *PASP* 51 (1939): 253. A slightly later work, N. T. Bobrovnikoff, *Reviews of Modern Physics* 16 (1944): 271, gives a highly technical yet smoothly readable account of advances in planetary spectroscopy and also includes a comprehensive set of references to original works on the subject.

20. Joseph N. Tatarewicz, *Exploring the Solar System: The Planetary Geosciences Since Galileo* (Baltimore: Johns Hopkins University Press, in press).

21. Donald H. Menzel, *Astrophysical Journal* 58 (1923): 65.

22. Harold Jeffreys, *Monthly Notices of the Royal Astronomical Society* 83 (1923): 350. Jeffreys, *MNRAS* 84 (1924): 534. A. F. O'D. Alexander, *The Planet Saturn: A History of Observation, Theory, and Discovery* (London: Faber and Faber, 1962), pp. 368–72.

23. Rupert Wildt, *Astrophysical Journal* 87 (1938): 508.

24. Henry Norris Russell, Raymond Smith Dugan, and John Quincy Stewart, *Astronomy: A Revision of Young's Manual of Astronomy*, vol. 1: *The Solar System*, revised edition (Boston: Ginn and Company, 1945), p. 368. This is a typical example of astronomers' widespread acceptance of Wildt's models.

25. Frank E. Ross, *Astrophysical Journal* 64 (1926): 243.

26. Frank E. Ross, *Astrophysical Journal* 68 (1928): 57.

27. See, for example, Donald H. Menzel, *Astrophysical Journal* 56 (1923): 65; D. H. Menzel, W. W. Coblentz, and C. O. Lampland, *Astrophysical Journal* 63 (1926): 177; Edison Pettit and Seth B. Nicholson, *Astrophysical Journal* 71

(1930): 102; Edison Pettit, *Astrophysical Journal* 91 (1940): 408. Edison Pettit, in Gerard P. Kuiper and Barbara M. Middlehurst, eds., *Planets and Satellites* (Chicago: University of Chicago Press, 1961), p. 400, surveys the Mount Wilson work.

28. Donald H. Menzel, *Astrophysical Journal* 63 (1926): 48. Gerard de Vaucouleurs, *Physics of the Planet Mars: An Introduction to Aerophysics* (London: Faber and Faber, 1954), pp. 99–102.

29. Menzel died long before this book was begun. However, in the late 1960s I had the opportunity to talk to him about the subject, and he was proud of the fact that his surface pressure estimate had held up so well over the years.

30. De Vaucouleurs, *Planet Mars,* pp. 102–104.

31. Ibid., pp. 125–25.

32. A letter from Gerard de Vaucouleurs to Ronald A. Schorn, June 23, 1994, gives explicit approval to cite this quote. As de Vaucouleurs honestly notes, "At the time one could only make educated guesses at these factors."

33. R. W. Wood, *Astrophysical Journal* 36 (1912): 75.

34. R. W. Wood, *Astrophysical Journal* 43 (1916): 310.

35. Donald K. Yeomans, *Comets: A Chronological History of Observation, Science, Myth, and Folklore* (New York: John Wiley, 1991), pp. 219–24, gives an excellent summary of spectroscopic investigations of comets during the first half of the 20th century.

36. P. Swings, *Astrophysical Journal* 95 (1942): 270.

37. Fred L. Whipple, interview, Cambridge, Mass., April 20, 1993. Whipple related the story earlier in *The Collected Contributions of Fred L. Whipple,* vol. 1 (Cambridge, Mass.: Smithsonian Astrophysical Observatory, 1972), pp. 3–11. For a more contemporary version of the situation, see Fletcher G. Watson, *Between the Planets* (Philadelphia: Blakiston Company, 1945), pp. 99–101.

38. W. L. Webb, *Brief Biography and Popular Account of the Unparalleled Discoveries of T. J. J. See* (Lynn, Mass.: Thos. P. Nichols & Son, 1913), pp. 181–83.

39. Webb, *Brief Biography,* plate opposite p. 74.

40. John Lankford, *Journal for the History of Astronomy* 11 (1980): 129, argues strongly that there is no evidence that See did so. On the other hand, William G. Hoyt, *Journal for the History of Astronomy* 12 (1981): 139, suggests that See might have gotten an "impression" of a lunar-type landscape. As it had long been known that the Moon and Mercury reflected sunlight similarly, this was not a ridiculous idea, and as it turns out it is correct. I have spent a lot of time observing planets visually with substantial telescopes in good seeing, and I can only comment that See just *might* have seen what he said he saw.

41. Herbert E. Ives, *Astrophysical Journal* 50 (1919): 245.

42. H. H. Ninnenger, *Out of the Sky: An Introduction to Meteoritics* (New York: Dover Publications, 1959), pp. 205–207.

43. Russell, Dugan, and Stewart, *Astronomy,* pp. 456–57. When Henry Norris Russell accepted something, most other astronomers usually fell into line!

44. Frederick E. Wright, F. H. Wright, and Helen Wright, in Barbara M. Middlehurst and Gerard P. Kuiper, eds., *The Moon, Meteorites, and Comets* (Chicago: University of Chicago Press, 1963), p. 1.

45. Clyde W. Tombaugh, Astronomical Society of the Pacific, leaflet no. 209,

1946. Tombaugh has written much about his discovery of Pluto, but this may be the shortest and sweetest description of all.

46. William Graves Hoyt, *Planets X and Pluto* (Tucson: University Press, 1980). This is the best and most complete description of the search for and eventual discovery of Pluto.

47. Robert H. Baker, reviser, *Simon Newcomb's Astronomy for Everybody* (New York: New Home Library, 1942), pp. 322–24.

48. Russell, Dugan, and Stewart, *Astronomy*, pp. 462–68, gives a typical description of thought on the matter at that time.

49. Lyman Spitzer, Jr., *Astrophysical Journal* 90 (1939): 675.

50. C. M. Jansky, Jr., *Proceedings of the Institute of Radio Engineers* 46 (1958): 13. Grote Reber, *Proc. IRE* 46 (1958): 15. Woodruff T. Sullivan III, ed., *Classics in Radio Astronomy* (Dordrecht, Holland: D. Reidel Publishing Company, 1982), pp. xxi, 5–9. In this work Sullivan reprints three of Jansky's papers on cosmic static from the *Proc. IRE.* See also Sullivan, in Sullivan, ed., *The Early Years of Radio Astronomy: Reflections Fifty Years after Jansky's Discovery* (Cambridge, England: Cambridge University Press, 1984), p. 3.

51. Jesse L. Greenstein, in Sullivan, ed., *Early Years*, p. 67.

52. I vividly remember how radio astronomers of the late 1950s, when I was a young graduate student, considered that Jansky's inability to follow up his early work, his untimely death, and his failure to receive appropriate recognition in his lifetime constituted a real human tragedy.

53. Grote Reber, *Proc. IRE* 46 (1958): 15.

54. Grote Reber, *Astrophysical Journal* 91 (1940): 621.

55. Grote Reber, *Astrophysical Journal* 100 (1944): 279.

56. Even in the late 1950s it took "special dispensations" from the department heads involved for an astronomy graduate student to take and get credit for courses in electrical engineering (or vice versa) in at least one case. I had to go and get such dispensations, even though cooperation between the two departments at the University of Illinois was unusually close for those days.

57. Sullivan, in Sullivan, ed., *Early Years*, p. 5. Greenstein, ibid., p. 67.

58. Robert H. Baker, *Astronomy*, 6th edition (Princeton, N.J.: D. van Nostrand Company, 1957). This book's 10-page, double-column index contains just five entries for radio astronomy.

59. Frederick Lewis Allen, *Since Yesterday: The Nineteen-Thirties in America, Sept. 3, 1929 — Sept. 3, 1939* (New York: Bantam Books, 1965), pp. 251–63. Allen does a concise job of fitting the Welles broadcast into the general context of its times.

60. Howard Koch, *The Panic Broadcast: Portrait of an Event* (New York: Avon Books, 1971.) Koch wrote the actual radio play and includes the complete script in his book (he later wrote the script for the movie *Casablanca*).

61. In the 1960s, the night assistants at Lick Observatory would sometimes play a tape of the Welles broadcast over a radio near a telescope observing position. The receiver was there to relieve the nighttime tedium and was supposedly tuned to a local commercial station. This was a popular sport when the observer was a rookie at Lick, and it fooled more than one professional astronomer for longer than they later cared to admit!

62. Raymond William Stedman, *The Serials: Suspense and Drama by Installment,* 2nd edition, (Norman: University of Oklahoma Press, 1977), pp. 97–106, sketches Gordon and Rogers' careers. Frederick C. Mish, editor in chief, *Merriam Webster's Collegiate Dictionary,* 10th edition (Springfield, Mass.: Merriam Webster, 1994), p. 148, defines "Buck Rogers" as "marked by futuristic and high-tech qualities: suggestive of science fiction."

63. Andrew T. Young, in M. Capaccioli and H. G. Corwin, eds., *Gerard and Antoinette de Vaucouleurs: A Life for Astronomy* (Singapore: World Scientific, 1989), p. 31.

64. Shapley, ed., *Source Book,* pp. xiii–xv.

65. Harlow Shapley and Helen E. Howarth, eds., *A Source Book in Astronomy* (New York: McGraw-Hill, 1929), pp. xiii–xvi.

66. Dunham, *PASP* 51 (1939): 253.

CHAPTER 7. THE LEGACY OF WAR

1. Richard Humble, *Hitler's High Seas Fleet* (New York: Ballantine Books, 1971), pp. 100–105.

2. J. S. Hey, *Nature* 157 (1946): 47. Woodruff T. Sullivan III, in Woodruff T. Sullivan III, ed., *Classics in Radio Astronomy* (Dordrecht, Holland: D. Reidel Publishing Company, 1982), p. 164.

3. Sullivan, *Classics,* pp. 141–44.

4. J. S. Hey, S. J. Parsons, and J. W. Phillips, *Nature* 158 (1946): 234.

5. Sullivan, in Sullivan, ed., *Classics,* p. 221.

6. H. I. Ewen and E. M. Purcell, *Nature* 168 (1951): 356. The "21-centimeter" radiation from interstellar hydrogen was predicted by H. C. van de Hulst, *Nederlandsch Tijdschrift voor Naturkunde* 11 (1945): 210. The van de Hulst article is difficult to find and even more difficult to read. A good English translation by Woodruff T. Sullivan III, is in Sullivan, ed., *Classics in Radio Astronomy* (Dordrecht, Holland: D. Reidel Publishing Company, 1982), p. 302.

7. See, for example, I. S. Shklovsky, Richard B. Rodman, and Carlos M. Varsavsky, translators, *Cosmic Radio Waves* (Cambridge, Mass.: Harvard University Press, 1960), pp. 191–201. Shklovsky gives a fine summary of the topic.

8. Jesse L. Greenstein, in Sullivan, ed., *Early Years,* p. 67. This is a succinct history of early radio astronomy. The Reber and Greenstein review article is in *Observatory* 67 (1967): 15.

9. *Proc. IRE* 46 (1958).

10. R. A. Schorn, C. D. Hendricks, and G. W. Swenson, *Proc. IRE* 46 (1958).

11. See Karl Hufbauer, *Exploring the Sun: Solar Science since Galileo* (Baltimore: Johns Hopkins University Press, 1991), especially chapter 5, for a good summary of this early work in the context of the times.

12. Robert H. Dicke and Robert Beringer, *Astrophysical Journal* 103 (1946): 375. J. H. Piddington and H. C. Minnett, *Australian Journal of Scientific Research, A,* 2 (1949): 63. A popular description of this early work is J. H. Piddington, *Radio Astronomy* (New York: Harper & Brothers, 1961), pp. 107–108.

13. A good summary of early work is Cornell H. Meyer in Gerard P. Kuiper and Barbara M. Middlehurst, ed, *Planets and Satellites* (Chicago: University of Chicago Press, 1961), pp. 445–55.

14. C. H. Mayer, T. P. McCullough, and R. M. Sloanaker, *Astrophysical Journal* 127 (1958) informed optical astronomers of the discovery. A second paper by the same three authors appeared in the *Proceedings of the Institute of Radio Engineers* 46 (260), familiarizing a different group of researchers of the results.

15. A good, short summary is Meyer, in Kuiper and Middlehurst, eds., *Planets and Satellites,* pp. 455–61.

16. Ibid., pp. 461–62 for a short summary.

17. Ibid, pp. 462–67.

18. B. F. Burke and Kenneth L. Franklin, *Journal of Geophysical Research* 60 (1995): 213. See also the same authors' paper in H. C. van de Hulst, ed., *Radio Astronomy* (Cambridge, England: Cambridge University Press, 1957), p. 394.

19. B. F. Burke, in Kuiper and Middlehurst, eds., *Planets and Satellites,* p. 473.

20. Meyer, in Kuiper and Middlehurst, eds., *Planets and Satellites,* pp. 467–68.

21. Van de Hulst, *Radio Astronomy.*

22. S. K. Mitra, *The Upper Atmosphere,* 2nd edition (Calcutta: Asiatic Society, 1952), pp. 176–78. This book is difficult to find but is a gold mine of information about studies of the upper atmosphere during the first half of the 20th century.

23. A. C. B. Lovell, *Meteor Astronomy* (Oxford: Clarendon Press, 1954), pp. 23–28. Bernard Lovell and J. A. Clegg, *Radio Astronomy* (New York: John Wiley, 1952), pp. 82–86. D. W. R. McKinley, *Meteor Science and Engineering* (New York: McGraw-Hill, 1961), pp. 13–23.

24. McKinley, *Meteor Science,* p. 22.

25. Lovell, *Meteor Astronomy,* pp. 28–30.

26. Ibid., pp. 155–211.

27. Ibid., pp. 212–47. McKinley, *Meteor Science,* pp. 157–71.

28. Lovell, *Meteor Astronomy,* pp. 358–59.

29. J. H. DeWitt and E. K. Stodola, *Proc. IRE* 37 (1949): 229. Z. Bey, *Hungarica Acta Physica* 1 (1946): 1.

30. Useful early surveys of radar studies are in J. L. Pawsey and R. N. Bracewell, *Radio Astronomy* (Oxford, England: Clarendon Press, 1955), pp. 293–305. Lovell and Clegg, *Radio Astronomy,* pp. 214–27.

31. Andrew J. Butrica, *To See the Unseen: A History of Planetary Radio Astronomy* (Washington, D.C.: NASA, 1996).

32. Willy Ley, *Rockets, Missiles, and Space Travel* (New York: Viking Press, 1951), pp. 213–19.

33. Literature concerning the history of rocketry is voluminous, but perhaps the best summary of the heroic early days is Willy Ley, *Rockets, Missiles, and Space Travel.* Representative descriptions of early scientific studies utilizing the V-2 are Jessie L. Greenstein, in Gerard P. Kuiper, ed., *The Atmospheres of the Earth and Planets,* revised edition (Chicago: University of Chicago Press, 1952), p. 112; and H. E. Clearman, ibid., p. 125. A detailed analysis of the first "rocket ultraviolet" solar spectra is given by E. Durand, J. J. Oberly, and R. Tousey, *Astrophysical Journal* 109 (1949): 1. These authors also give a short summary of the earliest work in this field along with references to the original publications.

34. See, for example, Ley, *Rockets,* pp. 250–56; and Milton W. Rosen, *The Viking Rocket Story* (London: Faber and Faber, 1956).

35. Gerard P. Kuiper, *Astrophysical Journal* 100 (1944): 378.

36. C. F. von Weizsäcker, *Zeitschrift für Astrophysik* 22 (1944): 319. I have never seen an original copy of this article, and the reference here is given for historical reasons alone. It is the only case in this work where I have not read the actual publication cited.

37. G. Gamow and J. A. Hynek, *Astrophysical Journal* 101 (1945): 249.

38. Boris T. Pash, *The Alsos Mission* (New York: Award Books, 1970), pp. 39, 249–56.

39. See, for example, E. C. Slipher and A. G. Wilson, Report on the Conference of the Mars committee (Held at Lowell Observatory, October 22, 23, 1953). Unpublished report, copy courtesy William M. Sinton.

40. Minutes of a Meeting of the Mars Committee held at the Headquarters of the National Geographic Society, Washington, D.C., March 29, 1954. Courtesy William M. Sinton.

41. Letter to William M. Sinton from the Secretaries of the Mars Committee by A. G. Wilson, October 4, 1954. Courtesy William M. Sinton.

42. Ewen A. Whitaker, *The University of Arizona's Lunar and Planetary Observatory: Its Founding and Early Years* (Tucson: University of Arizona, [sometime after August, 1985]), pp. 2–3.

43. Ibid. Whitaker's history was written for the 100th anniversary of the University of Arizona but for some reason has remained almost unknown, even among planetary astronomers. It is an excellent account of the early years at LPL by an insider.

44. Just how long was the "long-wavelength limit" is a moot point. Kuiper (Gerard P. Kuiper, *Astrophysical Journal* 106 [1947]: 251) mentioned that G. Herzberg had found the 1.2 micron carbon dioxide bands on Venus using Kodak 1-Z plates. But in the 1960s several observers (including Tobias C. Owen, Andrew T. Young, Louise L. D. G. Young, Edwin S. Barker, and myself) attempted to record them in the same way, using the same equipment that Herzberg did, the 82-inch reflector at McDonald Observatory and its associated spectrographs. Our photographic plates were all blank, and the best explanation that we have been able to come up with is that the emulsions we used had less sensitivity in that spectral region the earlier ones that Herzberg used.

45. G. P. Kuiper, W. Wilson, and R. J. Cashman, *Astrophysical Journal* 106 (1947): 243.

46. Gerard P. Kuiper, *Astrophysical Journal* 106 (1947): 251.

47. Carl Sagan, interview, Boulder, Colo., Oct. 19, 1993.

48. Whitaker, *Laboratory*, p. 5.

49. Gerard P. Kuiper, *Astrophysical Journal* 120 (1954): 603.

50. Kuiper, in Kuiper, ed., *Atmospheres*, pp. 358–60.

51. See, for example, J. Grandjean and R. M. Goody, *Astrophysical Journal* (1955): 548.

52. Gerard de Vaucouleurs, *Physics of the Planet Mars: An Introduction to Areophysics* (London: Faber and Faber, 1954), p. 125.

53. P. Swings and L. Haser, *Atlas of Representative Cometary Spectra* (Louvain: Ceuterick Press, 1956).

54. Jan H. Oort, *Bulletin of the Astronomical Institutes of the Netherlands* 11 (1950): 91.

55. Fred L. Whipple, *Astrophysical Journal* 111 (1950): 375.

56. Ingrid Groeneveld and Gerard P. Kuiper, *Astrophysical Journal* 120 (1954): 200. The application of the 1P21 phototube to astronomy in general is discussed in Gerald E. Kron, *Astrophysical Journal* 103 (1946): 326.

57. Edward Anders, in Barbara M. Middlehurst and Gerard P. Kuiper, ed., *The Moon, Meteorites, and Comets* (Chicago: University of Chicago Press, 1963), p. 402.

58. Willy Ley, *The Conquest of Space* (New York: Viking Press, 1952).

59. Joseph Kaplan et al., *Across the Space Frontier* (New York: Viking Press, 1952.

60. Whipple, interview.

61. Cornelius Ryan, ed., *Conquest of the Moon* (New York: Viking Press, 1953). The "within our lifetime" prediction appears on page 6.

62. Willy Ley and Wernher von Braun, *The Exploration of Mars* (New York: Viking Press, 1956). The confident "within a matter of decades" prediction is on page 85.

CHAPTER 8. TURN OF THE TIDE

1. See, for example, Willy Ley, *Rockets, Missiles, and Space Travel* (New York: Viking Press, 1951), pp. 257–316.

2. *What's Ahead in Space: America's Astronautical Timetable* (New York: Grosset & Dunlap, 1960), pp. 3–23. Under the title of *The Next Ten Years in Space, 1959–1969*, this was first published by the United States Government Printing Office as House Document No. 115 for the House of Representatives, 86th Congress, 1st Session. In addition to a comprehensive summary, this compilation contains the statements of a large number of prominent individuals concerned with space exploration.

3. Dean B. McLaughlin, *Journal of the Royal Astronomical Society of Canada* 50 (1950): 193.

4. C. C. Kiess, C. H. Corliss, H. K. Kiess, and E. L. R. Corliss, *Astrophysical Journal* 116 (1957): 579.

5. C. C. Kiess, S. Karrer, and H. K. Kiess, *PASP* 72 (1960): 256. C. C. Kiess, C. H. Corliss, and H. K. Kiess, *Astrophysical Journal* 67 (1962): 579. C. C. Kiess, S. Karrer, and H. K. Kiess, *PASP* 75 (1963): 50.

6. W. M. Sinton, *PASP* 73 (125): 1961. H. Spinrad, *PASP* 75 (1963): 190. J. V. Marshall, *Publications of the Lunar and Planetary Laboratory* 2 (1964): 167. The one lasting effect of the "nitrous oxides affair" appears in Ray Bradbury's science fiction opus, *The Martian Chronicles,* where these substances play a prominent part.

7. C. C. Kiess, C. H. Corliss, and Harriet K. Kiess, *Astrophysical Journal* 132 (1960): 221, 1960.

8. William M. Sinton, *Astrophysical Journal* 126 (1957): 231.

9. Ibid.

10. William M. Sinton, *Science* 130 (1959): 1234.

11. William M. Sinton, interview, Phoenix, Ariz., Jan. 4, 1993.

12. Ralph B. Baldwin, *The Face of the Moon* (Chicago: University of Chicago Press, 1949), p. 131.

13. Ralph B. Baldwin, *The Measure of the Moon* (Chicago: University of Chicago Press, 1963), especially p. 333 ff.

14. T. Gold, *Monthly Notices of the Royal Astronomical Society* 115 (1955): 585.

15. A good discussion is Baldwin, *Measure*, pp. 295–302. He points out that the dust hypothesis was originally proposed by T. J. J. See as far back as 1910.

16. N. A. Kosyrev [sic], *Sky and Telescope* 18 (1959): 561.

17. See, for example, Baldwin, *Measure*, pp. 416–18, for the view of one serious student of the Moon. Kozyrev freely discussed and wrote about his observation, and his detailed technical description is in Zdenek Kopal and Zdenka Kadla Mikhailov, eds., *The Moon* (London: Academic Press, 1962), p. 263.

18. *New York Times*, July 30, 1955.

19. *Time*, Jan. 16, 1956, p. 42.

20. *A Chronology of Missile and Astronautic Events* (Washington, D.C.: U.S. Government Printing Office, 1961), p. 28.

21. *New York Times*, Oct. 5, 1957. Almost every newspaper and news magazine in the world carried similar reports.

22. V. Petrov, *Artificial Satellites of the Earth*, trans. B. S. Sharma (Delhi: Hindustani Publishing Corp. [India], 1960), p. iv. The book's dust jacket bears the imprint Gordon and Breach Science Publishers, New York, 1961, presumably the United States copublisher.

23. Kurt R. Stheling, *Project Vanguard* (Garden City, N.Y.: Doubleday, 1961), pp. 17–25. This is perhaps the best overall review of the Vanguard project. Interested readers can check opinions of the time by looking at their hometown newspapers—wherever in the world that may be—of the day.

24. *New York Times*, Oct. 5, 1957. Walter Sullivan, for many years the dean of American science reporters, was only one of those who made this false assumption.

25. "The Impact of Sputnik on the Standing of the U.S. versus the U.S.S.R." (United States Information Agency, WE-57, Dec., 1957). See also "Post Sputnik Attitudes toward NATO and Western Defense" (United States Information Agency, Report No. 53, Feb., 1958). Again, a look at almost any contemporary newspaper or news magazine in the world will give a good perspective on public opinion at the time.

26. *Preliminary History of the National Aeronautics and Space Administration during the Administration of President Lyndon B. Johnson: November 1963 – January 1969*, final edition (Washington, D.C.: National Aeronautics and Space Administration, 1969), p. I-9.

27. Eugene M. Emme, *Aeronautics and Astronautics: An American Chronology of Science and Technology in the Exploration of Space, 1915–1960* (Washington, D.C.: National Aeronautics and Space Administration, 1961), p. 83.

28. Emme, *Aeronautics and Astronautics*, pp. 95, 98.

29. *Hearings before the Select Committee on Astronautics and Space Exploration: Eighty-Fourth Congress, Second Session, on H. R. 11881* (Washington, D.C.: U.S. Government Printing Office, 1958).

30. Ibid., p. 3.

31. Ibid., pp. 26–28.

32. *What's Ahead in Space: America's Astronautical Timetable* (New York: Grosset & Dunlap, 1960), pp. 3–23; Oran Nicks recalls that North American Aviation made a serious corporate proposal in 1958 to send two manned ships on (flyby) missions to Mars and return in 1964.

33. *Hearings on H. R. 11881*, p. 2.

34. Ibid., pp. 12–13.

35. Ibid., p. 13.

36. Ibid.

37. Ibid., p. 5.

38. Ibid., pp. 5–13, 220–21.

39. Public Law 85–568, 85th Congress, H. R. 12575, July 29, 1958, 72 Stat. 426.

40. "NASA to Take over NACA September 30" (Washington, D.C.: NACA Press Release, 1958).

41. Alex Roland, *Model Research: The National Advisory Committee for Aeronautics 1915–1958*, vol. 1 (Washington, D.C.: National Aeronautics and Space Administration, 1985), pp. 186–93, 296–303. Roland is quite candid about the NACA's good and bad points. On page 243 he describes the "exhaustive and exhausting" editing process undergone by NACA reports.

42. *First Annual Report to the Congress of the National Aeronautics and Space Administration* (Washington, D.C., U.S. Government Printing Office, 1959), pp. 42–43. In the same publication, pp. 81–84, is the text of the agreement between NASA and the army.

43. Henry C. Dethloff, *Suddenly, Tomorrow Came . . .: A History of Johnson Space Center* ([Houston]: NASA, Lyndon B. Johnson Space Center, 1993), pp. 17–33.

44. Ibid., pp. 27–29.

45. *What's Ahead in Space: America's Astronautical Timetable. Staff Report of the Select Committee on Astronautics and Space Exploration* (New York: Grosset & Dunlap, 1960).

46. *First Semiannual Report to the Congress of the National Aeronautics and Space Administration* (Washington, D.C.: U.S. Government Printing Office, 1959), p. 8.

47. *Hearings before the Committee on Science and Astronautics and Subcommittees Nos 1, 2, 3, and 4, U.S. House of Representatives, Eighty-Sixth Congress, First Session, on H. R. 6512*, p. 7.

48. Earl. C. Slipher et al., "Final Report," Contract No. AF 19(122)-162, Lowell Observatory, Sept. 30, 1952.

49. William M. Sinton, Ph.D. dissertation, "Distribution of Temperatures and Spectra of Venus and the Other Planets," Johns Hopkins University, Baltimore, Md., 1953.

50. *Map of the Moon* (Philadelphia: Missile and Space Vehicle Department, General Electric, 1959).

51. This was common knowledge among astronomers of the time. See Sinton, interview; *What's Ahead in Space: America's Astronautical Timetable* (New York: Grosset & Dunlap, 1960).

52. Sagan, interview; and see Gerard P. Kuiper, ed., *The Sun* (Chicago: Univer-

sity of Chicago Press, 1953). Gerard P. Kuiper, editor, *The Earth as a Planet* (Chicago: University of Chicago Press, 1954, 2nd impression, 1958). Gerard P. Kuiper and Barbara M. Middlehurst, eds., *Planets and Satellites* (Chicago: University of Chicago Press, 1961). Barbara M. Middlehurst and Gerard P. Kuiper, eds., *The Moon, Meteorites, and Comets* (Chicago: University of Chicago Press, 1963).

53. Gerard P. Kuiper, ed., *Photographic Lunar Atlas: Based on Photographs Taken at the Mount Wilson, Lick, Pic du Midi, McDonald and Yerkes Observatories* (Chicago: University of Chicago Press, 1960).

54. Kuiper, ed., *The Sun;* Kuiper, ed., *Earth as a Planet;* Kuiper and Middlehurst, eds., *Planets and Satellites;* Middlehurst and Kuiper, eds., *Moon, Meteorites, and Comets.*

55. Comments and notes from Oran Nicks, College Station, Tex., Mar. 15, 1995.

56. See, for example, Stanley P. Wyatt, *Principles of Astronomy,* 3rd edition (Boston: Allyn and Bacon, 1977), p. 197.

57. *New York Times,* Oct. 6, 1957.

58. Emme, *Aeronautics and Astronautics,* pp. 104–105.

59. *Preliminary History of NASA,* p. I-80.

60. Emme, *Aeronautics and Astronautics,* p. 120, 124.

61. *First Semiannual Report of NASA,* pp. 14–18.

62. Emme, *Aeronautics and Astronautics,* p. 106.

63. Emme, *Aeronautics and Astronautics,* p. 112.

64. J. B. Sykes, translator, *The Other Side of the Moon* (New York: Pergamon Press, 1960). N. P. Barabashov, A. A. Mikhailov, and Yu. N. Lipsky, eds., *An Atlas of the Moon's Far Side: The Lunik III Reconnaissance,* Richard B. Rodman, translator (New York: Interscience Publishers, 1961).

65. *Preliminary History of NASA,* p. I-19.

66. *Hearings on H. R. 11881,* pp. 18–22.

67. *A Chronology of Missile and Astronautic Events,* pp. 144–48. The Soviets have made it their general practice to launch probes to Mars and Venus in pairs.

68. *Chronology of Missile and Astronautic Events,* p. 130. Among Americans in the know, the joke at the time was that irritation over these failures was what caused Khrushchev to bang his shoe on the table at the U. N. General Assembly.

69. [Charles S. Sheldon II], *United States and Soviet Progress in Space: Summary Data through 1979 and a Forward Look* (Washington, D.C.: U.S. Government Printing Office, 1980), p. CRS-60.

70. Comments and notes from Oran Nicks, College Station, Tex., Feb. 22, 1995.

71. Oran W. Nicks, *Far Travelers: The Exploring Machines* (Washington, D.C.: National Aeronautics and Space Administration, 1985), pp. 96–101.

72. Ibid., pp. 141–43.

73. Ibid., pp. 124–26.

74. Ibid., pp. 124–40.

75. Oran W. Nicks, interview, College Station, Tex., Nov. 1994.

76. Nicks, *Far Travelers,* pp. 175–76; Linda Neuman Ezell, *NASA Historical Data Book,* vol. 2: *Programs and Projects 1958–1968* (Washington, D.C.: NASA, 1988), pp. 39–40, 331–38.

77. Ibid., pp. 13–16.

CHAPTER 9. THE NASA CONNECTION

1. Gerald A. Soffen, *Journal of Geophysical Research* 82 (1977): 3961. Many deserving names have been left out of this brief description, and my only defense is that to have included them all would have left this portion of the text looking like a telephone directory. My sincere apologies to those who were omitted.

2. William David Compton, *Where No Man Has Gone Before: A History of Apollo Lunar Exploration Missions* (Washington, D.C.: NASA, 1989), pp. 4–7.

3. *New York Times,* Aug. 1, 1961.

4. Ibid.

5. P[hilip] H. A[belson]., *Science* 140 (1963): 267.

6. *Scientists' Testimony on Space Goals* (Washington, D.C.: U.S. Government Printing Office, 1963), p. 1.

7. Ibid., pp. 5–6.

8. Homer E. Newell, *Beyond the Atmosphere: Early Years of Space Science,* (Washington, D.C.: NASA, 1980), pp. 223–42.

9. The issue was *Astromomical Journal* 69 (1964) and the articles were by L. Carpenter, p. 2; R. M. Goldstein, p. 12; W. K. Klemperer, G. R. Ochs, and K. L. Bowles, p. 22; D. O. Muhleman, p. 34; and F. D. Drake, p. 62. O. N. Rzhiga, in M. Florkin and A. Dollfus, eds., *Life Sciences and Space Research* (Amsterdam: North-Holland Publishing Company, 1964), p. 178.

10. L. R. Koenig et al., *Handbook of the Physical Properties of the Planet Venus* (Washington, D.C.: National Aeronautics and Space Administration, 1967), pp. 19–21, contains a succinct summary of the early radar work on Venus.

11. Ibid.

12. *Mariner-Venus 1962: Final Project Report,* (Washington, D.C.: National Aeronautics and Space Administration, 1965), pp. 11–13, has a short summary of the change in plans from a JPL point of view. Oran W. Nicks, *Far Travelers,* pp. 14–17, gives a view from NASA Headquarters.

13. *Mariner-Venus 1962,* p. 87. Nicks, *Far Travelers,* pp. 1–5.

14. *Mariner-Venus 1962,* pp. 1, 97–120.

15. [Charles S. Sheldon II], *United States and Soviet Progress in Space: Summary Data through 1979 and a Forward Look* (Washington, D.C.: U.S. Government Printing Office, 1980), p. 70.

16. *Mariner-Venus 1962,* pp. 327–37.

17. Carl Sagan, in Carl Sagan, Tobias C. Owen, and Harlan J. Smith, eds., *Planetary Atmospheres,* International Astronomical Union Symposium No. 40, held in Marfa, Tex., Oct. 26–31, 1969 (Dordrecht, Holland: D. Reidel Publishing Company, 1971), p. 116.

18. Ibid., pp. 313–27.

19. I must acknowledge Oran W. Nicks's reference to Murphy's Law in connection with the Ranger project. Murphy's law can be stated as: "If anything can possibly go wrong, it will."

20. See Nicks, *Far Travelers,* pp. 96–123.

21. *Investigation of Project Ranger* (Washington, D.C.: U.S. Government Printing Office, 1964). The interested reader should read this entire publication, for it reveals in detail how space missions were done.

---

22. Arnold S. Levine, *Managing NASA in the Apollo Era* (Washington, D.C.: NASA, 1982), pp. 15–16.

23. Ibid., p. 23.

24. *Ranger VII: A Special Report* (Washington, D.C.: National Aeronautics and Space Administration, 1964).

25. Nicks, *Far Travelers*, pp. 124–40.

26. [Sheldon], *Progress in Space*, pp. 57, 65.

27. Surveyor Scientific Evaluation and Analysis Team and associated working groups, *Science* 150 (1966): 1737–50.

28. L. D. Jaffe and R. H. Steinbacher, in *Surveyor Program Results*, compiled by Surveyor Program, Lunar and Planetary Programs Division, Office of Space Sciences and Applications (Washington, D.C.: National Aeronautics and Space Administration, 1969.

29. Nicks, *Far Travelers*, pp. 141–56.

30. Ibid., pp. 76–77. C. P. Sonett arranged and chaired that meeting, and he was dumbfounded at the result. For a terse yet illuminating account, see C. P. Sonett, *Journal of Geophysical Research* 99 (1994): 19,175.

31. At the time, one acrid comment on the situation was, "If you were Columbus, would you rather have an infrared spectrogram of the shore of the New World or a photograph?" As experience showed, the pictures win hands down every time.

32. A. Dollfus, *Comptus Rendus de l' Académie des Sciences 256 (1963):* 3009; *Mémoirs de la Société Royale de Liège*, 5th series, vol. 9 (1964): 392.; *Comptus Rendus* 261 (1965): 1603.

33. The Victoria failure to detect water on Mars is in H. Spinrad and E. H. Richardson, *Icarus* 2 (1963): 49.

34. H. Spinrad, *PASP* 75 (1962): 190. L. D. Kaplan, G. Munch, and H. Spinrad, *Astrophysical Journal* 139 (1964): 1.

35. Ronald A. Schorn, in Sagan et al., eds., *Planetary Atmospheres*, p. 223. This is a detailed history of the spectroscopic search for water on Mars.

36. Edward Clinton Ezell and Linda Neuman Ezell, *On Mars: Exploration of the Red Planet 1958–1978* (Washington, D.C.: National Aeronautics and Space Administration, 1984), p. 93. This proceedings of this meeting were never published and now appear to exist only in the memories of the participants. Although I arranged the meeting, I have no written or printed record that it ever happened! Ezell and Ezell give no citation for this gathering, but one can only praise them for their ability to find out about it.

37. Robert B. Leighton et al., *Mariner Mars 1964 Project Report: Television Experiment, Part I. Investigators Report: Mariner IV Pictures of Mars* (Pasadena, Calif.: Jet Propulsion Laboratory, 1967).

38. I have not succeeded in finding an original copy of this comic book, but the panels in question are reproduced in Jules Feiffer, compiler, *The Great Comic Book Heroes* (New York: Dial Press, 1965), pp. 151–52.

39. See, for example, Nicks, *Far Travelers*, p. 171. Also see Ezell and Ezell, *On Mars*, pp. 77–80.

40. Ronald A. Schorn, Crofton B. Farmer, and Steven J. Little, *Icarus* 11 (1969): 283. Ronald A. Schorn et al., *Science* 170 (1970): 1308.

41. *New York Times*, March 25, 1969. *Time*, April 4, 1969, p. 48.

42. Richard Goody, in Leo Goldberg, David Layzer, and John G. Phillips, eds.,

Annual Review of Astronomy and Astrophysics, vol. 7 (Palo Alto, California: Annual Reviews, 1969), p. 330.

43. *New York Times,* March 25, 1969. *Time,* April 4, 1969, p. 48.

44. Ezell and Ezell, *On Mars,* pp. 156–59.

45. There is a host of possible citations, but the "long dead Mars" view is concisely summarized in Ezell and Ezell, *On Mars,* pp. 175–80.

46. Ezell and Ezell, *On Mars,* p. 176 is but one of numerous possible citations.

47. See, for example, Ezell and Ezell, *On Mars,* pp. 175–80. There is also an excellent fold-out brochure containing a good selection of images and a concise summary of scientific results from the mission and titled *Mariner Mars 1969: Pictures and Results from Mariner VI and VII* (Publication details are obscure).

48. Ewen A. Whitaker, *The University of Arizona's Lunar and Planetary Laboratory: Its Founding and Early Years* (Tucson: University of Arizona, [sometime after August, 1985]), pp. 25–37.

49. Hyron Spinrad, interview, Moraga, Calif., June 6, 1993. On a personal note, I first became seriously interested in planetary astronomy as a graduate student in 1959, when I spent a summer at Yerkes Observatory at the time when Kuiper was still director.

50. Whitaker, *Laboratory,* pp. 37–46.

51. David S. Evans and J. Derral Mulholland, *Big and Bright: A History of the McDonald Observatory* (Austin: University of Texas Press, 1986), pp. 1–129. McDonald has one of the more interesting histories among observatories, and this is a good read.

52. Ibid., pp. 130–40.

53. Spinrad, interview.

54. Nicks, *Far Travelers,* pp. 58–60.

55. Joseph M. Tatarewicz, *Space Technology and Planetary Astronomy* (Bloomington: Indiana University Press, 1990), pp. 58–61.

56. Evans and Mulholland, *Big and Bright,* pp. 141–43. Interestingly, the authors of that book play down the fact that NASA and the American taxpayers paid for the cost of these improvements. As an aside, this author was the first observer to use the new coude spectroscope, and for the privilege had to spend an entire month helping to put the components of that instrument—which were laying on the floor in boxes—together. An observing assistant, Claude Knuckles, provided most of the expertise, but we both spent many 18 hour days getting the equipment into shape.

57. Whitaker, *Laboratory,* p. 37.

58. Gerard P. Kuiper, Memorandum to Homer P. Newell, June 18, 1960. University of Arizona Archives.

59. Whitaker, *Laboratory,* pp. 40–42.

60. Evans and Mulholland, *Big and Bright,* pp. 146–50. Tatarewicz, *Space Technology,* pp. 78–80. Harlan J. Smith, interviews by James M. Douglas, March–May, 1991, transcribed and edited by Oct. 17, 1992.

61. I have in my possession a photocopy of the original Texas proposal.

62. The bus was pulled out by the assistant observatory superintendent, George Grubb, who supplied the truck with the winch, and head electronics technician Fred Harvey, aided in part by yours truly. All three of us (and our wives) spent a pleasant three days marooned in a winter wonderland on Mount Locke

with Pol Swings (then the president of the International Astronomical Union) and his wife, along with other interesting guests. All in all, none of us would have missed it for the world.

63. Proposal for a 60-Inch Telescope (Pasadena, Calif.: Jet Propulsion Laboratory, 1963).

64. That morning, Smith called me at NASA Headquarters and said that he had to talk to the University of Texas regents that afternoon, and he had to tell them that NASA had approved the deal. My answer was that I had to talk to Newell and tell him that Texas had done the same. By chance, we both had to give our presentations simultaneously. We went ahead, gave assurances to both sides, and were vastly relieved later that afternoon when we learned by telephone that both NASA and the University of Texas had accepted the project.

65. Homer E. Newell, memorandum to Dr. [James C.] Fletcher, Oct. 26, 1971, JPL archives.

66. Ibid., pp. 43–45.

67. Tatarewicz, *Space Technology*, pp. 80–83.

68. Whitaker, *Laboratory*, p. 46.

69. *Ground-Based Astronomy: A Ten-Year Program* (Washington, D.C.: National Academy of Sciences—National Research Council, 1964). The interested reader can scan this entire publication and try to look for the few scraps of attention given to solar system studies. My survey makes it out as a small fraction of one percent.

CHAPTER 10. A GOLDEN AGE

1. Henry Norris Russell, Raymond Smith Dugan, and John Quincy Stewart, *Astronomy: A Revision of Young's Manual of Astronomy*, vol. 1: *The Solar System*, revised edition (Boston: Ginn and Company, 1945), p. 3.

2. The organizers of these gatherings did their best to separate the presentations into mutually exclusive categories, but sometimes there were problems. In 1966 I was nearly the victim of two of these parallel sessions at the Los Angles meeting of the American Astronomical Society. My papers (you could still give two back then), one on infrared planetary spectra and the other on radio observations of quasars, were scheduled for simultaneous sessions. Only fast footwork and willing accomplices prevented a fiasco.

3. Joseph W. Chamberlain, interview, Nassau Bay, Tex., April 13, 1993.

4. I did the yelling.

5. In the 1960s I was told in no uncertain terms by superiors at the Jet Propulsion Laboratory that my publications would not "count" unless they appeared in the *Astrophysical Journal* or *Astronomical Journal*.

6. I once held to this view, and so was completely surprised when a paper describing the confirmation of the presence of water vapor in the atmosphere of Mars—a paper of which I was the senior author—was not only accepted by the *Astrophysical Journal* but was published as a lead article, a position usually reserved for what the editors thought was the most important research result described in a particular issue.

7. One afternoon on the sidewalk next to the Astrophysics Building of the California Institute of Technology, I was corralled in just such a manner.

8. I was at the meeting, and if memory serves correctly (the proceedings were not recorded, to my knowledge), sentiment favoring DPS "adoption" of *Icarus* was general, with discussion pretty well limited to matters of detail, such as any financial liability that the division might have.

9. The meeting itself was held at the old Paisano Hotel in Marfa, Texas, which is 40 miles or so from McDonald Observatory—"just down the road a piece," as distances are judged in the Lone Star State. Some years earlier, the same hotel had been used by the cast and crew of the movie *Giant*, which was filmed in the vicinity. Foreign guests—particularly the Soviets—were suitably impressed by the many candid photographs of James Dean, Elizabeth Taylor, Rock Hudson, and other Hollywood stars that hung on the Paisano's walls.

10. Carl Sagan, Tobias C. Owen, and Harlan J. Smith, editors, *Planetary Atmospheres,* International Astronomical Union Symposium No. 40, held in Marfa, Tex., Oct. 26–31, 1969 (Dordrecht, Holland: D. Reidel Publishing Company, 1971). This book is well worth browsing through, as it gives an accurate picture of the state of planetary astronomy at the time.

11. A. P. Vonogradov et al., in Sagan et al., eds., *Planetary Atmospheres,* p. 3.

12. On seas, Willard F. Libby and P. Corneil, in Sagan et al., eds., *Planetary Atmospheres,* p. 55. At the end of their paper Libby and Corneil suggested that the clouds of Venus might be composed of acid-laden water droplets. They were on the right track. As regards life on the planet, see Joseph Seckback and Willard F. Libby, in Sagan et al., eds., *Planetary Atmospheres,* p. 63.

13. Gerard P. Kuiper, in Sagan et al., eds., *Planetary Atmospheres,* p. 91, advocated ferrous chloride ($FeCl_2$), while Carl Sagan, in the same book, p. 116, promoted water ice crystals. Both were off the mark. See also L. R. Koenig et al., *Handbook of the Physical Properties of the Planet Venus* (Washington, D.C.: National Aeronautics and Space Administration, 1967), pp. 89–98.

14. Sagan et al., eds., *Planetary Atmospheres.* On p. 189 L. D. Kaplan and L. D. Gray Young found that the carbon dioxide on Mars would give rise to an average surface pressure of about 5 millibars, while the carbon monoxide concentration was about one part per thousand by volume. Edwin S. Barker on p. 196 reported that results from the 1967 and 1969 apparitions yielded surface pressures from 4 to 8 millibars, and suggested that the CO_2 abundance appeared to vary by a factor of two as the Martian polar caps waxed or waned. Andrzej Woszczyk presented his work during the 1969 apparition, which indicated elevation differences on Mars amounting to 10 kilometers or so, in good agreement with the latest radar measurements from Earth, which were just beginning to get good enough to show actual height differences on the planet. D. P. Cruikshank also reported on attempts to use differences in the observed strengths of CO_2 bands to estimate elevation differences; in particular he found that the dark area known as Mare Acidalium was several kilometers lower than a bright area with which it was compared. However, this turned out not to be a general trend.

15. There are several articles on the subjects in Sagan et al., eds., *Planetary Atmospheres.* On p. 224, Ronald A. Schorn gives a history of attempts to detect water vapor; on page 237 Robert G. Tull reports on his studies of the latitude variation of the water vapor; S. J. Little relates what the water vapor was doing near Martian opposition in 1969 (not much variation, it turned out); and Andrew P. Ingersoll discussed the possibility of liquid water on the surface.

16. R. B. Leighton et al., in Sagan et al., eds., *Planetary Atmospheres*, p. 260.

17. J. D. Poll, in Sagan et al., eds., *Planetary Atmospheres*, p. 384.

18. Butrica, *To See the Unseen.*

19. See, for example, Gordon J. Pettengill, *Journal of Research of the National Bureau of Standards* 69D (1965): 1617.

20. For a clear explanation of this and other unusual solar motions as seen from the surface of Mercury see, for example, William J. Kaufmann III, *Exploration of the Solar System* (New York: Macmillan, 1978), pp. 396–97.

21. This excellent performance was due Harlan J. Smith's decisions to devote the resources—in people and money—necessary to get the image tube to work as perfectly as possible, and in particular to the skill and hard work of Robert G. Tull, an instrumental genius who spared no effort to obtain excellent spectra. I vividly remember looking for the first time through the back end of the McDonald image tube and actually seeing the infrared spectrum of Venus with my own eyes. This seemed impossible, but actually it was true. As a practical matter, this capability made it far easier than ever before to set up the spectrograph for imaging a particular spectral region. There *is* progress, it seems.

22. Gerard P. Kuiper, in Sagan et al., eds., *Planetary Atmospheres*, pp. 406–408.

23. William Shakespeare, *The Tragedy of Romeo and Juliet*, act 2, scene 2, line 109, in Sylvan Barnet, ed., *The Complete Signet Classic Shakespeare* (New York: Harcourt Brace Jovanovich, 1972), p. 498.

24. Books and substantial articles about the Apollo project number in the thousands. One well-written, comprehensive, and relatively recent review of the subject is William David Compton, *Where No Man Has Gone Before: A History of Apollo Lunar Exploration Missions* (Washington, D.C.: National Aeronautics and Space Administration, 1989).

25. Ibid., p. v.

26. Ibid., pp. v–vii.

27. Ibid., pp. 96–103.

28. Ibid., p. 97.

29. Dethloff, *Suddenly, Tomorrow Came*, p. 180.

30. Ibid.

31. Compton, *Where No Man Has Gone Before*, was my source for most of the detail following in this section of text. See especially pp. 98–109, 147–56, 177–91, 225–55.

32. Ibid., pp. 100–101.

33. Ibid., pp. 154–56.

34. Ibid., pp. 167–72. Of course there were voluminous newspaper and magazine articles on the subject, but citing them would only clutter up these endnotes. Compton, among others, gives a short and sweet summary of the conflict.

35. I was riffed early in 1973.

36. Compton, *Where No Man Has Gone Before*, p. 194. For a good summary of this doleful period, see Newell, *Beyond the Atmosphere*, pp. 193–95. I believe the mission could have been accomplished, and at less than an "astronomical" cost.

37. For an insider's view see Oran W. Nicks, *Far Travelers: The Exploring Machines* (Washington, D.C.: National Aeronautics and Space Administration,

1985), pp. 169–75. During development of the Mars Voyagers, Nicks's title at NASA Headquarters was changed from "Director of Lunar and Planetary Programs" to "Director of Voyager and Acting Director of Lunar and Planetary Programs," a switch that indicates the magnitude of the project. For a different perspective (but the same sad ending), with more discussion of why Voyager was killed, see Edward Clinton Ezell and Linda Neuman Ezell, *On Mars: Exploration of the Red Planet 1958–1978* (Washington, D.C.: National Aeronautics and Space Administration, 1984), pp. 83–118. As an aside, I once inspected a mockup of the Voyager landing vehicle at JPL—it was huge!

38. See, for example Ezell and Ezell, *On Mars*, pp. 175–80.

39. Charles F. Capen, a planetary observer in the 1960s and 1970s at JPL and later at Lowell Observatory, was an early believer in the possibility of such enormous storms happening whenever Mars was closest to the sun in its orbit, and thus solar heating was at a maximum. I remember Capen discussing the subject with great enthusiasm in the mid-1960s, buttressing his argument on telescopic observations dating back to the days of Percival Lowell. Ezell and Ezell, *On Mars*, p. 289, also mention Capen's early theorizing.

40. As an example of what was known at the time (the early 1970s), see an elementary textbook of the period on historical geology, William E. Stokes, *Essentials of Earth History: An Introduction to Historical Geology*, 3rd edition (Englewood Cliffs, N.J.: Prentice Hall, 1973), p. 225–26, where the oldest structurally preserved organisms are estimated to be at least 3.2 to 3.3 billion years old, while indirect evidence such as oil-rich rocks pointed to even more ancient life, perhaps as much as 3.6 billion years old. Since the early 1970s, the estimated age of the earliest life has not changed much. As our planet formed some 4.5 or 4.6 billion years ago, and for some time afterward was subject to intense bombardment by debris remaining from the formation of the major planets, it seems clear that life on our planet "came to stay" about as early as it could. The enthralling possibility that even earlier life was wiped out by cosmic collisions has become a popular speculation, but barring some exceptional discovery this alternative can not be proven. However, it is clear that life on Earth began at a very early stage of our planet's existence, when conditions were probably substantially different from what they are today.

41. Ezell and Ezell, *On Mars*, pp. 121–53. When reading their chapter, one wonders how Viking ever got going.

42. In the mid 1960s, Louis D. Kaplan, then my supervisor at JPL, commented that the Russians "would be surprised at how many people are rooting for them."

43. Ezell and Ezell, *On Mars*, pp. 317–61. After suffering through the seemingly endless early Ranger fiascos, I remember being incredulous at the dual success of Viking.

44. See, for example, Friedrich O. Huck et al., *Journal of Geophysical Research* 82 (1977): 4401. Their conclusion is that "contrary to commonly held belief, the red planet does not appear as red, as seen either from its surface or from earth."

45. The literature on the Viking project is enormous and still growing. To complicate the situation, successive scientific papers on the same subject, sometimes using the same data, and sometimes by the same authors, often came to different conclusions. It was fascinating to read of these veerings and haulings at the time,

but the subject is too complicated to be described in detail here. For a good review of the subject from the perspective of a later time, see, for example, Ezell and Ezell, *On Mars,* pp. 330–423. They give a good blow-by-blow account but, even in a book essentially devoted to Viking, do not have the room to discuss all the nuances. Preliminary results from Viking missions are in *Science* 193 (1976): 759–815, and 194 (1976): 57–104. For an early exhaustive review of the Viking results, see, for example, the special issue of *Journal of Geophysical Research* 82 (1977): 3959 ff.

46. A. P. Vinogradov et al., in Sagan et al., eds., *Planetary Atmospheres,* pp. 3–16.

47. *Mariner-Venus 1967 Final Project Report* (Washington, D.C.: National Aeronautics and Space Administration, 1971).

48. The progress of this debate is summarized in Ronald A. Schorn and Louise Gray Young, *Icarus* 15 (1971): 103. As an aside, the list of references at the end of this article provides an interesting example of the fact that, despite the increasing influence of *Icarus,* research of interest to planetary scientists was still appearing in a wide variety of publications (a situation that prevails to the time of this writing). Of 29 citations, 11 are to *Icarus,* while the rest are scattered among eight other sources.

49. P. Connes, J. Connes, W. S. Benedict, and L. D. Kaplan, *Astrophysical Journal* 147 (1967): 1230.

50. This section is largely based on a report by R. L. Newburn, Jr. and S. Gulkis, *A Brief Survey of the Outer Planets Jupiter, Saturn, Uranus, Neptune, Pluto, and Their Satellites* (Pasadena, Calif.: Jet Propulsion Laboratory, 1971). This succinct, 63-page summary is essentially complete up to February 15, 1971.

CHAPTER 11. DECLINING PROSPECTS

1. Dethloff, *Suddenly, Tomorrow Came,* pp. 209–22.

2. Linda Neuman Ezell, *NASA Historical Data Book,* vol. 3, *Programs and Projects, 1969–1978* (Washington, D.C.: NASA, 1988), pp. 93–108; and see Roland W. Newkirk and Ivan D. Ertel, with Courtney G. Brooks, *Skylab: A Chronology* (Washington, D.C.: NASA, 1977).

3. Ezell, *NASA . . . Programs and Projects,* pp. 102–108.

4. Newkirk, Ertel, and Brooks, *Skylab: A Chronology,* pp. 380–389.

5. Ezell, *NASA . . . Programs and Projects,* p. 96.

6. Ezell, *NASA . . . Programs and Projects,* pp. 108–13.

7. See, for example, Homer E. Newell, *Beyond the Atmosphere: Early Years of Space Science,* SP-4211 (Washington, D.C.: NASA, 1980), pp. 283–95. For many years, and in particular at the time when the important question was what to do after Apollo, Newell was in charge of all of unmanned space science at NASA Headquarters. A respected space scientist, he was highly placed in the agency but not directly involved with manned missions, and so his comments carry particular weight. William David Compton, *Where No Man Has Gone Before: A History of Apollo Lunar Exploration Missions* (Washington, D.C.: National Aeronautics and Space Administration, 1989), pp. 201–203, describes how budget cutbacks (widely criticized at the time as "penny wise and pound foolish") affected the

Apollo program. Dethloff, *Suddenly, Tomorrow Came,* pp. 205–26, provides an economic historian's view of the period when NASA began to experience falling budgets as a result of a change in the national priorities of the United States.

8. *Science* (March 29, 1974): 1289–1321.

9. Ibid.

10. Ibid.

11. Ibid. Even the initial reprints of the series of articles on the Mariner 10 encounter with Venus featured the "blue and white" Venus.

12. Henry S. F. Cooper, Jr., *The Evening Star: Venus Observed* (Baltimore: Johns Hopkins University Press, 1994), pp. 21–23, gives a compact summary of early Soviet and American probes of Venus.

13. John S. Lewis, *Earth and Planetary Science Letters* 15 (1972): 286. This was an obscure journal compared to *Icarus*, for example, but because there were so few planetary scientists at the time—perhaps a few hundred—Lewis's views spread rapidly among them.

14. Godfrey T. Sill, *Communications of the Lunar and Planetary Laboratory* 171 (1972): 191.

15. Andrew T. Young, *Icarus* 18 (1973): 564.

16. For an early review of the sulfuric acid model see, for example, Andrew T. Young, in James E. Hanse, ed., *The Atmosphere of Venus* (New York: Goddard Institute for Space Studies, no date but probably shortly after Oct. 17, 1974), p. 8.

17. The first I heard of the matter was when Louise Young came into my office and said simply, "It's sulfuric acid." As to many another planetary astronomer, it was clear to me at once that the problem was solved. In this case I knew everybody involved well, and my best guess is that both Geoff Sill and Louise Young thought of the sulfuric acid explanation independently and at about the same time.

18. James A. Dunne and Eric Burgess, in *The Voyage of Mariner 10: Mission to Venus and Mercury* (Washington, D.C.: National Aeronautics and Space Administration, 1978), provide a comprehensive account of the Mariner 10 mission.

19. For a typical, relatively early presentation of Pioneer results, see the special edition of the *Journal of Geophysical Research* (79 [1974]: 3487–3694) devoted to the Pioneer 10 encounter with Jupiter. For a mature, comprehensive revue of the Pioneer missions see Richard O. Fimmel, James Van Allen, and Eric Burgess, *Pioneer: First to Jupiter, Saturn, and Beyond* (Washington, D.C.: National Aeronautics and Space Administration, 1980). See also David Morrison, *Voyages to Saturn,* (Washington, D.C.: National Aeronautics and Space Administration, 1982).

20. The classic descriptions of the zodiacal light and the counterglow are in M. Minnaert, *The Nature of Light and Colour in the Open Air,* translated by H. M. Kremer-Priest, revised by K. E. Brian Jay ([New York]: Dover Publications, 1954), pp. 290–95. I have found the zodiacal light relatively easy to see from clear, dark sites, even at sea level. The gegenschein, however, is another matter. I have seen it only from high altitude observatories when conditions were just right and my eyes had been dark adapted for several hours. The problem seems to be that not only is the counterglow very faint, but it is also "fuzzy," with its brightness dropping gradually toward its edge.

21. Fimmel, Van Allen, and Burgess, *Pioneer,* p. 117.

22. See, for example, the original discovery paper by R. A. Brown and F. H. Chaffee, Jr., *Astrophysical Journal Letters* 187 (1974): L125. (Not everything about planetary astronomy was in *Icarus* even then.)

23. One of the original discovery papers is J. L. Elliot, E. W. Dunham, and D. J. Mink, *Nature* 267 (1977): 328. For a general review of the discovery and interpretation of the rings of Uranus, see A. Brahic, in Gary Hunt, ed., *Uranus and the Outer Planets* (Cambridge, England: Cambridge University Press, 1982), p. 211.

24. Stephen G. Brush, *Reviews of Modern Physics* 62 (1990): 43, gives an exhaustive and well-balanced review of the development in the period from 1956 to 1985—roughly the first three decades of the Space Age—of theories of the solar system's origin. The hundreds of references in this article include, as far as I can tell, every single useful publication on the subject from those years. My treatment here follows Brush's closely. Brush has also published a detailed study of the ups and downs of various theories of the Moon's origin; see *Space Science Reviews* 47 (1988): 211. In part because of the relatively large number of studies performed on actual Moon rocks in the past few decades, and the insights that those investigations provided, his review provides an excellent description of just how difficult it is to pin down the origin of anything in the universe.

25. There was tremendous media coverage of Comet Kohoutek during 1973 and the early part of 1974, and virtually every newspaper in America carried a number of articles about the cosmic visitor. A running account of how the situation developed—more informed than most media stories but still on a popular level—can be found in the pages of *Sky & Telescope* during that period: early brightness predictions, 46 (1973): 91; scaled down expectations, 46 (1973): 285; full-page Cunard advertisement for the special cruise of the *Queen Elizabeth 2*, 46 (1973): 307; and the letdown after the event, 47 (1974): 153 and later issues. A concise summary of the scientific results from the study of Comet Kohoutek is in Donald K. Yeomans, *Comets: A Chronological History of Observation, Science, Myth, and Folklore* (New York: John Wiley, 1991), pp. 227–29.

CHAPTER 12. VOYAGERS TO THE OUTER PLANETS

1. *NASA Pocket Statistics* (Washington, D.C.: National Aeronautics and Space Administration, Jan., 1994), gives a reasonably complete history of the funding levels from 1959 to 1993.

2. The literature churned out about the Grand Tour Mission at the time of its planning was immense, though mostly forgotten and neglected today for obvious reasons. For a succinct review of the rise and fall of the project see Oran W. Nicks, *Far Travelers: The Exploring Machines* (Washington, D.C.: National Aeronautics and Space Administration, 1985, pp. 241–42.

3. The popular and technical literature concerning the Voyager missions and their results is enormous and still growing. Moreover, as the planetary encounters were years apart, books and review articles tend to discuss individual flybys or groups of them. J. Kelly Beatty, Brian O'Leary, and Andrew Chaikin, eds., *The New Solar System*, 2nd edition, (Cambridge, Mass.: Sky Publishing Corporation, 1982), contains a broad view of what we knew about the solar system after the two Voyagers encountered Jupiter and Saturn. A good summary of what we knew

about many facets of Jupiter somewhat later is in Michael J. S. Belton, Robert A. West, and Jürgen Rahe, eds., *Time-Variable Phenomena in the Jovian System* (Washington, D.C.: National Aeronautics and Space Administration, 1989). Much of the material in this book depends upon Voyager observations.

4. The shadow of Jupiter's ring on the planet may have been detected many years before the Voyager missions as a "thin, faint, dusky line known as the Equatorial Band." See Bertrand M. Peek, *The Planet Jupiter* (London: Faber and Faber, 1958), p. 97.

5. Stanton J. Peale, Patrick Cassen, and Ray Thomas Reynolds, *Science* 203 (1979): 892. The tidal heating mechanism is fairly complicated, because Io tends to always has the same side facing toward Jupiter. This situation would raise a permanent tidal bulge that did not move with respect to the body of the satellite and as a result would produce no heating. However, there are other factors at work and that situation does not always apply exactly. The relatively small difference between exact and not quite exact provides the energy to heat Io.

6. When first seeing images of Europa, more than one planetary astronomer with a sense of history exclaimed that "Schiaparelli and Lowell just had the wrong planet!" To tell the truth, the similarity between those observers' drawings of Mars and the actual appearance of Europa is eerie.

7. As with all phases of the Voyager project, the literature concerning the Saturn encounters is voluminous, the scientific papers alone running into the hundreds at least. For a good review, see David Morrison, *Voyages to Saturn* (Washington, D.C: National Aeronautics and Space Administration, 1982) and Beatty et al., *New Solar System.*

8. A. F. O'D. Alexander, *The Planet Saturn: A History of Observation, Theory, and Discovery* (London: Faber and Faber, 1962) contains a reproduction of Antoniadi's 1899 drawing of Saturn showing dark spokes on the A ring as plate 9, while a reproduction of Lyot's 1943 drawing showing numerous ring divisions appears as plate 17.

9. Stephen Larson and John W. Fountain, *Sky & Telescope* 60 (1980): 356, provide a good summary of the situation regarding satellites of Saturn just before the Voyager 1 encounter.

10. See, for example, Morrison, *Voyages to Saturn,* pp. 143–48.

11. Ibid., pp. 152–66.

12. Gary Hunt and Patrick Moore, *Atlas of Uranus* (Cambridge, England: Cambridge University Press, 1989), p. 57.

13. Ibid., pp. 70–72.

14. Ibid., pp. 60–66.

15. Ibid., p. 86.

16. Ibid., pp. 78–84.

17. Eric Burgess, *Far Encounter: The Neptune System* (New York: Columbia University Press, 1991), pp. 6–7; Gary E. Hunt and Patrick Moore, *Atlas of Neptune* (Cambridge, England: Cambridge University Press, 1994), p. 28.

18. Burgess, *Encounter,* pp. 7–8; Hunt and Moore, *Neptune,* pp. 38–41.

19. Burgess, *Encounter,* pp. 54–55; Hunt and Moore, *Neptune,* p. 52.

20. Burgess, *Encounter,* pp. 59–72; Hunt and Moore, *Neptune,* pp. 37–48.

21. Burgess, *Encounter,* pp. 93–107; Hunt and Moore, *Neptune,* pp. 53–57.

22. Burgess, *Encounter,* pp. 107–12; Hunt and Moore, *Neptune,* pp. 58–61.

23. Burgess, *Encounter,* pp. 113–38; Hunt and Moore, *Neptune,* pp. 61–75.

24. Gerard P. Kuiper, *PASP* 62 (1950): 133.

25. A. J. Whyte, *The Planet Pluto* (Toronto: Pergamon Press, 1980), p. 63, mentions this suggestion, which evidently originated with the British theoretical scientist Sir James Jeans soon after Pluto's discovery and was revived two decades later by the American Dinsmore Alter. Several books have been written about Pluto, on both the popular and technical level, but many of them are devoted primarily to the history of its discovery. Whyte's work, while describing this aspect of the story, also gives a good summary of physical investigation of the planet up to the time of writing. Of particular importance is his extensive list of references to technical articles on the subject.

26. Ibid., pp. 57, 97.

27. James W. Christy and Robert S. Harrington, *Astronomical Journal* 83 (1978): 1005.

28. Ibid., p. 125.

29. Dale P. Cruikshank, Carl B. Pilcher, and David Morrison, *Science* 194 (1976): 835.

30. D. Chris Benner, Uwe Fink, and R. H. Cromwell, *Icarus* 36 (1978): 82.

31. Richard O. Fimmel, Lawrence Colin, and Eric Burgess, in *Pioneer Venus* (Washington, D.C.: National Aeronautics and Space Administration, 1983), give a complete description of the dual mission.

32. Henry S. F. Cooper, Jr., *The Evening Star: Venus Observed* (Baltimore: Johns Hopkins University Press, 1994), gives a detailed, popular account of the Magellan mission as well as brief summaries of earlier spacecraft missions to Venus. For a detailed survey of geologic interpretations of the radar results see John. P. Ford et al., *Guide to Magellan Image Interpretation* (Pasadena, Calif.: Jet Propulsion Laboratory, 1993).

33. As one can imagine, the literature about the latest appearance of Halley's comet is enormous and, in fact, even simple summary listings of the initial scientific results fill volumes in themselves. One good example is Zdenek Sekanina, ed., *The Comet Halley Archive Summary Volume,* ([Pasadena, Calif.?]: Jet Propulsion Laboratory, 1991), which thoroughly surveys the situation as of August, 1991.

34. John M. Logsdon, *Isis* 80 (1989): 254, gives a blow-by-blow account of the eventually futile plans of space scientists and others in the United States to mount a mission to Comet Halley. He has included all the important documented steps in this dismal story as well as incisive commentary and judgments (all of them all too true, in my view). It is also fair to add that during this period there was a wide variety of rumors circulating among those interested in space exploration about "what was really going on"—some of which even may have been true.

35. *Science* 232 (1986): 353–85, contains a number of articles decribing the initial results of the International Cometary Explorer's encounter with Comet Giacobini-Zinner.

36. C. M. Yates et al., *Galileo: Exploration of Jupiter's System* (Washington, D.C.: National Aeronautics and Space Administration, 1985), is one of many descriptions of the Galileo mission as originally planned.

37. *Science* 266 (1994): 1835–62, is a special issue containing several articles describing the Clementine mission and the initial scientific results.

38. Select Committee on Astronautics and Space Exploration, *The Next Ten Years in Space 1959–1969*, 86th Cong., 1st Sess., House Document No. 115 (Washington, D.C.: Government Printing Office, 1959), pp. 218–19.

39. The first formal meeting concerning a possible large space telescope in earth orbit was held at O'Hare Airport in Chicago in 1964, organized and chaired by myself. At the recommendation of Aden B. Meinel of the University of Arizona, a target of a primary mirror with a 120-inch diameter was selected, as that seemed to be the biggest that could be produced in the next few decades. When the shuttle was downsized much later, the diameter of the primary mirror was accordingly reduced.

40. *Space Telescope Science Institute*, Association of Universities for Researsearch in Astronomy, European Space Agency, National Aeronautics and Space Administration, n.d., n.p.; *NASA Pocket Statistics*, Jan. 1994, p. B-43.

41. *DPS Newsletter*, Summer 1993, pp. 6–8.

42. *NASA Pocket Statistics*, Jan. 1994, p. B-53; *DPS Newsletter*, Summer 1993.

43. Hubble Space Telescope News, Press Release No.: STScI-PR95-20.

44. Hubble Space Telescope News, Press Release No. STScI-PR95-16, March 21, 1995.

45. The entire episode was of course front page news around the world. However, as of this writing it is still too soon to give a general assesment of the scientific results of the impacts. To give just one example, at first there were no reported spectroscopic detections of water vapor at the crash locations. Eventually there was one, but that claim was later withdrawn. Later still, evidence for water was indeed found. While individual articles continue to appear in various scientific journals, a large number were gathered together in three issues of vol. 22 of *Geophysical Research Letters* in 1995. The particular citations are June 15, pp. 1555–1636; July 1, pp. 1761–1840, and Sept. 1, pp. 2413–40.

CHAPTER 13. PAST AND FUTURE IMPERFECT

1. Over the years, I have has asked many scientists just when they would place the beginning of planetary astronomy. A few opted for the eras of Galileo or William Herschel, but the overwhelming majority voted for a time as far back as astronomical records extend. By and large, planetary researchers take a broad view of the content of the extent of their field and the methods used, and in no uncertain terms they are proud to be part of a science with such a long and interesting history.

2. Doel has essentially finished his study of planetary astronomy in the United States from 1920 to 1960, and he generously sent me early, uncorrected galley proofs of his work. While we disagree on some matters, we agree on a great many others.

3. Solar System Exploration Committee of the NASA Advisory Council, *Planetary Exploration through Year 2000* (Washington, D.C.: National Aeronautics and Space Administration, 1983).

4. National Commission on Space, *Pioneering the Space Frontier* (Toronto: Bantam Books, 1986).

5. Solar System Exploration Subcommittee, Solar System Exploration Division, *Solar System Exploration: 1995–2000* (Washington, D.C.: National Aeronautics and Space Administration, 1994).

6. Committee on Planetary and Lunar Exploration, Space Studies Board, *An Integrated Strategy for the Planetary Sciences: 1995–2010* (Washington, D.C.: National Research Council, 1994).

7. NASA, "NASA Strategic Plan," Feb. 1995, 24 pp.

8. See, for example, *New York Times* (national edition), Dec. 4, 1996. However, almost any newspaper of the time that the reader may care to look up will have carried the story.

9. A good recent summary of the history of Martian climate is Aaron P. Zent, *American Scientist* (Sept.–Oct., 1996): 442. Zent points out that there may have been primitive life on Mars early in the planet's history, and that some forms may still exist in sheltered locations. Note that these statements were written *before* the the Allan Hills meteorite results were announced.

10. I looked over scores of newspapers from around the world for the dates Aug. 7–9, 1996, and the "Life on Mars" story was prominently featured in every single one. The *New York Times* (national edition) had excellent coverage on Aug. 7, and the "Good Gray Lady" even ran a lead editorial on the subject the next day. However, it is only fair to mention that the *Houston Chronicle,* probably because it was "on the spot," appears to have scooped everyone.

11. Such private views are, by their very nature, almost impossible to document, but I have "asked around" about these new claims and found only comments such as, "Well, it could be true."

BIBLIOGRAPHICAL
ESSAY

It is impossible to give anything approaching a complete bibliography of planetary astronomy in a single volume. To take a case in point, the 1959 second edition of Edward Rosen's *Three Copernican Treatises* contains an annotated Copernican bibliography that extends for sixty-nine pages although it includes only works published from 1939 to 1958. As another example, a bibliographic search completed in 1965 by the Jet Propulsion Laboratory on the narrow topic "Mars— Surface Features and Atmosphere," and containing only publications of the 1950s and early 1960s, resulted in two soft-bound volumes weighing a total of five pounds! Sadly, these references are virtually useless even to a Martian specialist, for the few significant items are literally buried under a mass of inferior work.

Thus, only those items that seemed to me especially useful or informative, or that I considered might be of special value to the reader, are discussed here. Their full citations can be found, along with those of other works that have proved helpful in researching and writing this book, in a bibliography at the NASA Headquarters History Office collections in Washington, D.C. Because that bibliography was completed and submitted to NASA in December, 1995, it lacks items that have appeared since then as well as a few that were unintentionally overlooked and are included here.

Not all the works mentioned in this essay or in the bibliography are cited in the main text. Those not cited were used to ferret out sources, furnish suggestions, or provide general background information. All have been read, however, either in full or at least those parts of voluminous and specialized publications that seemed to be needed for the present work. Similarly, not every work cited in the endnotes appears in the bibliography, let alone in this essay. In particular, many research articles published in professional journals appear only in the notes, and even there only as selected references, such as those reviewing the status of a field at a particular time.

The basic idea is to avoid duplication. My intent is to describe here the most important works on planetary astronomy and add others of lesser importance that are missing from the bibliography at NASA Headquarters, but to put the details in the reference notes. In addition, this essay and the bibliography are basically limited to materials written in English. English has virtually become the universal international language, especially in science and particularly in astronomy. Most recent planetary research and historical writing on planetary astronomy has been published in English.

For an introduction to the bibliographic history of planetary science, one can do no better than to begin with David H. DeVorkin's *The History of Modern Astronomy and Astrophysics: A Selected, Annotated Bibliography,* which roughly spans the period from when Galileo first aimed his telescope toward the heavens (late 1609 or so) to the end of 1980, with emphasis on the years between the middle of the nineteenth and twentieth centuries. While he covers all of astronomy, DeVorkin has grouped the planetary items in convenient separate sections and has chosen them well. There are also good listings of general histories, national and institutional histories, and journals, to mention a few of the other topics covered. Each entry has a short descriptive paragraph, which may also contain a quote or a comment. DeVorkin's bibliography is a good job and has been used as the standard against which to check the basic references in this work.

Other bibliographies are much more exhaustive in the length of time covered, the extent of topics included, and the number of entries. However, their very size and their generally less perceptive annotation make them harder to use, and with one exception none have been used extensively in preparing this book. For anyone who who cares to delve further, DeVorkin has an excellent selected list of other, more specialized bibliographies.

However, one specialized work should be mentioned: the *Astronomischer Jahresbericht,* published annually in Berlin from 1900 to 1969. This encyclopedic series aims to present no less than citations and short summaries for all the professional astronomical publications in the world. In 1969, bowing to the establishment of English as the universal scientific language, the German series was replaced by *Astronomy and Astrophysics Abstracts.* However, because of the increasing number of publications over the years, just finding something now in this compendium is getting to be a real chore.

Several histories cover the entire long sweep of astronomy in general, including planetary topics. Among reliable, well-written, overviews published in this century are: prominent solar astronomer Giorgio Abetti's *The History of Astronomy,* published in 1952; Peter Doig's 1950 book, *A Concise History of Astronomy;* and A. A. Pannekoek's *A History of Astronomy,* published in 1961 and produced by a first-rate astronomer, providing good coverage of often neglected topics such as Assyrian astrology, "New-Babylonian" science, and Chaldean tables, going into the subjects deeply enough to provide a good feel for them. Colin A. Ronan's *Discovering the Universe: A History of Astronomy* is a brief 1971 survey by a well-known popularizer of technical subjects. In a similar vein is *And There Was Light: The Discovery of the Universe,* by Rudolph Thiel, originally published in German in 1956, though the 1960 English version is the one I used.

The General History of Astronomy is an ambitious collective project under the general editorship of Michael Hoskin. When complete, it will cover astronomy from the earliest times to about 1950. Several volumes have already appeared, including volume 2, *Planetary Astronomy from the Renaissance to the Rise of Astrophysics, Part A: Tycho Brahe to Newton,* edited by René Taton and Curtis Wilson, and volume 4, *Astrophysics and Twentieth-Century Astronomy to 1950, Part A,* edited by Owen Gingerich.

Some earlier general histories are still useful for showing the prevailing attitudes, ideas, and states of knowledge in the eras when they were written. These works often seem dated, quaint, and even naive today. Still they demonstrate, on the one hand, how advanced astronomy was compared to the other sciences in earlier times, and on the other hand how primitive our knowledge was of the Sun's family, not to mention the rest of the universe, not so long ago. Interestingly, the older a work of this kind is, the larger the fraction of space it devotes to the solar system. One example is *Popular Astronomy,* W. H. Smyth and Robert Grant's 1855 translation of the expanded version of lectures that Francois Arago gave in Paris. Another is Arthur Berry's *Short History of Astronomy from Earliest Times through the Nineteenth Century,* published in 1898 and reprinted in 1961, a popular history and account of where astronomy stood at the beginning of the twentieth century. John F. W. Herschel, son of the discoverer of Uranus and a prominent astronomer in his own right, wrote a number of popular reviews, such as *A Treatise on Astronomy,* of which a new edition was published in the United States in 1844.

A "general history on a restricted theme" is Robert Grant's *History of Physical Astronomy, from the Earliest Ages to the Middle of the Nineteenth Century,* which was first published in 1852 and reprinted in 1966. Concentrating on celestial mechanics—how planets, satellites, comets, and asteroids move—from Newton onward, it is nonmathematical but authoritative.

Another such study is Steven J. Dick's 1982 work, *Plurality of Worlds: The Origins of the Extraterrestrial Life Debate from Democritus to Kant.* This is a fascinating account of the long early history of a subject that today is still of great general interest and that is now an active area of research.

A work in a class by itself is Owen Gingerich's enlightening and entertaining 1992 book *The Great Copernicus Chase and Other Adventures in Astronomical History.* This is a collection of items that first appeared as popular magazine articles on topics as diverse as the origin of the zodiac, the discovery of the spiral arms of the Milky Way, and how to tell if you have been fooled into buying a false astrolabe. The work was not intended to be comprehensive, but many of its sections relate to the history of planetary astronomy, and there are numerous examples of how "accepted" explanation turned out not to be true. It is a good read.

In a similar vein, but generally on a much more difficult level, is Otto Neugebauer's *Astronomy and History: Selected Essays,* a collection of his scholarly publications covering topics from ancient Egyptian to medieval and Renaissance astronomy, including Hindu, Ethiopic, and Tamil topics. Another selective but wide-ranging compendium is Harlow Shapley and Helen E. Howarth's *A Source Book in Astronomy,* published in 1929. The editors' aim was to collect in one handy volume most of the most important astronomical writings from Copernicus onward. Most of the selections relate to planetary astronomy, and the editors capture the essence and spirit of the works involved while avoiding technical details.

Histories of planetary astronomy are few, but a recent one is William Sheehan's *Worlds in the Sky: Planetary Astronomy from the Earliest Times through Voyager and Magellan.* Two short chapters summarize the history of the subject up the beginning of the Space Age, but most chapters are devoted to a single topic such as the Moon, Mars, and so forth. The accent throughout is on the growth of our knowledge about the solar system.

Another recent work is Stephen G. Brush's *A History of Modern Planetary Physics,* a monumental three-volume work giving a detailed description of the advances during the past two centuries in our knowledge of the origins of the solar system, the Earth, and the Moon. Ronald E. Doel's *Solar System Astronomy in America: Communities, Patronage, and Interdisciplinary Science, 1920–1960* gives a detailed and fairly rosy picture of the status of planetary studies during that period.

Once past the rather small number of more or less general histories and collections, there remain books and articles of limited scope. Not surprisingly, some eras or topics are more popular than others. Most of what has been written recently about the history and status of astronomy (including the planetary variety) concerns "modern" times, notably the twentieth century, with a heavy emphasis on events during just the past few decades, a subject on which the literature is enormous. The next most popular topics seem to be the era from Copernicus through Tycho Brahe and Johannes Kepler to Newton (roughly the sixteenth and seventeenth centuries), during which the "New Astronomy" was born, and the era of classical antiquity. Everything else seems to get less attention.

Approaching these specialized works chronologically, the first that must be mentioned is Otto Neugebauer's monumental *A History of Ancient Mathematical Astronomy*. His three large volumes treat the subject—predicting lunar and planetary motions as seen in our sky—from the time when late Babylonian (Chaldean) arithmetic techniques were able to make accurate eclipse predictions (roughly 400 or 300 B.C. in Neugebauer's view) through early Greek astronomy with its development of geometric methods, to Hipparchus, to Ptolemy, and down to the seventh century A.D. Only a few will want to or need to delve into the main part of this 1975 work, but the introduction offers a fine, succinct chronological survey that, among many other topics, covers Islamic and Hindu astronomy and the complicated ways in which classical astronomy was transferred to medieval Europe.

Liba Chaia Taub produced an interesting 1993 study on whether Ptolemy was really an "Aristotelian," as is often assumed. Her work provides an answer (though not until the last few pages!) and gives an engaging picture of the intellectual climate of those days.

Those who would like to try reading the original (or at least the English version) should get G. J. Toomer's *Ptolemy's Almagest*. This translation, which includes vital and informative annotations, has become the standard English version of the great work. It provides startling evidence of just how advanced mathematical astronomy was almost two thousand years ago compared to every other science. Even to someone trained in (modern) celestial mechanics, as I was, this is a daunting work.

J. L. E. Dryer's *A History of Astronomy from Thales to Kepler* came out in 1906, but it is still useful. Dover reprinted the second edition in 1953. Dryer's treatment is not nearly as thorough as Neugebauer's where the two overlap, and it makes no mention of Babylonian work, which was only dimly known a century ago. But there is enough detail to give the flavor of the early work and to demonstrate some of its complexity and cleverness.

Owen Gingerich covers some of the same ground in his *The Eye of Heaven: Ptolemy, Copernicus, Kepler*. This collection of articles is less comprehensive than Dryer's history, but it is much better written, embodies a great deal of modern research, and includes a number of interesting, "nonstandard" subjects.

For the period from Copernicus to Newton there are many books and articles at all levels from the popular to the most scholarly. Here is a selection that I think useful.

Alexandre Koyré's *The Astronomical Revolution,* the English translation of which came out in 1973, offers three essays, beginning with Copernicus, proceeding to Kepler, and including the (today) almost unknown Giovanni Borelli. In a related 1957 work, *From the Closed World to the Infinite Universe,* Koyré traces the development of western European thought from its conception of the relatively small, enclosed universe of pre-Copernican days to the perhaps infinite one of a few centuries later.

In *The Copernican Revolution*, Thomas Kuhn describes how drastically the scholarly European view of the universe changed from pre-Copernican times to the seventeenth century. Kuhn treats much more than strictly astronomical developments, also discussing the vast change undergone by Western civilization as a whole during the same period.

There are numerous examples of the "Great Man" school of history in the biographies and annotated reprints of the works of the scientific giants of this amazing era. We are lucky that some of the most important original works of that age are now conveniently available in modern, translated editions. Unfortunately, it is also true that many of those old works still take years of effort for anyone to understand, even in translated versions, for the computations at issue tend to be involved and the mathematical methods unfamiliar. As a result, these originals played no direct part in the writing of the present book. However, there are authors who have spent the time and effort needed to understand these works, and to "translate" them for the rest of us.

The five-hundredth anniversary of the birth of Nicolaus Copernicus in 1473 spawned a minor industry dedicated to new works related to the famous astronomer. One fortunate result of this interest was the 1992 paperback version of Edward Rosen's *Nicholas Copernicus: On the Revolutions,* perhaps the best English rendition of this earth-shattering work. Copernicus wrote this for professionals of his time, but it is worth looking at even today.

For a wider view of Copernicus, see Rosen's *Three Copernican Treatises* (the 1959 paperback reprint is the more affordable edition). Copernicus himself has been limned in many works. *Copernicus: The Founder of Modern Astronomy* is Angus Armitage's 1957 popular biography, while Jan Adamczewski's *Nicolaus Copernicus and His Epoch* (which bears no printed publication date but appears to have been printed in the early 1970s) describes in some detail the physical, political, and intellectual world in which the famous astronomer lived and worked. Armitage also wrote *The World of Copernicus* (the fifth printing appeared in 1956). This is a popular work that, while concentrating on the title character, tells the story of planetary astronomy from the earliest days to the time of Newton.

Of special interest is Michael J. Crowe's *Theories of the World from Antiquity to the Copernican Revolution,* which mainly deals with the question of whether an informed person of the time (about 1615) would prefer the Copernican theory or its then current competitors. This is a magnificent trip in a time machine, placing the reader right into the era when our concept of the universe was changing crucially.

Tycho Brahe is also the subject of an extensive literature. A good place to start would be Victor E. Thoren's 1990 book, *The Lord of Uraniborg: A Biography of Tycho Brahe.* An earlier work is John Allyne Gade's *The Life and Times of Tycho Brahe.*

Galileo Galilei was primarily a physicist, not an astronomer, though he probably would have protested that he was actually a natural philosopher. There is an enormous amount of published material relating to him. For someone wishing to peruse only one of his works, a good choice would be the 1955 abridged edition of his *Galileo Galilei Dialogue on the Great World Systems in the Sulusbury Translation,* revised and annotated by Giorgio de Santillana—the original of this book was what got Galileo into serious trouble, and it is worth careful study. The 1967 volume *Galileo: Man of Science* is a multiauthor collection of essays edited by Ernan McMullin, commemorating the four-hundredth anniversary of Galileo's birth. Stillman Drake's *Galileo: Pioneer Scientist,* published in 1990, carefully examines how the Italian scientist went about his work.

A good popular book about Kepler is *John Kepler* by Angus Armitage, which appeared in 1966. A deeper and more comprehensive view is the 1959 English version of Max Caspar's definitive *Kepler,* a scholarly work that reads like a novel.

For a historical work that is really a detective story, one cannot beat Rosen's *Three Imperial Mathematicians: Kepler Trapped between Tycho Brahe and Ursus,* a riveting saga showing that planetary astronomy is not the pure and noble story of the search for truth that legend and myth have made of it.

The three-hundredth anniversary of the publication of Newton's epochal *Philosophiae naturalis principia mathematica* brought an enormous increase to the already formidable body of work about him. Two good (and massive) biographies are Richard S. Westfall's 1980 book, *Never at Rest: A Biography of Isaac Newton,* and *In the Presence of the Creator: Isaac Newton and His Times* by Gale E. Christianson, published in 1984. The latter is on a more popular level, but both are impressive works of scholarship. An easier read is Westfall's shorter 1993 biography, *The Life of Isaac Newton.*

Interestingly, Newton's mathematical methods soon became outmoded (except for too long a while in Great Britain), because they generally required a Newton to use them. The result is that the *Principia,* despite its revolutionary impact, is rarely cited today, except by Newtonian scholars, and is read by few contemporary physical scientists. For these reasons it was not used in the preparation of the present work.

For the nineteenth century we are fortunate in having two useful works that neatly cover the era. The first is Agnes M. Clerke's *A Popular History of Astronomy during the Nineteenth Century,* which first appeared in 1885. Astronomy in her day was still such a small field that she could include essentially everything of importance in her time frame. In addition, the science was still primitive enough that she did not have to oversimplify research papers for her readers. (There were some exceptions, for topics such as the highly mathematical calculations of orbits did have to be "popularized.") Finally, she was highly respected by the astronomers of the time and was on friendly personal terms with a remarkably large number of them.

A similar work is Dieter B. Herrmann's 1984 study, *History of Astronomy from Herschel to Hertzsprung,* first published in German in 1973, and translated and revised by Kevin Krisciunas for a 1984 English edition. This is a fine description of how astronomy developed from the late eighteenth to the early twentieth century because Herrmann wrote with a historical perspective—knowing what had turned out to be *really* important—that Clerke could not have had. As it was written when the author lived and worked in the former East Germany, the occasional references to the interaction between astronomical advances and Hegel, Engels, and Marx lend this book a quaint air in places, though they do not interfere with most of the story. The place occupied by planetary studies naturally declines as the narrative proceeds, but good material remains.

The solar system plays a major role in *Other Worlds than Ours: The Plurality of Worlds Studied under the Light of Recent Scientific Researches,* by the popular English writer Richard A. Proctor. This work went through several editions after the first of 1870; it illustrates among other things how widespread was the belief in life on other planets at that time.

For a taste of the extreme specialization and daunting complexity of nineteenth-century celestial mechanics—the most prestigious type of astronomical and indeed scientific research in those days—one need only hunt down a 1912 third edition of W. Klinkerfues's treatise of some eleven hundred pages, *Theoretische Astronomie.* There is no need to read it—scanning a few random pages or even just attempting to pick up this weighty tome will give anyone who tries it the correct impression.

Another technical book on the same topic and covering essentially the same eras, but written to instruct rather to impress, is Forest Ray Moulton's *An Introduction to Celestial Mechanics.* This 1902 text is still useful for students (my well-used version is the thirteenth printing of the 1914 second edition) and also contains quite a bit of history as well as extensive annotated bibliographies. A general reader can profitably skip all the mathematics and just enjoy the physical descriptions.

The controversy over the existence of the canals of Mars was perhaps the most publicized dispute in planetary astronomy over the past hundred years. Percival Lowell's views on the subject are delivered in his *Mars,* which came out in 1895 and was reprinted in 1978; *Mars and Its Canals,* published in 1906; and *Mars as the Abode of Life,* which appeared in 1908. His 1909 work *The Evolution of Worlds* barely mentions the red planet but does present his views on the wider subject of planetary development. A comprehensive modern view of Lowell and the controversy is in William Graves Hoyt's 1976 biography, *Lowell and Mars.*

The "planetesimal hypothesis," which in the first half of the twentieth century temporarily supplanted the venerable "nebular hypothesis" as the favored explanation for the origin of the solar system, provoked a huge literature. Probably one of the most potent agents of change was the series of elementary textbooks on geology with Thomas C. Chamberlain, a cocreator of the new theory, as senior author. For decades his *A College Text Book of Geology* was extensively used across the United States. In the Texas A&M University library, to give just one example, I found a wide variety of different editions, all giving the planetesimal hypothesis prominent treatment.

As to the general state of astronomy in the first half of the twentieth century, Shapley edited another compendium, the 1960 work *Source Book in Astronomy: 1900–1950.* This book devotes only a little more than 10 percent of its pages to "the planetary system" in the widest sense, and nothing at all to the physical constitutions and characteristics of the planets, in stark contrast to his earlier source book. K. Lange and O. Gingerich edited an updated 1979 version with the title *Source Book in Astronomy and Astrophysics 1900–1975* (it is all too easy to confuse the three *Source Books*).

Astrophysics: A Topical Symposium Commemorating the Fiftieth Anniversary of the Yerkes Observatory and a Half Century of Progress in Astrophysics, edited by J. A. Hynek, appeared in 1951. This collection of articles aimed to, and in general did, give a fairly complete and detailed picture of the progress of astrophysics—including solar system work—up to that time. This is an interesting volume because it was one of the last effective efforts to cover all of astrophysics; afterward the field simply became too big.

The story of the discovery of Pluto has been written about many times, but perhaps the best telling of it is by William Graves Hoyt in his 1980 book *Planets X and Pluto.*

Three books not intended for professional scientists nevertheless contain excellent summaries of the state of planetary astronomy in the first half of the twentieth century, as well as illustrating yet again how little we knew about the subject not so long ago. *Astronomy: A Revision of Young's Manual of Astronomy,* volume 1, *The Solar System,* was intended as a textbook for an introductory university course. Written by Henry Norris Russell (then the dean of American astronomers), Raymond Smith Dugan, and John Quincy Stewart, it first appeared in 1926 with a revised edition in 1945. Despite its semipopular nature, this work is definitive for its era.

Fred L. Whipple's *Earth, Moon, and Planets* first appeared in 1941. Written by the scientist who became the world's foremost student of comets, it is an easy read but very reliable record of our knowledge of the subject at the time. Whipple's treatment of Earth as a planet is especially interesting. In a similar way, Fletcher G. Watson's *Between the Planets,* the first edition of which also came out in 1941, covers asteroids, comets, and meteors—the flotsam and jetsam of the solar system. A review of a somewhat later date, but still before space probes and other new techniques had significantly advanced our knowledge of the solar system, was V. M. Blanco and S. W. McCuskey's *Basic Physics of the Solar System,* published in 1961.

Until the Space Age got well into its stride, there were few professional level books written about planetary astronomy in this century. However, there were several titles that are important as benchmarks.

Gerard de Vaucouleurs's *Physics of the Planet Mars: An Introduction to Aereophysics* appeared in 1954 (an earlier French edition came out in 1951) and gives a detailed and rigorous picture of where our knowledge of the red planet stood at the time. The author, who was one of the handful of true planetary *scientists* in that era, makes clear how limited and uncertain our knowledge was. Gerard P. Kuiper edited and partly wrote *The Atmospheres of the Earth and Planets,* the two editions of which came out in 1949 and 1952. This collaborative effort presents what we knew of the subject back then. Most "old-time" planetary astronomers (those who go back three decades or so) have a dog-eared, falling-apart copy of this work on their shelves.

In addition, Kuiper made a conscious effort to provide a standard against which future scientists and historians could judge advances made in the era of direct planetary exploration that he foresaw. He edited, partly with Barbara M. Middlehurst, the four massive volumes of *The Solar System,* which appeared from 1953 to 1963. Unfortunately, the series was never completed as planned (there is nothing on planetary spectra, for example), but the work nonetheless served its purpose and remains a milestone.

Produced during the same period was William W. Kellogg and Carl Sagan's relatively slim but informative 1961 report, *The Atmospheres of Mars and Venus,* a rigorous review of the subject that was of much practical use in designing early planetary probes.

Another landmark, published in 1971, was *Planetary Atmospheres,* the proceedings of a 1969 symposium on planetary astronomy sponsored by the International Astronomical Union (the first such symposium ever devoted entirely to planetary studies—a telling fact). Edited by Carl Sagan, Tobias J. Owen, and Harlan J. Smith, the research reports in it are mostly dated by now, but it is still an important benchmark.

Books, not to mention articles and special editions of scientific journals, about the advances in planetary astronomy in the past three decades would fill a respectable library, and I can only mention a selection.

William J. Kaufmann III's *Exploration of the Solar System* presents a good review of the subject from ancient times to 1978, concentrating on recent developments. It was intended as a university textbook for non—science majors, and as such is clearly written without oversimplifying things to the point of creating errors.

For some reason, the study of comets, particularly their orbits and spectra, was never considered a second-rate occupation by the English-speaking astronomical establishment. Perhaps because of this attitude, literature on comets tends to be scattered thinly but widely through a large number of books, journals, and observatory publications. As might be expected, the last apparition of Halley's comet produced a flood of cometary literature. An excellent comprehensive collection of technical articles fills the two hefty volumes of *Comets in the Post-Halley Era,* edited by Ray L. Newburn, Jr., Marcia Neugebauer, and Jürgen Rahe. These books appeared in 1991, containing papers given at a 1989 conference.

The best and most comprehensive recent popular description of cometary research is Donald K. Yeomans's *Comets: A Chronological History of Observation, Science, Myth, and Folklore,* published in 1991. It is readable yet comprehensive and well documented from primary sources, and the present work leans heavily on it.

An extensive and relatively early survey of meteors is in the 1954 book *Meteor Astronomy.* The author, A. C. B. Lovell, was not an astronomer by training but became one of the founders of the new science of radio astronomy, which devoted much effort in the 1940s and 1950s to the study of the reflection of radio waves from meteor paths.

We also should mention Otto Struve and Velta Zeberg's 1962 publication, *Astronomy of the 20th Century.* This is a superb review of modern astronomy in general, but its importance for our purposes is the light it throws on the abysmal state to which planetary studies had sunk in the eyes of the astronomical mainstream. The text devotes a paltry few pages to the planets. A few special studies deserve particular mention. Ewen A. Whitaker's *The University of Arizona's Lunar and Planetary Laboratory: Its Founding and Early Years,* which appeared in the late 1980s, gives a lively account of the subject including some rare personal glimpses of the LPL founder, Gerard P. Kuiper.

For a good look at the American astronomical scene at the turn of the century, when reputable scientists still did planetary work as a matter of course, Donald E.

Osterbrock's 1984 biography, *James E. Keeler: Pioneer American Astrophysicist and the Early Development of American Astrophysics,* is unsurpassed. Osterbrock, a fine astronomer in his own right, not only gives an intimate view of Keeler's scientific accomplishments and personal life but also pens a superb picture of the development of science in general, and astronomy in particular, in the United States at the beginning of the twentieth century.

Henry C. King's *The History of the Telescope,* published in 1955 and reissued in 1979, is still the best study of the subject. It is an important story because the progress of planetary astronomy, even today, clearly depends strongly on improvements in telescopes and the auxiliary equipment used with them. This volume covers telescopes, pretelescopic instruments, and the development of auxiliary equipment such as spectrographs and photographic apparatus. In addition, King includes treatment of the history of astronomy in general.

Radio astronomy has become a popular field with a huge literature (though there does not appear to be any general history of *planetary* radio astronomy). Two books edited by Woodruff T. Sullivan give a good introduction to early development in the field. One is the 1982 *Classics in Radio Astronomy,* and the other is *The Early Years of Radio Astronomy,* published in 1984. An excellent survey of the development of radio astronomy from its beginnings is J. S. Hey's 1973 history, *The Evolution of Radio Astronomy,* written by a noted pioneer in the field.

Gerrit L. Verschuur's *The Invisible Universe Revealed: The Story of Radio Astronomy,* which first appeared in 1974 and had a second edition in 1987, is a popular and well-illustrated account. It contains a concise history of the field in general and also covers planetary studies, but emphasizes the spectacular and unexpected discoveries that radio observations have revealed about the vast universe beyond the solar system.

Before the field grew so much that the task was more or less impossible, there were several publications that provide "snapshots" of radio astronomy as a whole at specific times. One is *Radio Astronomy,* edited by H. C. van de Hulst, which appeared in 1957 and contains papers presented at an International Astronomical Union symposium held in 1957. A second is the January, 1958, "Radio Astronomy Issue" of the *Proceedings of the Institute of Radio Engineers.* (Note that this first collection of observational, theoretical, and equipment papers appeared in an engineering journal.) A third is *Paris Symposium on Radio Astronomy,* another IAU venture, this one edited by Ronald N. Bracewell. The meeting was held in 1958 and the book published in 1959.

The origins and development of the Space Age are described in numerous publications of various types, due to the great interest in the subject by the general public, historians, economists, engineers, and scientists of many kinds, including astronomers. Here I can only mention a few items that I believe are important.

Of particular interest is a set of four well-written and magnificently illustrated books on the topic, intended for the general public. Significantly, a substantial part of their contents first appeared in pages of the the popular *Collier's* magazine. The first, *The Conquest of Space,* written by rocket pioneer and historian Willy Ley, appeared in 1949. The second, *Across the Space Frontier,* was published in 1952 and edited by Cornelius Ryan. This book was a revelation, for in it top-ranked astronomers such as Fred L. Whipple, along with engineers and space enthusiasts, presented a panorama of new and exciting possibilities. *Conquest of the Moon,* also edited by Ryan, was published in 1953. Wildly visionary as it seemed to most at the time, it was not far off the mark in describing, and only sixteen years in advance, of the first manned Moon landings. The last was *The Exploration of Mars,* by Ley and rocket scientist Wernher von Braun. Well written and well illustrated, in large part by the amazingly prophetic paintings of artist Chesley Bonestell, these volumes inspired many young readers. Numerous planetary scientists trace the beginnings of their careers to reading those books, and I am no exception. To read them is to understand in part how and why the revival of solar system studies in the latter half of the twentieth century came about.

An old standard history of early rocketry is Willy Ley's popular level 1951 volume *Rockets, Missiles, and Space Travel.* There have been many treatments of various missiles, payloads, and programs, an early example being Milton Rosen's *The Viking Rocket Story,* first published in 1955. A different kind of work is *Aeronautics and Astronautics: An American Chronology of Science and Technology in the Exploration of Space 1915–1960,* assembled by Eugene M. Emme and published in 1961. This became an annual series.

Homer E. Newell's 1980 book, *Beyond the Atmosphere: Early Years of Space Science,* describes the origins of space science and the contributions of the National Aeronautics and Space Administration to the advancement of that field. This is an inside view, for Newell was the longtime head of NASA's Office of Space Science. *Far Travelers: The Exploring Machines,* published in 1985, tells the story of the development of lunar, planetary, and interplanetary space probes. Here is another inside story, for the author, Oran W. Nicks, was the head of NASA's Lunar and Planetary Program during the decade in which most of the U.S. space probes to date were launched.

The 1990 work *Space Technology and Planetary Astronomy* by Joseph N. Tatarewicz deals specifically with NASA's role in reviving planetary science. The author gives a detailed look at how and why things developed as they did in the 1950s and 1960s. He ends the story in the 1970s, when the "flush" times for planetary astronomy ended as suddenly and unexpectedly as they had begun. This work is one of a trio of parallel studies commissioned by NASA. The other two are Tatarewicz's *Exploring the Solar System* and Andrew J. Butrica's *To See the Unseen.* These authors have done their best to make their works complement one another's.

While most of its contents do not concern this study, the rise of modern planetary astronomy can be traced in the continuing series *Transactions of the International Astronomical Union,* the first volume of which appeared in 1922. For original research papers of the recent past, *Icarus* has been the premier journal of planetary astronomy since the early 1960s. Before then, and to some extent today, articles also can be found in publications such as the *Astronomical Journal, Astrophysical Journal, Journal of Geophysical Research, Monthly Notices of the Royal Astronomical Society, Nature,* and *Science.* Before World War I, *Astronomische Nachrichten* often carried announcements of current planetary research. Also, various papers can be found in a bewildering worldwide array of journals, observatory publications, monographs, and the like. A special case is *Communications of the Lunar and Planetary Laboratory,* begun by Gerard P. Kuiper in 1962, which lasted until the 1970s and was devoted to studies of the solar system.

In the past two decades there has been a torrent of what might generally be called symposium volumes, which happen like this. Someone calls a meeting on a specific topic ("The Atmosphere of Neptune," or some such theme) and various scientists present papers (which are usually read or summarized verbally) describing their latest research on the subject. These presentations are then collected and published as a hefty book, often without even being set in type, computer-produced camera-ready copy being used instead. Being accounts of research in progress, these volumes in most cases are soon out of date. For that reason, few are included in the bibliography.

On the historical side, the *Journal for the History of Astronomy* has carried many items of interest to this study since it first appeared in 1970. Other publications, such as *Isis,* also contain material about planetary astronomy, but these journals cover such a wide area of knowledge that material useful to this book appears only now and then.

Document collections have been important for this study and I used archives at NASA Headquarters History Office (particularly the William Brunk papers), the National Academy of Sciences, the University of Arizona (especially the Gerard P. Kuiper papers), the University of Texas (Harlan J. Smith papers), Lowell Observatory, the Jet Propulsion Laboratory, the Huntington Memorial Library (the Mount Wilson papers), and others.

Interviews with planetary and other astronomers provided much information that otherwise would have been unavailable for this book. Many significant details, whether intentionally or not, were never placed in the written record. For one thing, most planetary astronomers have never had the luxury of an ever present aide to take down all their words and writings. For another, conversations and decisions sometimes went unrecorded because they seemed visionary, unfounded on solid bases, or unlikely to result in anything positive. Of course, many important matters were never *meant* to be recorded. Then too, planetary atmospheres sometimes play a direct role: when Hurricane Alicia hit the Houston area of Texas in 1983, it destroyed a good part of the correspondence relating to the formation of the Division for Planetary Sciences of the American Astronomical Society.

For these reasons, I tape-recorded and had transcribed a large number of interviews with a broad array of astronomers. In selecting the interviewees, I tried to follow the sage advice of the astronomer and historian Donald E. Osterbrock. He strongly urged that I not limit my discussions only to planetary scientists, with the aim of producing a wider and more balanced range of views. Any failure to achieve that goal is, of course, mine alone. Those interviewed include:

Barnes, Thomas G.	Berkeley, Calif.	June 8, 1993
Barker, Edwin S.	Washington, D.C.	Oct. 13, 1993
Beebe, Rita F.	Boulder, Colo.	Oct. 21, 1993
Belton, Michael J. S.	Tucson, Ariz.	Apr. 23, 1995
Bergstrahl, Jay T.	Washington, D.C.	Feb. 23, 1993
Boyce, Peter B.	Berkeley, Calif.	June 7, 1993
Brandt, John C.	Berkeley, Calif.	June 8, 1993
Brunk, William	Washington, D.C.	Oct. 13, 1993
Chamberlin, Joseph W.	Nassau Bay, Tex.	Apr. 13, 1993
Chapman, Clark R.	Boulder, Colo.	Oct. 22, 1993
Cochran, William D.	Austin, Tex.	May 1, 1993

Cruikshank, Dale P.	Boulder, Colo.	Oct. 19, 1993
de Vaucouleurs, Gerard	Austin, Tex.	May 29, 1993
Franklin, Fred A.	Cambridge, Mass.	Apr. 22, 1993
Fink, Uwe	Tucson, Ariz.	Apr. 24, 1995
Havlen, Robert J.	Berkeley, Calif.	June 10, 1993
Hubbard, Willam B.	Boulder, Colo.	Oct. 21, 1993
Hunten, Donald M.	Tucson, Ariz.	Apr. 23, 1995
Jefferys, W. H.	Austin, Tex.	May 1, 1993
Johnson, Torrence V.	Boulder, Colo.	Oct. 20, 1993
Marsden, Brian	Cambridge, Mass.	Apr. 21, 1993
Newburn, Ray L., Jr.	Pasadena, Calif.	June 15, 1993
Nicks, Oran W.	College Station, Tex.	Nov., 1994
Rea, Donald	Washington, D.C.	Oct. 14, 1993
Roman, Nancy G.	Washington, D.C.	Mar. 24, 1995
Sagan, Carl	Boulder, Colo.	Oct. 19, 1993
Sinton, William M.	Phoenix, Ariz.	Jan. 4, 1993
Smith, Bradford A.	Berkeley, Calif.	June 10, 1993
Smith, Harlan J.	Austin, Tex.	March–May, 1991
Charles P. Sonnett	Tucson, Ariz.	Apr. 23, 1995
Spinrad, Hyron	Berkeley, Calif.	June 10, 1993
Tifft, William G.	Berkeley, Calif.	June 8, 1993
Trafton, Laurence M.	Austin, Tex.	May 2, 1993
Traub, Wesley A.	Cambridge, Mass.	Apr. 22, 1993
Tull, Robert G.	Austin, Tex.	May 1, 1993
Wells, Donald C.	Berkeley, Calif.	June 10, 1993
Whipple, Fred L.	Cambridge, Mass.	Apr. 20, 23, 1993
Whitaker, Ewen A.	Tucson, Ariz.	Apr. 24, 1995
Yeomans, Donald K.	Kingsville, Tex.	Mar. 28, 1994
Young, Andrew T.	College Station, Tex.	Mar. 26, 1994

The interviews with Harlan J. Smith were conducted by James N. Douglas in 1991; the remaining interviews were by me. Tapes and transcriptions are available at the NASA Headquarters History Office.

INDEX

Bobrovnikoff, N. T., 138
Bode, Johann Elert, 44, 50
Bode's Law. *See* Titius-Bode Law
Boeing Company, 205
Bond, George, 55
Bond, William Cranch, 54, 66
Bonestell, Chesley, 160
Bradley, James, 39–40
Brahe, Tycho. *See* Tycho Brahe
Brandes, H. W., 51
Braun, Wernher von, 160, 161, 173
Bredikhin, Fedor Alexsanrovitch, 79
Brown, Ernest W., 82
Brucia, 74
Brunk, William E., 219–20
Bunsen, Robert, 62
Burke, Bernard E., 147–48
Butrica, Andrew J., 151

California Institute of Technology
    (CalTech), 203–204, 218
Callisto, 276
Campbell, William W., 99, 100,
    101–103
Carr, Michael E., 194
Carte du Ciel, 72
Cassini, Jean Domenique, 30–33
celestial mechanics, 26, 32–37, 41–42
celestial sphere, description of, xii
Centaur rocket, 189, 190, 200, 204,
    205, 244, 291
Cepheid variable stars, 111, 116
Ceres, 50
Cernan, Eugene A., 238
Challis, James, 56–57
Chamberlain, Joseph W., 157, 225
Chamberlain, Thomas C., 105–107
Charles II (king of England), 33
Charon, 285–86
Charte der Gebirges des Mondes, 80
Chicago, University of, 213
China, astronomical knowledge, 5–6
Chladni, Ernst F. F., 51
Christy, James W., 285
chromatic aberration, 27, 37–38, 40
Clairaut, Alexis Claude, 41
Clarke, Arthur C., 160–61
Clementine mission, 292, 310

Clerke, Agnes, 79
clocks: chronometers, 39; pendulum
    regulation, 28
Coblentz, W. W., 124
Collier's, 160, 161, 255
Columbus, Christopher, 212
comets, xvi, 36, 52–53, 76–79, 109–
    10, 158–59; Arend-Roland, 268;
    Biela's, 53, 76; composition of, 78,
    109, 127; dirty snowball theory,
    158–59, 290; Donati's, 76, 77; of
    1811, 52; of 1843, 52, 126–28;
    Encke's, 52–53; of 1577, 18–19;
    Giacobini-Zinner, 290; Great Sep-
    tember of 1882, 77, 78; Great
    Southern, 76; Halley, 37, 41, 52,
    53, 109, 270, 289–90; Kohoutek,
    253, 269–71; nature, 78, 158–59;
    Oort cloud, 158; origin of, 79, 158;
    possible distant, quiescent nuclei,
    310; Shoemaker-Levy 9, 295; short
    period, 37, 53; spectra, 78, 158;
    sungrazers, 77, 78; Swift-Tuttle,
    76; tails, 79, 110; Tebbutt's of
    1861, 76; Tebbutt's of 1881; Tem-
    pel, 78; Temple-Tuttle, 78; water,
    270–71; Winnecke's, 78
Compton, William David, 232, 234,
    239
Comte, Auguste, 62–63
Conquest of Space, 160
Conquest of the Moon, 161
Conrad, Charles, Jr., 253
constellations, xvi, 3–4
contraction theory, 108
Copeland, Ralph, 78
Copernicus, Nicolaus, 17–18, 300
counterglow, 263–64
Cours de Philosophie Positive, 62
Cruikshank, Dale P., 286

Daguerre, Louis Jaques Mande, 64
D'Alambert, Jean-le-Rond, 41
D'Arrest, Heinrich Louis, 56
Darwin, George H., 82
Dawes, W. R., 55
deferent, 12
De Forest, Lee, 171

Grovers Mill, New Jersey, 137
Gruithuisen, F. von P., 54

Hagan, John P., 178
Hainaut, Olivier, 294
Hale, George Ellery, 97, 115, 226
Hall, Asaph, 87, 89
Hall, Chester Moore, 40
Halley, Edmond, 37–39
Halley's Comet probes: European
    Space Agency, 290; Japanese, 290;
    Soviet Vegas, 290; U.S. lack of,
    289–90
Hardie, Robert H., 285
Harrington, Robert S., 285
Harrison, John, 39
Harvard Observatory, 61-inch reflec-
    tor, 167
Haser, L., 158
helical rising and setting, xiv
heliocentric theory: of Aristarchus, 11;
    of Copernicus, 17–18; eventual gen-
    eral acceptance, 24; of Heraclides,
    11
Helmholtz, Hermann, 108
Henderson, Thomas, 58
Heraclides of Ponticus, 11
Herschel, John, 45, 55, 60, 64–65
Herschel, William, 43–45, 46–49, 50,
    265, 272
Hertzsprung, Ejnar, 111
Hess, Wilmot N., 234, 235
Hevelius, Johannes, 29
Hey, James S., 142, 144, 150
Himalia, 109
Hipparchus of Nicaea, 13–14
Hitler, Adoph, 136
Hooke, Robert, 30
Howarth, Helen E., 138
Hubble, Edwin, 116–17, 292
Hubble Space Telescope (HST),
    292–95; team science, 294–95
Huggins, William, 70–71, 73, 78, 85,
    88, 99
Hughes Aircraft, 204
Hull, G. F., 110
Huygens, Christian, 27, 28, 30–32
Hyperion, 54

Iapetus: discovery of, 30; bizarre sur-
    face, 30–31, 45, 279
Icarus, 227–28
ice worlds, 276, 281, 283
Ida, 291
image tubes, 230–31
impact studies, 80, 123–24, 128–30
infrared studies, 48, 123–24, 156–57
Integrated Astrategy for the Planetary
    Sciences: 1995–2010, 309
International Astronomical Union,
    Marfa, Tex., meeting, 228–31
International Geophysical Year, 170
International Sun-Earth Explorer 3,
    290
Io, 32; emission lines, 264–65; vulcan-
    ism, 275
Irwin, Jim, 238
island universes, 117
Ives, Herbert B., 129–30

James, Philip, 295
Jansky, Karl Guthe, 133–34
Janssen, Pierre Jules Cèsar, 77, 99
Jeffreys, Harold, 122
Jet Propulsion Laboratory (JPL), 178,
    189, 200, 203–204, 218, 244; 60-
    inch telescope proposal, 218
Johnson Space Center, 178, 234
Journal des Savants, 32
Journal of Geophysical Research,
    227
Juno, 50
Jupiter, 249; albedo of, 60; belts of,
    29; cloud features of, 262, 275;
    and collision with Comet
    Shoemaker-Levy 9, 295–96, 298;
    composition of, 167; Galilean
    moons, 21, 29, 249, 262, 276; inter-
    nal heat, 291; mass of, 35; oblate-
    ness of, 31; radiation belts of, 147;
    radio bursts, 148; Red Spot on, 85–
    86, 275; ring of, 275; rotation
    period of, 31; spectrum of, 85, 156,
    167. See also individual satellites
Jupiter-C, 174
Jupiter satellites, 109. See also individ-
    ual satellites

Mars (*cont.*)
208, 210, 229, 243, 246–47;
meteor from, 310; Nix Olympica
(later Olympus Mons), 211–12,
241, 242; photographs of, 95–96;
polar caps on, 31, 242, 246; radar
studies of, 244; river systems on,
243; rotation period of, 31, 55;
sand dunes on, 242; satellites of,
89; spectra of, 99–103, 157; surface features of, 29, 165–66, 190,
210–12; surface pressure of, 124–
26, 158, 209–10; volcanos on,
165–66, 210, 241; water on, 207–
208, 210–11, 229, 242–43
Mars, 95
Mars and Its Canals, 95
Mars as the Abode of Life, 95
Mars Committee, 155
Mars expeditions, 239
Marshall Space Flight Center, 178,
252
Mars Observer, 247, 289
Mars Pathfinder, 247
Mars 3, 242
Mars 2, 242
Marvin, Ursula B., 80
Masursky, Harold, 194
Mauna Kea Observatory of the Uni-
versity of Hawaii, 213, 216, 218–
20
Maunder, E. Walter, 97, 99
Maxwell, James Clerk, 55, 79
Mayer, Simon, 29
McCormack, John W., 176
McDonald Observatory of the Univer-
sity of Texas, 213–15; 82-inch
reflector, 213–14, 215; 107-inch
reflector, 216, 217–18
McKay, David S., 310
McLaughlin, Dean B., 165–66
Méchanique Analytic, 42
Melotte, Pierre, 109
Menzel, Donald H., 104, 124, 125
Mercury, 260–61; albedo of, 83; ano-
molous orbital motion of, 83–84,
118; brightness variations of, 83;

phases discovered on, 29; rotation
period of, 83, 230; surface features
of, 260
Mercury project, 179
Meteor Crater, 80, 130
meteorites, 51, 76; ages, 157
meteors, xvi, 75–76, 127; interstellar,
127; radio studies, 149–51
meteor showers, 51–52, 76; Leonid,
51–52, 76, 149; Perseid, 52, 76
Micrographia, 30
Milky Way, 21, 47, 116
Miller, George, 233
Miller, George F., 180
Miller, William A., 70, 73
Millman, Peter M., 139
Millochau, 100
Mimas, 44, 279
Miranda, 281
Mir space station, 254
Mitchell, Edgar, 238
Monatliche Correspondenz, 50
month, lunar, xiv
Moon, 168–70; age of, 236; albedo of,
60, 80–82; changes on, 81; composition of, 236–38; crater origins on,
30, 54, 81, 129–30, 168–69, 236;
daily and monthly motions of, xiii-
xiv; dust layers on, 169, 205; his-
tory of, 236–38; mapping, 29, 49,
54, 80–81, 204–205; maria, 236;
mascons, 233; naming features,
29–30, 49, 54; origin of, 82, 237,
238, 267–68; radar contact with,
151; radio observations of, 147;
and Soviet Mountains, 206; surface
of, 81–82, 204–206; tidal history
of, 82; volcanic activity on,
169–70; water ice deposits in polar
craters, 310
Moon Committee, 130–31
Moore, Joseph H., 104
Moore, Roger C., 215–17, 218
Morrison, David, 286
Moulton, Forest Ray, 105–107
Mount Palomar Observatory, 200-
inch reflector, 167

Shoemaker, Eugene M., 183, 295
Sidereus nuncius, 21
Sill, Godfrey T., 259
Sinope, 109
Sinton, William M., 167–68
Skylab program, 252–54, 271; scientific results, 253–54; Skylab 1, 253; Skylab 2, 253; Skylab 4, 253
Slipher, Earl C., 95, 104
Slipher, Vesto M., 100, 101, 111–12, 117
Smith, Bradford A., 194
Smith, Harlan J., 213–14, 215, 225–26, 231
Soderblom, Lawrence A., 194
solar motion, 47
solar system: age of, 108, 159; origin of, 42–43, 105–108, 132–33, 153–55, 266–67
Solar System Exploration: 1995–2000, 308–309
Source Book in Astronomy, A, 138
Source Book in Astronomy: 1900–1950, 138
Soviet challenges, 195–96
space probes, 187–88, 189–90; early attempts, 185–86. *See also specific missions*
Space Shuttle, 252, 254–55, 271, 291, 293, 294
Space Task Group, 178
Space Telescope Science Institute at Johns Hopkins University, 293, 294
spectra, stellar, 110–11
spectroscopy, 38, 61–64, 69–71, 72–74, 104–105, 119–22, 166–68
speed of light, 32
Spinrad, Hyron, 207–209, 213, 214, 218
Spitzer, Lyman, Jr., 133
Sputniks: I, 172–73; II, 174; IV, 187; V, 187; and American response, 174–77
stars, nightly motion of, xii–xiii
stellar evolution, 110
stellar energy sources, 108, 117–18
Stoney, G. Johnstone, 103, 210
Storrs, Alex, 294

Struve, F. G. Wilhelm, 58, 225–26
Struve, Otto, 146
Sun: annual motion of, with respect to the stars, xiv; daily motion of, xiii
Surveyor program, 188–89, 204–205; Surveyor 1, 205
Swings, P., 158
synchrotron radiation, 145
Syntaxis. See Almagest
Systema Saturnium, 30

teams, science, 192–94
telescopes, 67–68; and achromatic lenses, 40; and photographic refractors, 65; as reflecting, 37–38, 44, 59, 116; slow initial development of, 27
Tethys, 30
Thales of Miletus, 8
Themis, 88
tidal friction, 81
Titan, 30, 153, 250, 263, 278, 310
Titania, 44, 280
Titan rocket, 292
Titan III rocket, 244
Titius, Johann Daniel, 49
Titius-Bode Law, 49–50, 57, 267
Titov, Gherman S., 195
Tombaugh, Clyde W., 132
Traité de Méchanique Céleste, 42
transits of Mercury, 28
transits of Venus, 28, 41
Treatise on Electricity and Magnetism, 79
Triton, 58, 153, 283
Tycho Brahe, 18–19, 300

ultraviolet, 48, 300
Umbriel, 55, 280–81
Uranus, 43–44, 55–56, 250, 279–81; albedo of, 60; cloud features of, 280; radio emission from, 279–80; rings of, 265–66, 280; rotation period of, 104, 280; satellites of, 44, 88, 280. *See also individual moons*
U.S. Geological Survey Astrogeology Center, 183